16 99

Behavioural
Gerontology

Behavioural Gerontology

Central Issues in the Psychology of Ageing

D. B. Bromley

Department of Psychology, University of Liverpool, UK

JOHN WILEY & SONS

Chichester · New York · Brisbane · Toronto · Singapore

Copyright © 1990 by John Wiley & Sons Ltd,
Baffins Lane, Chichester,
West Sussex PO19 1UD, England

Other Wiley Editorial Offices

John Wiley & Sons, Inc., 605 Third Avenue,
New York, NY 10158–0012, USA

Jacaranda Wiley Ltd, G.P.O. Box 859, Brisbane,
Queensland 4001, Australia

John Wiley & Sons (Canada) Ltd, 22 Worcester Road,
Rexdale, Ontario M9W 1L1, Canada

John Wiley & Sons (SEA) Pte Ltd, 37 Jalan Pemimpin #05-04,
Block B, Union Industrial Building, Singapore 2057

Library of Congress Cataloging-in-Publication Data:

Bromley, D. B. (Dennis Basil)
  Behavioural gerontology : central issues in the psychology of
ageing / D. B. Bromley.
    p.   cm.
  Includes bibliographical references.
  ISBN 0 471 92747 3
  1. Aging—Psychological aspects. 2. Aged—Psychology. I. Title.
BF724.8.B688   1990
155.67—dc20   90–35765
                                                                    CIP

British Library Cataloguing in Publication Data:

Bromley D. B. (Dennis Basil)
  Behavioural gerontology : central issues in the psychology
of ageing.
  1. Old persons. Ageing. Psychological aspects
  I. Title
  155.67

  ISBN 0 471 92747 3

Typeset by Photo·graphics, Honiton, Devon
Printed and bound in Great Britain by Biddles Ltd, Guildford, Surrey

Contents

Preface

The aim of this book is to provide a framework for and a critique of those areas of scientific inquiry which constitute the psychology of human ageing. This requires the relevant concepts, methods, findings, and applications of psychology to be reviewed in the context of the multidisciplinary study of ageing known as gerontology. Reference to this multidisciplinary context, however, must necessarily be brief since, as the title indicates, we are concerned with central issues in behavioural gerontology.

The term 'behavioural gerontology' has been adopted in order to emphasize that adult development and ageing constitutes a relatively new but now substantial branch of mainstream psychology, comparable to that other branch of the discipline—child development. Another reason for adopting the term 'behavioural gerontology' is that it expresses the considerable emphasis given to scientific method in psychology—in particular the emphasis on behavioural data when dealing with covert psychological processes such as cognition, motivation, and emotion. At the same time I have tried to fit the traditional and somewhat narrow methodological preoccupations of social and behavioural gerontologists into the wider framework of scientific method. The third reason for adopting the term 'behavioural gerontology' is to label certain central topics in the psychology of ageing and to help define the boundaries between this area of psychology and related disciplines, in particular those related to the biology of ageing at one extreme and those related to social gerontology at the other.

Different authors use different terms to refer to this branch of psychology. We do not have a convenient word or phrase to refer to the psychological changes that take place after the person has reached maturity. The word 'senescent' is usually used in connection with mental impairment in late life. The words 'growth' and 'development' are well-understood and widely used in connection with juveniles but take on a somewhat different meaning when used in connection with adults. The word 'ageing' is somewhat negative and restrictive. Terms such as 'geropsychology', 'gerontological psychology', 'post-developmental psychology' and 'behavioural gerontology' can be used more or less interchangeably to refer to the psychology of adult life and ageing.

vii

Behavioural gerontology shifts the focus of psychology away from the 'normal adult' (a static and artificial notion) in an attempt to take account of age changes and individual differences in adults.

My hope is that the book will appeal to academics, practitioners, and postgraduate students working in or interested in the psychology of ageing. The wider readership, however, might well include those in other areas, such as the biomedical aspects of ageing, social gerontology, adult education and training, counselling, and indeed anyone who aspires to a scientific or professional level of understanding the psychological aspects of human ageing.

As far as readability is concerned, I have done my best to find the right technical level—not an easy task in view of the multidisciplinary nature of both psychology and gerontology. Readers who want more specialized, detailed, or technical information can consult the appropriate references. I would appreciate having my attention drawn to errors of fact or interpretation.

Acknowledgements

I am grateful to Mrs Dorothy Foulds for organizing the necessary
secretarial services, and to Mrs Anne Halliwell who has carried the main
burden of typing and retyping numerous drafts.

I am also grateful to the librarians at the University of Liverpool for
their never-failing help in solving problems of document retrieval.

Many authors have kindly responded to requests for reprints, for which
I thank them. Restrictions on the size and scope of the book have
prevented me from citing many interesting and important articles. Where
numerical data are shown in tables and graphs, the aim is to illustrate
and summarize, in a general way, the issues raised; readers interested
in precise, technical details should consult the relevant references.

My deepest debt of gratitude is to my wife Roma whose support and
affection seem to be unlimited.

Chapter 1

Introduction: A Conceptual Framework for Behavioural Gerontology

WHY STUDY HUMAN AGEING?

There are several reasons why human ageing is worth studying. To begin with, adult life occupies three-quarters of the human lifespan, and in some advanced societies there are now as many people in retirement as there are children at school, roughly 16–20% of the population. There is a great deal going on during adult life and old age that is of scientific interest. For example, there are physiological changes that have implications for psychological functions, there are differences between individuals in the way their behaviour and experience change over the adult years, there are psychological disorders characteristic of later life, there are all sorts of social factors—institutional practices, social attitudes, interpersonal relationships, and so on—which provide a context for and condition our behaviour as adults and as old people.

Another reason why human ageing is worth studying is that its later stages are often accompanied by infirmity and dependency which most of us regard as undesirable and would avoid if possible. There is therefore a major scientific challenge for psychologists in finding ways to retard and ameliorate these unwanted effects of ageing. As far as extending the lifespan beyond its present upper limit of about 120 years is concerned, this is mainly a challenge for biologists, especially geneticists—see Cutler (1981). Through the achievements of biology and medicine, and through the achievements of science generally, education and standards of health and social welfare have improved over the years, so that more people are surviving into the later years of adult life. However, this gradual improvement in life-expectancy (including the increased further expectation of life for adults of all ages) is of little use if it is not accompanied by improved health, functional capacity, productive activity, and personal well-being. It is in these areas that psychologists, and some other scientists and professionals, can make their mark.

The infirmity and dependency of later life, like other sorts of human need, present moral challenges as well as scientific challenges—see Meier and Cassel (1983). That we have a duty to look after the health and welfare of children, whoever they are, is taken largely for granted in civilized societies; there is possibly an instinctive basis for such altruism. Similarly, it can be argued that we have a moral duty to look after the health and welfare of the infirm elderly. However, the biological, psychological, and social bases of this sort of altruism seem to be rather more complicated and confused than the sort that protects and nourishes children—see Bromley (1978). So here we have a characteristically double-knotted psychological-cum-ethical problem—why do people behave as they do in relation to ageing and the elderly? How *ought* people to behave in relation to the elderly and how *ought* the elderly themselves to behave?

Acceptance of the principle that older people have rights (as well as duties, of course) implies some level of economic and social support. The provision of goods and services to the elderly in the form of pensions, health and welfare services, and so on, is a major element in the social policy of advanced societies, and has important political and economic effects. Psychologists, and other social scientists, have a part to play in planning the provision of goods and services older people need. Psychologists have a particular part to play in so far as specialist psychological knowledge is needed—as for example in health education and promotion, in staff training, in running social organizations, in making psychological assessments, in treating individual cases, in carrying out experiments and other sorts of investigations to advance scientific knowledge, and in evaluating the effectiveness of policies and procedures.

Finally, human ageing is a natural, universal phenomenon, and is psychologically interesting because most of us can expect to participate in it—to grow old, or at least survive until late middle age! Having foreknowledge of what ageing means—in terms of its likely psychological, social, and biomedical effects—is to be forearmed. We should be in a better position to avoid, delay, or minimize some of the adverse effects in our own case. This personal involvement gives the subject added interest because of its direct, practical relevance. Usually, of course, one's scientific knowledge and professional skills will serve the public interest too.

Briefly, the answer to the question, 'Why study human ageing?' is that it is scientifically interesting, there is an underlying moral obligation, it offers practical benefits to society at large, and there are personal advantages to be derived from one's understanding of this natural phenomenon.

THE NATURE AND SCOPE OF ADULT DEVELOPMENT AND AGEING

It is convenient to define adult development and ageing as that set of psychobiological processes that begins with the transition from late adolescence to early adult life and continues thereafter until the terminal stage of life which ends with death.

Mortality statistics for western industrial societies show that about half the people born in recent years will survive to 74 years (men) or 81 years (women). They also show that the further expectation of life for women retiring at the age of 60 is about 21.3 years, and for men retiring at the age of 65, about 13.5 years. Other statistical and research sources show that illness and disability (morbidity) increase substantially from early middle age, say 40 years, but that a considerable amount of productive activity—economic, domestic, scientific, cultural, educational—is carried on throughout adult life and into old age.

There are many diverse sources of information on the statistics of mortality and morbidity in relation to ageing and their interpretation. They include, for example, Alderson (1986), Brody and Brock (1985), Bromley (1988a), Central Statistical Office (1986, 1989), Manton (1982), Office of Population Censuses and Surveys (1986), US Department of Health and Human Services (1982), Verbrugge (1984).

The figures and tables illustrate some of the statistical data available on population ageing for the United Kingdom. It would take us too far afield to compare the statistics on ageing from different countries, or regions of the U.K., although such comparisons might well have implications for behavioural gerontology, for example with regard to variations in life-style, intergenerational relationships, employment and retirement practices.

Figure 1.1 shows the actual age and sex structure of the U.K. population in 1987, together with projections for the years 2001 and 2025. The age structure of a population is determined by a number of factors, including birth-rates, death rates and migration. Table 1.1 shows the estimated resident population of England and Wales aged 50 and over in 1987. Figure 1.2 compares the death rates for age and sex in the U.K. for the years 1901 and 1987. Notice that improvements in life expectation and

4

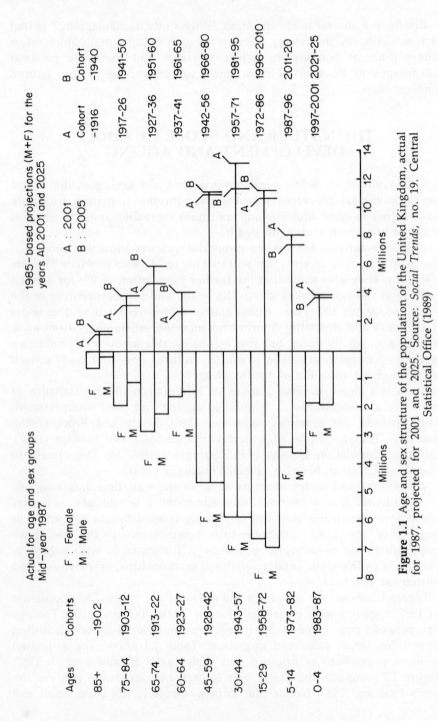

Figure 1.1 Age and sex structure of the population of the United Kingdom, actual for 1987, projected for 2001 and 2025. Source: *Social Trends*, no. 19. Central Statistical Office (1989)

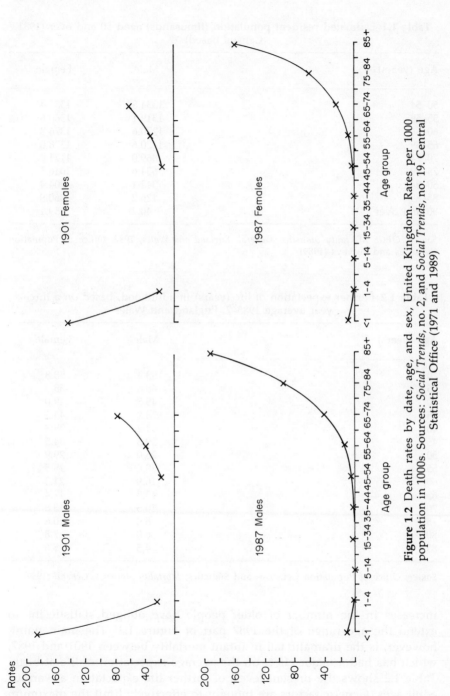

Figure 1.2 Death rates by date, age, and sex, United Kingdom. Rates per 1000 population in 1000s. Sources: *Social Trends*, no. 2, and *Social Trends*, no. 19. Central Statistical Office (1971 and 1989)

Table 1.1 Estimated resident population (thousands) aged 50 and over (1981 Census based)

Age (years)	Male	Female
50–54	1334.8	1333.4
55–59	1319.1	1360.6
60–64	1270.6	1376.3
65–69	1120.6	1328.0
70–74	869.0	1171.0
75–79	634.6	1016.3
80–84	342.1	704.4
85–89	126.2	360.9
90 and over	40.2	159.1

Source: *OPCS Mortality Statistics, General, England and Wales, 1987.* Office of Population Censuses and Surveys (1989)

Table 1.2 Further expectation of life (years) in adulthood, based on a three-year average 1985–7, England and Wales

Age (years)	Male	Female
20	53.4	58.8
25	48.6	53.9
30	43.8	49.0
35	38.9	44.1
40	34.2	39.3
45	29.5	34.5
50	25.0	29.9
55	20.8	25.5
60	16.9	21.3
65	13.5	17.4
70	10.5	13.8
75	8.0	10.6
80	6.0	7.8
85	4.5	5.6

Source: Office of Population Censuses and Statistics, *Mortality Statistics, General* (1989).

increases in the number of older people have obliged statisticians to extend the age range of the 1987 part of Figure 1.2! The main point, however, is the dramatic fall in infant mortality between 1901 and 1987, which has had a major effect on the average expectation of life at birth. Table 1.2 shows the present levels of further life expectation at various adult ages. Genetic factors are thought to effectively limit the maximum length of life even under good conditions and to lead to an exponential increase in mortality from the middle years.

The psychological study of adult development and ageing is concerned with the behaviour and experience of people from about the age of 18 to 20 years onwards. It is concerned with the systematic study of what is sometimes called 'the ordinary activities of daily life' (at work, at home, at leisure), as well as with the results of laboratory experiments, clinical investigations, and social surveys. These sorts of investigations describe and analyse human actions in natural or in contrived situations in order to advance our understanding of the differences between individuals and to explain the causes of age-related changes in behaviour and experience in adult life and old age.

As a behavioural science, psychology is concerned with the behaviour of animals as well as humans. The study of animal behaviour comes into the picture when we consider some of the basic biological processes of ageing—for example genetic and physiological processes—see Lamb (1977) and Behnke et al. (1978). Mankind's evolutionary relationship with the rest of the animal kingdom means that we can learn a great deal about human ageing from animal studies, apart from the interest such studies have for understanding ageing generally, since ageing is a major feature of organic life and inorganic matter.

However, the psychological study of human ageing also has to take into account social factors, by which we mean the way society prescribes appropriate forms of behaviour for adults at different times of life, and sets up institutional arrangements dealing with career paths, retirement practices, pensions, health and welfare services, dying, and death. These factors provide a context for and condition the behaviour of everyone, but in different ways at different ages—see Harris and Cole (1980) and Harris (1985) for an introduction to the sociology of ageing and an annotated bibliography.

Psychology provides a kind of bridge between the biological and the social sciences. This is particularly true where the study of ageing is concerned. Gerontology is the scientific study of ageing. Behavioural gerontology is the study of the behaviour of organisms, including humans, in the adult phase of their life. In psychology nowadays, the word 'behavioural' is often used in a methodological sense, i.e. in the sense that although we need concepts referring to covert psychological processes (perceiving, thinking, desiring, remembering, imagining, and so on), these processes have to be anchored in publicly verifiable behavioural observations if they are to be dealt with scientifically.

The scope of the psychological study of adult development and ageing is as wide as psychology itself. In fact, behavioural gerontology has had the effect of *extending* the boundaries of psychology by introducing an additional dimension—adult ageing—which raises a large number of issues which are relatively new to psychology. For example, there are issues such as adult ontogenesis, age-related biological and psychological changes, stressful life-events, and the social role of the elderly. These issues figure hardly at all in introductory psychology textbooks, which nevertheless devote a great deal of space to juvenile development. The psychological processes described in such books are often attributed to that imaginary and static creature the 'normal adult'.

Adult development and ageing is concerned with the central problem of psychology. It attempts to describe and explain the organization of behaviour and experience in relation to the problems of adjustment (adaptation) at all adult ages, and especially to describe and explain *changes* in the organization of behaviour and experience at successive ages.

A NOTE ON TERMINOLOGY

The word 'gerontology' means simply 'the scientific study of ageing'. It is essentially a multidisciplinary science; that is to say, it incorporates concepts, methods, and findings from a wide variety of scientific disciplines and professional practices in so far as they have a bearing on ageing. So, for example, gerontology incorporates information from physics and chemistry, biology and medicine, psychology and the social sciences, mathematics and statistics.

The word 'ageing' refers to a process which is not confined to living things, it is a process found throughout nature from stars to spiders' webs. It is, in one sense, the antithesis of development, i.e. decay. As far as organic, living, things are concerned, ageing undoes the work of growth and development. The process seems not to be similarly 'programmed', but rather to be 'accidental and consequential'. The basic association between ageing and decay has had unfortunate consequences for the study of human ageing, because it led to a natural interest in the adverse effects. This, in turn, increased people's aversion to the prospect of ageing, increased pessimism, and led to a neglect of the positive (beneficial) aspects of adult life. It also underestimated the prospects for reducing the adverse effects of ageing through biomedical, social, or psychological intervention.

Age is measured in terms of 'time', but time as an aspect of cosmology is well beyond our immediate interest. Age, measured in calendar years, is not in itself a causal variable. It is simply a time-marker. Hence, when we talk about the 'effects of ageing' we are really talking about age-related effects. The underlying causal factors are mechanisms or processes of one sort or another—cell loss, psychological stress, social transitions, or whatever.

The term 'geriatrics' is derived from the same root as 'gerontology'. It refers to the medicine of later life, in particular the medicine of old age, where we observe not only the emergence of new diseases (diseases not seen at younger ages), but also chronic (long-lasting) disorders, the cumulative adverse effects of 'normal' ageing, and changes in the way diseases and injuries generally present themselves in the context of an ageing body (and person)—Brocklehurst and Hanley (1976). The term 'psychogeriatrics' obviously refers to the psychiatric disorders of late life, for example, diseases such as senile dementia of the Alzheimer type (SDAT), late-onset schizophrenia, and late-onset depression.

The application of behavioural psychology in geriatric medicine has given rise to an area known as 'behavioural geriatrics'—see Hussian (1981). The aim of behavioural geriatrics is to apply the concepts and methods of behavioural management in the treatment of mentally infirm elderly patients. For example, the behaviour of patients who cannot respond to ordinary incentives and forms of persuasion can be 'shaped', to some extent, by the same sorts of techniques that are used successfully with young patients who are mentally retarded. Environments too can be designed and managed to meet the changed needs and reduced abilities of elderly infirm people.

The term 'behavioural gerontology' refers to a much wider area than the term 'behavioural geriatrics'. Behavioural gerontology is, in effect, the whole of psychology that relates to the processes of ageing, and conversely the whole of gerontology that has a bearing on psychology. It is a scientific enterprise which is calculated to extend the boundaries of psychology beyond its traditional frontiers. The 'central issues' covered in this book by no means exhaust the scope of behavioural gerontology— see 'The Multidisciplinary Context', below.

An alternative title, 'gerontological psychology', is not the sort of phrase which is likely to appeal to the masses, but it is no more jargonistic than 'physiological psychology' or 'developmental psychology'. It makes sense to use it when we wish to draw attention to or to emphasize the wider context of gerontology (the multidisciplinary science of ageing) within which the psychology of adult development and ageing operates. For example, theory construction in this area calls for the development of new concepts which bridge two or more branches of gerontology, or at least assimilate concepts from one area to those of another. Similarly, professional practice has yet to develop the role of 'gerontologist', except perhaps in the combined areas of research and teaching where the term is more widely used. At present, professional roles in work with the elderly are usually variations on existing roles, e.g. in social work, nursing, medicine, or housing. A term like 'gerontological psychology', therefore, anticipates considerably more cohesion in theory and in practice than exists at present. We can already see the emergence of specialist roles in psychological work with the elderly. These roles are analogous to the roles of child and educational psychologist in developmental psychology. An examination of the activities associated with these roles helps to identify the similarities and differences between these two scientific and professional areas.

THE MULTIDISCIPLINARY CONTEXT

Table 1.3 portrays behavioural gerontology as an interdisciplinary area linking gerontology and psychology. Panels, 1, 2, and 3 list the topics that make up the three disciplines in such a way as to align their common themes or interests. These common interests imply at least some degree of similarity or connection in the respective concepts, methods, findings, and applications.

Space does not permit an exhaustive treatment of the topics listed in panel 2 of Table 1.3, but it seems worthwhile to select some of them for brief discussion so as to provide a context for the 'central issues' dealt with in subsequent chapters.

Historical background

Mankind's concern with mortality dates back to the beginnings of recorded history, in particular to the Sumerian legend of Gilgamesh. The earliest attempts to deal with the problems of disease and ageing were naturally limited by ignorance and by reliance on pre-scientific modes of reasoning. This gave rise to ideas and practices based on folklore and beliefs in what we now call the 'supernatural', i.e. magical and spiritual agencies invoked to explain what would otherwise remain inexplicable. Primitive forms of thought—relying on metaphors, analogies, simple resemblances, coincidences, and the like—were not subject to rational scientific appraisal. Consequently, many errors of observation and interpretation were made, some of which persisted through the ages. Primitive forms of thought are normal or natural modes of reasoning, easily observed in children and in adults lacking the benefits of training in science and logic. This helps to explain the presence, even in modern times, of all sorts of misconceptions about the nature of ageing, and especially about the possibility of rejuvenation. The prevailing scientific view, however, is that rejuvenation, or a substantial extension of the human lifespan, is unlikely, at least in the foreseeable future, and the most we can hope for is an amelioration of the effects of ageing and a shortening of the period of late-life infirmity.

The beliefs and practices of the physician–priests of Sumeria and Egypt, based on magic, religion, and folklore, gave way partially and temporarily to Greek science and medicine, which brought better empirical observation and reasoning to bear on the problems of ageing and disease. This nascent scientific spirit persisted, albeit less vigorously, in Rome but was virtually overwhelmed during the Dark Ages. During this period, earthly life was subordinated to a concern with the eternal life hereafter. Life expectancy was put at 'three score years and ten' but this estimate probably discounted childhood deaths.

Religious beliefs, together with the social arrangements that evolved, imposed some order and structure on human behaviour. Chronological age was associated with various norms governing adult status, marriage, seniority, retirement, and of course with relationships between generations within families. Old age dependency would be a family matter, except where aged retainers (servants) might be maintained by their masters. Then as now, no doubt, the beliefs and practices that were prescribed by society were not adhered to fully by all its individual members. Thus it is difficult to ascertain how the elderly lived in those remote times. It seems likely that very few survived into late life, and those that did survive would quickly succumb to one or other of the many causes of death.

A persisting feature of mankind's attitude to ageing has been ambivalence. That is to say, people have regarded it with mixed feelings because on the one hand it seems to have adverse effects on appearance, health, and competence, but on the other hand it seems to be a sort of achievement, and for a time at least often brings wisdom, status, and improving living standards.

Another persisting feature of mankind's attitude to ageing has been the search for rejuvenation—a cure for ageing. This was a major focus of alchemy, which grew out of the philosophies of Empedocles and Hippocrates, since it was believed that a 'fifth essence' would make it possible to transmute base metals into gold and provide an elixir of life.

Although fairly high standards of health and hygiene, based on the more effective medical practices of the Greek and Roman tradition, were achieved in some segments of society, and although institutions akin to hospitals came into existence before Roman times, the health and welfare conditions for the elderly infirm generally were probably very poor.

The classical works on philosophy and medicine were rediscovered by the West in the fifteenth and sixteenth centuries, and the way was cleared for the emergence of a scientific and humanist approach to the problems

Table 1.3 The multidisciplinary context

Panel 1 Gerontology	Panel 2 Behavioural Gerontology	Panel 3 Psychology
Definition the scientific study of ageing.	Definition: the psychological study of adult development and ageing.	Definition: the scientific study of behaviour and mental processes.
Nature and scope of gerontology.	Nature and scope of behavioural gerontology.	Nature and scope of psychology.
History of gerontology.	History of human ageing.	History of psychology.
Fundamental processes of ageing: physical, chemical, biological.	Adult ontogenesis.	Developmental psychology.
Biomedical aspects of ageing: some specialties in biology and medicine, such as epidemiology, psychiatry, geriatrics, pharmacology, nursing, neurology, and endocrinology, have a greater involvement in ageing than do others.	Psychophysiological processes: bodily functions; sensory and motor functions.	Physiological psychology: including sensory and motor processes, neuropsychology, psychopharmacology.
	Psychological processes: cognitive, affective, learning, knowing, and forgetting.	Higher mental processes; including perception, cognition, language, learning, and memory.
Behavioural and psychological aspects of ageing: see centre panel.	Methods of investigation.	Psychological methods.
Mathematical and statistical models of ageing.	Quantitative and qualitative methods.	Quantitative methods: psychometrics and statistics.

Age-related pathologies.	Age-related psychological disorders. Personal adjustment and individual differences. Social behaviour.	Abnormal and clinical psychology. Personality and adjustment; motivation and emotion. Social psychology.
Social gerontology: social history, sociology, politics, economics, social administration and the law, geography, architecture and planning, adult and continuing education.		
Comparative gerontology: animal models of ageing.	Animal behaviour. Theories of human ageing.	Comparative psychology.
Theoretical gerontology: philosophical and explanatory accounts of ageing at any level of organization—molecular, cellular, organ, organismic, collective.	Philosophy: ethics; lifestyles; social policy.	Theoretical psychology: system-building; high-level explanations of behaviour. Philosophical psychology: theories of mind; morality.
Ageing in art and literature.	Ageing in art and literature.	Aesthetics.
Applied gerontology: those areas of intervention associated with the cumulative effects of ageing, mostly but not entirely in late life—geriatric medicine and nursing, health and welfare services in the community, health education and promotion, housing and transport, rehabilitation, social support, and leisure.	Applied behavioural gerontology.	Applied psychology: clinical, occupational, educational, community psychology, forensic, military, industrial, environmental.

of ageing. Developments in anatomy, physiology, and pathology, together with those in political arithmetic, gradually took over from traditional approaches left over from classical and medieval times. The seventeenth and eighteenth centuries brought significant developments in science and medicine which were important in understanding the physical basis of ageing and disease. Advances in social medicine in the nineteenth century brought about improvements in public health. The reductions in infant mortality and epidemic diseases led to increases in life-expectancy, and to changes in the size, composition, and age structure of the population.

The scientific study of human ageing was firmly established in 1873 when Thoms's book on longevity was published (Thoms, 1873). The words 'gerontology' and 'geriatrics' were introduced early in the twentieth century. Scientific optimism gave rise to extravagant claims at first, but gradually the complexities of biological ageing were revealed and greater realism prevailed. The psychological study of ageing has developed rather slowly and unevenly, partly in response to developments in medicine and physiology, rather than in response to social needs as revealed by surveys. Military and industrial factors promoted research into mental abilities and human performance. The concept of intellectual deterioration provided a link between the study of normal adult intelligence and the study of psychiatric disorders, especially dementia.

Developments since 1950 have been massive, at least in terms of published literature. One reason for this was the expansion of psychology itself as a science and profession. A second reason was a shift of emphasis in medicine towards the diseases of middle age and late life. A third reason was the growing awareness that changes in the age structure of populations, namely an increasing proportion of elderly infirm people, were producing large-scale health and welfare demands, and economic problems, that psychological services could help to meet.

The social history of ageing illustrates a number of topics in social psychology and serves as a reminder of the ways in which social psychology relates to behavioural gerontology. Until Elizabethan times the State made no general provision for old-age infirmity. Care of the elderly was mainly a family responsibility; those without family might look to former employers, friends, the church, and charity. The Poor Law distinguished for a time between the deserving and the undeserving poor in the kind of relief provided. As economic conditions worsened, political reforms were introduced to deal with the social problems that arose. Social attitudes towards people in need have been somewhat ambivalent, because of the tendency to attribute blame for misfortune to the person rather than to circumstances. Old age pensions were introduced near the turn of the century in several countries. Pension provision continues to be an important aspect of social and economic policy. It reflects, in a way, the 'worth' that society assigns to its elderly. The welfare state was intended to remedy social injustices, including those suffered by the elderly. However, in most countries it has not proved possible to meet the income, health, and welfare expectations of the elderly, because national resources have to be allocated across other areas of concern too. In modern western society the elderly constitute a sizeable fraction of population—in the UK they exceed the number of children at school. Survey techniques have been used extensively in social gerontology as an aid to advocacy and policy-making.

Until about 1940 the history of human ageing had not been systematically studied. Subsequently, F. D. Zeman (1942–50) published a series of articles dealing with the medical history of old age in the *Journal of Mount Sinai Hospital*. See Bromley (1974a, b) for a full list of the Zeman references and for a summary account of their contents, together with an extended treatment of and additional references to the history of human ageing. See Bromley (1989) for a history of human ageing from a psychological perspective.

Other useful recent references include Freeman (1979), *Ageing and Society* (1984), Conrad (1978), and Stearns (1982). G. S. Hall's *Senescence: The Last Half of Life* was published in 1923, but Gilbert's (1952) *Understanding Old Age* was perhaps the first modern attempt to write a textbook on the psychology of ageing.

Biomedical factors

The biological processes of ageing provide a necessary basis for understanding the psychological and social aspects of ageing. This is because the anatomical and physiological changes which underlie behaviour and experience in adult life and old age are themselves the result of more fundamental causes operating at the biophysical level, i.e. at the molecular level. Furthermore, it seems that any interventions affecting life-expectancy, well-being and functional capacity throughout adult life must depend ultimately on improvements in the physical basis of behaviour. This is why the biological and medical aspects of ageing are so important. In a sense the social and psychological contribution to human ageing is to ameliorate the conditions that biology and medicine cannot deal with. In another sense it is to promote the sort of behaviour and the sort of society that minimizes the adverse effects of biological ageing.

Human beings, like other animals, have a characteristic lifespan under given environmental conditions. Mortality and morbidity statistics make it possible to investigate the causes of, and changes in, the age structure and health of whole populations.

Experimental studies with animals show that it is possible to lengthen or shorten the characteristic survival curve of a species by changing the environmental conditions. Similarly, genetic studies show that genetic factors influence health and longevity. The problem is to discover precisely how genetic and environmental factors operate and interact to produce the psychological effects that interest us. Some biological changes are thought to be normal in the sense of natural, universal, and inevitable, whereas other changes are thought to be pathological in the sense of increasing disability and hastening death through disease, injury, and deprivation or stress. The aim of researchers is to maximize health and longevity so that the intrinsic processes of ageing can be more easily revealed. For example, we may find that the human genome has design limitations, or that there is a built-in 'clock' or 'timetable' which sets off events that bring about the effects we refer to as 'ageing'.

Changes in the physical health and age structure of populations are relatively slow. Even so, societies may be even slower to adapt their institutional arrangements to these changes. For this reason people may not develop the sorts of beliefs and practices that are conducive to good adjustment in later life, and there may be confusion and disagreement about the rights and duties of different age groups.

A biological approach to the study of adult life and old age involves some areas of knowledge that are familiar to students of psychology. These include the central nervous system, the autonomic nervous system, the endocrine system, and the special senses. Ageing, unfortunately, affects these and other tissues and organs of the body too; and some of these changes have important psychological consequences, either directly or indirectly. This is an example of the way in which the study of ageing has the effect of reshaping psychology, i.e. changing its boundaries and its links with other scientific disciplines.

For the most part, adult ageing has adverse effects on human anatomy and physiology. Consequently, the adult's functional effectiveness declines (more in some respects than in others), and he or she has to adapt to changes in physical appearance, health, and fitness. Such adaptation typically takes place slowly and in a social context which may or may not be supportive.

Methodological difficulties hinder investigations into the normal and pathological effects of ageing on the physical basis of human behaviour. Wide differences between individuals limit the accuracy and generality of research findings.

Age changes in the skeleton, the muscles, and the skin are numerous and diverse in character, and seem to arise from a variety of causes.

Some of the effects are unavoidable—for example, wrinkles, greying hair, dental wear and decay—although cosmetic and prosthetic measures may do much to disguise or compensate for these changes. The body image continues to be an important part of the self-concept, but there is probably a shift from concern with sexual attractiveness to concern with functional competence. The physical appearance of the aged may well affect social attitudes.

The effects of ageing on the circulatory, respiratory, and digestive systems are also numerous and diverse in character. Fortunately, for a large part of adult life most people are normally provided with 'biological reserves' which enable them to cope with the ordinary demands of daily life reasonably well. The biological reserves are called into play in times of stress. As we move into later life, however, our reserves are reduced, our ability to cope with even the basic functions of self-care is reduced, and we are forced to rely on other people's resources. Eventually we are deprived of one or another biological function essential to life. We die of heart disease, cancer, respiratory infection, kidney failure, or some other ailment. There is some hope of finding ways to retard and ameliorate these effects, not only through medication and surgery but also through physical exercise, diet, and lifestyle.

The psychological significance of age changes in the autonomic nervous system has received remarkably little attention. This is surprising considering the importance of motivation and emotion in adjustment to the opportunities, constraints, and stresses of later life. The ANS has to be considered in relation to the endocrine system. The general pattern of age effects is to reduce homeostatic stability, to reduce the capacity to mobilize physiological resources for action, and to recover from the effects of physical and psychological stress. However, the anatomical and physiological changes which underlie the effects of ageing are far from clear, partly because of the complexities and interdependencies within and between the ANS and the endocrine system.

Our present understanding of neuropsychology and neurotransmitter substances provides some guidance as regards the use of psychoactive drugs with adults. The effects of ageing, however, complicate the picture by changing the ways in which drugs are metabolized and excreted.

The menopause provides a unique biological marker for the effects of ageing. It has been studied mainly in relation to minimizing the inconvenience caused by its somatic symptoms and to managing the psychological disturbance it precipitates in some women. The hormonal mechanisms have been identified, in the sense that the ovaries eventually produce insufficient oestradiol to stimulate the menstrual cycle in spite of compensatory hormonal reactions. The menopause seems not to provide a model for age changes in the reproductive capacity of males, although there are changes in the complex hormonal balance associated with sexual behaviour in males. The overall effect of ageing is to reduce sexual and reproductive capacity. However, long-term relationships between men and women depend upon factors other than the sexual relationship. There is usually a complex cost/benefit exchange pattern involving family relationships, work and leisure, mutual attraction, and respect, set in context of social norms and expectations. Such exchange relationships can be expected to vary as people grow older.

The total amount of sleep taken seems to change little if at all during adult life, although in later life especially, the distribution of sleep periods may shift to a polyphasic pattern. Sleep appears to be less deep and more prone to disturbances. This may be another example of the gradual breakdown of the regulatory functions of the body as age increases.

The effects of ageing on the central nervous system are particularly important in behavioural gerontology because of their consequences for the organization of complex patterns of behaviour (Terry, 1987; Ulatowska, 1985). Thus, reductions in the blood supply to the brain, reductions in the number of neurons, weakening of synaptic connections, disturbances in supporting structures and neurotransmitter processes, and so on, can be expected to impair high-level performances in reasoning, memory, language, and perceptual-motor skills. Brain failure is demonstrated dramatically in senile dementia of the Alzheimer type.

The psychological assessment of neurological impairment is of considerable interest and importance, but the complexities of neuropsychological processes make it difficult to identify the specific effects of ageing. Technological and psychometric developments promise to change this situation.

In terms of relative size and importance, behavioural gerontology can be thought of metaphorically as a minor planet circling the giant star of biomedical gerontology. Consequently in choosing references one is faced with an embarrassment of riches. Brief elementary introductions to the biology of ageing include Lamb (1977), and Cunningham and Brookbank (1988). A more advanced text directly related to psychology is Whitbourne (1985). Rothstein (1983) has edited a review of biological research in ageing; see also Warner et al. (1987) and Schneider (1982). Finch and Schneider (1985) have edited the second edition of the Handbook of the Biology of Aging. Birren and Schaie's (1985) Handbook of the Psychology of Aging contains several chapters relating to the biology of ageing. See Brocklehurst and Hanley (1976) and Bromley (1988a, pp. 69–88) for brief elementary introductions to the biomedical aspects of ageing.

Sensory and motor processes

It is difficult to say exactly how ageing affects each of the sensory systems. This is because research in this area is relatively new, and faces difficult methodological problems apart from those normally associated with research in ageing. For example, the instrumentation required to study sensory processes can be quite elaborate and the procedures time-consuming. They are therefore unsuited to large-scale screening or establishing age-norms for performance.

The safest assumption seems to be that ageing has adverse effects on all sensory systems at every level of organization—from the anatomy and physiology of the end-organs to the central nervous integration that gives rise to perceptual experience and response. However, there are wide differences between individuals (each individual is anatomically and physiologically unique), and individuals change over adult life. Consequently, it is difficult to reach precise conclusions applicable to adults generally.

The effects of normal or intrinsic ageing are difficult to disentangle from the effects of disease, injury, and special circumstances such as genetic predisposition.

Worsening vision is a familiar experience even in the early years of adult life. Older people tend to become long-sighted (presbyopic) in that stimuli in near vision become blurred because the focal point lies behind instead of on the retina. Various aspects of visual performance—static visual acuity, dynamic visual acuity, colour vision, dark-adaptation, depth perception, flicker fusion, and so on—tend to deteriorate. Chronological age, however, is not a good guide to a person's visual competence. Ophthalmic examination and testing are necessary to establish the nature and extent of visual impairment, and even this assessment may not accurately predict how well a person will cope with the visual world outside the clinic and laboratory. Fortunately, there appears to be a considerable amount of help available from professional and voluntary workers in the area of visual handicap.

Loss of hearing is also a familiar aspect of ageing, although there seems to be insufficient recognition of the early stages of hearing loss—say by the age of 50 years—which may be sufficient to impair hearing in the ordinary activities of daily life. The main losses appear to be in the inner ear and in the associated nerve processes up to and including the auditory cortex. Hearing loss for pure tones does not necessarily predict hearing loss for meaningful sounds, such as spoken words. In addition to hearing loss, there is an increase with age in disturbances of hearing. For example, tinnitus is a condition in which noise is experienced in the absence of auditory stimulation—ringing, buzzing, whining, voices, or even loud music. This can lead to considerable psychological upset. Practical help and advice for people with hearing loss appears to be relatively less well developed than for people with visual impairment. For example, the prevalence of hearing loss could be given more publicity, as could methods of communicating more effectively whilst still using the spoken word.

Speech sound frequencies lie within the range 250–3000 Hz, and are less adversely affected by age than the high frequencies. Speech perception is more a matter of cognitive interpretation than of sensory discrimination, in the sense that we can give meaning to degraded or incomplete stimuli provided we can bring correct expectations and appropriate knowledge to bear on the task. Speech perception tends to take place in contexts where factors such as background noise, cross-talk, hesitations, and variations in speech production occur. Loss of hearing means that we have to listen more attentively in such conditions; this is effortful and may give rise to diminished interest and reduced performance (Rabbitt, 1986). The speech of older people tends to become more hoarse, tremulous, weaker, and breathier.

Losses in the sense of balance and movement are particularly important in later life because they predispose to falls and other accidents. As with the other senses, there are adverse age changes at every level from the end-organs to the cortex. Poorer vision, slower reactions, weaker muscles, postural hypotension, and so on increase the likelihood of loss of balance. In the absence of other remedial measures, physical exercise, practice in movement, and attention to safety in the everyday environment may help.

As we grow older through adult life, we tend to lose muscular strength, speed, and endurance because of reductions in muscle fibres and innervation. Disuse aggravates these losses, whereas physical training does much to maximize the functional effectiveness of muscles. The loss of fine motor control, of course, results in tremor and poorer coordination, with the risk of accident. Ageing seems to affect the different stages in the organization of response in different ways, presumably because of differences in the biological process underlying these stages.

The senses of taste and smell are difficult to investigate and so relatively little is known about the specific effects that ageing has on them, although they do seem to deteriorate in later life. This would happen partly as a consequence of adverse anatomical and physiological changes in these sensory systems, and partly as a consequence of adverse changes in the central neuropsychological processes which underlie our ability to interpret—make sense of—taste and smell stimuli.

Flavour is a mixture of taste, smell, and other sensations. Older people are less able to identify smells, tastes and flavours.

Temperature regulation is a complex physiological process. It may be of critical importance in late life if an elderly person is subjected to cold stress. Hypothermia in the elderly receives considerable publicity during cold winter weather. An elderly person is less able to register a drop in temperature and less able to respond to it appropriately. At the other extreme, an elderly person is less able to cope with heat stress, not necessarily because of a reduced ability to lose heat through sweating or failing to register a rise in temperature, but because excess body heat is not effectively transferred to the surface and lost.

The decline with age in proprioception contributes to reductions in the ability to maintain a proper posture and balance, and to move quickly and efficiently. These losses are very obvious in late life. Earlier in adult life one may also observe increased tremor, unsteadiness, and lack of speed, strength, and coordination, but to a lesser extent. Physiotherapy and physical exercise may help to retard or ameliorate these losses.

The effects of age on pain perception (nociception) are not well understood. The basic anatomy and physiology of pain are still obscure, and there are obvious ethical constraints on pain research. Pain sensitivity and pain tolerance are subject to the limitations of subjective response biases.

The reason for not devoting a whole chapter to physiological processes and to sensory and motor functions is that effective treatment of these topics would require excursions deep into biomedical gerontology, although these topics can be justifiably regarded as 'central' to behavioural gerontology. They are described fully elsewhere (see later references) and are perhaps better understood and less controversial than other central topics.

In reviewing the effects of ageing on sensory processes we must not lose sight of the fact that age-related changes arise from a variety of causes and that the differences between individuals are very wide. A loss in one sensory system does not necessarily indicate losses in other sensory systems. It may prove possible, through a combination of technological and psychological means, to further retard, alleviate, or compensate for these effects.

Sensory and motor processes are dealt with extensively in the biology of ageing because of the associated anatomical and physiological factors. General references to ageing of the sensory systems include Corso (1981), Hinchcliffe (1983), Ordy and Brizzee (1979), and Whitbourne (1985). See Bromley (1988a, pp. 33–68) for a brief elementary introduction to the anatomy and physiology of the ageing sensory and motor processes. The effects of ageing on motor processes are dealt with in Mortimer *et al.* (1982).

Social gerontology

The social psychology of ageing might well be regarded as one of the 'central issues' in behavioural gerontology. The reason for not devoting an entire chapter to this topic is partly lack of space and partly the difficulty of defining the boundary between social psychology and some of the other social sciences that comprise social gerontology.

Socialization to old age is the process whereby we come to develop certain beliefs, attitudes, values, and practices that lead us to conform to the prevailing norms and institutional arrangements governing retirement and dependency. This process varies somewhat as between men and women, and different socioeconomic classes. There are differences between individuals in the extent to which social adaptation is achieved.

Social attitudes towards old age are largely negative, even if attitudes towards particular elderly individuals are not. Prejudice is expressed in the usual ways—discrimination, stigmatization, abuse, ridicule, stereotyping, and neglect. It seems unlikely that there is any sociobiological or instinctive basis for altruism in relation to the elderly; it is more likely to rest on tradition and social learning. Our social attitudes and values are embedded in the forms of language we ordinarily use and in social practices that we take for granted.

Adult life and old age can be viewed as a series of social transitions, some entered into voluntarily, some imposed by circumstances. Social readjustment consists in coping with these transitions—including retirement and bereavement. Factors such as age discrimination, poverty, and isolation can hinder social readjustment. The general trend is towards disengagement from important central roles, possibly accompanied by more involvement in peripheral roles and social activities of a more personal nature.

Social interaction leads to the emergence of social roles, statuses, and norms. To the extent that age differences affect the extent of social interaction, there is likely to be some age differentiation in social roles, statuses, and norms. Age norms prescribe the sorts of behaviour and characteristics expected of people at different age levels. Social change and generational differences in experience are likely to reinforce age differences in values and attitudes. At later ages, retirement, infirmity, and selective survivorship act to impose minority status, with the likelihood of discrimination and segregation, even if mitigated by the provision of health and welfare services.

The emergence of a substantial proportion of elderly infirm people is a relatively new social phenomenon, and the social arrangements needed to deal with it are still being evolved. The main problem is how to integrate the elderly into the wider society when their functional contribution has ceased and they have become dependents. If the dependency of the elderly is contrasted with the dependency of children the social, psychological, and economic aspects of the problem of integration become clear. One view of this problem is that the elderly on the whole are socially integrated, at least to the extent that there are economic, health, and welfare provisions for them. Another view is that the elderly are not socially integrated because their living standards tend to be low and there is evidence of widespread prejudice, exclusion, and neglect. A third view is that the social integration of the elderly is a matter of degree and that ways can be found to improve social integration. However, although it is difficult to bring about major changes in the way societies are organized, changes are likely to come about gradually through the effects of several factors: changes in the age structure of populations, changes in the health and functional capacities of older people, and the activities of advocates and pressure groups. One of the barriers to change is the tendency for social attitudes and values ingrained in adult life to be carried forward into later life, as a kind of self-inflicted handicap. The problem of the social integration of the elderly is not simply an economic problem, although it has major economic implications. It is also an ethical problem.

A major contribution to the social integration of the elderly would be through the development of a range of lifestyles suited to their characteristics and circumstances. We need to demonstrate, by means of 'behavioural models', the sorts of options available, particularly for ordinary people who may otherwise remain ignorant of the possibilities open to them. In free democratic societies this depends on public policy (affecting adult education, leisure, employment, health, and so on) and on pressure groups and advocates working through elected representatives and the media. If the problem of social integration is a question of enabling the elderly to develop more satisfying lifestyles, it is also a question of persuading other age groups, particularly working adults, that the costs involved and the social changes required are in the best long-term interests of the community as a whole. Improved social integration of the elderly might include a degree of self-segregation— through retirement communities, sheltered housing, and so on—provided such arrangements maintain mutually satisfying relationships between the elderly and the wider community.

The factors affecting the formation and maintenance of social relation- ships in later life seem to be much the same as in earlier adult life, except for the obvious changes in personal characteristics and circumstances. The interaction between people of the same age and people of different ages can be described in terms of exchange relationships (costs and benefits)—Dowd (1980). Consider, for example, friendships in later life, family relationships, relationships at work, and the relationships between the elderly infirm and their care-givers.

It is possible that the instinctive mechanisms that seem to underlie adult/child relationships have no parallel in adult/elder relationships. In this case the latter would be based entirely on social learning and may be highly specific, i.e. confined to particular elders, usually the parents.

Social relationships are rule-governed. The rules are usually implicit but can be uncovered by scientific inquiry—by direct observation and inference, the examination of 'accounts', experimentation, and so on. Social relationships can be modified by counselling and training. The termination of 'special attachments' in later life—through bereavement, illness, relocation—tends to provoke emotional reactions such as depression and desolation. Social isolation is a serious risk in later life; social support is a key factor in recovery from illness and stress.

The scope of social gerontology in the UK is illustrated in Tinker (1985); see also Bromley (1988a, pp. 89–148). There is a *Handbook of Aging and the Social Sciences* edited by Binstock and Shanas (1985). One of the few books on human ageing with 'social psychology' in its title is by Marshall (1986). Hendricks and Hendricks (1977) cover an area of overlap between the social psychology and sociology of ageing. Rosow (1974, 1985) presents an interesting perspective on the social aspects of ageing.

ETHICAL ISSUES

Psychology's deep concern with human problems means that ethical issues are hardly ever out of sight. Ethical considerations set limits to scientific investigations with both animals and humans. Professional work in psychology is governed by an explicit code of conduct, as for example in the British Psychological Society (1985) or the American Psychological Association (1982). In our dealings with adults and older people, especially relatives, in the ordinary activities of daily life, we normally feel bound by the obligations and duties that our social training has imposed on us. The ethical standards we live by are in large measure traditional. That is to say, they have evolved gradually through a complex process of social history involving science, religion, politics, philosophy, economics, jurisprudence, and common sense. The difficulty is that old-age dependency on a large scale is a relatively new phenomenon and is giving rise to ethical problems for which there are no obvious or agreed solutions. Consider, for example, the question of the relative costs and benefits of medical care for the elderly infirm, the question of euthanasia and the right to die, the question of compulsory retirement, the question of living standards for retired people, the question of the quality of life for the mentally impaired in institutional care, and of informed consent. These important questions cannot be answered by means of scientific research (one cannot derive 'ought' from 'is'). However, scientific findings form part of the context within which ethical issues may be resolved. The issues are so salient in social gerontology that a great deal of scientific and professional effort is devoted to advocacy—defending the rights and promoting the interests of the dependent elderly. This kind of altruism expresses people's moral outlook, and is to be commended provided it does not misdirect or misrepresent behavioural gerontology. In any event, concern for the health and welfare of the elderly is highly compatible with self-interest in the long run!

Further consideration of the ethical and legal issues in social and behavioural gerontology would take us too far afield. Readers interested in this area are referred to Downing and Smoker (1986), Estes (1986), Hellman (1985), Norman (1980), Rachels (1986), and Rosoff and Gottlieb (1987).

The nature and scope of behavioural gerontology can be formulated as the scientific enterprise concerned with basic advances in our knowledge and understanding of the ways in which psychological and behavioural processes tend to change with the passage of time in adult life, especially the post-reproductive period. In pursuing this aim, gerontological psychology takes its place alongside a wide range of other sciences and professions in the multidisciplinary area of research known as gerontology. Psychology contributes its own concepts, methods, and findings to the pool of knowledge and shares in those contributed by other sciences. Gerontological psychology is also a social enterprise concerned with the application of scientific knowledge and methods to the solution of social problems, and to the improvement of standards of living, often referred to as 'quality of life', especially in relation to the elderly. In pursuing these aims, gerontological psychology becomes associated with a variety of other social enterprises, for example voluntary organizations concerned with leisure and welfare in later life, institutions concerned with legal and ethical issues, economic and political policies, and schemes for continuing education, training, and employment.

Just what this definition of behavioural gerontology means, and what its current status as a basic and applied science amounts to, should become clearer with each section and chapter that follows.

THE SCIENTIFIC LITERATURE ON AGEING

We have emphasized the multidisciplinary nature of gerontology—the scientific study of ageing. Textbooks on human ageing tend to have a multidisciplinary character, even when they have psychology as their main focus of interest. There is a wide range of recent introductory textbooks, most of which attempt to integrate the biological, sociological, and psychological aspects of human ageing. They include: Belsky (1984), Botwinick (1984), Bromley (1988a), Butler and Lewis (1982), Cunningham and Brookbank (1988), Hayslip and Panek (1989), Kermis (1984), Perlmutter and Hall (1985), Rogers (1986), Santrock (1985), Schaie and Willis (1986), Stevens-Long (1984), Turner and Helms (1986), Whitbourne (1986), and Woodruff-Pak (1988).

There are books of a more advanced sort, for example the following recent publications: Binstock and Shanas (1985), Charness (1985a), Birren and Schaie (1985), Eisdorfer *et al.* (1985), Finch and Schneider (1985), Kausler (1982), Kenney (1982), McGaugh and Kiesler (1981), Maddox (1986), Poon (1980), Riley *et al.* (1983), P. Robinson *et al.* (1984). McKee (1982) reviews some philosophical issues. Theories are reviewed by Birren and Bengston (1988) and Burbank (1986).

Recent references on lifespan developmental psychology include the following recent contributions: Baltes *et al.* (1986, 1987), Brodzinsky *et al.* (1986), Datan *et al.* (1986), McCluskey-Fawcett and Reese (1984), Munnichs *et al.* (1985), and Sorensen *et al.* (1986).

From time to time the *Annual Review of Psychology* contains a chapter on the psychology of ageing. A list of English-language periodicals is shown in Table 1.4.

SUMMARY

Human ageing is worth studying because adult life occupies about three-quarters of the lifespan, and in some advanced societies older adults account for nearly one-fifth of the population. Normal ageing has profound and widespread effects on behaviour and experience. Many of these effects are of an adverse sort; so psychology faces the challenge of retarding and ameliorating those effects that fall within its sphere of influence. One aim is to minimize dependency by maximizing health and functional capacities. Another aim is to help clarify the ethical issues associated with old-age dependency. The scientific aim is to advance knowledge of the psychology of ageing through systematic empirical observation and the development of concepts, methods, and theories.

The upper limit of human longevity is about 120 years. In advanced societies the expectation of life at birth is about 74 years for men and 81 years for women. The psychological study of adult development and ageing forms an important bridge between the biology of ageing and the social sciences concerned with ageing. It has the effect of extending

Table 1.4 A list of English-language periodicals on ag(e)ing relevant to behavioural gerontology

Abstracts in Social Gerontology
Activities, Adaptation and Aging
Age and Ageing
Ageing and Society
Ageing and Work (Industrial Gerontology)
Ageing International
International Journal of Aging and Human Development
(Aging and Human Development)
American Journal of Geriatrics
Annual Review of Gerontology and Geriatrics
Archives of Gerontology and Geriatrics
Canadian Journal on Aging
Clinical Gerontologist
Clinics in Geriatric Medicine
Comprehensive Gerontology (new Munksgaard journal)
Death Studies (formerly *Death Education,* not confined to ageing)
Dementia (new John Libbey Journal)
Developmental Psychology (juvenile development and adult ageing)
Educational Gerontology
Experimental Gerontology
Generations (Bulletin of the British Society of Gerontology)
Geriatric Nursing and Home Care
Gerontology and Geriatrics
The Gerontologist
Human Development
International Journal of Aging and Human Development
International Journal of Behavioral Development
International Journal of Geriatric Psychiatry
International Journal of Technology and Aging (new Human Sciences Press
journal)
Journal of Ageing Studies (new JAI Press journal)
Journal of Aging and Health
Journal of Applied Gerontology
Journal of Clinical and Experimental Gerontology
Journal of Cross-cultural Gerontology
Journals of Gerontology
Journal of Geriatric Drug Therapy
Journal of Geriatric Psychiatry
Journal of Gerontological Social Work
Journal of Housing for the Elderly
Journal of Nutrition for the Elderly
Journal of Religion and Aging
Journal of the American Geriatrics Society
Mechanisms of Aging and Development
Omega: Journal of Death and Dying
Psychology and Aging (new APA journal)
Research on Aging

the boundaries of traditional psychology. The central problem is how to describe and explain the many changes in behaviour that take place from the end of the juvenile period of development to the terminal stage of life. This includes the study of individual differences in ageing. A lifespan development approach attempts to integrate the study of juvenile development and adult ageing.

In presenting a relatively new branch of basic and applied psychology it is necessary to introduce some technical words and phrases. These include the following: gerontology, geriatrics, psychogeriatrics, behavioural geriatrics, behavioural gerontology, gerontological psychology. The word 'ageing' has to be used with care.

The context for the study of the psychology of ageing comprises an extensive historical background, a huge literature in biology and medicine (including closely related work in sensory and motor processes), and an array of contributions from the social sciences. Ageing produces a variety of ethical and legal problems. References are provided for each of these areas.

Behavioural gerontology is a basic as well as an applied scientific enterprise pursued in the context of other scientific disciplines and within the current social framework.

The scientific literature in behavioural gerontology comprises books ranging from elementary introductions through more advanced specialized texts to vast handbooks. There are at least 30 scientific journals devoted to the study of ageing.

Chapter 2

Adult Ontogenesis

INTRODUCTION

Psychologists use the word 'ontogenesis' in connection with the study of child development. It refers to the historical development of an individual as an organized entity. Juvenile development works out a sort of 'genetic blueprint' as the individual matures biologically, and his or her characteristics find (or fail to find) expression in the given environment. By the time we reach early adulthood, however, the genetically controlled programme of development is virtually complete, except perhaps for the expression of some late-acting genes, and for the long-term consequences of genetic characteristics. Effects which make their appearance after the adult reproductive period will exert no, or very little, selective effect in the evolutionary sense.

We can make the following contrast between juvenile development on the one hand and adult development and ageing on the other. Juvenile development is a systematic, orderly, fairly predictable sequence of genetically regulated changes culminating in biological maturity in late adolescence. This does not mean that biological growth as such ceases in late adolescence. Biological growth (as well as psychological and social 'growth', metaphorically speaking) occurs throughout adult life, but mainly in connection with cell turnover rather than in connection with increased biological resources. Adult development and ageing, by contrast with juvenile development, is a relatively unsystematic, disorderly, and somewhat unpredictable sequence of adverse changes resulting from a variety of intrinsic and extrinsic factors such as loss of non-replaceable cells, injury, and disease. Apparently little is known about the long-range connections between juvenile development and adult ageing, which is one reason why the 'lifespan' approach to the psychology of ageing, mentioned in Chapter 1, will not be adopted in this book. The other reason is that the central issues in ageing have little in common with those in development.

It is possible to calculate the further life-expectancy of normal individuals and of those who have suffered from particular diseases or physical injuries in childhood, e.g. epilepsy, Down's syndrome, diabetes, although such information is not widely publicized. In the absence of evidence to the contrary, we can assume that common childhood illnesses and injuries have negligible effects on health, performance, and well-being in adult life and on longevity.

By contrast, it is assumed that psychological learning experiences and stresses during the formative years have long-lasting effects on behaviour in the adult years. Normal childhood experiences, together with the shaping effects of education and social influence, are assumed to give rise, eventually, to stable adult characteristics. Individual differences are attributed to genetic variations in association with differences in environmental conditions during development. Psychological explanations of maladjustment in adult life often propose causal sequences that have their origins in childhood. However, it is difficult to validate arguments based on life-history data. One should not confuse an historical interpretation, which deals with 'distal' events, with a functional explanation, which deals with 'proximal' events. One way of reconciling these two sorts of accounts is to distinguish between predisposing factors and precipitating factors. Predisposing factors are influences which increase the probability that a person will react in one way rather than another in a given set of circumstances. So, for example, genetic endowment and 'formative influences' in childhood help to direct and delimit our behaviour—inclining us to seek out certain kinds of situations and to avoid others, to react in this way rather than that. Precipitating factors are the 'proximal' or 'immediate' conditions which 'trigger' a reaction, as for example a mother reacts to protect her child in a hazardous situation, or a person commits suicide in a given set of circumstances, or a marriage breaks up because events lead to a situation which is intolerable to one or both parties.

The study of adult ontogenesis consists in describing and explaining patterns and sequences of behaviour and experience in the post-developmental years, even though some of the predisposing factors are attributed to genetic endowment or to formative influences in the juvenile years. The methods used to identify the relevant genetic factors are simply those used in behavioural and medical genetics, e.g. the study of family resemblances and twins.

The scientific study of adult ontogenesis consists in part of searching for conceptual systems that impose order and coherence on a multitude of observations. Much of what happens to people in adult life and old age is 'common knowledge' and can be taken for granted. Hence our main interest is in those aspects of ageing which are more difficult to understand, or with matters which we think are different from what is commonly believed. So social and behavioural gerontologists are interested, among other things, in intergenerational relationships, life stresses, some adult psychiatric conditions, the menopause, achievement, and centenarians.

The study of adult ontogenesis can be pursued in two contrasting ways. One way—let us call it the *simple stage approach* (SSA) is to regard adult life as a succession of rather broad stages, rather like childhood can be conceptualized as a series of developmental stages for the purposes of describing intellectual or social development. Normal adult life is then seen to consist in an orderly progression through successive stages, each of which is associated with its own special sorts of behaviour patterns, forms of experience, and environmental circumstances. Another way— let us call it the *complex sequence approach* (CSA)—is to regard adult life as a somewhat disorderly and unpredictable affair, in which there are wide differences between individuals and their circumstances, and into which a large element of chance intrudes. The result is a very wide variety of individual adult-life patterns because of the unlimited possibilities for interactions between many variables over extended periods of time.

It is obvious that the first of those two approaches (SSA) has to proceed at a very high level of abstraction and generality, and may neglect the wide range of differences between individuals, the deviant, and the exceptional cases. It is also obvious that the second approach (CSA) has to proceed at a very low level of empirical description, i.e. at the level of the individual case, and may neglect features and trends common to some or all of the individual cases. The implication is that we must somehow operate at both levels simultaneously. We must find ways of conceptualizing adult life and ageing so that we can make sense of individual cases, and deal with individual cases in ways that enable us to abstract their common features and reach conclusions which can be applied at some level of generality. This last requirement is an essential feature of scientific investigation.

SIMPLE STAGE APPROACH

It is natural to describe processes which occupy substantial amounts of time in terms of a limited number of successive stages. Thus we identify historical periods, stages in a manufacturing process, and seasons of the year. Not surprisingly, therefore, attempts have been made to divide the human lifespan into fairly distinct periods—Levinson (1978, 1981, 1986);

Lowenthal *et al.* (1975). One attempt draws an analogy with the four seasons:

Spring	Childhood and adolescence
Summer	Early adult life
Autumn	Late adult life
Winter	Old age

The associations with growth, flowering, fruition, and dying are easy to see.

Perhaps the most well-known literary description of the stages of human life is Shakespeare's seven ages of man. Not all traditional conceptualizations of the life-course have been in terms of stages. Some of the more potent images—like that of the burning candle or the emptying cask—see life as a continuous process, not one marked by abrupt transitions and discontinuities.

An early scientific study of the stages of human life was that of Charlotte Bühler and associates in the 1930s—see Bühler and Massarik (1968). Using biographical and autobiographical material they tried to identify commonalities and regularities in the lives of the people they studied. Sensibly, they tried to link social and psychological changes in life with biological changes. The result was a five-stage theory, based on 400 biographies. The first stage (i) was that of childhood and early adolescence from birth to 15 years. The remaining four stages were as follows:

 (ii) Ages 15–25—basically preparation for the transition to adult life, together with explorations in self-development and aspirations.
(iii) Ages 25–45—clarification and stabilization of life-goals and personal qualities together with effort directed towards achievement.
(iv) Ages 45–65—life review and self-assessment in relation to actual achievements and circumstances.
 (v) Ages 65 and over—feelings of satisfaction or dissatisfaction with life's outcomes, leading to contrasting patterns of adjustment to later life.

The corresponding biological characteristics were as follows:

 (ii) Completion of physical maturation together with sexual and reproductive capacity.
(iii) Stable biological functions.
(iv) Reduction in sexual and reproductive capacity.
 (v) Biological deterioration.

It is not difficult to see the limitations of both this early scientific attempt and the pre-scientific attempts to devise a conceptual framework for the human lifespan in terms of stages. Briefly, the schemes are not sufficiently detailed, especially as regards the interaction of biological and social factors, and they neglect the wide range of differences between individuals; they take no account of the fact that many lives end well short of the later stages.

Other authors, like Jung, have drawn attention to changes in motivation, as expressed in terms of interests, values, and attitudes, in adult life. These clearly differ as between young and old adults. The question is whether the age trends reveal gradual shifts, which are not coordinated, across a wide range of activities, or whether there are comprehensive and stepwise changes—discontinuities—at particular ages. It should be noted that stepwise changes averaged out over a sample of subjects may give a misleading impression of gradual age trends. Age-related effects can be examined in relation to biological changes, e.g. the menarche or the menopause, by plotting changes relative to these markers (which occur at various chronological ages but within fairly narrow limits). Unfortunately, there are few objective functional or biological markers in adult life, and we are obliged to resort to chronological age as our standard of comparison. Most social arrangements and transitions are geared to chronological age, for example many sorts of occupational seniority, retirement, and, earlier in adult life, voting, military service, and legal responsibility.

The term 'middle age' continues to be somewhat ill-defined, but interest in this topic has given rise to a number of recent publications including Berado (1982), Fiske (1979), Neugarten and Associates (1980), Troll (1985). The psychology of early and early-middle adult life will not be reviewed here, simply because its main features—personal adjustment, psychological processes, psychopathology, family life and interpersonal relationships, employment, and so on—are part of mainstream psychology or one of its branches.

Sex differences in ageing have been studied but not in a systematic way. A current tendency is to examine age effects in women, focusing on issues particularly relevant to women—Baruch and Brooks-Gunn (1984), Lesnoff-Caravaglia (1984), Notman (1979), K. Robinson (1986).

One could regard juvenile development and early adult life as a process whereby a person develops his or her potentialities in a context of expanding opportunities, and contrast this with late adult life as a process whereby a person's potentialities are reduced (through the adverse cumulative effects of ageing) and his or her opportunities for action are increasingly curtailed. Although these propositions are true in a rather abstract and general sense, they are subject to many reservations and qualifications as soon as one tries to apply them to real individual lives.

As argued elsewhere, it may be scientifically counterproductive to look for common age trends across different sorts of people, and different sorts of functions, and over long periods of lifetime. A more productive strategy might be to de-emphasize research into the adult lifespan as such, and concentrate instead on much more limited issues *within* adult life. In other words, one would study particular processes, in relatively homogeneous samples of people over short segments of adult life. In time one could build up a mosaic of findings which, in total, should reveal the main features of adult life and old age.

Jung was, perhaps, the first to draw attention to what is now sometimes called the 'mid-life crisis'. This is a period when some individuals experience a fairly radical change of outlook, following a revaluation of their past life and their prospects for the future. Such crises may be associated with substantial alterations in health and personal circumstances. Again, a notion like the 'mid-life crisis' has its uses as a sort of conceptual shorthand, and may be perfectly appropriate in some cases. It would probably be a mistake, however, to regard it as a key feature in normal adult development, or to bracket it with the menopause.

More importantly, Jung also drew attention to the problem of the meaning and purpose of life at later ages. This issue has been discussed in detail by Rosow (1974), who attributes many of the social and psychological problems of ageing in modern society to the lack of productive (useful) roles for older people.

Economic production and sexual reproduction provide much of the meaning and purpose to early adult life. But what remains when these functions have been fulfilled? Moral and religious frameworks of belief may be supportive in part, and for some people, but in an increasingly humanistic and scientific world there is a great need for a 'philosophy of human life' which is compatible with both our physical and our social nature. It is, of course, possible or even likely that cultural changes in morality will lead to values and practices in relation to ageing that would not be acceptable today—for example, with regard to euthanasia and low levels of medical and social support.

Erikson's views on stages in the life course are widely known—see Erikson (1963, 1978) and Fitzpatrick and Friedman (1983). Erikson identifies four adult stages, each of which is marked by a conflict of interests:

  (i)   identity versus role confusion
 (ii)   intimacy versus isolation
(iii)   generativity versus stagnation
(iv)   integrity versus despair.

(i) The first adult stage, in the late teens and early 20s, deals with the transition from childhood dependence to adult independence, i.e. with the transitions from education to employment, from single to married state, from childlessness to parenthood. The typical individual at this stage is unclear about his or her future and may have no long- or medium-term plans. The individual has relatively little first-hand experience of what it means to be 'adult'; and without well-established social relationships and economic resources the individual will not have clearly defined roles or a recognizable social identity. The surrounding social and environmental conditions provide a context of opportunities and constraints, of incentives and disincentives, within which the individual attempts to establish satisfying patterns of adjustment. For Erikson, satisfactory adjustment means securing a stable identity within the community of one's choice, and so fulfilling the functions that seem appropriate (those that are socially prescribed) at that time of life.

(ii) The second adult stage, from the late 20s to early middle age, say age 40, is typically concerned with establishing and consolidating close relationships, especially within the new nuclear family, but also with friends and neighbours, and at work. These close personal relationships and the activities they are associated with—sexual, parental, cultural, economic, recreational—make up what is called 'lifestyle' and underlie feelings of 'life satisfaction'. It is, of course, possible to make a satisfactory adjustment to life at this stage without conforming completely to the prevailing social norms—see Kimmel (1980). Erikson's point is that without the intimacy of close and lasting personal relationships the individual is likely to suffer a sense of social isolation that is damaging to health and welfare. We have to recognize that personal characteristics and circumstances over which the individual has little control may prevent or hinder the establishment of close social relationships, or lead to the breakdown of relationships that have been formed. There is obviously considerable scope for individual differences, and no guarantee that relationships will last for ever.

(iii) The third adult stage, middle age and later adult life, in normal circumstances, would be a fairly settled period of life in which the parents would see their children through school and into adult independence. It would be a period in which one would achieve high, possibly maximum, levels of achievement—for example, seniority at work, in income and living standards, in social status, and in some areas of intellectual or artistic activity. It goes almost without saying that differences between individuals at this stage of life are wide, and that the accidents of history and circumstance sometimes disrupt not just individual lives but whole communities of adults, as when war, economic recession, or a local disaster strikes. From an Eriksonian point of view one could say that this stage of life is concerned with what the person contributes to society, i.e. with the benefits they confer on family and interpersonal relationships—furthering other people's interests, with their economic productivity and other achievements, with what they add to the sum total of human health and welfare. The feeling that one has been of help to others or that one has contributed something of benefit to society is valued and likely to promote well-being. By contrast, the feeling that one has failed, or not made the most of one's abilities and opportunities, is unpleasant and likely to have the opposite effect.

Erikson's account of the crises at various stages of adult life may incline one to suppose that everyone carries out some sort of periodical self-analysis in an attempt to resolve successive conflicts of interest. However, many people no doubt are not reflective in this way, or not unduly concerned with the moral issues which underlie Erikson's approach. Others may experience these conflicts and emotions in relation to specific problems of adjustment without being able to conceptualize them explicitly.

(iv) The fourth and final adult stage is that which normally occurs at a late age and culminates in death. It is a function of the individual's awareness of the nearness of death. Such awareness is natural in the face of increasing physical infirmity, old age, and the various 'losses' likely to have been experienced. There is usually ample time to reflect on one's life, and to try to come to terms with what it has been. One would expect the majority of people, those who have been reasonably well-adjusted, to feel at least moderately satisfied with the life they have led, even if they have not been particularly fortunate. One's sense of integrity is based on how one copes with situations, not with the situations themselves (unless these are of one's own making). Failures in coping effectively because of flaws in oneself may give rise to a sense of despair or futility, particularly when there is no longer any time to make up for one's past mistakes and inadequacies.

One could argue that Erikson's contribution is culturally and historically circumscribed, that it conflates scientific and ethical ideas. Thus the conflict between integrity and despair is a hypothetical state of mind—it may or may not arise, and if it does it can take many different forms. No doubt moral conflicts other than those identified by Erikson could be proposed—for example, a conflict between enjoyment and responsibility, or between personal freedom and security. One could further argue that his system of ideas is not sufficiently rigorous and penetrating to serve as a platform for empirical research or further theoretical analysis. But one could say this of many contributions to psychology. Its main value has been in promoting professional and scientific interest in adult life and old age.

COMPLEX SEQUENCE APPROACH

The most basic level of observation and description is that which deals with the raw facts of the behaviour and experience of an individual over a short period of time. We can ignore, for the time being, the way such 'raw facts' are processed through observation and report by investigators who not only perceive selectively but also interpret and report in terms of their preconceptions. Descriptions and explanations of human behaviour, in other words, are 'socially constructed' and the phenomena to which they refer can be construed in various ways.

One can think of the course of adult life as a series of behaviour episodes or events—see Bromley (1986, pp. 80–1). Each episode involves not merely overt action, but all kinds of psychological processes— perception, motivation, emotion, cognition, learning and memory, atti- tude, and expectation. Each episode also occurs in some kind of environmental context and it may be crucial to our understanding of the person to know what the circumstances are and how he or she interprets the situation. Many episodes involve not only the person we are interested in studying, but also other people; so that it is necessary to take these social relationships into account. Retrospectively, the person may 'reconstruct' an episode in his or her personal history so that it seems different, in recollection, from the way it actually was. Prospectively, at any particular moment, a person has a number of possible futures, although of course only one such future is actually realized.

If a narrative corresponding to an actual sequence of life events is examined it will be seen to be composed of many different sorts of events from simple routines like washing, dressing, and feeding, to complex or significant episodes like quarrelling with someone, being ill, feeling betrayed, or being interviewed for a job. The variety is infinitely wide, hence the uniqueness, in the last resort, of the individual life.

Many episodes are trivial or mundane, and have no particular psychological significance. They may go unnoticed by observer and subject alike. Such episodes are, as it were, 'taken for granted' and fail to capture our interest or attention. This explains why our 'autobiographical memory'—see Chapter 6—usually cannot retain the details of such episodes, although we may very well assume that such-and-such an event happened and that we behaved in such-and-such a way, because that is how we would normally behave in those circumstances.

At the moment of observation the person is in a particular situation and engaged in a particular sort of activity—eating, sleeping, walking the dog, visiting mother-in-law, or whatever. This episode is the latest in a series that stretches back through time to the beginning of the individual's life. This is the series of episodes that the individual has actually lived. It is possible to conceive that the person's life could have been different—if this had happened rather than that, if the person's characteristics had been other than they were, and so on. In other words, one can conceive of a number of 'possible' lives that the individual might have lived. These 'possible' lives feature from time to time in the individual's imagination, since they represent reflections on previous actions and circumstances which might well affect attitudes to and actions in the future, as for example in making friends, giving advice, spending one's money, or dealing with one's children.

As mentioned above, our recollections about our life so far are, in part at least, reconstructions of what happened, not a literal record of events. It is not at all clear how reminiscence and autobiographical memory work—see Chapter 6. What is clear, from what we know about counselling, and the writing of case-studies and life histories, is that people may change their minds about what happened to them in the past. It is not unusual to be faced with incontrovertible objective evidence about the past which obliges us to revise our ideas about where we were and what we were doing some time ago.

The future holds a large number of possible life paths, only one of which will be actually realized. It follows that as the individual approaches closer to the limit of his or her further expectation of life, the scope for alternative life paths is reduced, and eventually none is left.

The complex sequence approach to adult ontogenesis is designed to draw attention to the existence of a variety of life-paths, and to the problems of abstracting from the empirical data on adult development and ageing and generalizing widely about age trends. Thus, even if one could identify near-identical episodes, one person's previous history and physical and psychological make-up would almost certainly lead to a reaction different from that of another person, and to different consequences for future life. A further complication is that small effects at time t_1 may have cumulatively larger effects at time $t_2, t_3 \ldots t_n$. This is why generalizations and long-range predictions about human behaviour are unreliable.

This is not to say that abstraction and generalization are not possible in the study of events in adult life and old age, but rather that proper allowances must be made for individual differences and variations in circumstances when attempting to impose a theoretical framework of inference on a body of empirical data. Take, for example, the view that bereavement is a stressful life event that reduces the life-expectancy of the surviving spouse, at least in the first year of bereavement. Or take, as another example, the view that unemployment leads to a lowering of physical and mental health. It used to be thought that the menopause was a physically and psychologically stressful period of life, but recent work suggests that its effects are less marked than had been supposed, and much more varied. Other examples of the way in which close examination of adult lifestyles (through the study of life events and daily routines) might lead to better understanding of and better control of human health and welfare in the later years can be found in studies of nutrition, alcohol intake, smoking, physical exercise, occupational hazards, and so on.

The account we have given suggests that there is no intrinsic 'plan', 'structure' or 'pattern' to a person's life-history, except that which the person subjectively constructs for himself or herself and tries to conform to, or that which the investigator constructs *post hoc* from the information available. The individual can be regarded as the locus of one actual person, as compared with an infinite number of other 'possible persons', namely, those that he or she might have become had things been different from what they actually were. The variety of individual lives seems limitless. Perhaps the best way to make sense of all this actual and possible variety is to see individual lives as somehow 'selected' in an evolutionary sense through the interaction of personal characteristics and situational factors. Of course, chance factors may play a not inconsiderable part in determining outcomes in successive episodes—see Fiske (1961). Also, people learn from experience, make plans, and act in anticipation of results. To this extent people have some control over their own fate. However, there are many important factors that we are unaware of or are unable to control, so self-management is severely curtailed.

It could be argued that for many people self-directed planning in adult life plays a relatively minor role as compared with the effects exerted by factors outside their personal control. For the most part we react automatically or habitually with little thought of the overall structure or pattern of our life. Pirandello, the dramatist, presents the course of human life as a process of improvisation in response to the vagaries of circumstance. Research on locus of control indicates that people differ in the extent to which (and circumstances in which) they attempt to assert personal control. Although ageing in later life reduces the range of behavioural options available to us, a sense of personal control continues to be an important factor in good adjustment—see Rodin *et al.* (1985).

To the extent that people share common characteristics and common circumstances we can expect to find interesting and important regularities in the way adult lives unfold—see Runyan (1982, 1984) and *Journal of*

Personality (1988). For example, one could investigate the patterns and sequences of events that lead to marriage, or to divorce, or to entering or moving through a particular career. On the basis of this information one could calculate all the different possible pathways to these outcomes. One would surely find that these different pathways are not equally likely to be followed, and that the lives of most people would be distributed over a relatively small number of 'usual' pathways—see Herbst (1970). It is in comparison with these normal or usual pathways that we identify unusual cases—age-discrepant marriages, religious conversions, high-fliers or career failures, psychological and criminal deviations.

The life-history method, like the case-study method, is essentially an exercise in detective work—an attempt to make sense of a unique pattern of facts. The evidence consists of any information which is relevant to the inquiry. It may include interview data, standardized test data, personal documents, archival material, testimony from informants, direct observation, and so on. However, even a good life-history can establish only a tiny fraction of the empirical facts. There may be no way of telling what has been omitted, invented, or misconstrued. At best, therefore, the life-history method can provide us with only rough approximations and inconclusive knowledge. The importance of the life-history method is that it goes much more deeply into the facts than is possible with brief survey instruments. One aim is to illuminate the ontogenesis of adult behaviour by close description and analysis of individual lives. Another aim, which is much more difficult to achieve, is to identify relatively normal patterns of adult development and ageing, and to constrast these with deviant or exceptional patterns.

In view of what we have said about the indeterminacy of adult life, it is obvious that accounts which attempt to impose a 'pattern of meaning' on individual lives are essentially 'socially constructed'. That is to say, they are *post-hoc* interpretations of whatever evidence is available, made in terms of the concepts and theories available to an investigator who wants to make sense of data and to persuade others of his or her point of view.

Thomae and Lehr (1986) offer an account of adult life in terms of stages, crises, and conflicts. They use a biographical method. In a review of previous literature they refer to the emphasis on conflict and stress initiating change followed by periods of relative stability. Some idea of the variety of adult lives can be seen from their work. An analysis of the biographies of 1311 men and women showed an average of 17.5 memorable events with a range from 5 to 26. Naturally, the number of significant events reported in a life-history can vary according to the depth of an inquiry and the range of issues raised. Many of the events reported were similar to those commonly referred to in the current 'life-event' literature—for example, marriages, births, deaths, illnesses, changes of address, friendships, employment, retirement—see the section on 'Life-events'. Family and occupational events predominated; other sorts of events related to political and economic circumstances. However, the same objective circumstances would tend to be understood and reacted to in an individual subjective way.

Consequently, Thomae and Lehr question the validity of any stage theory of adult development and ageing, i.e. any theory which reduces the emphasis on individual variation in favour of broad abstractions and generalizations. So, for example, generalizations about parenthood, grandparenthood, the menopause, the 'empty nest', bereavement, retire-ment and so on, must be dealt with circumspectly. In particular, one needs to examine the methods used to collect the data, the way the subjects are selected, and the way the data are collated and interpreted. It may prove to be the case that the spread of individual differences is wide, and that the variables of interest do not account for much of the variance even if they are statistically significant.

In their inquiry into conflict and stress, Thomae and Lehr report that women obtained higher scores than men, and younger people higher scores than older people. There were also differences between these groups in the frequencies with which certain kinds of conflict and stress were experienced, e.g. conflicts with children, and occupational conflicts. There is some indication that the frequency and intensity of stress diminishes sharply from early adult life to a fairly stable level from the 30s to the 50s, with a possible increase later.

Historical, environmental, and cultural factors provide the 'ecological' context within which individuals live their lives. Hence we would not expect to find great similarity between widely spaced cohorts, or between urban and rural populations, or between distinct cultural groups. Although there is some biographical and autobiographical material available, e.g. accounts by slaves, concentration camp victims, immigrants, soldiers, and so on, it is not readily accessible and seems not to have been organized as a body of knowledge.

The essential point is that adult ontogenesis is a process of adaptation and/or maladaptation to a series of unfolding and somewhat unpredictable circumstances—Block (1971), Conley (1985).

THE ADULT LIFE-PATH

This section considers a conceptual framework for understanding adult life and old age that combines features of both the simple stage approach and the complex sequence approach. Like other attempts to describe and analyse adult life, it is culturally and historically circumscribed. In other words it refers to normal adult members of westernized industrial societies in the second half of the twentieth century. It is not presented as a 'theory' of ageing, but rather as a descriptive framework which lists some of the main features of ageing as known at present, alongside a chronological scale in years. It acknowledges the importance of group and individual differences, and draws attention to the fact that while many social and psychological functions are 'age-related', this does not mean that chronological age itself is a causal factor. Ageing occurs *in* time through the interactions of a variety of biological, environmental, social, and behavioural factors.

The conceptual framework is set out in the form of a detailed timetable—see Table 2.1. The adult life-path does not lend itself to division into clear-cut biological, social, or psychological stages. Differences in personal characteristics, and in life-history and circumstances, make for considerable diversity both in the duration of lives and in the sequences of events that comprise them. The intention of the scheme set out below is to draw attention to some of the main normative characteristics associated with successive adult ages. It is based partly on common knowledge and social practice, and partly on theoretical ideas and empirical findings. Age changes may be gradual or abrupt, but averaged out they do not seem to call for a generalized 'stage theory' of adult life. A better approach seems to be to look at specific sorts of people over relatively short segments of life with regard to particular functions. In other words, to disaggregate older people and to study particular processes or life-events (not stages) and their consequences over discrete periods.

Table 2.1 may be summarized as follows:

Stage no.	Age in years	Title
1	18–21	Transition to adult independence
2	22–25	Early adulthood
3	26–40	Middle adulthood
4	41–54	Late adulthood
5	55–60	Transition to (pre-)retirement
6	61–65	(Pre-)retirement
7	66–75	Young–old
8	76–85+	Old–old
9	86–120	Very old
(10	—	Terminal stage)

In the summary table the terminal stage is listed as stage 10. However, we know that death can occur at any age. In fact, we can expect half the population born into a particular cohort to have died by the age of 74 (men) and 81 (women). Some of these individuals (about 1.5%) will have

Table 2.1 The adult life-path

Approximate age (years)	Stage	Main characteristics, ignoring wide differences between individuals and effects of circumstances
18–21	Transition from adolescence to early adult life.	Acquisition of adult rights and responsibilities, relative economic independence through employment or welfare; high levels of delinquency, but also of social concern.
22–25	Early adulthood	Engagement in various social roles: in intimate family or personal relationships, home-making, paid employment, leisure, education and training, and voluntary (value-oriented) activities. High athletic achievement in many areas. High levels of crime. Early adult identity formation.
26–40	Middle adulthood The mid-point of the male working life is about 40 years. The term 'mid-life crisis' is best reserved for any life crisis which coincidentally occurs at around the age 40–50 years and mainly involves a radical psychological readjustment or 'identity crisis'. The age of 40 is popularly thought to be an important social marker for women, but has no particular biological or psychological significance.	Selection, establishment, and consolidation of main social roles, especially those related to occupational and family matters, i.e. earning money, having children. Clear identity. Peak years for intellectual achievement. Some loss of physical and mental capacity apparent in tests of maximum performance. Noticeable effects of disuse of functions. More obvious external signs of ageing.
41–54	Late adulthood The average age for the menopause is about 49 years.	Continuation of established occupational and other social roles. Achievement of seniority in many areas, such as work, social movements (religious, political, recreational), i.e. increased social

(Continued)

Table 2.1 (*Continued*)

	Note historical changes in patterns of activity regarding employment, especially for women. The rate of mortality doubles approximately every seven years during adult life.	status and authority. Shift in family responsibilities with departure of children and increased dependence of (grand)parents. But concern for the future for others, especially younger people, indicates 'generativity' as contrasted with 'stagnation' which is indicated by preoccupation with one's own immediate well-being. Re-entry of women into occupational roles outside the home as a consequence of relief from child care. Menopause: loss of reproductive function in women. Further loss of physical and mental capacities, interaction with lifestyle, e.g. diet, exercise, stress. Problems for men in finding new employment. Relatively rapid increase in mortality rate and in disorders of middle and later life. Shift in time perspective: greater awareness of later-life prospects. Loss of (grand)parents. Grandparenthood.
55–60	Transition to retirement or pre-retirement. The usual retirement age for men is 65 years and for women 60 years. This is likely to change to a common retirement age of 63 years with flexible arrangements between age 60 and 70.	High levels of social achievement and authority for some kinds of activity. Pre-retirement preparation for women; possibly early retirement for men. Health limitations may encroach on occupational and other activities, especially those that are physically or mentally demanding. Reduction in sexual attractiveness and activity. Obvious age effects on appearance. Some role confusion in balancing personal preferences and social and occupational demands.
61–65	Pre-retirement for men; retirement for women.	Peak years for some kinds of social achievement—status, prestige, authority, wealth. Increasing disengagement from occupational roles and community affairs. Shifts in the allocation of time, money, and energies to interests which are more central to the self. Readjustment of self-concept (personal identity) in relation to withdrawal from long-standing social roles and lifestyle.

The changing health status of old people, and the gradual improvement in their social status, is leading to a refinement of the concept of old age, which nowadays applies to the 'old-old' and the 'very old', i.e. to people who, because of infirmities associated with ageing, are substantially dependent on others for their activities of self-maintenance and daily living.

66–75	Young-old	The term 'young-old' is used to refer to those aged about 66–75 years who are relatively fit and healthy and independent.	Increasing susceptibility to disorders of late life. Continuing gradual accumulation of impairments to sensory and motor functions, and to central organizing functions. Increasing loss of age peers. Changes in lifestyle and living standards associated with chronic disabilities and reduced living standards. Retirement, total or substantial withdrawal from occupational and community responsibilities (disengagement). Increased involvement in personal and family social relationships. Increased opportunity for leisure and recreational activity. Further increase in susceptibility to physical and mental disorders of late life. Increases in widow(er)hood. Terminal illness likely. Increased acceptance of prospect of death if a sense of 'integrity' (satisfaction with one's life) has been achieved; otherwise 'despair' (depression, anger, disgust) may result.
76–85+	Old-old	The term 'old-old' is used to refer to those aged 76–85+ years whose advanced age is responsible for their relatively poor health and their dependence on others for the activities of daily living. People may be dependent for reasons other than the infirmities of old age. Life-expectation at birth in the United Kingdom in 1985–7 was 72.1 years for men and 77.8 years for women.	Physical and mental inadequacy. Considerable dependency. A proportion of people, the so-called elderly 'elite', manage to maintain relatively high levels of physical and mental performance and relatively low levels of dependency. A proportion of people suffer from chronic disorders and disabilities. Terminal illness very likely.

(Continued)

Table 2.1 (*Continued*)

	Within the foreseeable future, given the expected 'rectangularization' of the survival curve, life expectation at birth should rise to about 85 years.	
86–120	Very old. The apparent upper limit of human longevity is marginally above 120 years. High final ages are achieved by those with the required genetic endowment and life circumstances.	Few survivors. Very high levels of dependency. Terminal illness – a final breakdown of critical biological functions and death.

Note: A small number of causes are responsible for many deaths; a much larger number of causes are responsible for the remaining deaths. Close analysis of mortality and morbidity data suggests that future prospects for the average life-expectation and the maximum lifespan may have been considerably underestimated.

died during the juvenile period, i.e. without passing through any adult stage of life.

One now begins to appreciate the problem of making comparisons between people at different stages of adult life. The older members, by definition, are survivors, and they are likely to differ in a number of respects from non-survivors, for example in physical health, education, psychological functioning, and socioeconomic status. The older the individual, the more likely he or she is to have undergone a variety of biological, psychological, and social changes which, in some ways, set him or her apart from other individuals of the same age, but at the same time, in other ways, make them more alike.

LIFE-EVENTS: CONCEPTS, METHODS, AND FINDINGS

Concepts

The idea of a 'life-chart', i.e. a record of the important episodes in a person's life, has been traced to Adolf Meyer, who advocated its use in medical diagnosis. The psychological study of adult life-events could be said to have begun with the publication of a Social Readjustment Rating Questionnaire (SRRQ) by Holmes and Rahe (1967), although life-events as such have always featured in accounts of personal adjustment in adult life and old age, as for example in studies of suicide, divorce, illness, bereavement, and retirement. It seemed that close examination of life-events would show a relationship between overall recent stress and subsequent physical and mental health, e.g. heart disease, depression.

The interest in life-events arose out of earlier work on stress which revealed the intimate associations between physiological functions and behaviour, particularly in relation to strong and persisting emotions such as anxiety, anger, and depression. The difference perhaps lies in the current concern with the way in which the relatively ordinary, common stresses of daily life may have cumulative effects.

Of particular interest to social and behavioural gerontologists are life-episodes which take the form of stresses, changes, upsets, persisting difficulties, or daily difficulties. It is believed that episodes of this sort contribute to physical and mental ill-health, partly as a result of their cumulative effects on the body's physiological and psychological defences.

Consider the following stressful life-events:

Being partly responsible for a traffic accident in which a child is injured.

Being removed from office pending an inquiry into one's competence.
Being threatened at knife-point and raped.
Moving house.
Winning a competition.
Achieving public recognition for bravery.

These examples illustrate the diversity of stressful life-events. They also illustrate that each brief statement covers not a particular episode which is identical from one person to another, but rather a *type* of episode within which there are many different individual patterns of behaviour and circumstances. Attempts have been made to assign values to commonly occurring stressful life-events. This can be achieved without too much difficulty by pooling the subjective judgments of a panel of subjects, either individually, or communally following discussion of those aspects of each episode to be taken into account. Naturally, panels composed of one sort of subject, e.g. middle-income retired men, are likely to give subjective values somewhat different from panels composed of a different sort of subject, e.g. young low-income women. Even so, depending upon the selection of life-events used, there is usually good general agreement on the rank-order of the events in terms of their stressfulness.

Consider next the following daily difficulties:

Being held up in traffic on one's way to work.
Overcooking a cake.
Accidentally tearing one's clothing.
Having a slow puncture in a car tyre.
Mislaying one's spectacles.
Having one's television entertainment interrupted by a telephone call.

The remarks we have made in connection with stressful life-events apply to daily difficulties too, since there is probably only a difference in degree between the two. Much depends on the actual details and the surrounding circumstances, and the psychological significance or meaning of the event.

Attention is drawn to the fact that life-events which are regarded as forms of fulfilment or achievement or good fortune can also be 'stressful' in the sense that they engender strong emotional reactions and changes in lifestyle. So too, presumably, daily difficulties, minor satisfactions, life's little ups and downs, may affect our health and well-being.

Relatively little is known about the effects of adult ageing on motivation and emotions—but see Malatesta and Izard (1984) and other references in Chapter 7. Emotional reactions, like other sorts of reactions, are partly a function of predisposing factors—temperament, motivation, habits, and so on—and partly a function of precipitating factors—usually a change in circumstances signifying a loss or a gain, or a threatened loss or hoped-for gain. Adult emotions also have a time-course, in the sense that the intensity and quality of the emotion changes as it moves from its initial onset to its status as a part of one's autobiographical memory.

A further form of stress can be observed in what can be called 'persisting difficulties'. These are not 'events' that occupy a brief period of time, but rather 'conditions' that endure for months or years. Consider the following persisting difficulties:

> Looking after a handicapped person, e.g. an elderly impaired parent.
> Having impaired vision, hearing or balance or being otherwise disabled.
> Being a combatant in military operations.
> Being unhappily married.
> Being poor.

It is obvious that such difficulties are likely to engender stress so long as they persist, even though some people may achieve a tolerable level of adaptation, i.e. 'learn to live with' the situation.

There is disagreement about the effects of desirable life-events. One would naturally assume that 'desirable' events bring about positive effects, i.e. improved health and well-being. However, some events which are regarded as desirable, e.g. getting married, migrating, increasing one's income, may involve a change in lifestyle which brings unanticipated problems of adjustment, even in the short term.

The study of life-events obviously fits well into what we have called the complex sequence approach, where we referred to adult life and ageing as a 'stream of behaviour' divided up into successive segments or episodes describable in terms of an ordinary-language narrative of events. However, behavioural gerontologists are not content with descriptive accounts of individual cases. They try to impose some sort of systematic explanatory framework on them, and in so doing they are obliged to talk in terms of common characteristics and trends, at least for specified types of people. To that extent, therefore, the study of life events is compatible with the simple stage approach since a number of life-events are common to large numbers of people at particular times of life. Consider, for example, the following list of adult life-events:

> Leaving full-time education.
> Finding temporary employment and/or unemployment.

Establishing main employment.
Change of address (relocation).
Shifts in living standards.
Marriage.
Parenthood (successive stages).
Occupational change or redundancy.
Marital readjustment.
Health changes.
Retirement.
Bereavement.

Similarly, our account of the adult life-path—see Table 2.1—identifies a variety of circumstances and events that normally characterize each stage, and could be associated with varying degrees of stress, illness, and maladjustment or, by contrast, with happiness, health, and success.

The key concepts mentioned so far include the concept of life-event itself, and the closely associated concepts of life-changes, daily difficulties, and persisting difficulties. The concept of stress links them together because of the psychophysiological mechanisms which are thought to underlie reactions to stressful life-events and changes. Another important concept is the meaning or psychological significance of an event or episode. One expects different sorts of people to react in different ways to the same sort of situation. One reason for this is that some people see as a challenge what other people see as a threat. Some people have deeper emotional attachments than others. Some are more intelligent, more experienced. For some the events are 'on time' and have been anticipated; for others the events come as a surprise. Obviously, we react to situations in terms of what those situations 'mean' to us. Thus the psychological significance of an event is one factor which mediates the effect of that event. This fact raises problems when it comes to making comparisons between people in terms of the kinds of stresses to which they have been subjected.

Methods

(a) One method uses clinical interviews and life-history data to compile lists of memorable events and circumstances associated with some kind of adaptive (or maladaptive) reaction on the part of the individual concerned. As we have seen, such events are psychologically significant, not routine, run-of-the-mill episodes of daily living. Some of the events reported are stressful, others are regarded as rewarding. In either case they induce some sort of life-change.

Perusal of the information culled from life-history investigations reveals a variety of specific life-events (memorable episodes). These events can be grouped under broad headings such as the following:

Death of a close friend.
Change of occupation.
Personal injury or illness.
Prosecution.
Change in leisure activities.
House improvement.

It is possible to scale these types of life-event subjectively according to their stressfulness or according to the degree of life-change they induced.

Holmes and Rahe (1967) compiled a list of 43 items which were then rated using a magnitude estimation procedure—with 'marriage' arbitrarily assigned a value of 500. This procedure requires that other events be assigned values relative to that standard. Thus an event which was regarded as requiring only half the amount of readjustment that marriage calls for would be assigned the value of 250. Holmes and Rahe obtained quite high correlations between their various subsamples. However, although subjects may agree generally on the rank-order of stressfulness of these events, they may differ as regards their absolute level. The use of more than one anchorage-event or comparison-event should help to control for variations in the level of scores.

The subjectively estimated stress/change values obtained from a standardization exercise can be used to examine the number of stressful life-events and the total amount of stress that people experience. These observations in turn can be examined in relation to levels of physical and mental health—see Dohrenwend and Dohrenwend (1974).

There are a number of difficulties with this first method, including the following: the omission of relevant or representative items from a scale; variations in the way subjects interpret an item or identify an appropriate event or recall it; variations in the psychological significance of an event; the occurrence of multiple events of the same sort. Considerable care is needed in the construction, standardization, and administration of a life-event scale—Davies et al. (1987, 1989). Davies et al. (1989) have compiled a 'dictionary' of life events and difficulties to help resolve some of the many methodological difficulties in research on ageing and life stress. For example: there is the problem of distinguishing between 'events' and 'difficulties', and between 'objective conditions' and 'subjective meanings'; there is the problem of summing multiple events or difficulties; older people may rate certain types of stress differently from younger people. Different procedures are likely to produce different results.

(b) Another method uses the same sort of life-history interview method, but retains the uniqueness of the episodes as reported. Recall is usually restricted to the previous six or 12 months. These episodes are then examined and discussed by a panel of judges who arrive at a consensus regarding the magnitude of the life-change involved in each episode. Various scaling methods can be used, including magnitude scaling. The advantage of this method is that it can take contextual features into account, including to some extent the psychological significance of the event. The disadvantage is the time and effort required to score the episodes, and the difficulty of making comparisons between different sorts of samples. It is possible to use a panel of older judges to assess the life-episodes reported by older subjects, and to compile a 'dictionary' of life-events and difficulties which illustrates the diverse sorts of stresses to which older people are exposed.

Both methods enable an investigator to arrive at an estimate of the total number of stressful life-events experienced in a given period of time, and to sum the values assigned to each event to derive a total score. The two scores are usually closely correlated. Naturally, different scaling methods will yield quantitatively different results, although the findings may be in general agreement.

Perhaps the most important problem with life-event methodology is that of separating out cause from effect. For example, to what extent is marital discord the cause or effect of a psychological maladjustment? To what extent may a depressive illness increase the likelihood of recall of stressful events? Some investigators have argued that only prospective studies are worthwhile.

Findings

The recent literature on stressful life-events is extensive, e.g. Dohrenwend *et al.* (1987), Dohrenwend and Shrout (1985), Holmes and David (1984), Tennant (1983), so we can indicate only a few of the findings relevant to adult life and ageing. In general, investigators have found consistent but low positive relationships between life-stress and physical and mental health. There is some conflict of opinion about whether 'desirable' events can be interpreted as stressful, in the sense of leading to adverse consequences. The research findings seem to point in the opposite direction, as with common-sense expectations, in that desirable events lead to better health and well-being—see Aro and Hanninen (1984).

Some studies have attempted to relate particular sorts of life-stresses to particular sorts of distress—for example, losses such as bereavement are thought to increase the risk of depressive illness, and occupational stresses (high workload, low control) are thought to increase sickness absence. McLanahan and Sorensen (1984) examine theoretical and methodological issues in the study of life-events, and report the results of a large-scale longitudinal study. In general the stresses considered— residential, occupational, familial—had adverse effects on feelings of self-satisfaction, optimism, and effectiveness. They found that 'exits' or 'losses' were more stressful than other kinds of life-change, but much depended on whether the changes were voluntary or not.

As pointed out earlier, a person's behaviour is a function of predisposing factors (located within the person) and precipitating factors (usually defined in terms of environmental events). In clinical practice, however, as well as in daily life, it is not always possible to identify the nature and extent of the causal processes that produce a given reaction, e.g. student or occupational failure, marital breakdown, suicide, or depression. Hence the need for valid and discriminating methods of measuring physiological, psychological, and social (including environmental) charac-teristics. Life-event methodology is concerned with quantifying the kinds and degrees of stress (or life-change) that people experience. Retrospective studies are suspect. Longitudinal prospective studies offer considerable advantages, as they would, for example, in relation to the study of the effects of exercise during adult life—see Thornton (1984). Longitudinal studies make it more likely that the investigator will detect cases where event-related effects induce other events with similar or different effects, as for example poor health may aggravate occupational stress which gives rise to marital discord which leads to financial stress and to poorer health.

Cornell et al. (1985) draw attention to the importance of information about 'baseline' levels of stress. In fact, relatively little is known about the general level of stress in the community at large, although people may have formed strong impressions of the stress experienced by some groups of people in some circumstances, e.g. ethnic minorities, the elderly poor in inner-city areas, single parents, and certain occupational groups. One consequence is that when a person reveals his or her life-circumstances, as in a clinical interview which focuses on stressful life-events, the clinician is likely to overestimate the influence of such events in producing physical illness or maladjustment, simply because he or she is not aware of the extent to which other, normal, adults encounter difficulties in life. Another consequence is that if there are baseline differences in stress levels between two groups which are being compared, then such differences need to be taken into account when assessing the relationship between levels or types of stress and concurrent or subsequent physical illness or maladjustment.

Cornell et al. (1985) show that the number of stressful life-events increased from a baseline level (one to two years before the onset of psychiatric illness) to a pre-onset level (up to one year before the illness). Patients diagnosed as suffering from so-called reactive depression had a higher initial baseline level of stress than the patients with 'endogenous' depression, but experienced roughly the same increase in stress in the pre-onset period. In other words, the reactive depressives seemed to be subject to chronically high levels of stress. In percentage terms, patients with reactive depression seemed to be more prone than endogenous depressives and controls to stress involving work, financial problems, and interpersonal difficulties. However, the statistical analysis shows that the relationships are by no means so simple—for example, the baseline levels of the groups (endogenous, reactive, controls) varied across different sorts of stress.

Zimmerman (1983) has reviewed a variety of methodological issues in research on life-events. Since the publication of the Holmes and Rahe (1967) scale, several investigations have been carried out to test its reliability and validity, and to develop improved concepts and methods for studying life-events and their effects. For example, assigning different 'weights' to events which seem to differ in the degree of stress they bring about has little or no advantage over 'unit' weights. Although the relative order of magnitude is clear, the absolute values assigned as scores vary from person to person and from group to group. Scales which contain more life-events, and describe them more specifically, tend to be more reliable and valid than shorter scales containing broad, general items. It has been pointed out that subjective ratings of stress are confounded by the person's feelings about the subsequent effects of that stress. Another complication is that some life-events that can be anticipated produce stress long *before* they actually occur, e.g. a change of occupation, divorce, moving house. Physical ill-health or psychological disturbance may cause certain life-events. Hence it may be difficult to work out the relationships between causes and effects, especially when the relevant dates may be in some doubt. Some investigators have argued that statements describing physical and psychological 'symptoms' should not form part of a life-event schedule.

In general, undesirable events tend to be given higher subjective 'stress', 'upset', or 'change' scores than desirable events, and to be more closely associated with subsequent ill-effects. But this still leaves open the question of what actually causes the ill-effects. Although the early research work assumed that even desirable or positive events might have ill-effects because of the demands of readjustment, this aspect of the problem of life-events is even less well understood than that of negative events.

It seems reasonable to suppose that the way we experience a life-event—how we interpret its significance—is important in determining the score we assign to it. However, control subjects who have not experienced a particular event seem not to differ greatly from those who have experienced it, in terms of the score they assign to it. It is possible that subjects who assign relatively high scores to stressful life-event items may be indicating a susceptibility to react adversely. This possibility can be examined prospectively by testing subjects well before some event, e.g. an examination, selection interview, or driving test, and measuring post-stress reactions.

Zimmerman (1983) reviews articles on the interesting issue of the extent to which informants, other than the person/patient being interviewed, provide additional information. Estimates of the amount of information added range from 10% to 29%. Of course, much depends on the kinds of information sought and the characteristics of the persons studied.

There are indications that some of the adverse consequences of stress on health are mediated by the ANS and the immune system. This is a technical area outside our present concern, but referred to in several of the references to the biology of ageing listed at the end of the book.

OTHER ASPECTS OF ADULT DEVELOPMENT AND AGEING

The social and ecological framework

A neglected aspect of adult development and ageing is the way our lives are locked into a number of natural cycles associated partly with the physical world and partly with the social world we inhabit. Thus we calculate our lifetime in terms of annual solar cycles; certain important activities are geared to tidal cycles and seasons of the year. In addition, there are a number of social cycles when activities occur at weekly, sessional, annual, or longer intervals. In education we are locked into termly (semester) cycles; in religion, into periodic festivals and ceremonies. Economically, we are subject to natural cycles of supply and demand, expansion or recession, which are only partly understood. Biologically, we are normally subject to diurnal rhythms of sleeping and waking, eating and excreting, and the monthly menstrual cycle (until the menopause). These and other psychobiological periodicities give rise to regular patterns and sequences of behaviour shared, in a broad sense, by large numbers of people.

As we move into the period of dependency in late life because of physical and mental infirmity, we are necessarily subjected to a variety of constraints arising from the need to fit in with the circumstances and behaviour patterns of our care-givers. Unfortunately this may give rise to institutional types of environment which seem to encourage dependency, apathy, and loss of personal control. Such environments may fail to provide the therapeutic and supportive services which maximize and prolong those aspects of human life most highly valued at earlier ages. If we manage to avoid institutionalization in late life, and attempt to live in the community, then unless we can integrate our own daily and periodic activities with those of other people, we are unlikely to benefit fully from the support services that others can provide, and so suffer the consequences of neglect or predation.

Personality development and the self-concept in adult life and old age

Although I have outlined the main features of adult development and ageing in general terms, I have not dealt with the organization of individual behaviour, i.e. with 'personality'. This topic is taken up again in Chapters 3 and 4. All that needs to be said at this stage is that it is difficult to make statements about personality changes over long periods of time (or about personality differences between people of widely different ages). One reason for this is because the way we behave is partly a function of the situations in which we find ourselves, and our circumstances change substantially throughout adult life. Also, it is not easy to make comparisons between personality characteristics (dispositions, abilities, values, habits, attitudes, beliefs, interests, etc.) at different ages, because we cannot be sure that our measuring instruments are equally valid at these different ages. The evidence, such as it is, suggests that changes in 'personality' during adult life are normally small. However, if there are substantial changes in the physical basis of behaviour or in the individual's environment, then naturally one can expect to see substantial changes in the organization of behaviour, i.e. in personality. So, for example, alterations in bodily functions account for senile dementia of the Alzheimer type, and some forms of depression. Also, excessive stress may result in abnormal psychological reactions, such as apathy, suicide, or sexual dysfunction.

The already massive literature on the self-concept and self-perception is being added to as a consequence of studies on the effects of ageing— Grellner (1986), Haemmerlie and Montgomery (1987), *International Journal of Behavioral Development* (1985), McCrae and Costa (1988), Mueller and Ross (1984).

We shall take the self-concept to be, quite simply, the impression that the individual has formed of himself or herself. This impression has a manifest content, i.e. those explicit ideas and feelings the person has, and a latent content, i.e. those implicit assumptions and feelings the person is unaware of, which nevertheless influence his or her behaviour. Access to these ideas and feelings by an outside observer is essentially inferential, in the sense that the person's public statements about himself or herself may not correspond with the person's private opinions. Furthermore, we are not fully cognizant of our own characteristics because of the effects of ignorance, stupidity, and emotional defences. Having said this, it seems reasonable to suppose that the self-concept, defined in terms of how the person would describe himself or herself, or how privileged and competent observers would describe the person's self-concept, changes during adult life and old age in an adaptive way, partly in response to the demands of the real world, partly in response to internal demands for consistency, fulfilment, and conflict resolution—see Maddi (1980). The self, of course, has a developmental history through juvenile and adult life, so the basic questions are: 'What are the functions of the self-concept in adult life and old age?' and 'In what ways does it change?' Normally we can recognize and acknowledge the continuity of self over long periods of the lifetime. But in some respects there may be a sense of discontinuity or 'otherness' in relation to certain periods of life, in that we distance ourselves from, or no longer quite understand, the person we used to be. Such discontinuities may be accounted for in terms of radical changes in circumstances, or conversion experiences (religious, political, moral, scientific, or cultural). The tendency in psychology has been to emphasize the consistency of the self-concept and personality, whereas a great deal of the scientific evidence, and common experience, suggests that the behaviour of individuals is better thought of as 'adaptive' (in the broad sense that includes defensive coping), and adaptation may very well give rise to inconsistencies in behaviour and discontinuities from one occasion to another.

Reminiscence, life-review, and autobiographical memory

These issues are closely connected with the self in adult life and old age. A sense of historical continuity can be maintained as long as the functions of autobiographical memory remain intact. That is to say, the individual should be able to recall events which are psychologically significant, and particularly events which are socially shared. This last point deserves amplification. In conditions of mental infirmity in late life we may become incapable of recognizing or remembering things that enable us to relate to other people—their faces, names, identities, functions, relationships, locations, and so on. This happens in senile dementia of the Alzheimer type when we may become disoriented for time, place, and person. We then become incapable of adapting to our environment without massive support from others. In losing our social identity we lose our personal identity.

Normally, throughout adult life, we engage in the autobiographical memory functions known as reminiscence and life-review. These are familiar functions in daily life. They are adaptive in the Piagetian sense of accommodating the individual to the facts of life and enabling him or her to assimilate information relevant to the self. Reminiscence can fulfil a number of functions—see Coleman (1986) and Chapter 6. For example, it can be used in the interests of social solidarity, or to entertain, or to express one's feelings, or to compensate for current insufficiencies. Life-review (Butler, 1963) is a rather more systematic exercise in autobiographical recall. It is associated more with middle age and later than with early adult life. It tends to occur on occasions when people are faced with making important decisions about what to do with themselves in the future, as for example when the last child is about to leave home, or when retirement is in prospect, or when illness or job change necessitates a radical readjustment. Life-review tends to be a reconstructive process, a process of putting things into perspective, or rethinking the past in order to deal more effectively with the future. In the later stages of life, of course, when one's future is greatly foreshortened, the process of life-review is more concerned with finding some psychological significance in, and personal satisfaction with, the life one has led, or rather with the story of one's life that one has constructed. This refers back to Erikson's notion of a conflict between integrity and despair when faced with the prospect of one's own death.

The life-review can take many different forms. It can be a fairly casual, intermittent sort of reverie. It can be a deliberate systematic attempt to reorganize one's lifestyle. It can become a literal autobiography or life-story. The life-history method used, for example, in clinical, psychological, and social research can be adapted for counselling purposes, so that in establishing the life-story, the patient can be helped to review and readjust his or her life.

SUMMARY

The term 'adult ontogenesis' refers to the historical development of an individual after completion of the juvenile period. One can contrast the relatively orderly, genetically regulated process of juvenile development with the relatively disorderly and the somewhat diverse and unpredictable process of adult development and ageing. Little is known for certain about the long-range effects of development on adult life and old age. A distinction can be drawn between predisposing factors and precipitating factors in the explanation of adult behaviour, and between distal and proximal factors. Attention should be paid to the diversity of issues of theoretical or practical interest in adult life, and to the diversity of methods used to investigate them.

The simple stage approach regards adult life as a succession of broad stages. The approach has its origins in natural common-sense forms of reasoning, and has a long history. There have been several attempts to put this approach onto a scientific footing, as with the work of Buhler, Jung, and Erikson. These attempts have drawn attention to interesting and important aspects of ageing but have not resulted in significant conceptual or empirical advances in behavioural gerontology. It is noted that, apart from the menopause, there are no distinctive biological markers for any of the proposed life-stages. These stages are invariably defined in terms of psychological and social characteristics, and the boundaries between them are virtually obscured by variations between individuals. It is possible to argue that the attempt to look for common age trends across different sorts of people and over long periods of adult life may not be the best scientific way forward.

The complex sequence approach regards adult life as a somewhat disorderly and unpredictable affair in which there are wide differences between individuals and their circumstances, and into which a large element of chance intrudes. The result is a very wide variety of individual adult life-patterns. The study of adult lives calls for methods that will do justice to the way human behaviour is organized in relation to real-life circumstances, especially when such behaviour is distributed over a considerable period of time. This has tended to rule out the usual sorts of brief experimental investigations, and to give more emphasis to prospective longitudinal surveys, naturalistic observation, clinical investigations, and life-history methods.

Adult life can be represented as a series of psychobehavioural episodes. Many of these are mundane and taken for granted as part of the ordinary activities of daily life. The episodes or life-events which are scientifically interesting are those which are psychologically significant for a range of individuals, change their behaviour substantially, and help us to understand and deal more effectively with the determinants of human behaviour.

The simple stage approach and the complex sequence approach can be reconciled by recognizing their advantages and disadvantages, and combining their best features. The best feature of the simple stage approach is its attempt to develop a comprehensive account of adult development and old age at a high level of abstraction and generality. The best feature of the complex sequence approach is its concentration on the actual details of individual lives. Our account of the adult life-path offers not a theory of ageing but rather a descriptive framework whereby many different sorts of psychological issues can be brought into relationship with one another to make up an overall pattern. The relationship is, metaphorically speaking, the relationship that individual pieces have to a complete mosaic. Table 2.1 shows how the adult life-path can be divided into 10 age-related stages, each having a typical set of biological, social, and psychological features, the last one being the terminal stage. The wide range of differences between individuals limits the extent to which one can generalize about age trends or about the factors affecting adult behaviour.

The study of life-events has always been a necessary part of biographical and autobiographical work. However, Holmes and Rahe put it on a scientific footing when they constructed a scale in which 43 possible life-events were assigned numerical values according to the degree of life-change induced. It was supposed that any sort of substantial life-change, i.e. psychological readjustment, would be stressful and might help bring about adverse consequences in physical and mental health. It was also supposed that the stresses induced by several life-events might have cumulative effects, because of the relationship between stress and the body's physiological and psychological defences. Subsequently, distinctions were drawn between life-stresses, life-changes, persisting (chronic) difficulties, and daily difficulties. One method in life-event research is to compile a standard list of events and to attach to each a standardized stress value. Another method is to collect personal accounts of life-events and have a panel of judges rate the severity of each event, relative to certain standard comparison events. Unfortunately, methodological difficulties make it unwise to draw firm conclusions from this empirical research.

There is a difference between the objective event and the psychological significance or meaning it has for the individual. There are problems with life-stress scales as psychometric instruments. The study of life-events obviously fits in well with the complex sequence approach to adult life, but it also fits in with the simple stage approach, since it attempts to identify life-events which are common to large numbers of people, and some of these life-events are more common at some age levels than at others. In general, stressful life-events have been shown to have adverse consequences for physical and mental health, although the relationship is not strong. There are also indications that particular sorts of stress lead to particular sorts of distress.

Other aspects of adult development and ageing include the following: the ecological and social frameworks which impose sequential patterns of behaviour on adults at every age; personality development and the self-concept; reminiscence, life-review, and autobiographical memory.

Chapter 3

Psychometric Assessment

INTRODUCTION

There are methods of psychological assessment which are not quantitative, i.e. not psychometric. For example, case-studies, life-histories, psychiatric diagnoses, social reports, and other useful forms of assessment are qualitative in the sense of not containing any measurements. Such assessments are usually reported in a mixture of ordinary language and the technical language appropriate to a particular area of professional expertise. What we look for in qualitative assessments is not measurement as such, but accuracy. An accurate qualitative assessment is one in which the statements correspond with the facts and discriminate between similar but non-identical cases. Psychometric assessment, by contrast, is quantitative, but the measurements derived from psychometric assessment have to be interpreted in the wider context of psychological assessment.

Psychometrics can be regarded as one of psychology's outstanding achievements, and yet it is probably no exaggeration to say that, outside the realm of intelligence and attainment testing, the practical applications of this technology leave much to be desired. Kline (1986, p. 207) goes as far as to say 'Simple as good psychometrics are, it remains an unfortunate fact that a huge majority of psychological tests are both invalid and unreliable.'

Reference is made elsewhere in this book to the need for objective and exact assessments of the psychological effects of ageing. Reference is also made to some of the problems associated with the construction of psychometric instruments for use in adult life and old age. In this chapter we deal with the way psychometric theory and practice may have to be modified to cope with the problems of psychological assessment in later life, and conversely with the way such assessment may benefit from closer adherence to psychometric methods. This is essential if progress is to be made towards exact and objective observation, whether for the purposes of research, diagnosis, prognosis, monitoring, or outcome evaluation—see Kane and Kane (1981), Mangen and Peterson (1982a, b).

The elderly present particular problems as regards psychometric assessment. Their behaviour, their health and living conditions, are usually the result of a multiplicity of contributory causes (rather than of one or a few)—biomedical, psychological, social, and environmental. A critical feature of their behaviour is the extent to which they can function independently in spite of their disabilities and disadvantages—see Fillenbaum (1984).

The elderly, especially the infirm and the so-called 'old–old', change fairly rapidly over time and fluctuate in performance, often unpredictably. Such changes and fluctuations may be useful as indicators diagnostically or in evaluating the effectiveness of a treatment. Hence, sensitive measures capable of repeated application are needed.

The sorts of measures thought to be appropriate are often not available, or have been developed for other purposes or standardized on non-elderly subjects. Few norms or standards have been established. Measures of performance prior to assessment, e.g. premorbid measures, may not be available. Those that are available may not be sufficiently valid or reliable for practical purposes. For examples of developments in psychometric assessment in behavioural gerontology, see Aiken (1988), Bell and Gilleard (1986), Cresswell and Lanyon (1981), Golden et al. (1984), Rabbitt (1982b), O'Carroll and Gilleard (1986).

Some measures are suitable for the assessment of individual cases; other measures are suitable for the assessment of groups or organizations. A major incentive for the development of valid measurements is the expectation that economies can be made in the use of resources, and that services can be made cost-effective.

Psychometric assessment of an individual case should help improve the management of that case by facilitating a comprehensive and individualized programme of treatment and support. Assessment may need to be comprehensive because many diverse factors are relevant to adjustment in later life, and because one is likely to be dealing with the 'person as a whole' on a long-term basis, i.e. for the rest of his or her life. Assessment also needs to be relevant to specific issues in the particular case.

Psychometric assessment should meet the usual requirements of reliability, validity, and utility. Ideally, assessment methods should be economical, portable, easy to use, quick to administer and interpret, replicable, and acceptable to users and subjects alike.

It is easy to forget that a psychometric measure is only the means of operationally defining a concept. Operationally defining intelligence or personality in terms of a particular test does not exhaust the general meaning of the concept of intelligence or personality. Thus the measure may be reified (assumed to measure something real) or misconstrued (assumed to indicate something it does not in fact indicate), e.g. well-being, life-satisfaction, or depression. This is a particular danger where the assessment instrument consists of a few self-report items, since a plausible alternative set may fail to give the same result. Also, items culled from questionnaires designed for younger subjects may not have the same psychological significance for older subjects.

Elderly subjects may have difficulty in understanding and following even simple instructions. Also, routine and repeated assessment may be assigned to care-staff who may need training and supervision in the use of psychometric tests, even simple rating scales and checklists. Their duties may leave little time for the administration of such tests. A particular advantage is gained in other contexts, e.g. in research, if the tests can be self-administered reliably and validly.

In general, psychometric measurements should not be regarded as equivalent to biomedical measurements such as weight, pulse rate, or blood count. They are usually based on different principles and have a less direct relationship with the processes they are designed to measure. However, this is not to say that biomedical measures need not meet the usual requirements of reliability, validity, and utility—see Thienhaus *et al.* (1985), Waters *et al.* (1987).

Psychological measurements, like other measurements, have a number of uses: they provide descriptive data; they can be made into standardized diagnostic or assessment instruments; they can be used for 'screening' purposes to identify patients at risk or patients likely to benefit from a particular type of treatment; they may provide comparable measures over several occasions for the same person and thus help to reveal changes over time; they can be used actuarially to forecast outcomes. Psychometric assessment may be helpful in guiding a variety of treatment or management programmes—for example, monitoring the effects of drugs, or of recreational and occupational therapy, counselling, and so on.

Among the important considerations to take account of are base rates. A base rate is the frequency of occurrence of a condition, e.g. depression in community-dwelling women aged 70–80 years. Diagnostic tests which cannot show an improvement over base rate estimates have little or no value. Similarly, tests which fail to score patients correctly are, to that extent, unsatisfactory.

The sort of comprehensive, in-depth, and continuing long-term assessment needed in work with the elderly raises ethical and administrative problems, apart from technical, conceptual, and economic problems. Record-keeping and communication between carers may break down in the absence of effective management. It may be difficult to demonstrate the 'psychological benefits' of care for some patients, especially those reduced to a vegetative state. Considerations such as these cannot be settled by reference to empirical data, although empirical data may help to clarify the ethical issues involved. Psychometric assessment, together with other 'qualitative' sorts of assessment, helps to clarify cause–effect relationships, provided an appropriate explanatory framework can be developed.

Psychometric tests for the elderly can be adapted from existing instruments used for other purposes with other age groups. However, this involves virtually reconstructing a test so as to ensure that its various features—item content, length, instructions, scoring standards, norms, and so on—render it reliable, valid, and useful when applied to elderly subjects. There is a need to develop tests designed to measure aspects of behaviour relevant to understanding and dealing with the mental health and social welfare of the elderly. Some of these tests will be similar to those used with younger age groups (especially the physically and mentally handicapped), but others will deal with aspects of behaviour and psychological functioning peculiar to late life, e.g. the assessment of dementia or stroke, attitude to retirement, risk factors, and social support.

The range of issues that have already been the subject of psychometric investigation is enormous. Consider the following selective list, and bear it in mind when considering the concepts, methods and findings of psychometric assessment in relation to later life.

(1) *Biomedical functions*: health, vision, hearing, balance, other senses, mobility, fine motor control, speech, neurological functions, sleep, bladder and bowel functions.
(2) *Psychological functions*: life-satisfaction (morale, happiness and well-being), social attitudes and relationships, intelligence and memory, language, motivation, feelings and emotions, psychiatric state, personal control, reminiscence and life-review, self-concept, attitude to the future and to other issues, subjective health, activities of daily living, and leisure interests.
(3) *Environmental conditions*: accommodation and living standard, social support, communications and transport, income and expenditure, availability and quality of services, risk factors, nutrition, 'quality of life', stress.

Some factors can be assessed fairly objectively and with some precision (blood pressure, accommodation, language) whereas others depend upon subjective judgments by the subject or observer (sleep, stress, mental state), which may be difficult to quantify.

RELIABILITY AND VALIDITY

It is generally accepted that a psychological measure should be reliable and valid and should discriminate clearly between different individuals. However, its utility, i.e. the practical benefits it brings for the professional user, is less often considered. Instead, reliance is placed on the results of experimental investigations and standardization trials, often using small samples, selected subjects, and neglecting cross-validation. Follow-up studies investigating the results of practical applications under routine conditions appear to be relatively rare. Some studies have shown that psychometric tests, other than intelligence and attainment tests, are by no means widely used in professional practice. Other studies have shown that single-occasion measures of psychological functions are unsatisfactory, although data aggregated over several occasions can produce satisfactory levels of reliability and validity—see Epstein (1983). The not-uncommon failure to replicate experimental findings in psychology means that the measures used are not sufficiently robust for practical purposes; they are too sensitive to unimportant differences between subject characteristics and situational conditions.

There are reasons for believing that our behaviour becomes more variable (unstable) as we grow older, even although the range of our responses is reduced in many respects—as for example in response speed, physiological reactions, and some aspects of emotion and motivation. It would therefore be helpful to develop measures and procedures which would enable us to separate out an older person's characteristic or maximum performance from the intrinsic variation (or instability) with which it is associated. This means constructing tests which are more reliable than those used with younger adults, where subject variability is assumed to be less of a problem.

Performance in later life is thought to be less stable because of the wide range of adverse effects that accumulate with age. Well-practised performances, of course, may not suffer to the same extent. The point is that any increase in such intrinsic variation—through fatigue, inattention, discomfort, memory lapse, and so on—may lower the apparent reliability of a test. This is particularly important with regard to 'difference' scores, which compound the unreliability of both tests—see Chapman and Chapman (1978).

The usual method for increasing the reliability of a test is to increase its length, i.e. the number of items. This then raises problems with item selection and test fatigue. Thus, in order to keep a test reasonably short, extra effort has to go into making each item a good and relatively independent indicator of the function being tested. That is to say, items should correlate well with the criterion or with the total score (and load strongly on the factor represented by the test), but have relatively low correlations with each other. Of course, there is no point in increasing the reliability (internal consistency) of a test at the expense of its validity. The relationship between reliability and validity is particularly important in the measurement of change over time—an essential feature of longitudinal studies of ageing.

Although psychological tests are said to require measurement of at least interval scale level, opinions differ about the legitimacy of using certain mathematical operations on numbers derived from procedures which give essentially ordinal (ranked) values. 'Forgetting where the numbers came from' (Lord, 1953) may ease the computations but undermine one's interpretation of the results. Provided there is a logic to the procedure it should be possible to find legitimate methods of scaling and statistical analysis. The important thing is to explain clearly and exactly how the measures (numbers) were arrived at.

When it comes to making comparisons between age groups, raw score differences may be misleading and proportional effects may be more revealing. For example, a change in score from 20 to 24 is a 20% improvement, whereas a change from 50 to 54 is only an 8% improvement. The question is 'What do these differences mean?' The question arises regardless of whether the scores are objective, e.g. time taken, number correct, sum of weighted items, and regardless of any transformation, e.g. z or square-root scores. Perhaps the best approach is to make full use of exploratory data analysis as well as modern computer-assisted statistical analysis, whilst remembering that empirical observations can be interpreted in a variety of ways. The aim is to find the most sensible interpretation, i.e. the one that most fully explains the data, stands up to close examination, and opens up new areas of inquiry.

The minimum test–retest reliability is said to be 0.7. Although the standardization trials may reach or exceed this value, it is possible that in practice, with minor variations in administration and subject characteristics, the reliability may be lower. It is important to remember that the validity coefficient cannot exceed the square of the reliability. Unreliability thus sets a limit to validity, but a highly valid test must necessarily have high reliability. So, it is argued, validity should be the main aim in developing a psychometric test.

Unreliability can arise for a number of reasons related to the processes of ageing. First, individual items may not be equally applicable to subjects of different ages. Second, opportunities for guessing may advantage one age group rather than another. Third, the format and administration of the test may affect people differently—for example, tests containing many items may be tiring for older subjects, the instructions and the phrasing of items may have differential effects. Fourth, ageing may affect the extent to which responses are omitted or subject to biases of one sort or another.

A number of points can be made about validity. First, although face validity is regarded somewhat contemptuously by psychometricians, it nevertheless exerts a profound influence on those who want to interpret the psychological significance of a test performance. So, for example, the content of items in measures of locus of control, anxiety, or life-satisfaction is used to argue the nature of the function tested. It can be shown, however, that the meaning of a person's opinions and actions depends on the context in which they occur. In self-report measures the context is often not revealed. Hence it does not follow that a particular trait, e.g. internal locus of control, is being expressed by the person taking the test—see Gergen *et al.* (1986). One advantage of a test which has apparent face validity (even if this is misleading) is that it helps to secure the cooperation of subjects in enabling them to 'see the point' of the exercise in which they are taking part. Motivation and cooperation are clearly important in the study of older people who may have difficulty in understanding what they are supposed to do, may be unfamiliar with psychological tests, and need to be kept interested in the task.

As far as concurrent validity is concerned, the point to remember is that a test which is a valid measure of a psychological function at one age may not measure the same function at a later age, or may not measure it to quite the same extent. Hence, tests constructed for young adult ages should be revalidated at several later age levels. This raises difficult conceptual and methodological problems because it seems likely that the organizaton of cognitive and personality functions changes with age, and problems or items which were dealt with in one way earlier in life may be dealt with differently at a later age. Our present understanding of personality and cognitive operations is insufficient to enable us to construct exact measures of these operations.

Berg and Sternberg (1985) have proposed a new approach to the study of adult intelligence. They emphasize: the practical applications of intelligence to the problems encountered in daily life; the organization of behaviour over time; the formation of cognitive schemata (crystallized intelligence); and the identification of basic cognitive operations (fluid intelligence). It seems likely that this new approach will be most profitably explored through the study of infant and juvenile development, but it does at least offer a fresh perspective on adult intelligence, in the sense of directing our attention to aspects of cognition other than those traditionally studied under this heading—learning and memory, intelligence test performance, mental skills, mental speed. New methods of assessment should arise from new ways of conceptualizing adult intelligence. These new methods will, of course, have to be validated.

As we have seen, face validity is relatively unimportant except as a feature which helps to establish cooperation with subjects. In so far as existing tests of adult intelligence are measuring what they are supposed to measure they can be used, initially at least, to demonstrate the concurrent validity of any new tests. Should it prove possible to identify any important 'objective' correlates of intelligence, e.g. physiological indices, then obviously these too might be used to assess the concurrent validity of new tests. The identification of objective criteria against which psychological tests can be validated is a continuing problem in most areas of assessment.

It is sometimes forgotten that a test should not correlate with variables other than those which it is supposed to measure. For example, a test which measures spatial reasoning may inadvertently reflect personality characteristics also. It is important to get rid of these extraneous influences if one's aim is to establish the validity of the test as a measure of spatial reasoning alone. This is not to say that there is no place for tests which measure a combination of psychological characteristics. Such tests may be very useful for practical purposes—in selection, for example, or in following up treatment effects. However, their value is limited if one does not have a clear idea of the extent to which a test measures each relevant variable. Ideally one should have separate, independent measures of each variable. This problem illustrates the connection between theory and practice—between the way psychological processes are conceptualized and the way we operationalize them for the purposes of empirical research and professional practice.

The usual ways of identifying psychological processes measured psychometrically is by one or another form of factor analysis or cluster analysis. Confirmatory factor analysis is designed to enable an investigator to revise his or her theory in the light of empirical data.

Another way of looking at the validity of psychological measures used in the study of adult life and ageing is to examine the extent to which such measures predict future outcomes. This is known as predictive validity. So, for example, a measure designed to test a subject's rate of cognitive deterioration (excluding effects arising from drugs or other medication, or from certain pathological conditions) should enable one to predict a future score and to predict future differences between individuals. Successful prediction and discrimination provide convincing evidence of the validity of a test. Although here too theoretical considerations affect arguments about validity; the problem is not simply one of collecting empirical data.

As with concurrent validity, the difficulty in demonstrating a test's predictive validity lies in finding suitable criteria, i.e. independent, objective indices of the variable being measured. This difficulty, in fact, helps to explain the existence of psychological tests, and the bootstrapping methods needed to improve their validity.

Any psychological measure rests on a number of assumptions. These assumptions need to be made explicit and developed into a theory, a detailed statement of how the measure is supposed to work. This theory should carry certain implications or reasonable expectations about what should be observed empirically in certain circumstances. So, for example, a measure of 'sense of personal control', based on the assumption that loss of control over the events in one's life has adverse psychological consequences, might be expected to discriminate between subjects who are known to differ in their self-confidence, and might be expected to be associated with beneficial changes following treatment which in fact increases their control over events. Confirmation of these implications and reasonable expectations adds to what is called the test's 'construct validity'. Construct validity can be attacked either by pointing to defects in the theory underlying the design of the test or by pointing to empirical results which run counter to expectations.

Construct validity, predictive validity, and concurrent validity are in a sense interrelated, and improvements in one are likely to improve the others. A distinction has been drawn between face validity and content validity, where content validity is concerned with demonstrating that test items are genuine and representative examples of a well-defined area, such as mathematical knowledge, vocabulary, and speed of mental processing. The contribution made by any individual item depends upon the other items in the test and the characteristics of the subjects taking the test.

PRACTICAL PROBLEMS

Psychological tests are used for different purposes at different stages of adult life and old age—see Chapter 2. Young adults have moved into relatively independent styles of life and have taken on occupational and family responsibilities. At this period, therefore, one can see considerable scope for tests in occupational selection and guidance, in training in industry or the armed forces, in marriage guidance and family counselling, in the assessment of disability, in mental health and subnormality, in the treatment of offenders, in market research and consumer behaviour, and in social and behaviourial research. These same areas of psychometric application hold throughout the working life. As we move closer to old age the emphasis shifts towards diagnostic psychological testing, the assessment of degrees of disability, dependency and life-satisfaction, the measurement of treatment effects, and reactions to institutional care.

Although administratively inconvenient, it is probably advisable, on scientific grounds, to develop tests designed to measure specific characteristics (rather than compound functions) and designed for narrowly defined types of subject rather than older subjects in general. However, administrative needs may necessitate the development of performance indicators which may have no clear-cut relationships with psychological characteristics. So, for example, direct, objective performance indicators, like dietary intake, medication, mobility, daily activities, social contacts, or expressed life-satisfaction, may provide the sorts of information needed to decide on the allocation of resources. These sorts of measures too can be judged by psychometric standards and should not be taken at face value.

One attempts to standardize a test on subjects who are comparable to the sorts of subjects to whom the test will be applied in practice, e.g. suspected dementia patients. In addition, one needs data on 'normal' or other 'control' subjects, since one needs to discriminate between subjects with dementia and those without. The performances of all these subjects provide the norms and standards in terms of which the performance of new suspected dementia patients can be interpreted.

Any deviation in performance outside the range of normal or comparison subjects could be reasonably attributed to the patient's condition, e.g. dementia, although one must rule out other possible reasons for the observed deviation. Wechsler used a similar sort of reasoning in identifying subjects who had a DQ (deterioration quotient) greater than that expected on the basis of standardized data.

One difficulty with psychometric theory that seriously affects the use of psychological tests in later life is the problem of defining and selecting from all the possible items those that are to be incorporated in a test. In the case of a self-report measure of self-esteem or life-satisfaction, for example, how does one define self-esteem or life-satisfaction statements and select a representative sample from all the statements that truly indicate the characteristic? In practice, what often happens is that many items are constructed intuitively—with the assistance of traditional practice and clinical experience—see Table 3.1. Then ideally, out of this larger pool of items, one or more subsets are selected following critical scrutiny and statistical analysis of the items. Failure to incorporate important relevant items early in the procedure means that the final selection will be sub-optimum.

A further complication is that the items which are effective for one sort of group or at one period of life may not be so effective for another sort of group or at a different period. Thus reliability and validity coefficients are not properties of tests as such, but rather indices of the accuracy of the test in relation to particular groups of subjects. Hence

Table 3.1 Examples of the sorts of items used in a self-esteem questionnaire

1.	I am satisfied with my life most of the time.	T	F
2.	Most people think reasonably well of me.	T	F
3.	All things considered, I have done as well in life as could be expected.	T	F
4.	I do not make much effort to help other people.	T	F
5.	I sometimes feel that my life has been a waste of time.	T	F
6.	I do not try hard to improve my behaviour.	T	F
7.	I am not as happy as I used to be.	T	F
8.	My time is fairly fully occupied.	T	F

Note: One should not accept test items at face value. A procedure known as 'item analysis' will show the extent to which the items are associated with each other and with any common factor. One set of items may not be equivalent to an apparently similar set in terms of reliability, validity, and utility; these have to be established independently. Similar sorts of items appear in a measure of 'life-satisfaction'; so the title given to a measure should not be taken too literally. One needs to know what a test does not measure, as well as what it does measure. See text for further discussion of the problems of constructing psychometric tests for use with the elderly.

also the need for different 'forms' of a test, and separate norms for different groups of subjects.

As far as administrative convenience is concerned, tests should be brief, i.e. consist of a small number of items that can be dealt with in a few minutes. Unfortunately, short tests are likely to be unreliable (and to that extent invalid) unless designed with considerable skill and care. Also test norms are unlikely to be accurate unless they are based on relatively large and representative samples of subjects.

It should be clear by now that psychometric assessment presents some formidable problems as regards testing the effects of ageing. Even so the assessment of psychological states, personal qualities, and social relationships cannot be avoided, although it can be carried out in an oversimplified and misleading way—as when we rely on casual subjective impressions.

There are issues of fundamental importance in the way society reacts to chronic disorders—see Plough (1986). These issues have to do with reconciling the often-conflicting interests of individual patients, family and friends, professional care-givers, scientific researchers, industrial technologists, government, and government agencies. Psychometrics cannot settle these issues, but it can help to generate the sorts of empirical data that clarify them. These objective and standardized data are superior to subjective impressions and to indirect or apparently 'obvious' indices in so far as they are quantified, discriminate between subjects, are reliable, valid, relevant, theoretically sound, and predictive. Generally speaking, actuarial prediction is superior to clinical (subjective) judgment, partly because of the many faults and biases in natural reasoning.

A person's score on a psychological test depends upon the extent to which the items index the variable of interest, e.g. intelligence, depression, aggressiveness, motivation, dementia, and the strength of that variable for that person. This poses practical and technical problems in psychometrics, because of the way the difficulty level or the index value of an item is related to the subject's characteristics. For example: a subject with low interest in a task will not express his or her ability to the same extent as someone with a high interest; a cognitive item which is easy for a normal subject will be difficult for a patient with dementia. The problem then is to devise tests which avoid ceiling and floor effects, which avoid missed items, which discriminate well between subjects, and distribute items so that the majority of subjects to whom the test is administered are correctly indexed relative to each other and relative to the appropriate norms or performance criteria.

Some tests permit a sort of psychophysical method of administration whereby a stepwise up-and-down method of item presentation enables the examiner to use fewer items across a narrower range to quickly pinpoint a subject's score. So, for example, with a matching-to-sample or vocabulary task, one could quickly make a rough estimate of a subject's ability and then, using many items over a narrow range, find an exact score (although still only an estimate of the hypothetical true score).

Technological advances in communications and computing are greatly increasing the scope for psychometric assessment. We can look forward to testing-at-a-distance, to self-administered computer-assisted testing, to highly standardized routine and repeated testing on a nationwide basis, to new sorts of tests, and to automated scoring and interpretation, e.g. Acker and Acker (1982), Beaumont and French (1987), Psychological Corporation (1986). The automated (computer-assisted) Geriatric Mental State examination, Copeland et al. (1987), is a development of the Present State Examination (PSE) and the Present State Schedule (PSS). It employs questions designed to elicit information regarding symptoms experienced in the previous month. Apparently, the addition of biomedical information and a medical history add little to its diagnostic efficiency. Several clusters of symptoms have been identified and scaled: organic; paraphrenia; manic-depressive; obsessional; hypochondriacal; phobic, anxiety state. The symptom profile of organic patients is different from that of functional patients, who tend to improve over time.

We have noted the relative unreliability of single-occasion methods of assessment. Changes in performance with training and practice are common. We can therefore distinguish between an initial (baseline or first-occasion) measure, a rate of learning measure, and an eventual steady-state measure of performance, as for example in a reaction time task or a memory task, or even a self-report personality questionnaire. It is up to the investigator to decide which of these three sorts of performance is most indicative of the variable he or she is trying to measure. All three may be of interest. Generally speaking, a practised performance is closer to the subject's best or maximum performance (provided it is unaffected by fatigue or loss of interest). A first-occasion measure, on the other hand, may help to reveal the causes of low initial performance. A measure of rate of learning may reveal the subject's inability to profit from training or, if improvement occurs, reveal individual differences in learning and in maximum performance.

It goes almost without saying that tests should have clear instructions, a clear format, and be acceptable to subjects.

TEST CONSTRUCTION AND ADMINISTRATION

Perusal of some of the more accessible tests illustrates the diversity of item content and format even within a single domain, such as personality, intelligence, or social attitudes. With reference to ageing, we note that items with a complex format may inadvertently tap intelligence, and items which depend on particular sorts of knowledge or experience may produce cohort effects or social class differences.

Research in psychometrics has identified a number of so-called 'response sets' or biases in performance—a tendency to choose a neutral (or an extreme) response, a tendency to agree (or presumably to disagree), a tendency to lie, to be defensive or to give socially desirable answers. It is possible, even likely, that such biases may affect the responses of certain types of adults and older people on certain types of test. It is probably unwise to attribute any particular response bias to the elderly in general but see Kozma and Stones (1987), Ray (1988). Response biases have to be identified empirically, and then eliminated by revising the item contents and formats, or by changing the instructions and method and administration. So, for example, a 'Don't know' response bias could be eliminated by omitting this response option, or by instructing subjects to rethink their response or to guess.

Test instructions such as 'Work quickly, don't think too deeply about your answer' are likely to give different results from test instructions which invite subjects to 'Think carefully before answering' and to 'Revise your answers if necessary'. The investigator's choice of instructions should reflect the theory on which the psychological test is based, as well as his or her knowledge of the subjects to be tested.

Considerable importance attaches to objective tests because they are independent of the subjective judgments of either the subject (giving a self-report) or the observer (giving an 'examiner's estimate'). There are many kinds of characteristics which lend themselves to objective measurement—a person's natural rate of walking or talking, reaction time, diet, visual acuity, strength of grip, arithmetic performance, social contacts. Some characteristics are more difficult to measure than others; and clearly some may not be informative except in a research sense. Questionnaires cannot be regarded as objective unless the subject is unaware of what they are intended to measure, and even then he or she is likely to exercise some sort of subjective interpretation in responding to them. Some measures, like vocabulary, may be regarded as objective under certain conditions.

Individual differences in motivation or interest are not easy to control; but some control can be achieved through differential incentives and test administration. Research studies in ageing usually employ volunteer subjects whose motivation can reasonably be assumed to be high. There is little evidence that low motivation is a major factor in the decrease with age of various performance levels.

For research purposes particularly it is convenient to be able to administer tests to groups of subjects rather than to individuals. This tends to be less easy with older subjects than with younger subjects because of problems with vision, hearing, attention, and individual differences in the ability to follow instructions. Small groups permitting some individual supervision are feasible. Age norms are likely to be biased by the selective effects of mortality, morbidity, and non-volunteering.

Self-report measures which require subjects to keep records—for example on how they spend their time or their money, or what kinds and amounts of social contact they have—may be biased not only by voluntary or involuntary selection of the information to be recorded, but also by the modifying effects on behaviour of keeping a record. Absolute measures of this sort—of food intake, hours worked, memory lapses— have to be interpreted with care because of the different contexts or circumstances within which each individual is responding. However, if subjects are acting as their own controls, as in the experimental study of single cases, then such measures should be much easier to interpret.

Perhaps the clearest contrast with objective tests are tests which ask subjects to report directly on their present state of mind, as in saying how they feel or what they are thinking about. This is not the same as asking them to give reasons for their actions or to make a statement about their personal qualities. It can be shown that subjects are sometimes mistaken about the reasons or statements they give, even though they may be answering in good faith. Statements about one's present state of mind, however, seem to be incorrigible for subjects who are not attempting to mislead the investigator. Even so, the demand characteristics of the situation, and the subject's ability to reflect on his or her state of mind and to express this in words (free description, checklist, or rating), may mean that even here direct access is not assured.

It is sometimes forgotten that the results obtained by administering tests to one group of subjects may not be replicated when the same tests are administered to a comparable group of subjects, under the same conditions. Cross-validation, i.e. cross-checking the validity of one's results, is essential in test construction.

It is possible that a relatively small number of basic variables will account for individual differences in a wide range of age-related psychological effects. On the other hand, these effects may be the result of many different and somewhat unrelated variables. For example, many age differences in cognitive processes are attributed to a decline in general intelligence in association with a differential decline in fluid and crystallized abilities. But if it becomes possible to identify specific neuropsychological functions underlying complex cognitive processes, we may find that different effects are attributable to specific functions. The basic research necessary to identify any such specific neuropsychological functions is probably not best pursued in the context of ageing, since the effects of ageing seem more likely to obscure than to reveal such functions.

The task of establishing that a test is a valid measure of a particular characteristic for all subjects of a given sort is laborious and complicated. It involves finding criteria against which the test can be validated—criteria which are not open to the same criticisms as the test itself. It also involves demonstrating that the test does *not* reflect other characteristics which, on any reasonable interpretation, might also produce the same results. Thus a self-report measure which is claimed to measure quality of life or sense of control or depression or anxiety, or even a test of cognitive function, might in fact reflect characteristics like defensiveness, anger, attention-seeking, or the effects of disuse through inactivity.

From this, it follows that the availability of norms and standards does not guarantee the validity of a psychological measure. Tests which are criterion-referenced have been constructed specifically to measure variables which can be assessed independently and objectively. Unfortunately, criterion-referenced tests do not provide a perfect solution to the problems of validation and standardization. The criterion itself may not be sufficiently reliable or valid. For example, the diagnosis of dementia of the Alzheimer type may be wrong, especially if the physician is trying to identify early cases. The disorder itself is subject to changes of definition. Another example would be the attempt to find criteria for personality characteristics such as extraversion or locus of control. The kinds of objective external criteria that might persuade one that such tests are valid for younger adults might not apply so well in older age groups. As Kline (1986, p. 176) points out, test items which are selected simply on the basis that they discriminate between two contrasting groups of subjects may reflect not one particular difference but several; so one cannot tell what that set of items is measuring. Of course, one may be fortunate or clever (or both) and hit upon one or more important variables along which the two groups differ. Even so, one must still cross-validate these findings and determine that the test is *not* measuring other possible variables.

Objective indices of physical and mental health can be constructed in terms of criteria such as the presence or absence of signs and symptoms. A sufficiently comprehensive assessment of this sort might enable one to assign an overall rating or score for health, or to plot a profile across several dimensions of health. Subjective indices of health, based on self-report, may differ substantially from objective assessments. Similarly, objective indices of social and psychological characteristics may differ substantially from subjective assessments. The reasons for the mismatch between objective and subjective indices arise in part from biases in the subject's understanding of his or her behaviour, state of mind, or circumstances. The subject may also lack the sort of information that can be obtained by objective examination, may not be aware of his or her standing relative to other comparable people, and may have become adapted to what, by objective standards, is a low level of health or standard of living. Thus normative data and objective criteria are important in establishing a test's validity and utility.

The information collected about an elderly person can be presented in various ways. If the individual items (in a test, questionnaire, rating scale, or whatever) correlate positively with each other, and therefore with total score, then the individual's total score or average score, in a sense, 'represents' the function, or functions, sampled by the test items. Of course, the test items may not be a good sample of the functions they are supposed to measure—that is the problem of validation. If the individual items fall into clusters, such that items in the same cluster correlate with each other more highly than they correlate with items in different clusters, then the items are clearly measuring more than one distinguishable social or psychological function (even though the cluster scores are themselves correlated overall). In this situation a set of scores (one score for each cluster or subset of items) provides a 'profile' which, when drawn as a graph, provides a quick and convenient representation of the areas of interest covered.

Some items are more closely correlated with total (or subtotal) score than others, or more closely correlated with the criteria used for validating the measure—consider, for example, items in a self-report measure of mood or life-satisfaction. In theory, such items can be given greater weight in the calculation of total or average score. In practice, however, unit weights are simpler to use and appear not to lose significant information.

Some measures may have cut-off points. These are score levels which separate out those subjects who can be assigned to one category from those assigned to another, e.g. brain-damaged or not, depressed or not, in need of domiciliary services or not. Such cut-off points may be arbitrary, in the sense that they can be adjusted to suit the criterion set by the investigator or the resources available for treatment. In other words, there may be no absolute measure of the subject's social and psychological condition—but psychometric measures may at least provide some sort of indication of, and some justification for, decision-making.

There are several problems in constructing a test intended to be applicable across a wide age range. The first and most obvious problem is that of defining and getting access to the population of interest. Any claim that the sample used in the construction and standardization of a test represents the general population of adults must be viewed with considerable scepticism. It is difficult, if not impossible, to select a fully representative sample of a large heterogeneous community. The usual result, in studies of ageing, is that volunteer subjects are recruited by means of a variety of incentives and persuasive pressures. It can be shown that volunteers differ from non-volunteers on a variety of demographic characteristics and so do not represent the wider population—see Chapter 8.

The second problem is that of selective survival. Older subjects are, by definition, survivors, and survivors too can be shown to differ in several respects from people who failed to survive. Thus older subjects do not fully represent the complete cohort to which they belong. Also, the willingness to volunteer for, and the ability to participate in, research studies changes with age, so that we get a selective drop-out over time. The result is that when these constraints are taken into account, we can no longer claim to be dealing with representative samples drawn from specified populations. Instead, we are obliged to try and reconstruct the characteristics of the population we wish to refer to from what we know of our sample and the constraints that limited recruitment.

It will be seen therefore that research studies using small samples of subjects of unspecified or vague origin are not likely to give rise to results which can be usefully generalized. The best way forward, if one is restricted to small-scale studies, is to select as representatively as possible from a small narrowly defined section of the population to which full access is possible, and to generalize one's findings to that section only. An alternative strategy, which one could use in relation to those sections of the population which are relatively inaccessible for research purposes, is to use a detailed case-study method. This means getting access to those individuals who are available and, through a process of careful comparison and contrast, begin to establish 'prototype' or 'typical' cases. These will constitute first approximations to a taxonomy within that section of the community towards which the research is directed, e.g. menopausal women, elderly male offenders, retired unmarried female schoolteachers, ethnic minority elders. Other investigators interested in the same area may also have limited access to that section of the population, and they too could add to the growing body of case law in the area. The procedure rests on the assumption that studying a relatively small number of cases in detail enables one to develop a theory that will account for their behaviour. The study of further cases leads to an elaboration of the theory and eventually to generalizations to 'cases of that sort', or perhaps reveals subsets of cases which require somewhat different accounts. The point is that successive comparisons and contrasts between cases should lead to closer approximations to the facts, and to better understanding of the subpopulation of interest. Thus representative samples and case-studies approach the same problem from different vantage points—see Bromley (1986).

Few, if any, psychometric tests meet the standards required for representative sampling, especially across adult age groups. The problem of representative sampling in studies of ageing is not simply the problem of resources. As we have seen, there are conceptual problems concerned with defining the population of interest and devising ways of representing it and generalizing about it.

The general lack of external, objective criteria for assessing psychological characteristics means that most psychological tests are exploratory measures of doubtful reliability, validity, and utility. It might seem that factor analysis or some other kind of multivariate statistical analysis could be used to clarify what it is that tests are measuring and to improve their effectiveness. This approach certainly has much to recommend it, but large-scale testing is extremely costly in time and money, especially if one is interested in the way factor structures in different domains change with age, e.g. personality factors or cognitive factors. Elaborate studies like these are hardly supportable without good theoretical guidelines or clear practical benefits. So far, factor-analytic studies of intelligence seem not to have converged onto neuropsychological studies of cognition—see Moses (1985) for a comparison of neuropsychological and intelligence tests.

The advent of computer graphics and statistical packages, together with advances in telecommunications, has meant that these technological facilities can be used in the design, construction, administration, scoring, and even the interpretation of psychometric tests. It is too soon to say how this technological revolution is affecting psychological assessment in relation to ageing, but it seems reasonable to suppose that, properly understood, it will bring considerable advantages—see Sarteschi et al. (1973).

Another, rather different, aspect of psychometric testing concerns attempts to deal with the problem of individuality. It is easy enough to devise ways of simplifying and shortening a procedure so that time is not wasted in administering items responses to which would not be informative, e.g. items above or below a certain level of difficulty, or items that are inappropriate for subjects with given characteristics (including prior responses of a certain kind, as in a diagnostic interview schedule)—see Golden et al. (1984), for example. More difficult, perhaps, is the task of constructing individualized tests based on a single subject's characteristics. Such tests are normally used for longitudinal follow-up studies—quasi-experimental or single-case designs—to see to what extent a person has changed as a consequence of treatment or the passage of time. Thus, a test designed to measure a person's self-concept, or the way an individual spends his or her time or money, could consist of items many of which would be unique to that person. Constructing such a scale requires a considerable amount of time, but may pay off in terms of providing a sensitive tailor-made measure of the effects of age or treatment. To the extent that the test consists of behavioural items, the problem of finding criteria to validate the test is eased. If the test is of the subjective self-report variety, it at least provides a standardized record over several occasions of a subject's expressed opinions (feelings, expectations, relationships, and so on).

COGNITIVE FUNCTIONS

Why do we need to assess the cognitive functions of the elderly? First, because cognitive processes are of central importance in the organization of behaviour. Second, because impaired mental functions have significance for the diagnosis, treatment, and management of psychological disorders. So, for example, mental impairment may render the person incapable of performing even relatively routine activities in daily life, with the result that patients are frequently confused and a danger to themselves and others. Also, mental impairment in some patients may be secondary to some other condition, e.g. depression or a physical disorder, and may disappear if the underlying condition can be effectively treated. For further discussion on how and why we assess cognitive functions, see Kendrick (1982), Rabbitt (1982a), Volans and Woods (1983).

The assessment of patients according to their degree of cognitive impairment may be useful in advising care-givers about the kind and amount of care a patient needs. Clearly, objective and accurate measures of mental functions are needed in order to avoid differences of opinion based on subjective estimates, and in order to monitor changes in performance as the disorder progresses or as treatment brings improvement.

There are many connections between physical health characteristics and mental functions. For example, psychological stress can produce physiological changes, and conditions such as hypertension or drug side-effects can produce mental confusion. Motivational and emotional states can also have adverse effects on mental functioning, as for example in depression and apathy. In combination with other sorts of psychometric test, tests of mental functioning may help to provide relatively individual-ized assessments, and not just global diagnostic labels. Impairment in the elderly is characteristically multiple; so that the pattern of impairment may be important diagnostically and in terms of how the patient might react to a particular form of treatment. Another advantage of individualized and comprehensive assessment is that it tends to avoid a stereotyped negative attitude towards the elderly mentally infirm; one of its aims is to identify the residual assets and abilities of patients, so that these can be taken advantage of in the kind of treatment and care provided.

In passing, we should note that adult age changes in intelligence are widely recognized among behavioural gerontologists, especially the differential decline of fluid and crystallized abilities. If systematic changes of this sort can occur in one area of mental life, there seems to be no reason why they should not occur elsewhere, for example in personality and social attitudes. We have perhaps tended to overemphasize the stability and consistency of personality characteristics by failing to take proper account of changes that can occur over time, especially in relation to 'formative' life-events. The extensive literature on intrapersonal conflict also points to the fact that personality characteristics need not constitute a coherent system.

A further complication is that it is not always easy to distinguish between 'states' and 'traits', i.e. between temporary states of mind and more enduring dispositions, as in assessing anxiety or depression. Dispositional characteristics must also be distinguished from 'ability' characteristics; the former determine what the person is *inclined* to do, the latter determine what the person is *able* to do.

Psychological assessment can be carried out rather casually by means of unstructured clinical appraisal. A professional and scientific approach, however, calls for a more objective and systematic, preferably quantitative, inquiry. In some instances one may need to carry out a comprehensive case-study and to view the psychometric data in this wider context. In other instances, where one is dealing with relatively routine cases, a more limited, standardized assessment procedure may be all that is required.

One should not confuse a 'mental state' examination, which looks at all relevant aspects of the individual's state of mind (in the context of his or her behaviour, circumstances, and life-history), with a more narrowly focused inquiry into the individual's cognitive capacity, i.e. his or her current intellectual abilities, sometimes confusingly referred to as a 'mental status' examination. Thus, cognitive abilities can be judged simply and clinically by presenting simple tasks like counting forwards or backwards in threes, or giving the meanings of proverbs or asking simple questions, such as: What day of the week is it? How many counters are there on the table? What does the word 'lamp' mean? The intention is to estimate the extent to which the person's residual mental ability, and orientation to reality, is sufficient to cope with the ordinary demands of daily life. The sorts of items used in tests of residual cognitive ability in the elderly are those found at the lower end of standard tests of intelligence, such as the Wechsler Adult Intelligence Scale (WAIS) subtests, or below even that level.

The reliability and validity of such brief clinical appraisals of residual intelligence are likely to be low because the items used may be too few and too unrepresentative to adequately 'sample' the individual's abilities. In addition, patients may suffer from sensory and motor deficits which hinder communication, and patients may be more variable in performance than healthy younger people. They may also be affected by medication, depression, anxiety, or concurrent illness. Generally speaking, self-administered or group tests of residual cognitive capacity cannot be used with the elderly mentally impaired.

Professional care staff, as well as a patient's relatives and friends, may be able to provide information about what the patient can and cannot do, and about the patient's premorbid mental ability—see, for example, Rozenbilds *et al.* (1986), Lawton *et al.* (1982). Information about *changes* in performance is very useful in that it may have diagnostic significance or indicate the effectiveness, or otherwise, of treatment. Such information should be of an observational nature, describing what the patient actually said and did (or failed to do) in a given situation, not simply giving a vague subjective impression. However, different observers may well provide conflicting evidence. If they are asked to rate the patient's mental abilities, their ratings may well be affected by the usual sorts of biases such as availability or halo effect. Ratings based on systematic observations over a period of time can be expected to be more reliable and valid than *ad-hoc* ratings. The form of rating used, and even the instructions, may well affect the ratings given by observers. Self-ratings by patients can also be useful—see Mossey and Shapiro (1982), Stoller (1984), Zung (1965). Self-assessments can be individualized and used for repeated measures.

Tests of general intelligence were developed in the contexts of education and employment (including selection and training and the Armed Forces). Tests of adult intelligence, such as the WAIS-R and Raven's Progressive Matrices Test have simply extended the age range over which the tests have been standardized and are thought to be valid. No attempt appears to have been made to redefine 'intelligence' in terms of the context of adjustment to later life—but see Berg and Sternberg (1985). It has been assumed that intelligence, operationally defined and measured by the usual sorts of tests, remains essentially the same process over the lifespan even if there is an overall reduction in capacity and some differential decline across the range of abilities. It is clear, however, that intellectual development during the juvenile years can be construed as a sequence of stages over which the 'structure' and 'functions' of intelligence change. It seems reasonable therefore to suppose that the adult period, and especially the later adult period, might be accompanied by changes in the structure and function of intelligence (cognition). Indeed, some of the changes in structure and function are obvious: the differential decline of mental abilities means that cognitive performance is likely to depend more on crystallized verbal abilities; speed of response tends to slow down, apart from any reduction required in order to maintain accuracy; short-term memory impairment hinders problem-solving; the greater effort involved in the exercise of fluid abilities may lead to a decline in performance evaluation; practice and experience modify some functions and maintain them at a very high level, whilst other functions may decline substantially through disuse.

From a practical point of view, what we need is a survey of the kinds of cognitive functions needed to cope with common problems of adjustment to later life, including the kinds of compensatory or metacognitive functions needed to offset age-related losses in intellectual capacity—such as flexible control of speed and accuracy, skills in learning and remembering, rehearsal or practice to offset disuse of basic intellectual functions. A survey of this kind ought not to be too difficult to carry out. It would be a matter of exploring areas of adult interest and knowledge—health, welfare, housing, transport, leisure, social relationships, domestic arrangements, lifestyle, and so on—and identifying the sorts of cognitive functions needed to solve the problems that arise in these areas.

Tests administered to older adults need to be fairly short, otherwise performance may be adversely affected by fatigue. But we must remember that 'mental stamina' (the ability to work at problems continuously over long periods of time) may be an important ability—see Belmont (1983). Convenience of administration may be increased by resorting to automated testing procedures using a simple keyboard and a suitably large clear visual display unit and/or clear auditory signals. Automated testing procedures can usually be arranged so that the test can be administered, scored, and interpreted in a standard way, and so that a hard copy of the results is available.

All this, however, hardly touches on the basic question of whether intelligence in later life is to be conceptualized and operationally defined differently from juvenile and young adult intelligence. Wechsler's (1986) approach to this problem in his handbook on the WAIS-R is to retain his original broad definition of intelligence as a global ability to think rationally, but to set intelligence in the wider context of personality (non-intellectual factors). He is not prepared to distinguish absolutely between dementia and normal ageing, but obviously intelligence must operate differently in the context of later life if only because of changes in non-intellectual factors (sensory and motor deficits, changes in motivation, energy level, experience, and so on).

The work of Berg and Sternberg (1985) and Sternberg and Wagner (1986) indicates some of the ways in which such a 'contextual' view of 'practical' intelligence might be applied to adult life and old age. Briefly, Berg and Sternberg consider three psychological aspects of intelligence. First, people either change their behaviour to accommodate to environmental demands, or change their environment so that it more nearly matches their requirements, or move to a more suitable environment (situation). Second, behaviour is modified by learning, such that after repeated experiences of a given situation what was initially a 'problem' to be solved by the exercise of intelligence becomes a routine or automatic performance based on experience. Consideration of this second aspect means that a task or a performance may involve more or less intelligence and more or less experience, depending upon how the individual uses his or her mental resources. The connection with the familiar notions of fluid and crystallized abilities is obvious. The third aspect is perhaps more difficult to deal with, since it concerns the very structures and processes of intelligence—the central problem in the study of intelligence. To be intelligent is to be alert to the possibilities implicit in the situations we encounter; it is the ability to plan and implement appropriate courses of action (strategies of adjustment), to monitor the progress of events and to work out the connections between events (reasoning and learning) making the necessary changes (tactics of adjustment), and to evaluate outcomes.

The relevance of Berg and Sternberg's approach to the study of adult intelligence is as follows. The main period of adult life is marked by a considerable increase in experience and usually by the gradual evolution of a relatively routine lifestyle. This is reflected in the tendency to rely on crystallized intelligence, i.e. familiar well-practised cognitive schemata or strategies of adjustment. Later on in life, however, the adverse effects of ageing reduce the individual's physical and psychological resources and so restrict his or her behavioural repertoire and environmental opportunities. Adult intelligence therefore operates in part in the context of a process of adaptation to these changes—ideally, being alert to their implications, planning and implementing alternative or compensatory strategies of adjustment, monitoring the effects of one's actions and evaluating outcomes, and readjusting one's behaviour accordingly.

The limitations of existing methods of testing adult intelligence are well known. As mentioned above, they are based on a relatively narrow conception of the nature of intelligence—the ability to profit from formal education and general occupational training. Many of the subtests, and items within subtests, may have historical and cultural limitations. As we have seen, they do not cater specifically for the interests, abilities, and circumstances of older persons.

Intelligence is essentially a 'central' process; hence tests which penalize older subjects because of their sensory and motor disabilities are, to that extent, not measuring intelligence. The relation of mental speed and 'mental energy or stamina' to intelligence is still being worked out. The reduction with age in mental speed is well documented and a clear indication of a decline with age in adult intelligence. Mental energy or stamina is a more obscure notion—perhaps best thought of as the ability to maintain cognitive functions over time, or alternatively as the ability to mobilize cognitive functions, i.e. 'mental power'. Speed/power relationships have received limited attention in the study of intelligence, as compared with the speed/accuracy trade-off. The indications are that mental speed and mental power are closely correlated, and that power may be a function of speed.

It is sometimes forgotten that intelligence often has to be exercised over long periods of time and distributed over different aspects of one's adjustment to the environment. Indeed, the ability to shift attention and resources according to the demands of the environment without losing control of the several 'streams of behaviour' (courses of action) that are under way is a central feature of intelligence. It may be that any general reduction with age in intellectual resources means a reduction in the ability to manage those resources. There appears to be no evidence that ageing as such has particular effects on the 'control' of mental abilities, except in so far as mental resources are reduced. Breakdowns of that sort, however, may be characteristic of psychopathological states, including dementia in late life. Performance self-evaluation may decline, although there has been little research in this area.

The distinction between normal ageing and pathological ageing is conceptually blurred; in practice it usually means identifying a condition specifically associated with a known pathology, e.g. SDAT or focal brain injury, as a condition which is abnormal in the medical–statistical sense, a condition outside the 'normal' range. Mental abnormalities are of particular interest in relation to intervention because of their diagnostic and treatment/management implications. The primitive and concrete forms of thought found in conditions of mental disease and brain damage are also to be found in some apparently normal older subjects.

Even relatively simple cognitive tests may be useful if consistent records can be kept of a patient's performance over time, since repeated measures may reveal variations in performance associated with physiological condition, environmental circumstances, or treatment. The construction, administration, and interpretation of psychometric tests calls for considerable technical expertise, otherwise elementary errors arising from unreliability, lack of validity, base rates, ceiling and floor effects, and so on, can arise. Several references to the assessment of cognitive and other functions in the elderly are given in Kane and Kane (1981). The effectiveness of a test, like that of any tool or instrument, depends in part on the way it is used and the circumstances in which it is used. Both reliability and validity vary with circumstances—the sample used, the method of administration and scoring, modifications to suit local conditions, and so on. Tests should not be administered routinely unless there is good reason to suppose that they will reveal useful findings, as with properly validated screening tests or in research. They should be administered in order to collect data relevant to particular issues in particular cases.

Tests can be constructed on the basis of virtually any cognitive function: orientation to time, place, and person; vocabulary and general knowledge; short-term learning and memory; attention; following instructions; problem-solving; numerical, verbal, and spatial reasoning; neuropsychological functions; fluency; mental speed. Given a sufficient spread of ability, cognitive tests correlate positively with each other. The common factor(s) responsible for these correlations have been used to define 'general intelligence' or 'g'.

It is not necessary to deal in detail with the psychometric tests used in assessing cognitive functions in the elderly, such as the WAIS-R (Wechsler, 1986) or the Kendrick Battery (Gibson and Kendrick, 1979). The main aim is to discriminate between subjects with relatively low cognitive capacities, but to do so in a way that is acceptable to subjects and relevant to diagnosis and/or treatment. Tests used for diagnostic purposes may misclassify patients—erroneously identifying cases as members of a diagnostic class, or failing to identify cases belonging to that class. Correct classifications should be substantially better than base-rate values, and better than convenient methods already in use. For example, one might want to construct a test to improve diagnostic differentiation between dementia and depression, or to distinguish between different types of dementia, or to monitor the effects on cognition of a new drug. It is particularly important to establish the criteria against which the tests themselves are validated.

Sternberg (1985) identifies a number of component processes in cognitive functions—encoding incoming information, assimilating (mapping or representing) it, making connections, drawing inferences, and organizing a response. The component cognitive processes may vary somewhat independently of one another in terms of their efficiency. Similarly, individuals may differ constitutionally in terms of their ability to handle different sorts of information—spoken or written language, numerical or spatial relationships, rhythms, pictorial representations, sequences or arrays, and so on—see Gardner (1985). Indeed, elementary cognitive functions may depend upon highly specific neurophysiological processes, which become reorganized (or break down) as the individual's life progresses.

MOTIVATIONAL AND AFFECTIVE STATES

The problems of assessing motivational and affective states objectively in quantitative terms are even more difficult than the problems of assessing cognitive functions. A general review of motivation and emotion in later life is given in Chapter 7. Briefly, one psychometric difficulty is that of assessing performance characteristics (as contrasted with self-reports) which are clearly associated with identifiable affective states, such as anxiety, depression, guilt, anger, suspicion. Another difficulty is that of diagnosing psychiatrically significant affective states, e.g. reactive depression, neurotic anxiety, paranoia. The criteria listed in the *Diagnostic and Statistical Manual* (DSM III-R)—American Psychiatric Association (1987)—provide the 'official' standards for a variety of psychiatric conditions, including depression, but it is not uncommon for researchers to challenge both the underlying concepts and the particular criteria listed.

We know very little, if anything, about age changes in motivational and temperamental characteristics, mood states, and emotional reactions in the adult population, although 'life-satisfaction' has been a major area of research in social gerontology—see Gurland *et al.* (1983), Jacobs *et al.* (1986), Kaszniak and Allender (1985), Larson (1978), Schuessler (1982), Zisook *et al.* (1982). We know something about sex differences in these characteristics, and how they are affected by health and circumstances. In general, however, there are few if any reliable norms and standards for assessing motivational and affective states in older subjects. Anxiety and depression are probably the affective states most thoroughly investigated psychometrically.

Cognitive impairment can distort an elderly subject's responses to the assessment of his or her motivational or affective state, as in failing to understand instructions or questions, or being unable to formulate an appropriate response. Sensory and motor disabilities, and unfamiliarity with the situation, may also hinder assessment.

Kane and Kane (1981) list and review a variety of measures designed to assess affect in the elderly. Such assessment usually occurs in the context of a sociomedical and/or psychiatric examination. The Geriatric Mental State Examination—see Gurland *et al.* (1976) and Copeland *et al.* (1984)—is an example of current developments in this area. In long-term care (institutional) settings, direct observation by care staff using standardized methods can contribute to clinical and psychometric assessment.

PERSONALITY AND SOCIAL ADJUSTMENT

Personality

The word 'personality' is used in psychology to refer to stable dispositions which bring about consistency in the individual's behaviour and mental states in different situations, and stability over relatively long periods of time—Costa and McCrae (1980, 1986). The dispositions themselves arise from the interaction of genetic factors and formative experiences. A particular pattern of behaviour is taken to be the outcome of some kind of interaction between the person (seen as an organized system of dispositions and abilities) and the particular situation (seen as a set of opportunities, constraints and contingencies) allowing for the operation of temporary states of mind. Maturation, ageing, and learning give rise to changes in the organization of behaviour. The effects of ageing on personality and the self-concept are dealt with in Chapters 2 and 4.

The assessment of personality dispositions has proved to be much more difficult than the assessment of abilities and performance. The traditional methods, using subjective, self-report measures, observer ratings, projective 'tests', and so on, have been severely criticized not only on the grounds of unsatisfactory levels of reliability and validity but also on conceptual and ethical grounds.

Although some attempts have been made to re-establish personality assessment—using 'objective' tests and using aggregated data (rather than relying on single-occasion measurements)—these seem not to have resulted in substantial developments, either in personality research or in professional practice. Much of the published literature still relies heavily on outmoded theories and methods.

It follows that personality assessment in relation to adult ageing is difficult to review. There has been relatively little effort to standardize existing 'tests' on older age groups. It should be noted that most self-report, questionnaire methods are *not* actually 'tests' or 'measures' of the traits indicated by the face validity of the items used; they are merely standard ways of eliciting 'opinions' from subjects. Such opinions are not necessarily truthful, valid, or direct. Almost any opinion or action can be subjectively linked to almost any personality trait, and explanations in terms of personality traits can result in circularity. Recent psychometric studies of ageing and personality include Conley (1984a, b), Costa and McCrae (1988), Lachman *et al.* (1982), McCrae and Costa (1984), Nilsson (1983), Nilsson and Persson (1984), Robinson (1985), Shanan (1985), Swenson (1985).

Social adjustment

Social adjustment is a basic human value; it interacts with physical health, self-esteem, and competence in the ordinary activities of daily life. Social adjustment can be indexed in various ways—positively through measures of life-satisfaction, morale, and self-esteem, and negatively through measures of anxiety, depression, life-stress, and loneliness. The usual sorts of psychometric techniques are employed: questionnaires, rating scales, observational checklists, projective tests. Kane and Kane (1981) list and briefly describe a range of measures for assessing social resources and interaction.

Social adjustment is not clearly defined in social gerontology, partly because its features vary with age, sex, socioeconomic class, culture, and personality. Consequently, social adjustment has to be operationally defined to suit a particular purpose. That purpose might be to help identify older persons 'at risk' in the community, or to evaluate a treatment programme in a residential home, or to compare the social networks of women before and after the death of their husband. Since subjective well-being is such a central component in social adjustment, it is necessary to consider why some people's feelings of satisfaction with their social arrangements may seem not to correspond with their actual social circumstances. Obviously, high or low expectations, habit, selfishness or generosity, dependency or independence, may play a part. The important thing is to identify the factors over which some control can be exercised, so that more satisfactory social adjustment can be promoted—see Eagles and Whalley (1985), Fillenbaum (1984), Flanagan (1979, 1982), Maddox (1985), Nydegger (1977), Sarason et al. (1983).

As with the treatment of physical disorders, there are limits to what can be achieved by way of improvements in social adjustment. However, counselling may be of value in raising subjective feelings of satisfaction; advice, education, and counselling of professional staff and family care-givers may improve actual social relationships. Other remedial measures—behaviour modification, the provision of facilities and services for recreation and social interaction—may be possible. In long-term care the aim is to provide a 'therapeutic environment'—Canter and Canter (1979), Lawton et al. (1982), Kettel and Chaisson-Stewart (1985)—which supports and compensates for patients' physical and social limitations, but tries, where possible, to bring patients closer to 'normal' ways of life. In these ways, in community as well as in institutional settings, the relationship between elderly people and their social environment can be made more effective and satisfying, provided the necessary evaluation studies can be carried out.

Serious social maladjustment is indicated by withdrawal, apathy, depression, or anxiety on the one hand or by aggressiveness, suspicion, and uncooperativeness on the other. The passivity characteristic of the first of these may lead to its being overlooked.

Wide differences between individuals, variations in their circumstances, and changes over time make it difficult to establish norms and standards for social adjustment in late life, except perhaps in relation to severe social maladjustment—isolation or hostility. In these extreme circumstances one would look for evidence that the person was at risk through neglect or abuse, or constituted a danger to self or others. Thus, although it is possible to collect data relevant to the assessment of social adjustment, it is not easy to make quantitative comparisons between cases. For example, simply counting the number of social contacts per week does not allow for the quality or intensity of those contacts; exchanges which are important in one case may be trivial in another; expectations present in one case may be absent in another. Such diversity is not a particularly serious problem in applied social and behavioural gerontology, since the need for individualized assessment and treatment is widely recognized (if not always met). Awareness of the nature and causes of diversity should improve our understanding and management of individual cases, even if we are unable to measure their social adjustment in psychometric terms.

Case-studies focused on social adjustment can generate perfectly good arguments for or against some particular theoretical interpretation of the facts or some practical recommendation about what should be done. Indeed, it may be a mistake to suppose that we can construct reliable and valid measures of social adjustment applicable across such a heterogeneous population as the elderly. The individual case-study approach, with its emphasis on relatively small homogeneous subgroups or 'prototype' cases, provides an acceptable and practical method of dealing with the problem of assessment. The case-study approach can incorporate quantitative (psychometric) data, baseline information, and even take account of reservations about the reliability, validity, and utility of such data. As mentioned in the introduction to this chapter, what we must look for is 'accuracy', if not in numerical terms then qualitatively in verbal description.

A sense of personal control over one's life is an important factor in social adjustment, since an inability to manage material resources, environmental circumstances, and social relationships is likely to result in feelings of inadequacy and helplessness. See Rodin (1983) for a report on self-control training for the elderly; see also Rodin and Langer (1977), Rodin et al. (1985) and Schulz (1976).

PHYSICAL HEALTH

The notion of physical health is not confined to matters of anatomy and physiology. Physical health is functional, it refers to performance capabilities—what the person is *physically capable* of doing. Physical health therefore may be obscured by psychological and social factors— by attitudes and expectations. For example, blood pressure or headaches associated with alcohol and diet may be falsely attributed to occupational stress. Older people may misjudge their physical capabilities, and so accept sickness and disability more readily than younger people, or take unnecessary risks.

The assessment of physical health in later life takes account of the person's medical condition in the usual ways—through a medical examination and laboratory tests. The person's performance capabilities can be assessed through his or her daily activities—washing, dressing, moving around, and communicating with others. Community-dwelling individuals, of course, need to be assessed on activities basic to survival—self-care, shopping, transport, security.

The same medical diagnosis may cover a wide range of differences between individuals, not only in the physical condition of the patient but also in the psychological and behavioural accompaniments of illness or disability. Psychological factors obviously affect self-reports of physical health, leading to under- or overestimation in some instances even if, as a general rule, subjective self-reports provide a rough guide to objective health status.

It appears that a considerable amount of ill-health in the elderly is unreported and ineffectively treated. Such conditions come to light when, for some reason or another, a medical examination becomes necessary. Screening instruments and standard medical tests are obviously useful in identifying some common disorders in late life, but they are by no means effective in every case and may not be cost-effective on a large scale. The term 'excess disability' has been coined (Brody et al., 1971), to refer to a tendency to overestimate functional impairment in the elderly; this may have the effect of unnecessarily restricting their activities of daily living and increasing their dependence on others.

Assessments of physical health and performance vary. Some cover a wide range of characteristics, others are more selective and detailed. Some health characteristics can vary independently of one another; so that an overall or average score may or may not convey useful information, and two measures of a given characteristic may not be closely correlated. Objective measures of ill-health and dependence are useful in assessing the workload of care staff and family in looking after a dependent elderly person.

Current theory promotes the idea that the elderly should be encouraged and enabled to reduce their dependence on others to a minimum. In practice, however, this may increase their exposure to risks; it raises ethical and legal questions and creates administrative difficulties in institutional settings, e.g. with regard to surveillance and catering.

Kane and Kane (1981) review a number of widely used procedures for assessing physical health and performance in a wide range of life-situations. A measure of 'health knowledge' would be useful in connection with health education and health promotion for the elderly.

GENERAL-PURPOSE MEASURES

Comprehensive assessment procedures have advantages in relation to patients who have multiple disabilities and who need services over an extended period of time. They diminish the likelihood that an important aspect of the individual's adjustment will be overlooked; they can be used to monitor progress and costs; they can provide detailed computerized personal and institutional records.

General-purpose measures of social and psychological functions, like more specific measures, depend to some extent for their effectiveness on the ability and experience of the persons using the measure. In some instances, say in relation to dental or nursing needs, professional training is clearly essential. In other instances, say in relation to psychological or social needs, the professional training needed may seem to be less obvious but is nevertheless important, if only because the indicators and remedies are less clear. The development of automated methods of assessment based on expert systems of knowledge should gradually enlarge the scope and improve the quality of routine assessment. In the meantime, the effectiveness of assessment, and of service provision, depends very much on how well each individual contributes to the work of the team of people involved in care, whether short-term or long-term. The social and psychological factors that affect teamwork in caring for the elderly are interesting and important in their own right, but outside the scope of our present concern.

One possible disadvantage of comprehensive assessment procedures is that they may be more comprehensive than they need be in a particular case, and therefore wasteful of time and effort. However, to omit items or sections in the interests of economy is to prejudge the outcome and to defeat the purpose of the procedure, which is to ensure comprehensive coverage in the inquiry. A comprehensive assessment procedure is, in effect, a sort of checklist of matters to be investigated; it is an attempt to routinize the assessment of a certain category of patient, namely those for whom the assessment procedure was designed, e.g. the elderly mentally infirm. Such routinization is obviously possible. The question is whether the comprehensive assessment procedures that have been developed are adequate and efficient in relation to all the cases to which they are applied.

The connection between an individual case-study and a comprehensive assessment procedure can be expressed in the following way. The individual case-study is essentially an exercise in problem-solving. It attempts to answer the question of what is wrong with this particular patient and what can be done about it. The comprehensive or general-purpose assessment procedure is essentially a routine inspection procedure which enables an investigator to apply appropriate remedies, if they are available. The individual case-study uses a flexible method to deal with an ill-defined and open-ended situation. The general-purpose assessment procedure uses a standardized method to deal with a more or less well-defined segment of the population; its effectiveness depends upon the extent to which the items cover the issues relevant to the health and welfare of the particular patient to whom it is applied. Problem-orientated procedures are well-established in medicine (as are routine medical examinations), but less so in social and behavioural gerontology. A systematic case-study approach, together with the development of a comprehensive assessment procedure for the elderly infirm, might do much to remedy this state of affairs—see Nahemow and Pousada (1983).

Where facilities and services are in short supply, the assessment may reduce to a simple screening procedure designed to ensure that patients meet the essential criteria regarding needs, functional level, and circumstances—see Cresswell and Lanyon (1981). Kane and Kane (1981) draw attention to the fact that screening can be used for case-finding, but that the results from screening tests do not necessarily apply to the wider population.

Like other psychometric instruments, general-purpose social and psychological assessment procedures rely on a variety of observational techniques—self-report in response to structured interviewing, ratings and reports based on direct observation of the subject in his or her normal (home or institutional) surroundings, clinical and laboratory tests, documentary records, and so on.

It may be difficult to assess a patient's suitability for one sort of environment whilst he or she is in another sort of environment. Consider, for example, assessments to determine whether an elderly patient is suitable for sheltered accommodation, or can be discharged from hospital to the community, or will benefit from attendance at a day centre. Follow-up evaluations are needed to examine the validity of such assessments, but lack of benefit does not necessarily invalidate the assessment (it may reveal a deficiency in the new environment). Evaluation research is complicated, and a major area of study in its own right—Cronbach and Associates (1980), Cordray and Lipsey (1987).

Where several observers are engaged in the task of assessing a patient, disagreement may arise. This is because different observers may observe different aspects of the patient's behaviour, or elicit different reactions, or have different frames of reference for making judgments. One way out of this difficulty is simply to average the results from two or more observers. Another way is for them to 'compare notes' and arrive at a consensus. Items which consistently give rise to disagreement between observers need to be revised. For example, items about a patient's dispositions and mental states may have to be replaced by items about actual behaviour in specified circumstances.

Economy of time and effort in the assessment of social and psychological characteristics is highly desirable but not easily achieved. The problem is to identify those stable characteristics of the patient, and his or her circumstances, which are important in relation to the facilities and services which could be made available in the interests of the patient's future health and welfare. The problem is dealt with by assessing health, sensory and motor abilities, personal hygiene, cognitive capacity, coping strategies, social support, financial resources, accommodation, and so on. As with physical health, some aspects of social adjustment are more important than others and take priority, as it were, in deciding what services to provide. In the last resort, given limitations on service provision, it may be a question of identifying emergency and urgent cases. In more spacious circumstances, however, thought can be given to preventive measures and to improvements in the scale of facilities and services with the aim of improving the 'quality of life' in the later years— a long-standing aim of gerontology and geriatrics—see Flanagan (1982).

Among the more widely known general-purpose assessment instruments are the following:

(1) The Stockton Geriatric Rating Scale—Meer and Baker (1966).
(2) The Comprehensive Assessment and Referral Evaluation (CARE)— Golden *et al.* (1984), Gurland *et al.* (1984), Gurland and Wilder (1984), Teresi *et al.* (1984a, b).
(3) The Older Americans Research and Service Center Instrument (OARS)—Fillenbaum and Smyer (1981), Lawton *et al.* (1982), Pfeiffer (1978).
(4) Clifton Assessment Procedures for the Elderly (CAPE)—Gilleard and Pattie (1979).

More recently, Helmes *et al.* (1987) and Pruchno *et al.* (1988) have reported on a multidimensional scale for assessing elderly subjects.

Further details and references can be found in Kane and Kane (1981), who draw attention to the many difficulties that underlie social and psychological assessment.

OTHER ASSESSMENT ISSUES

Several sorts of scientists and professional practitioners are involved in the assessment of the elderly, but their interests may differ considerably according to whether they are concerned with fundamental research, the provision of medical or social services, economic and political policy issues, the evaluation of facilities and services, case-management, and so on. They differ, therefore, in the kinds of assessment they wish to make, in how the assessments are carried out, and in the uses to which they put the information gathered.

It seems unlikely that any one instrument will satisfy all these diverse interests, particularly when the subject populations are of many different kinds. There are, of course, some useful basic indicators—for example of physical health, cognitive function, affective state, social adjustment—which enter into many different sorts of assessment. But, in general, an assessment procedure needs to be tailored to meet the aims of the investigation. Ideally, one would like to have access to a wide range of psychometric instruments with known properties as regards reliability and validity, especially in relation to their use with elderly subjects. For example, a programme designed to improve the quality of life of elderly infirm people in a sample of residential homes needs instruments which provide baseline measures of physical and mental health, if only to identify residents capable of benefiting from the programme and capable of providing self-reports. Additional measures linked to the programme, such as time-sampling of activities, social relationships, mood states, and self-reported satisfaction, would be needed in order to monitor changes forecast by the programme advocates. The programme might well affect the behaviour of residential staff; so that instruments to monitor this aspect of the investigation would also be desirable. This example begins to give some indication of the complexities involved in the assessment of psychological and social factors in the elderly.

One advantage of having a range of standardized instruments is that data could accumulate on the usefulness or otherwise of each instrument, and modified versions could be developed for particular purposes, thus increasing the range of 'psychometric products' available. This is what has happened, in effect, but with little or nothing in the way of 'standards' or 'consumer advice' to improve the utility of the products.

One should not overlook the fact that an assessment procedure itself may have an effect on the outcome of an investigation apart from any 'treatment'. For example, care staff may be alerted to matters of which they were unaware, patients may respond to increased attention, family members and visitors may increase (or decrease) their support. Where possible, independent observers should be used in situations where knowledge of one set of observations may contaminate another set—for example staff ratings of patients' sleep behaviour before and after changes in diet and physical activities.

The practical purpose of an assessment is a decision about what is to be done about the subject/patient. Decisions can be arrived at in all sorts of ways—individually or collectively, intuitively or with reference to hard evidence and rational decision-making. Modern decision theory provides a recursive method of considering the available options in relation to possible outcomes so as to assign an optimum subjectively estimated utility (SEU) to one of the options. This method enables conflicts of opinion to be resolved provided the people involved are rational and consistent. In relation to social and psychological issues, it helps to clarify the beliefs and value that underlie professional and lay opinions.

SUMMARY

Psychometrics is a well-established branch of psychological assessment emphasizing measurement, normative data, and statistical analysis. Psychometric assessment has so far been the approach preferred by psychologists in spite of some serious weaknesses in relation to assessing the elderly. Qualitative forms of assessment—brief clinical appraisals, life-histories and intensive case-studies—are admissible in behavioural gerontology, and valuable provided the statements made are accurate and discriminating.

Psychometric assessment of the elderly has to deal with a number of difficulties. First, tests have to be specially designed to assess those behavioural characteristics that have some theoretical interest or practical importance. Second, allowances have to be made for age-related impairments which affect test performance but are not relevant to the assessment. Third, it is difficult to obtain the large representative samples necessary for adequate standardization. Fourth, it may be difficult to separate out fluctuations in the elderly subject's performance from unreliability in the method of assessment. Fifth, the items in a test may need to be adjusted to permit better discrimination throughout the scale. Sixth, in adult life, age-related changes tend to be cumulative, and may be quite rapid in late life, so that a test which is valid for one age group may not be valid for another age group; a test which is valid under one set of conditions may not be valid under another set. Different sorts of assessment are needed at different stages in adult ontogenesis.

Psychometric assessment should meet the usual requirements for reliability, validity, and utility. The range of age-related characteristics investigated is very wide and includes biomedical functions, psychological functions, social factors, and environmental conditions. A good psychometric test should be sensitive and discriminating in relation to the behavioural characteristics it is designed to measure. At the same time it should be robust, in the sense of being insensitive to other behavioural characteristics or minor variations in conditions.

As far as practical applications are concerned, the principles of psychometric assessment can be applied widely, for example to physiological measures as well as to measures of institutional performance.

Increasing the number of items in a test usually improves reliability and validity, but may be counter-productive in assessing the elderly because of the effects of fatigue. On the other hand, short periods of training and practice may produce an improved and more consistent performance from an elderly subject. Improvements in psychometric assessment can be expected to lead to greater efficiency in the use of resources for the health and welfare of the elderly. Technological advances in computing and communications should increase the scope for standardized psychometric assessment.

Many sorts of tests can yield quantitative data. Some are objective and behavioural, in the sense that no subjective judgment is called for. Others are based on self-report or on clinical interpretation, e.g. questionnaires or projective tests. There are advantages and disadvantages to both sorts of test. The suitability of a test for use with the elderly has to be decided on empirical grounds. There may be factors, such as response biases, specific disabilities, or the acceptability of a test, which affect the performance of older subjects.

Group testing is hardly feasible except for the healthiest and brightest of the elderly. The elderly are a heterogeneous population; they need to be disaggregated—divided into more homogeneous subgroups—so that psychometric assessment can be developed for their specific requirements, e.g. retirement counselling, bereavement counselling, stroke, suspected dementia, depression or other psychiatric ailment, stress management. It seems unlikely that one test will be equally applicable across both sexes, various age groups, different marital statuses, different socioeconomic groups, different educational levels, and different health conditions. Disaggregation should help to solve the problems of sampling and standardization.

Where there are no adequate norms and standards it may be possible to obtain repeated measures experimentally on an individual case. So, for example, one might test whether a particular drug is effective in alleviating depression or disturbed sleep. Psychometric tests can be specially constructed for individual cases.

Even without the benefit of quantitative data, one may still make an assessment which is 'accurate' in the general sense of being reliable, valid, and discriminating. What is called for here is a good command of language, both natural and technical, to describe and interpret the evidence.

Tests of cognitive functions (intelligence and memory) are probably the best-known psychometric measures in behavioural gerontology. General intelligence is a major factor in other measures of cognition and memory. The effects of age on intelligence are moderated by health and education, and probably by lifestyle (involving the use or disuse of cognitive functions). The age-related differential decline of fluid and crystallized abilities, as measured by traditional psychometric tests, is well established. However, recent longitudinal studies and cohort studies, using the same or similar tests, have raised awkward questions of interpretation—see Chapter 5. Furthermore, doubts have been raised about the validity and utility of traditional measures of adult intelligence. The argument is that the exercise of intelligence in solving artificial problems is very different from the exercise of intelligence in solving real-world problems, especially in view of the fact that many real-world problems are extended in time, and involve significant personal characteristics and environmental conditions. Nevertheless, measured intelligence often correlates well with measures of personal adjustment in late life, as well as with other measures of cognition and memory.

Much could be done to improve the content and structure of tests of adult intelligence. It is even possible that the definition of intelligence, or at least the definition of 'practical intelligence', may have to be modified to take account of cognitive changes during the adult years. Qualitative changes in the level or mode of operation of adult intelligence have not been studied to anything like the same extent as quantitative changes. Qualitative changes—the emergence of concrete forms of thought and irrelevant associations—are often seen in mentally impaired elderly. We need to develop tests of residual mental ability and of cognitive pathology.

Motivational and affective states are difficult to assess psychometrically because of the subjective nature of these states and the complications governing their behavioural expressions and physiological accompaniments. The well-researched areas include depression, anxiety, stress reactions, and life-satisfaction. Self-report measures of affect are commonly employed; so too are ratings by observers.

Traditional psychometric measures of personality generally show little significant change with age. One question is whether such measures are insensitive to actual changes in personality, i.e. stable dispositions, or whether there is normally little change with age. Another question is whether current concepts and theories of personality are helpful in understanding changes in the organization of behaviour in adult life. If one makes a distinction between personality characteristics which are central and those which are peripheral, it is possible to see the peripheral characteristics—certain interests, values, attitudes, and so on—as more responsive to environmental influence (and possibly ageing) than the central characteristics. However, the psychometric assessment of personality has been the subject of considerable criticism; so the issue of age-related changes in personality is far from settled.

Measures of social adjustment can be derived from self-reports, from observers' ratings, and sometimes from objective data in the form of records of visits, social contacts, and use of time. Apart from physical health, social adjustment is regarded as the key to life-satisfaction. Lack of social support puts an elderly person in the community 'at risk'. A common complaint about institutional life for the elderly is that social interaction is minimal. This comes about in part because staff are busy with routine duties and may find social contact with residents rather one-sided and unrewarding. In addition, even though social activities may be a regular part of life in the institution, many of the residents may be unable to initiate or sustain other forms of social interaction since, for one reason or another, it has become too effortful.

Social withdrawal and apathy on the part of the frail elderly is a risk, whether they are in residential care or in the community. Social assessment consists in identifying the nature of the social isolation with a view to finding remedies for it. This means finding new opportunities for social interaction and ways of remotivating the individual.

The use of psychometric methods in the assessment of physical health presents fewer problems than in other areas of psychometric assessment—mental health, personality, and so on. The assessment of physical health depends upon the interpretation of various signs and symptoms—blood pressure, reflexes, complaints of headaches, pains, and so on. These are often tangible enough to permit reasonably reliable scaling. These measures can then be used in practice to test the effectiveness of treatment, or used in research to explore the implications of a theory. Subjective assessments of physical health may differ substantially from objective assessments. This is because the physician and the patient are making their judgments within rather different frames of reference.

Attempts have been made to develop comprehensive assessment procedures for use in areas where there are facilities for routine assessment and where there is opportunity to examine the interrelationships between the different areas of assessment. This kind of assessment is important in relation to the evaluation of health and welfare services. An alternative to routine, comprehensive, standardized assessment is an individual case-study, which is in effect a problem-solving exercise.

The other main issues in the psychometrics of behavioural gerontology seem to be concerned with practical applications rather than theoretical matters, although research and development are needed in order to improve existing measures. People who work directly with the elderly—nurses, care staff, volunteers, relatives—are in a good position to administer simple psychometric tests, but they have to be trained and persuaded of the benefits to be gained from assessment. The aim of psychometric assessment is to facilitate good decision-making.

Chapter 4

Clinical Psychology

INTRODUCTION

The term 'clinical' in its narrow sense refers to the practical assessment and treatment of individuals with reference to the signs and symptoms they exhibit at the onset and during the course of a disorder. The term is derived from the Greek *klinikos*, pertaining to a bed; hence the familiar phrases 'clinical procedure' and 'bedside manner'. The two features to take special note of are: that a clinical approach focuses on an individual's problem(s), and that it takes account not only of relevant objective 'signs' but also of relevant subjective 'symptoms'. For example, a patient put on a diet and an exercise regimen to reduce weight and improve cardiac functions may objectively lose weight, but show no cardiac changes and subjectively feel less happy and sleep less well. The clinician's task is to use all the relevant evidence in assessing the patient's condition and progress, and in prescribing the treatment most likely to achieve the desired state of affairs.

A clinical approach to the psychological problems of ageing therefore is simply an approach which deals with the older person as an individual (not simply as a member of a particular category), and takes into account the physical and social context of his or her problem, including its history, and its subjective meaning to the person—Lewinsohn and Teri (1983), Woods and Britton (1985). A problem-centred clinical approach identifies the specific problems affecting an older person's health and welfare, sorts them into related groups, and orders them in terms of treatment priority.

The clinical approach to the management of difficult 'cases' can be adapted to deal with problems of health and personal adjustment that fall within the normal range of experience. In situations which are problematical and somewhat stressful, but nevertheless fairly common in later life, simple forms of counselling and advice directed towards good self-management will ordinarily help the individual to make a rational assessment of his or her problems and to arrive at a common-sense ordering of priorities. Thus, for example, in the event of bereavement, an individual faces a number of problems, apart from the problem of dealing with grief. Reactions vary because of differences between individuals and their circumstances. Usually the individual, with help and advice from others, orders his or her priorities in a fairly sensible way—for example by expressing or inhibiting grief appropriately, by attending to the necessary legal and financial formalities, by conforming to the social prescriptions associated with bereavement, by postponing less important goals, by delegating some personal responsibilities, and so on.

Geriatric clinical psychology is developing along two main lines. Firstly, it is taking on the task of developing techniques for the behavioural management of 'difficult' patients—patients who are aggressive, apathetic or uncooperative, confused, and so on. Secondly, it is developing psychometric assessment procedures for diagnosing late-life disorders and evaluating treatment methods. However, Bender (1986), surveying the British journals of psychology, reports a continuing relative neglect of problems of ageing.

Only a small proportion of elderly people find their way into geriatric medical or social settings, e.g. hospitals or residential homes. The vast majority of the elderly live at home in the community, and yet have problems that have psychological aspects, such as physical illness and disability, loneliness, insecurity, unsatisfying lifestyles. Physical disability is particularly widespread among older people. The professional clinical psychologist is not necessarily the person who can deal most effectively with the older person's problems of adjustment. Such problems may be facets of a more complex issue, such as bereavement, physical illness, or relocation. These may be dealt with better in a multidisciplinary way through teamwork with other professionals, such as psychiatrists, geriatricians, neurologists, general practitioners, residential care workers, nurses, social workers, and occupational or recreational therapists. Relatives and voluntary workers may also be involved. The psychological component of the problem may be a specific difficulty needing specialized treatment, as in neuropsychological impairment, but more often it is a matter of helping other professionals to appreciate the way psychological and social factors can affect their efforts to help people cope with their problems.

Some elderly people suffer from disorders which are primarily psychological, especially emotional disturbances arising from stress, conflict, frustration, or personal inadequacies. Some of the disorders, however, can be traced in part to illnesses, injuries, and breakdowns in physiological functions, in which the psychological disturbance is secondary, as in depression associated with surgical disfigurement or malnutrition. Psychological disturbances, whether primary or secondary, also have an adverse effect on interpersonal relationships.

The clinical psychology of ageing is concerned with two main issues: assessment and treatment. I shall devote most attention to depression and dementia, and look first of all at the epidemiology of these conditions.

EPIDEMIOLOGY

The word 'prevalence' means the number of cases exhibiting a particular characteristic, e.g. a disease, in a population at a given time. The word 'incidence' refers to the rate of occurrence of such a characteristic, i.e. the rate at which new cases are occurring, usually per year. Prevalence therefore is incidence multiplied by the duration over time of the characteristic. A characteristic, e.g. SDAT, which is increasing in duration (because of all-round improvements in life-expectancy and the treatment of late-life disorders) will therefore increase in prevalence even if incidence remains the same.

A crude estimate of the extent of psychiatric disorders in patients aged 65 years or older would be that about 30% suffer from affective psychosis (depression, mania, or bipolar illness), about 30% suffer from senile dementia, about 10% suffer from paraphrenia, 15–20% from acute confusion, 5–10% from arteriosclerotic dementia—see Blessed and Wilson (1982).

THE EXTENT OF MENTAL DISORDERS IN LATER LIFE

The following estimates of the extent of mental disorder in later life in urban populations are based on various sources (see references cited). The data derived from epidemiological research depend upon many factors including the degree of severity of the conditions studied, the characteristics of the populations and the way they are sampled, and the diagnostic categories and methods used. In some instances the figures have been rounded off, combined, or otherwise adjusted for the purposes of comparison and ease of comprehension. They are at best rough approximations. Both the component figures and the totals reflect the considerable uncertainty associated with epidemiological research in this area. An early estimate was that about 13% of persons aged 75 and over and living in the community suffered from some degree of chronic brain syndrome (dementia associated with irreversible brain disorder). The

Table 4.1 Prevalence estimates for psychiatric disorders (based on Copeland *et al.*, 1987)

Category	Percentage	Sex differences
Depression	13–23	Males < females
Mania	0–1	Males ≤ females
Organic	2–10	Males < females
Neurosis	1–3	Males ≤ females
Alcoholism	1–2	Males > females
Other	n.a.	
Total	17–39	
Organic (all levels)	6–14	

Table 4.2 Prevalence estimates for neurosis (based on Copeland *et al.*, 1987)

Category	Percentage
Hypochondriasis	0.5– 1.0
Obsessional	1.0–10.0
Phobic	1.5– 2.0
Anxiety	17.0–19.0
Total (excluding depressive neurosis)	20.0–32.0

Table 4.3 Prevalence estimates for depression (based on Copeland *et al.*, 1987)

Category	Percentage
Moderate to severe	1.5– 3.5
Mild (neurotic depression)	14.0–16.5
Borderline	13.0–14.0
Total (all levels of severity)	28.5–34.0

estimates given in Tables 4.1 to 4.13, together with the sources referred to, illustrate some of the complications and variations found in studies of the extent of mental impairment in later life.

Data shown in Copeland *et al.* (1987) suggest the prevalence estimates for moderate to severe psychiatric disorders shown in Table 4.1. The prevalence estimates for neurosis including mild cases are as shown in Table 4.2. The prevalence estimates for depression are shown in Table 4.3.

Table 4.4 Prevalence (percentage) of severe mental disorders (based on Copeland
et al., 1987)

Age (years)	Organic	Depression
80 and over	15–22	15
90 and over	50	—

Table 4.5 Age trends for severe dementia and related disorders (based on
Bergman and Cooper, 1986)

Age (years)	Percentage
65–69	2– 5
70–74	3– 6
75–79	5–12
80–84	10–20
85 and over	21–35

It is possible that epidemiological surveys of community residents
underestimate the prevalence of late-life psychiatric disorder because
non-respondents seem likely to contain a higher proportion of subjects
with psychiatric disorder. Epidemiological studies based on hospital
admissions may also underestimate prevalence because it is believed
that much mental illness goes unreported and untreated. Conversely,
epidemiological studies of both sorts may use criteria which overestimate
the extent of maladjustment. The relative infrequency of some psychiatric
disorders means that very large samples are needed in order to obtain
reliable estimates of prevalence.

The prevalence of severe mental disorders increases from age 60. Data
from Copeland *et al.* (1987) suggest the estimates shown in percentage
terms in Table 4.4. Bergmann and Cooper (1986) examined several
epidemiological surveys. Their results suggest age trends for all severe
and moderately severe cases of dementia and related disorders (see Table
4.5). Jorm *et al.* (1987) provide data based on a survey of prevalence
studies of mental disorder in later life (age 65 and over). The estimates
shown in Table 4.6 summarize their findings. Sixty per cent of dementia
in late life is attributed to Alzheimer's disease, and the remaining 40%
to other conditions (see below).

Figures indicating age trends in the prevalence of dementia given
by Radebaugh *et al.* (1987) and Jorm *et al.* (1987) can be summarized as
shown in Table 4.7. Jorm *et al.* (1987) conclude that there is an exponential

Table 4.6 Prevalence studies of later-life mental disorder (based on Jorm *et al.*, 1987)

Category	Percentage
Organic (moderate to severe)	4–14
Organic (mild)	5–50

Table 4.7 Age trends in the prevalence of dementia (based on Radebaugh *et al.*, 1987 and Jorm *et al.*, 1987)

Radebaugh *et al.* (1987)		Jorm *et al.* (1987)	
Age (years)	Percentage	Age (years)	Percentage
		60–64	0.7
65–74	4	65–69	1.4
		70–74	2.8
75–84	13	75–79	5.6
		80–84	10.5
85 and over	34	85–90	20.8
		90–95	38.6

increase in the prevalence of dementia from about the age of 60. The rate doubles every five years (4.5 years for SDAT and 5.3 years for MID).

Even a substantial increase in the proportion of very old people, say 85 and over, suffering from dementia would not dramatically affect the prevalence for the population aged 60 and over because very few people survive beyond age 85. So, for example, with a measure of mental impairment which indicates that 5% of people aged 75 or older are impaired, the prevalence could still rise six-fold over the 10 years to 85 or older, from say, 2% at age 75–79 to 12% at age 85 and over.

Data given in Romaniuk's (1983) survey suggest age trends in prevalence in percentage terms (see Table 4.8). For community and nursing-home residents the estimates shown in Table 4.9 can be offered. Kastrup (1985) studied patients age 65 and over admitted to hospital for psychiatric treatment. The results suggest the estimates shown in Table 4.10. Table 4.11 shows estimates in the general population aged 65 and over.

Variations in the estimates of psychological disorder in later life are wide. Pfeiffer (1978) suggests that about 15% of the elderly suffer moderate to severe psychopathology. Blazer (1981) suggests that 5–10% suffer severe psychiatric impairment, 10–40% suffer mild to moderate

Table 4.8 Age trends in prevalence (percentages) (based on Romaniuk *et al.*, 1983)

Age (years)	Intellectual impairment		Functional disorder	
	Mild	Moderate to severe	Borderline	Definite to severe
60–64	3.5	1.0	4	15
65–74	5.7	1.2	13	17
75–84	10.2	2.6	19	22
85 +	16.0	16.0	16	22
Overall	6.3	2.1	14	18

Table 4.9 Age trends in community and nursing-home residents (based on Romaniuk *et al.*, 1983)

Category	Percentage
Organic	3.5–5.5
Functional	3.5
Neuroses	6.0–10.5
Personality disorder	5.0

Table 4.10 Age trends in relation to psychiatric admissions aged 65 and over (based on Kastrup, 1985)

Category	Percentage	Age differences	Sex differences
Schizophrenia	0.5–1.5	Old < young	Male < female
Manic depressive psychosis	8–11	Old = young	Male < female
Senile organic disorder	64–78	Old > young	Male > female
Functional psychosis	6–11	Old < young	Male < female
Neuroses	2–7	Old < young	Male < female
Personality disorder	0.5–3	Old < young	Male < female
Other	3–6	Old < young	Male > female

Table 4.11 Age trends in the general population (based on Kastrup, 1985)

Category	Percentage
Psychotic	7.0
Some kind of psychiatric disorder	38.0
Mild dementia	15.5

Table 4.12 Annual incidence of severe dementia, per 1000 population (based on Nilsson, 1984)

Age (years)	Males	Females
From 70 to 75	10–28	0–10
From 75 to 79	15–49	14–37

impairment, and 10–25% suffer neuroses. Kay and Bergmann (1980) suggest that 5–8% are severely demented, 6–22% are mildly to moderately demented, 1–4% suffer from schizophrenia or affective psychoses, and 4–9% suffer from neurosis.

The annual 'incidence' of dementia in later life, i.e. the rate at which new cases are notified, is estimated to be of the order of 1.9–2.3 per 1000 males and 2.1–3.0 per 1000 females. This rate increases with age from about 1.0 per 1000 at age 60 to 2.5 at age 70, to 7.5 at age 80 and above. These figures are probably underestimates because they do not include unreported cases. By comparison a survey method of assessing annual incidence might give an overall estimate of 10–16 per 1000, rising from 5 per 1000 at age 60, to 15–20 at age 70, to 30–60 per 1000 at age 80 and above. Estimates of the incidence of mental disorder in later life based on population surveys may be six or seven times higher than estimates based on hospital admissions. Epidemiological estimates are made more difficult by the high rates of morbidity and mortality from various causes in older age groups.

Nilsson (1984) followed up subjects aged 70 over a period of 10 years. Allowing for mortality, the annual rates of incidence of severe dementia can be represented as lying between the ranges shown in Table 4.12. Eagles and Whalley (1985) studied the age of first onset of affective disorders in Scotland. A section of their data suggests first admission diagnoses per 1000 population by age and sex as shown in Table 4.13 Mortality rates for those suffering from dementia appear to have declined in recent years; also, more people in general are living longer, with the associated increase in the risk of dementia and other disorders of late

Table 4.13 First admission diagnoses per 1000 population (based on Eagles and Whalley, 1985)

Age (years)	Depression		Mania		All affective psychoses	
	Male	Female	Male	Female	Male	Female
60–64	0.264	0.438	0.044	0.064	0.338	0.531
65–69	0.261	0.475	0.052	0.055	0.349	0.564
70–74	0.271	0.482	0.046	0.066	0.339	0.588
75 and over	0.310	0.402	0.074	0.092	0.412	0.509

onset. Consequently, one would expect an increase in both the prevalence and incidence of dementia in later life, although the conceptual and methodological difficulties encountered in epidemiology seem to forbid any firm conclusion. Improvements in the control of hypertension, and in diet, health education and lifestyle, have been associated with a reduction in stroke and multi-infarct dementia (MID).

Older patients are more likely to have an organic disorder. Patients in institutional settings are surviving longer. Community residents are likely to be referred for examination only some time after the onset of the disorder—maybe a year or so. Åkesson (1969) estimated a prevalence rate for senile dementia of 380 per 100 000 aged 60 years and over, and for arteriosclerotic dementia of 520 per 100 000. Epidemiological studies of psychological disorders in later life are difficult to carry out—Haynes and Feinleib (1980), Jorm et al. (1987), Nilsson (1984), Romaniuk et al. (1983).

Estimates of the prevalence of depressive symptoms in later life vary with the severity of the condition and the type of population studied. Depressive symptoms are more common in women than in men, for various reasons. Age differences in depression are at present unclear, although the probability of a recurrence of a depressive episode increases over time. Social factors, e.g. divorce or unemployment, appear to have some relation to depression. Depression as a psychiatric diagnosis is less prevalent for men than for women, again depending upon the diagnostic criteria used.

Hitherto, depression as a psychiatric condition has usually been thought of as characterized by the following: sadness, depressed mood and feelings, tendency to feelings of guilt and anxiety, pessimism, suicidal thoughts, reduced self-esteem and life-satisfaction, reduced energy and activity, loss of initiative, slowness and difficulty in coping with usual activities, sleep disturbances, early waking, loss of appetite and weight.

These characteristics vary in number, severity, and duration from case to case, and none seems to be an essential marker of depression. Feelings of depression can mask other, underlying, feelings, e.g. anger, guilt, disappointment, grief. See Frijda (1986) for a detailed examination of the problem of categorizing feelings and emotions—see also Chapter 7. The symptoms may relate to more than one condition.

There are indications that mild and moderate levels of depression have increased in the post-war years, although severe depression seems, if anything, to have decreased. There are many reasons why trends may occur over time in psychiatric disorders—changes in medical practice, environmental factors, social changes. See Bebbington (1978) for a wide-ranging review of the epidemiology of depression and associated methodological problems.

Depression is by no means confined to later life. Stressful life-events are thought to be implicated, although it seems likely that predisposing factors are involved too. The peak years for depression in women are 35–45 years, with no increase associated with the menopause. The age trend for men is less clear, but there is some indication of an increase. Men are more likely to commit suicide than are women. The social factors which are suspected of contributing to depressive disorder include the following: family history of depression, stressful childhood, recent stress (particularly losses or 'exits'), alcoholism, lack of confidant(e). Postnatal factors may contribute to depression.

Mania or manic-depressive psychosis is much less common than depression, with a prevalence of less than 1%. The effects of age, sex, and social factors are uncertain, possibly because of distortions in the data, e.g. clinicians tending to identify more episodes as 'manic' for women than for men, or for people from one cultural background rather than another.

Self-report measures show that persons with depressive symptoms have an increased risk of mortality compared with persons without depressive symptoms. Note also that participants in surveys and screening checks are, on the whole, physically and mentally healthier than non-participants.

A depressive episode, on average, lasts for about eight months, but may persist for two years. Older patients seem not to experience longer episodes than younger patients. The condition may respond to counselling, to treatment by means of drugs, or, in otherwise intractable cases, to electroconvulsive therapy.

Depression in late life may be misdiagnosed as dementia, i.e. pseudodementia. It is probably in the nature of depression that its prevalence is underestimated because of under-reporting.

Although dementia (or dementias as a group of conditions) increases in prevalence with age, yet no firm epidemiological patterns or risk factors have been identified—see Brody (1982). Various possible causes have been investigated including chromosome 21 abnormality, aluminium toxicity, neurotransmitter disorder.

The possibility of a genetic link between Alzheimer's disease and Down's syndrome via chromosome 21 is currently of considerable interest, although the findings are not all consistent with one another—Ball (1987), Breitner et al. (1986a, b), Eisner (1983), Hewitt et al. (1985), Kay (1989), Oliver and Holland (1986), Renvoize et al. (1986), Wright and Whalley (1984).

A major problem in epidemiological studies is that it is not always possible to distinguish between different sorts of late-life dementia (senile or pre-senile), or even between multi-infarct dementia and Alzheimer's disease. Indeed, Alzheimer 'pathology' could yet prove to be a normal long-term effect of ageing. That is to say, many people may have the underlying condition, but only some exhibit severe psychological dysfunction.

A crude estimate of the prevalence of severe or obvious dementia is 4–14% of the population aged 65 and over. A further 20% or more exhibit mild dementia. Prevalence for the severe forms increases rapidly in later life, reaching about 20% or more at the age of 80 years and above. However, diagnostic criteria vary, and diagnostic results are not perfectly reliable. The selective effects of mortality, and the unrepresentativeness of samples chosen for autopsy studies, mean that there is no firm evidence of age trends.

Although the further expectation of life of dementia patients is relatively short, say about six years, patients suffer from other disorders, so that SDAT itself may not be fatal. Improvements in the treatment of otherwise fatal conditions, e.g. pneumonia, have had the effect of prolonging the life of patients with SDAT.

Since there are many more elderly women than elderly men, there are more women patients with dementia. However, it is not clear that there is a true sex difference in susceptibility. There is no clear indication that geographical, socioeconomic, ethnic, or occupational factors are significant in dementia, although they may affect the likelihood of referral and institutional care.

Autopsy studies of dementia patients indicate that: about 50% have SDAT neuropathological changes; about 20% do not have SDAT neuropathological changes but do have severe atherosclerosis (SDAT is not a vascular disease); about 15% have both SDAT and atherosclerosis; about 10% show other pathology; 5–10% show no distinctive pathology. By contrast at least 10% of non-dementing people exhibit SDAT neuropathological changes.

There is some evidence that the degree of psychological impairment is correlated with the degree of neuropathological damage. It is not clear that the location of neuronal loss is significant in dementia. The degree of psychological impairment fluctuates. This suggests some sort of variation in brain chemistry or in one or more of the body's physiological systems.

As indicated above, dementia may have something in common with other disorders—Parkinsonism or Down's syndrome, for example. Maternal age is a risk factor both for Down's syndrome cases and cases with SDAT. Research into possible genetic and environmental factors is continuing. The inadequacy of current methods of psychological assessment is one obstacle to effective research into the epidemiology of dementia. It is also possible that we need to rethink our research methods in this area—see Brody (1982, 1984).

The importance of epidemiological studies is appreciated more when looked at in relation to population trends. In westernized societies the proportion of elderly people will remain fairly constant until about AD 2010–2020, when individuals born in the post-war years 1945–55 (years of high birth rate) reach retirement age. By about AD 2030 the elderly will constitute about 17% of the population. This figure is well below that already reached in some retirement areas in America and Europe. The greatest percentage increase is for the over-75 age group. Although this group is small in absolute numbers, it requires considerable medical and social services. The savings to be achieved, in terms of financial and human resources, by reducing the extent of depression and dementia and/or delaying their onset, are enormous.

DEPRESSION

Depression, unlike dementia, is a condition which, in its occasional, relatively mild reactive forms, is a familiar aspect of everyday life. It is experienced as dejection, disappointment, gloominess, despair, grief, sadness, unhappiness, low spirits, tearfulness, apathy, pessimism, desolation, or some other comparable state either because of unsatisfactory external circumstances or because of some change in our internal environment (infection, endocrine dysfunction, reaction to alcohol or other drugs, and so on). There seem to be no equivalent everyday experiences of dementia, i.e. periods during which we become mentally confused, forgetful, disoriented, and lacking intelligence. For this reason, perhaps, dementia is perceived as a more dramatic and characteristic feature of late life. It is at present a relatively intractable disorder. By contrast, depression in the elderly is seen as a not-unnatural response to the multiple losses and stresses associated with ageing. These include bereavement, diminished physical attractiveness, poorer health, restricted opportunities, and disengagement from mainstream socioeconomic activities.

However, depression in later life can be more profound, more long-lasting, and more disabling than the familiar forms of depression in everyday life referred to above. Such depression may or may not be clearly associated with the losses and stresses of later life. In other words it may be endogenous, i.e. arise from factors internal to the person. There are clearly wide differences between people in their temperamental characteristics—some are naturally disposed to be active, happy, and optimistic; others to be lethargic, dull and pessimistic. Some part is undoubtedly played by genetic factors, but it is not clear how ageing affects the expression of such factors. Age changes take place in virtually every aspect of the internal environment, as we have seen. Of particular relevance to the issue of depression in the elderly are age changes in the limbic system, the autonomic nervous system, the endocrine system, and the neurotransmitters. But such changes are extremely complicated and not well understood.

The study of depression in later life is complicated by the fact that depression may not be expressed in an easily recognizable way. It may present in the form of complaints about physical ill-health and discomfort, apathy and withdrawal, helplessness and agitation.

A particularly difficult problem is to distinguish between patients with true dementia (those with irreversible organic brain impairment) and patients who 'seem' to have the condition (because their behaviour and mental state is similar) but who are in fact exhibiting symptoms secondary to some other disorder. If this primary disorder can be treated promptly and effectively, the symptoms of 'pseudodementia', as it is called (McAllister, 1983; Bulbena and Berrios, 1986) disappear, leaving the patient in more or less the same mental state as before the onset of the primary disorder. It is obviously important that pseudodementia be ruled out as a diagnosis before a diagnosis of dementia is confirmed. This requires expert psychogeriatric assessment, since there are many disorders which can give rise to pseudodementia. Depression, unlike dementia proper, can be treated with a considerable degree of success; so it is most important not to confuse the apathy and mental slowing that accompany depression with those that accompany dementia.

A further complication in the study of depression in the elderly is separating out the normal from the abnormal conditions, since these seem to be less sharply differentiated than normal cognitive impairment is from dementia. Treatable depression is widespread in the community elderly—possibly as high as 25%. As we have seen, epidemiological studies of the prevalence (number of cases of a disease in a population at a given time) and incidence (rate of occurrence of a disease) of depression in the community vary widely in their estimates. This is because they differ in their assessment procedures, sampling methods, populations of interest, and so on. Even so, the extent of severe depression in late life is thought to be great enough to warrant the same degree of concern that is felt for dementia.

Suicide increases substantially in later life, more so for men than for women. Suicide 'attempts' are more successful than at younger ages. Unfortunately, the social and legal considerations associated with suicide make it difficult to draw conclusions with any confidence from the available statistics, but see Osgood and McIntosh (1986), Pollinger-Haas and Hendin (1983). Suicidal thoughts and a loss of interest in life commonly accompany severe depression. Suicide is not a socially accepted way of dying in most countries, although it is much less frowned upon nowadays than in previous times. The idea of a 'right to die' is gradually gaining ground, as is euthanasia, interpreted as 'letting die' when the life-support needed seems excessive in relation to the quality of life achieved—see Annas and Glantz (1986), Downing and Smoker (1986), Meier and Cassel (1983), Rachels (1986). These developments, however, are not immediately relevant to suicidal tendencies in severely depressed individuals, since such tendencies are symptoms of the disorder and are likely to disappear if the condition is treated effectively.

Both dementia and depression in late life create widespread, costly, and often severe personal problems in the community. They are not conditions which can be dealt with entirely within a medical context. Of the two, it may be depression which poses the greater challenge because, although it is more responsive to treatment, it is also more variable in its manifestations and perhaps more closely related to general socioeconomic and cultural factors. So depression, like dementia, is of concern not only to psychogeriatricians and to physicians generally, but also to all those other professionals who work with the elderly, voluntary workers, and of course to the elderly themselves and their care-givers.

Depression reduces one's subjective sense of well-being and one's 'quality of life'. It impairs the activities of daily living, employment, leisure and social relationships. Depression is in part a social ailment— the result of a mismatch between expectations and realities or a failure to secure the sorts of living conditions that make life bearable. This may result from personal inadequacies or unsatisfactory social circumstances or both. Consequently, depression is not uncommon at any age; but for obvious reasons it is more likely to increase with age in adult life.

Behavioural gerontologists are interested not only in late-life depression which is intrinsic (biological or medical in origin), but also in late-life depression which is extrinsic (resulting from losses and stresses). Some forms of depression are the product of both intrinsic and extrinsic causes. We can expect to find a wide range of differences between individuals and possibly little scope for generalization.

It appears that few if any of the traditional indicators of depression—early waking, mental slowing, poor appetite—are wholly reliable, and much remains to be done to improve assessment procedures. The main psychological impairments are fairly obvious; what remains to be done is to measure them more effectively and to identify early indicators of the condition. Technological developments of the brain-scan variety and in brain chemistry can be expected to throw considerable light on the biological basis of this disorder.

Diagnosis

Depression conceived of as a psychological or psychiatric disorder is difficult to diagnose. Depression can be expressed in different ways; it can vary over time; it can arise for a variety of reasons; its expression is influenced by personality characteristics, by social circumstances, and by concomitant physical or mental illness. The psychometric tests used to diagnose depression and measure its severity are open to criticism on the grounds of inadequate reliability, validity, and utility. At present no theories seem capable of integrating the wide assortment of views on the nature and scope of depression in the elderly. It is extremely difficult to investigate the causal links between physiological and psychological processes which must underlie the psychosomatic aspects of depression. Depression is possibly not a single identifiable disorder, but rather a range of effects attributable to a variety of disorders exhibited in different contexts. However, attempts to establish unambiguous physiological indicators for one sort of depression or another, such as the dexamethasone suppression test (DST), continue.

Depression, as a negative (socially and personally undesirable) emotion, may not be recognized as such by the individual, may not be expressed directly, and so may not be effectively dealt with either as a normal response to loss or stress or as an abnormal (disproportionate, unduly prolonged) response. Consider, for example, a recently widowed woman expressing the view that life has little or no meaning since her husband died, and that it does not matter much because she does not have long to live anyway. Such a view may be expressed in a calm matter-of-fact way without other obvious signs of depression; some signs of agitation, and long periods spent alone, may be seen merely as an expression of long-standing personality characteristics. The advantage of considering depression as a factor in this case is that it alerts one to possibilities for intervention that one might not otherwise consider. In this instance it may simply require some co-counselling, or gentle continuing persuasion on the part of family or other care-givers, to encourage a more constructive attitude on the woman's part. Other cases of depression are more problematical. They may present as psychosomatic or neurotic ailments, psychotic breakdowns, or dementia. The problem then is that of differential diagnosis, and particularly that of ruling out or effectively treating conditions which produce depressive symptoms as secondary effects, e.g. physical illness, life-stress, toxic drug reactions, nutritional deficiencies, endocrine disorders.

Theory

In view of the complexity of the subject and the apparent lack of integration of research methods and findings it is not possible to present a coherent and detailed theory of the relationship between age and depression in later life. All that can be offered is a general framework, together with the speculative notions set out in Chapter 7.

The obvious starting point for a conceptual analysis is the assumption that man is a biosocial creature. We can expect depression to arise from some combination of biological and social–environmental factors. In addition—because the human lifespan can be conveniently sequenced as juvenile, adult, and senescent—we can expect depression to take different forms at different stages of life. The situation is further complicated by the presence of sex differences, genetic variations in temperament and physical characteristics, and by individual differences in life-history.

The ANS, the endocrine system, and the CNS provide the control systems which regulate the body's internal states and our response to the environment. Of particular interest are the genetic factors affecting the physical basis of personality which predispose individuals with a 'melancholy' disposition rather than individuals with a 'sunny' disposition to reactions of a depressive sort.

Also of interest are the many neurotransmitters which influence mood, motivation, and other psychobehavioural processes. Depression and its polar opposite state—mania—appear to be related to levels of brain amines. Reserpine blocks brain serotonin, and norepinephrine has a depressive effect. Monoamine oxidase inhibitors (MAOs) have the opposite effect and alleviate depression. The study of neurotransmitters is technically complicated and is developing rapidly, not merely in the sense of accumulating detailed empirical findings but also in the sense of revolutionizing our ideas about the way the brain works. Depression seems to be tied in with the functions of the ANS and the immune system, as do stress reactions and psychosomatic disorders.

Depression, as a neuropsychological process, obviously has direct effects on behaviour, and possibly on physical health because of the involvement of the immune system. In addition, depression, and any associated loss, disruption or stress, may disturb the normal adaptive routines of daily living through self-neglect, resort to alcohol or other drug abuse, and so aggravate the situation. Conversely, periods of stress, self-neglect, and a maladaptive lifestyle may bring about physiological changes resulting in depression.

Unfortunately, the mechanisms underlying psychosomatic relationships are difficult to identify. The area does not lend itself to controlled experimental investigation, with humans at least, but evidence from the study of physical illness, natural life-stresses, disasters, military operations, and the like, seems to confirm the general picture which will become clearer as we learn more about the physiology of the body and the specific variables associated with depression. It may be necessary eventually to abandon 'depression' as a technical term, and substitute for it one or more operationally defined entities.

The existence of manic-depressive psychosis suggests an obvious bipolar dimension. The manic state, however, appears to be much less prevalent than the depressive state. Both could be construed as variations along a continuum of disinhibition–inhibition. Looked at in this way the behaviour of some elderly patients, not usually categorized as manic, could be regarded as contrasting cases. These would be the overactive, abusive, aggressive, wandering, restless patients.

The behaviour of the severely depressed elderly patient has been construed as self-protective—the equivalent of 'freezing' in animal behaviour—see Chapter 7. The silent, reclusive, timid, relatively motion-less individual, under this interpretation, is keeping a 'low profile' in the face of a hostile and unmanageable environment, not in a deliberate, rational way but as a stereotyped reaction to a no-solution situation.

The study of life-events as a topic in social gerontology has been pursued vigorously for many years—see Chapter 2. Depression, even physical ill-health and mortality, have been thought of as effects which arise partly as a consequence of life-events. Depressed patients report many more negative events than controls, but then their depression predisposes them to search for negative rather than positive events, and incidentally to notice more negative features about themselves and their circumstances than do normals.

Medication or other physical intervention is used to counteract the physical basis for the depression. Counselling and behavioural management techniques are used to re-establish normal patterns of behaviour.

It is interesting to speculate on the possible evolutionary adaptive value of depression as a reaction to loss, stress, or frustration. Does it elicit intervention and support from others? Does it express the conservation/recovery phase following a major emotional reaction? Does it express a continuing (unresolved) motivational orientation towards an object or outlet which is no longer available (yearning in grief and separation)? Does it express, as suggested above, an attempt to escape further stress by 'freezing'?

It can be argued that there is a connection between depression and anger—depression can be suppressed anger, anger can be expressed depression (despair, grief). Anger directed inwards, towards oneself, in the form of self-hate, self-criticism, self-punishment, is a psychoanalytic explanation of depression.

In view of the need to encourage older people to have a voice in their own affairs we need to distinguish between anger as irrational emotion or loss of control, and anger as an assertion of personal rights. Depression and apathy seem comprehensible as reactions to enforced dependency and deindividuation.

The terms we use to describe and explain depression and other sorts of emotion are taken almost entirely from ordinary language. The way we think about these things is a largely automatic process, the result of many years of immersion in the cultural life of the community to which we belong. It is not surprising, therefore, that many of the research results we obtain, on reflection, look very reasonable—they reflect in a quantitative and technical way what we already knew implicitly. The problem is how to move beyond a common-sense understanding of depression to ideas which may be counterintuitive and yet supported by empirical investigation.

Psychological assessment

The psychological assessment of depression in the elderly tends to concentrate on three methods: structured and unstructured interviewing, self-report inventories, symptom checklists. The difficulties are fairly obvious. Brief interviewing is notoriously unreliable, especially in relation to the assessment of complex and ill-defined conditions. Elderly subjects may experience difficulty with self-reports, which in any event need to be properly standardized. Symptom checklists depend not only on a valid rationale supported by empirical evidence, but also on reliable and effective observers—see Hughes *et al.* (1982). The general problem is that of identifying response characteristics which are indicative of depression in the elderly and at the same time indicative of the nature and source of the depression. Depression is assumed to be multifaceted in origin and expression. Depression scales cover topics such as sleep, appetite, work, appearance, and physical health. The Zemore and Eames (1979) results suggest that depression in the elderly may be overestimated by undue reliance on somatic complaints as indicators of depression. See also Chaisson-Stewart (1985b), Hughes *et al.* (1982), Murphy (1983), Sartorious and Ban (1986), Schatzberg *et al.* (1984).

It is perhaps worth mentioning at this point that interpreting someone's behaviour as 'depression' is achieved through a psychological process of attribution (on the part of the observer) which is itself complicated, subtle, and by no means entirely rational. Attribution and social judgment are interesting areas of study in themselves, but we cannot go into them here at all, except perhaps to mention the common implicit assumption that the elderly are more depressed because ageing is accompanied by depressing effects! If one expects a person to be depressed, one will look for confirmation; without such expectation one is less likely to notice symptoms of depression or other abnormal states.

In severe depression, somatic complaints are not uncommon—fatigue, sleeplessness, gastrointestinal upsets, loss of appetite, headaches, for example. However, somatic complaints are found in patients who are not 'depressed' in the clinical sense. Depression illustrates the close and complicated relationships between physiological and psychological functions. It also illustrates the difficulty of separating causes from effects. Treatment outcome may be used to validate diagnosis.

Electroconvulsive therapy (ECT) and antidepressant drugs have proved to be effective in the treatment of some depressive conditions throughout adult life. Counselling and the behaviour therapies appear to be widely used, especially in connection with mild reactive depression, as in grief following bereavement, depression as a reaction to physical illness or social stress. These interventions appear to be based largely on face validity—common sense—and could be regarded as making good what is deficient in the way of normal environmental support—emotional relationships, opportunities to talk through important personal matters, advice and guidance on redirecting one's life, and so on.

It is possible that subcategories of depression can be identified and that these will be characterized by a particular time course and possibly by a normal age of occurrence. At present, however, one can only speculate. Freedman *et al.* (1982) consider the possibility of a late-life depressive crisis for women in their late 60s and men in their early 70s.

Elderly depressed patients may be less alert, less interested, less attentive, slower, more easily distracted. On test they may seem to be mentally impaired. The danger then is failing to consider all the possibilities that could give rise to poor cognitive performance, and assuming what is felt to be most likely, e.g. dementia. Failure to provide the appropriate treatment could then have very serious consequences for the depressed elderly patient, leading perhaps to dementia proper.

A condition which may be found in association with depression is hypochondriasis—a morbid concern with one's physical health. Since ageing brings about an increase in ill-health, increased anxiety is not unnatural. The risk is that the social and psychological factors may be obscured by the more salient somatic factors. Reassurance and an opportunity for the patient to refer to 'other matters' that may be troubling him (or her) may give some hint of depression or other tension state.

The *Diagnostic and Statistical Manual of Mental Disorders*, DSM III-R (American Psychiatric Association, 1987) provides the diagnostic framework within which the psychiatric disorders of later life, including severe depression, are defined. However, even DSM III-R leaves out of account some of the considerations that make depression in late life different from depression at earlier ages and, of course, it is not concerned with those forms of depression that fall within the normal range of ordinary experience. It is mainly concerned to classify mental disorders and to define conditions as fully, exactly and objectively as possible.

The psychological evidence or data used in assessment and psychiatric diagnosis can be drawn from a wide array of methods ranging from casual observation and clinical interviewing through self-report measures, symptom checklists, and behavioural observations to experimental findings and psychometric test results. These data may vary widely in their reliability, validity, and utility according to the effectiveness of the method, the competence of the investigator, and the particular circumstances of use.

In the context of DSM III-R, severe or neurotic depression is an affective disorder, the central feature of which is a disturbance of mood not attributable to any other physical or mental disorder. In some cases, depression may be connected with manic episodes—hence the diagnosis 'bipolar disorder'. Manic episodes are found early in adult life. It is not clear whether the term applies to older age groups in the same way, since the usual behavioural indicators—hyperactivity, flight of ideas, pressure of speech, reduced sleep, recklessness, and so on—might be different, or masked by the effects of ageing.

Severe depression is usually expressed directly via facial expression, posture, movement, and state of mind (the patient's statements, tone of voice, lack of interest, slowness, tearfulness, hopelessness, suicidal tendencies, and so on). However, a variety of other indications may be found—disturbances of sleep, appetite, and sexual behaviour; tiredness; somatic complaints. The main point, however, is that severe depression in the elderly may express itself differently from severe depression at younger ages; consider, for example, apathy, restlessness, self-neglect. Also, some physical disorders of late onset may bring about loss of weight, fatigue, sleep disturbances, and other conditions in the absence of depression. Adverse reactions to drugs may also play a part, because many older people take a variety of medications. Poor living conditions, social isolation or stressful social relationships, and so on, may induce chronic states of depression in the elderly. The increased incidence of physical ailments in later life, together with reduced physiological 'reserves', means that hypochondriacal complaints may be difficult to distinguish from genuine somatic ailments—see Costa and McCrae (1985). It is possible that hypochondriasis may express depression indirectly without the patient being aware of the substitution.

Depression need not be so severe as to warrant the label of 'major depression'. Instead, less extreme maladjustments may be diagnosed, e.g. dysthymic disorder (depressive neurosis). The general pattern of symptoms is the same but less severe, although dysthymia is regarded as a disorder of early adult life. Not all patients necessarily fit neatly into the DSM III-R diagnostic categories. Individual case-studies reveal considerable complexity and borderline conditions—see Baldwin and Jolley (1986), Barker and Eccleston (1984), Kaszniak *et al.* (1985), Murphy (1983), Schatzberg *et al.* (1984), Shulman and Silver (1985), Umlauf and Frank (1987).

Often a persistent and moderately severe depression can be precipitated by a critical loss or stress, as in bereavement or physical disability. Its essential feature is its excessive or prolonged character relative to what is regarded as a 'normal' reaction to such loss or stress. Although normal depression following bereavement may be persistent and moderately severe in some cases—because of the range of differences between individuals and their circumstances—one would not expect to find evidence of pathological functioning: psychomotor retardation, feelings of worthlessness, chronic fatigue.

Like other subjects, the elderly can be expected to respond well to explanation, reassurance, and reward. The point is that more care is needed in assessment because there are more ways in which things can go wrong. Fatigue, incomprehension, response biases, unfamiliarity with the situation, inappropriate test materials, and lack of age-appropriate normative data may substantially reduce the reliability and validity of an assessment procedure.

Among the more traditional assessment procedures for depression are the following:

(1) The Hamilton Rating Scale for Depression (HRS-D)—see Hamilton (1967), Mowbray (1972), Sarteschi *et al.* (1973). Although this test reveals an increase with age in depression scores, it needs to be properly validated on older age groups. The reason for this, as already suggested, is that some of the symptoms which are regarded as indicative of depression—e.g. fatigue, disturbed sleep, somatic complaints—increase with age possibly independently of predisposition to depression.

(2) The Geriatric Mental Status Interview (GMS) is a general-purpose assessment schedule which incorporates a depression scale (factor)—see Gurland *et al.* (1976). It is especially designed to take account of some of the problems of assessing elderly patients; it has been used in cross-national comparisons, and is being developed in the direction of an automated system—see Copeland *et al.* (1984).

(3) Instruments like the following: (a) the Comprehensive Assessment and Referral Evaluation (CARE)—see Gurland *et al.* (1984); (b) the Older Americans Resources and Services Questionnaire (OARS)—see Fillenbaum and Smyer (1981), Liang *et al.* (1989); (c) the Philadelphia Geriatric Center Multilevel Assessment Instrument (MAI)—see Lawton *et al.* (1982). These are general-purpose assessment schedules which may nevertheless be useful in showing the wider psychological and social context within which depression occurs.

(4) The Minnesota Multiphasic Personality Inventory (MMPI) is a self-report procedure which can be automated. The MMPI reveals higher depression scores for older subjects, but not much significance can be attached to this observation as the scales have not been standardized on older age groups—but see Leon *et al.* (1981), Swenson (1985), and Koeppl *et al.* (1989).

(5) The Zung Self-rating Depression Scale (ZDS)—see Zung (1965), Zung and King (1983)—has been widely used, although reliability and validity reports have been mixed. The test illustrates the way in which one particular assortment of items may produce results which, even if reliable and valid in its own way, may record age effects different from a test with some other assortment of items. What is needed is a theory or rationale for the 'contents' of depression measures, so that we can establish a profile of depression characteristics (similar, presumably, to those listed in DSM III-R), and observe how this profile changes with age.

(6) The Beck Depression Inventory is another widely used assessment procedure—see Beck (1988), Beck *et al.* (1961, 1988). It appears to have better-than-average reliability and validity for tests of this sort, but elderly depressives may be sensitive to the particular item content.

(7) The Geriatric Depression Scale (GDS) is a relatively new test with some improved design features—see Yesavage *et al.* (1982–83).

(8) The Stockton Geriatric Rating Scale (GRS) is another general purpose assessment procedure for elderly institutional patients. Its main factor is apathy/withdrawal; the second a factor of disruptive/antisocial behaviour. See also: the Clifton Assessment Schedule—Gilleard and Pattie (1979), the London Psychogeriatric Rating Scale (LPRS)—Hersch *et al.* (1979).

DEMENTIA

Dementia in later life is a pattern of signs and symptoms, including intellectual impairment, mental confusion and memory loss, which point strongly to organic involvement in the absence of more direct evidence (Terry and Davies, 1980). Personality changes are also found (Rubin *et al.*, 1987). The terms 'organic mental disorder' or 'organic brain syndrome' may be substituted once the physical impairment to the brain can be identified as the underlying cause, through physical examination and laboratory tests. The condition is increasingly referred to as senile dementia of the Alzheimer type (SDAT) if similar conditions, such as multi-infarct dementia (MID), can be ruled out.

Dementia is the result of irreversible physical impairment to the brain, and must be distinguished from temporary but severe mental impairment, such as delirium, which may be a secondary consequence of infection, malnutrition, dehydration, or adverse reaction to drugs. Dementia also needs to be distinguished from the mental impairment that accompanies severe depression, since such impairment appears to be a sort of inhibition of, rather than a failure of, cognitive function, and disappears if the depression can be effectively treated.

In general, dementia in later life exhibits a number of cognitive features including: (1) general intellectual disability, (2) memory loss, (3) loss of judgment and self-control, (4) mental slowing, confusion and disorientation, and (5) proneness to concrete and primitive forms of thought. These may be present to a greater or lesser extent, and some may not be apparent except on close examination. Normal ageing can bring about similar effects; so the question is whether the severity and extent of the impairments indicates a qualitative (marked, stepwise) deterioration in the individual's state of mind. It is necessary to rule out conditions which mimic dementia, known as pseudodementia. Case-history material revealing previous psychiatric disturbance may contribute to the diagnosis.

Dementia in later life is partly accounted for by disease of the Alzheimer type (SDAT). This primary degenerative dementia refers to a pattern of neuropathology: neuronal loss, senile plaques, neurofibrillary tangles, and granulovacuolar degeneration (Tomlinson, 1982). Senile plaques are areas of neuronal degeneration. Neurofibrillary tangles are degenerative changes in the neuronal microtubules thought to affect metabolism in the neuron. Granulovacuolar degeneration refers to swelling of the cell with empty spaces and lipofuscin granules. This pattern is not characteristic of elderly depressed patients. However, intellectual disabilities may also occur in multi-infarct dementia (MID), possibly in combination with SDAT.

The onset of SDAT is slow and insidious; there may be more than one type (Jorm, 1985). The disorder becomes progressively worse and until recently many patients died within a few years of admission to hospital. Multi-infarct dementia (MID) is said to follow a more uneven course with periods of remission, although the eventual outcome is similar to that of SDAT. Differential diagnosis may be difficult—confirmation depends on post-mortem findings.

In contrast to SDAT and MID, depression in the elderly responds well to treatment and most patients survive longer. The main risk seems to be that of confusing depression with the very early stages of dementia when cognitive impairment and organic involvement are not well-defined. It is, of course, possible for these several disorders, or others, to coexist, further complicating the diagnostic problem. Depression, apparently, may occur at any stage as the dementia progresses.

Intellectual functions can now be assessed with considerable accuracy, or at least with more accuracy than for other psychological functions. Dementia brings about a generalized intellectual disability—mental slowing, forgetfulness, inability to reason, and so on. Abnormal thought content appears not to be particularly noticeable in dementia unless the condition is accompanied by other mental disorder, in which case hallucinatory, delusional, and pathological intrusions may occur. Concrete and primitive reactions to test materials are not uncommon even in 'normal' elderly subjects. With some demented patients impairment is so great that it is difficult to establish any sort of reliable psychometric baseline against which treatment effects can be compared. It is possible, however, to use performance on choice reaction time and matching-to-sample tasks as measures of residual cognitive capacity even with those patients who score zero or near zero on a simple verbal test of mental status.

For routine assessment, several measures of intellectual performance are available: the WAIS-R—see Wechsler (1986), the Wechsler Memory

Scale (WMS-R)—see Wechsler (1987), Gilleard (1980), the Kendrick Battery—see Gibson and Kendrick (1979), the Set Test—see Binks and Davies (1984), and the National Adult Reading Test (NART)—see Binks and Davies (1984), Nelson (1982), Nelson and O'Connell (1978). Ideally, tests of intellectual deficit should indicate both pre-morbid and morbid levels of performance, so that the extent of loss can be assessed—see Hart et al. (1986), Hersch (1979). However, it is obviously difficult to be confident about estimates of pre-morbid levels of performance, since the functions which are relatively resistant to the effects of ageing, i.e. 'hold-up' with age, may not be equally resistant to other sorts of effects, such as those arising from focal brain damage or disturbances of brain biochemistry. In general, it is difficult to identify particular patterns of cognitive deficit for particular types of dementia.

Two factors complicate the problem of cognitive assessment in dementia. One is education; there is a tendency for subjects of better education to get higher scores. The other is physical health; healthier subjects are likely to get higher scores. In general, measures of dementia are not well-standardized and much remains to be done in the way of constructing reliable, valid, and useful tests and in establishing norms and standards which take into account factors such as health, education, sex, and diagnostic category.

An interesting difference between dementia and depression is that although memory loss in dementia is marked it may be ignored or covered up by the subject, whereas in depression the memory loss appears to be less marked than the subject's complaints indicate. This may be understood in part as the result of an inhibitory process which increases the depressed person's uncertainty and tendency to withhold response, especially in more difficult (effortful) tasks. This would fit in with the idea of depression being a disposition to 'give in'. In dementia, on the other hand, the failure is partly one of not recognizing how badly one is doing—a failure of performance self-evaluation. A quite separate line of argument is that performance on cognitive tests may have little or no bearing on the patient's complaints about his or her reduced abilities or their performance in daily life. The assumption, however, is that memory impairment in depression is reversible whereas in dementia it is not. Efforts are being made to discover methods of physical treatment that will alleviate dementia, for example by increasing the brain's uptake of oxygen.

There are several neurological disorders of later life which are associated with depression and may present problems of differential diagnosis. They include Parkinsonism, Huntington's disease, infections affecting the brain, and brain cancer.

Neuropsychological assessment

The main anatomical and physiological changes in the ageing brain include diminished size and weight, differential loss of neurons and other types of cell throughout the brain and nervous system, reduced dendritic processes and fewer synaptic connections, alterations in neurotransmitter functions, neuronal changes of the Alzheimer variety. It is not clear exactly how these neurological changes relate to changes in psychological capacity, although there seems to be an overall relationship between the extent of neurological impairment and psychological deficit. Neither is it clear how these neurological changes come into being.

A neuropsychological examination comprises a series of investigations focusing particularly on brain–behaviour relationships in the context of a medical case-study. Any procedure thought relevant to the examination may be incorporated, e.g. simple clinical tests, unstructured interviews with the patient and informants, psychometric and neurological tests, laboratory tests, and so on. The evidence collected in these ways may need careful interpretation in relation to the norms, standards, and guidelines available.

Some neurological impairments are obvious from the patient's posture, movements, and general appearance. Reflex functions may be abnormal. Motor and sensory functions may be impaired in specific ways, e.g. tremor and an inability to coordinate different sensory modalities. Language and comprehension may also be impaired, thus presenting particular problems for communication.

Effective brain function, of course, depends on a stable and intact internal environment, so that changes in bodily functions—for example in temperature regulation, respiration, circulation, and so on, brought about by ageing, injury or disease—can be expected to have adverse effects. Age-related changes in metabolism may affect the way drugs are taken up, used, and excreted.

The electroencephalogram (EEG) has shown that the alpha rhythm decreases on average from about 10 cps to 8.5 cps from middle to late life. Evoked potentials (brain reactions to sensory stimuli) are somewhat retarded at later ages and also less well-defined. These points are of interest because it appears that the speed and accuracy of neurological functions may have a closer relationship to general intelligence than had hitherto been supposed. EEG patterns may contribute to the diagnosis of cerebral disease.

In recent years there have been rapid developments in technology which have made it possible to image the brain and its physiology. Computerized axial tomography (CAT) scanning reveals large ventricles and wider cortical sulci, although only the latter appears to be functionally related to cognitive impairment. The inhalation of radioactively labelled xenon makes it possible to examine cerebral blood flow. Positron emission tomography (PET) makes it possible to examine some aspects of cerebral metabolism which are apparently sensitive to changes of the Alzheimer variety. Nuclear magnetic resonance (NMR) imaging is capable of very fine resolution—to the level of the molecular composition of tissue, and therefore holds considerable promise for the study of neuropathology. These more recent developments should not obscure the value of more traditional forms of laboratory testing—whether biological or psychological—that may have value in the diagnosis of dementia or depression. For further discussion and references see Kaszniak *et al.* (1985).

Recent advances in CAT have generated new measures such as brain volume and ventricular volume separately for each hemisphere. Thus an estimate of the loss of brain tissue can be made by taking the difference in volume between cranial capacity and brain size. Bigler *et al.* (1985) report on a series of relationships between volumetric measures of the brain and intellectual performance measured by the WAIS, and the Wechsler Memory Scale (WMS). The comparisons were not between normals and patients with SDAT, but rather within patients with SDAT in its early stages. Some of these patients exhibited relatively normal gross brain anatomy. Bigler *et al.* found that ventricular volume was about 60% greater than the normal upper limit. No relationship was found between ventricular enlargement and intellectual functions. However, relationships were found between measures of overall cortical atrophy and WAIS performance IQ, but not other measures (WAIS verbal IQ, Wechsler Memory Scale), except that patients with greater atrophy had relatively poorer WAIS scores and showed poorer associate learning on the Wechsler Memory Scale.

Studies of this sort demonstrate the importance of developing sensitive measures of those psychological functions which appear to be adversely affected by SDAT (and other conditions), and are closely correlated with identifiable brain states. This means improving the psychometric properties of diagnostic tests, especially neuropsychological tests.

Dementia in late life may not be a single disease entity but a pattern of symptoms arising from a variety of causes. The salient symptoms are as follows: a deterioration in cognitive capacities substantial enough to impair social relationships and normal adaptive behaviour; memory impairment; impairment of abstraction and generalization; neuropsychological deficits; adverse changes in personal conduct and self-management; adverse changes in mood and mental state. These persisting symptoms should not be confused with any arising temporarily from depression, delirium, or unrecognized physical disorders such as dehydration, stroke, or the side-effect of medication. Cerebral arteriosclerosis leading to multiple cerebral infarctions accounts for only a minority of dementia patients, the majority suffer from the primary degenerative disorder known as Alzheimer's disease. A small proportion suffer from dementia associated with known factors such as head injury or chronic alcoholism.

The fact that intellectual deterioration is a prominent symptom in dementia of the Alzheimer type does not mean that cognitive symptoms are the only sorts of behaviour associated with this disorder. There are disturbances of personality and emotional and motivational behaviour, as in aggression or wandering or sexual misbehaviour. Even vegetative functions may be affected. Some SDAT patients exhibit EEG sleep abnormalities, sleep apnoea (temporary cessation of breathing during sleep), and sleep disturbances (sometimes associated with confusion); sleeping pills may aggravate the condition which may be related to cognitive impairment.

The specific features of SDAT are of two sorts: psychological and neuropathological. The psychological features are as follows: poor memory, especially for recent events; disorientation (for time, place, person, and activity) even in familiar surroundings and for familiar people, confabulation (making up accounts to hide psychological impairment), loss of inhibitory controls. Common neuropathological features include the following: senile plaques, neurofibrillary tangles, granulovacuolar bodies, Hirano bodies, congophilic angiopathy, and decreased dendritic arborization. The neuropathology is found mainly in the hippocampus, fornix, and mammillary areas of the brain. There are also indications of adverse changes in neurotransmitters, which may respond to drugs. Attempts are being made to implant foetal brain tissue.

In multi-infarct dementia the brain damage (cell death) arises from many small infarcts, and not from the chronic ischaemic state (local temporary anaemia) arising from changes in the large cerebral blood vessels. The risk factors for cerebrovascular disorders include hypertension, impaired cardiac functioning, and diabetes.

ASSESSMENT AND TREATMENT

Among the behavioural problems commonly encountered in the elderly mentally infirm are the following: accidents; non-compliance with advice or requests; apathy; confusion (regarding time, place, person); wandering; suboptimal performance (excess disability); antisocial behaviour (physical and mental abuse, intrusion). Some of the problems may arise as consequences of undiagnosed illness, faulty diagnosis, sensory impairments, poor nutrition, faulty medication, or stress. Usually, problems cannot be dealt with effectively unless they are properly formulated. Hence the need for close observation and careful reasoning. Once the diagnostic information is available and correctly understood, it is usually possible to apply specific treatments and evaluate their effects. In some cases medication or surgery is appropriate. In other cases, psychological treatment in the form of behaviour modification, environmental management, recreational therapy (including reminiscence and reality orientation) may produce beneficial effects so long as treatment is maintained.

Clinical assessment, i.e appraisal of the specific problems in an individual case in the context of its occurrence, can be carried out in different ways. Brief direct observation of the patient in a clinic or in the patient's home surroundings, together with a few questions, tests and reference to clinical records, may provide sufficient information on which to base a provisional diagnosis and to recommend treatment. By contrast, clinical assessment may be based on extensive observations over a long period of time by several members of a team of investigators. They may interview the patient at length, and carry out extensive tests, seek information from relatives and other informants, and then try to interpret this mass of information in relation to some sort of theory which will account for the patient's disturbed behaviour. Although it is usual to attempt to arrive at one or more of the recognized diagnostic categories, i.e. to identify what sort of 'case' it is, it may also be desirable to adopt a 'problem-oriented' attitude, in which the patient's problems are identified, arranged in order of importance, and dealt with in appropriate ways, with the help of clinical decision theory.

Both psychometric and qualitative forms of psychological assessment can be employed for diagnostic purposes, as in examining for depression, SDAT, or focal neurological damage.

Single case experimentation means using an elderly patient as his or her own control to obtain baseline measures of behaviour, and then observing how this behaviour changes over time in response to variations in treatment or circumstances. Such studies are particularly useful in cases where one particular aspect of behaviour is problematical, and is susceptible to modification, as for example feeding, wandering, phobic reactions, aggression—see Hersen and Barlow (1976), Hussian (1981), Patterson et al. (1982, 1983), Vaccaro (1988), Wisner and Green (1986), Wisocki (1984).

Clinical assessment uses the full range of observational methods and tests. However, older people, like younger people, may react in ways which invalidate the method employed. Thus, for example, if a psychological test seems meaningless or difficult, then elderly patients may not cooperate fully or may feel anxious or confused. Observational methods which are time-consuming are not likely to be used, and reliance on 'short forms' of assessment may be unwise because of the poorer reliability and validity of such assessments.

Quite often, psychological assessments using standard procedures—interviews, tests, ratings, and so on—are carried out not by psychologists but by others—nurses, doctors, care assistants—who may not fully appreciate the technicalities of psychological assessment, and so may not administer the procedures or record the behaviour in the proper manner. Also assessments which rely on the casual observations of staff may be distorted by the selective nature of such reports—observers tend to notice what is of interest to them personally, and not necessarily what is important for the purposes of assessment.

Naturally, observational methods which rely on the self-reports of elderly patients may have to be used from time to time, but the results obtained by such methods must be treated with considerable care. One suspects that the older person's reduced cognitive capacities—affecting attention, reasoning and remembering—would impair the process of self-report, as for example in reporting food intake, drug consumption, or social contacts. The elderly person's abilities to self-observe and keep records could also be impaired.

Some elderly patients are so impaired cognitively that self-reports serve only to indicate how confused the patients are—not knowing their names or their whereabouts. In cases like these one has to resort to indirect methods—obtaining reports from relatives, care staff, and others. Sometimes informants' reports may be selective and distorted because of the nature of their personal involvement with the patient. Any discrepancy between subjective reports by patients or informants and objective evidence is worth investigating for the further implications of such a discrepancy, for example between self-reported health and medical evidence.

One important problem in the clinical assessment of the elderly is that a patient's state of health or well-being is likely to vary from one occasion to another even over a relatively short period of time. Elderly people tend to have fewer 'reserves' in the sense that they are normally operating closer to their physiological and psychological limits than are younger people. Thus environmental demands—accidents, infections, emotional stresses—are likely to produce more serious consequences. Perhaps for the same reason, elderly people are thought to be more unstable or variable in performance than younger people. The problem for assessment then is how to determine whether a significant change, for better or

worse, has taken place against a background of increased variability—
see also Chapter 8.

Brief methods of psychological assessment—see Crook (1979), Gurland
et al. (1984), Loewenstein *et al.* (1989), Mattis (1976), Nelson *et al.* (1986)—
may be used for the purposes of screening, but some are not sufficiently
reliable or valid for practical purposes, such as diagnosis or monitoring
changes in performance.

Methods which purport to measure the same psychological function
sometimes fail to correlate well, as in personality assessment. It is usually
necessary to collect as much data as possible and from independent
sources so that, on aggregate, a valid and reliable assessment is more
likely. We saw in Chapter 3 that psychometric measurement is a large
and technical area of psychology; knowledge of its possibilities and
limitations is essential for anyone attempting to quantify the effects of
ageing on human behaviour and psychological processes.

There are many sorts of psychological indicators of age-related changes.
Among the more obvious are those related to cognition, memory, speed
of mental processing, and language; these are functions which are thought
to reflect the central organizing processes, as contrasted with sensory
and motor functions which, although impaired by ageing, are generally
less significant in relation to coping with the psychological problems of
adjustment. Some neuropsychological assessment procedures, however,
use sensory and motor impairments as indicators of localized brain
lesions. Impairment of the central organizing functions in later life may
be associated with both diffuse and localized brain damage, e.g. in
perceptual or memory processes.

Psychological assessment usually implies, implicitly or explicitly,
normative standards against which a particular person's performance can
be compared. So, for example, measures of mental status, vocabulary,
reaction time, memory, mood, and well-being, may compare an individual's response with the level and spread of scores for comparable people.
Unfortunately, few clinical psychological tests used with the elderly have
been properly constructed for the purpose or adequately standardized
on an appropriate elderly normal sample. Readers will recall that even a
'normal' population of elderly people is a population of survivors.
Survivors are not representative of their cohort.

The assessment of patients in relation to normative standards may
provide data of theoretical interest, as for example in showing the effects
of ageing or disease on cognitive functions or personality characteristics.
However, the motivation for assessment of the elderly is more often
concerned with practical action improving the health, welfare, and well-
being of patients.

Attempts have been made, and continue to be made, to assess premorbid psychological functions, i.e. a patient's personal characteristics prior to the onset of age-related impairment—see Eppinger et al. (1987), Klesges and Troster (1987), Larrabee et al. (1985), O'Carroll (1987), O'Carroll and Gilleard (1986), O'Carroll et al. (1987), Ruddle and Bradshaw (1982). The most familiar method of assessing pre-morbid intelligence, for example, is to assess current vocabulary. This is based on the assumption that vocabulary and intelligence are correlated in early adult life and that vocabulary level is relatively resistant to the effects of ageing. Vocabulary and reading, however, reflect not only intelligence, but also education, interests, and localized brain functions. As far as language functions are concerned the general pattern seems to be as follows. Syntax, phonology, and oral reading seem to 'hold up' with age relatively well, whereas semantics (word meanings), object-naming and discourse coherence seem to hold less well. The National Adult Reading Test (NART)—see Binks and Davies (1985), Cummings et al. (1986), Nelson (1982)—has been used to assess premorbid cognitive ability (assuming normal educational provision). The test requires subjects to read words with irregular spelling, e.g. yacht, nought. Correct pronunciations indicate previous acquaintance with those words even if the patient cannot use them spontaneously or give their meaning.

Other, more elaborate tests of mental impairment, such as the Kendrick Battery (Gibson and Kendrick, 1979; Kendrick, 1985), use the same sort of idea; namely, a discrepancy between cognitive functions which are relatively robust and those that are sensitive to the effects of ageing, disease, or other disruptive conditions. The Set Test—Binks and Davies (1984)—requires subjects to list examples of items belonging to different categories, e.g. fruits, towns. Fluency declines with age, and especially with dementia.

Assessments based on a single occasion of measurement without patients being given the opportunity to familiarize themselves with the materials or to practise their performance will almost certainly reveal age differences, but possibly for reasons other than those the test was designed to reveal. Age differences obtained from practised subjects may well be different—Beres and Baron (1981), Rabbitt (1980).

Referral and assessment constitute the first stage of treatment, for it is often the case that the prospect of help and the opportunity to benefit from advice and 'first-aid' measures bring about an improvement in well-being which may be interpreted by the patient and by his or her care-givers as an improvement in health—a sort of placebo effect. We should note, in passing, that different 'placebos' (used for control purposes in experimental treatment studies of elderly patients) may produce different effects and so obscure the results of treatment.

Treating the elderly patient's physical health is usually only part of the overall treatment and management. The aim of treatment is to maximize the patient's capacity for independent living. This aim is pursued in several ways: first, by mobilizing the necessary social support and professional services; second, by improving the patient's physical environment; third, by motivating and teaching the patient the sorts of skills needed to cope with daily activities and problems of adjustment.

The information needed in connection with medical treatment and improving the patient's life is not confined to that obtained in clinical or laboratory settings. Much of it depends on systematic observation of the patient in his or her natural surroundings, carrying out the ordinary activities of daily life. Thus, actual behaviour in relation to a diet or drug treatment may be different from the behaviour required by the prescription or reported; promises of support made by care-givers or professionals may prove to be short-lived or under-fulfilled.

A situation frequently arises in which an elderly patient is regarded as physically fit enough to leave hospital following a course of treatment. This implies that the specialized medical and nursing treatment, in the hospital setting, has been completed, and that the patient is capable of being transferred to a more normal environment. However, 'normal' environments vary widely in their suitability for elderly people who are physically and mentally frail, and it may be difficult to arrange for a patient to be discharged to a suitable location. The patient's own home may need adapting, residential homes may be unwilling or unable to cope with cases of more severe physical or mental infirmity, it may prove difficult to mobilize the social support and community services needed to maintain the patient outside hospital.

The aim of behavioural assessment is to provide accurate descriptions of what patients are able to do in specified circumstances. Among the more obvious areas of inquiry are: mobility and sensori-motor capabilities; social interaction and communication; and basic functions such as sleeping, feeding, hygiene, toileting, safety and security, and motivation. Observers may use rating scales and checklists in order to ensure that their observations are standardized, systematic, comprehensive, and replicable. Naturally, the observations should fulfil the usual requirements of reliability, validity, and utility.

It is particularly important to make full use of the patient's residual physical and psychological resources, i.e. to maximize his or her independence and sense of personal control. This may be difficult to achieve, of course, because of differences between individuals in the nature and extent of their dependency and in their ability to cope with stress. However, the point is to capitalize on the patient's abilities and not to be steered into an attitude of 'therapeutic nihilism' by focusing too narrowly on the patient's disabilities and the prospect of a progressively worsening condition. This sort of attitude is likely to result in forms of 'treatment' which are largely custodial, lacking in human dignity and worth, neglectful of individual differences, and even harmful to the patient's physical health and psychological well-being.

It is worth commenting at this point on the relatively low priority assigned to the health and welfare of the mentally and physically infirm elderly. The resources needed to provide good medical and social services are often not sufficient—shortage of staff, inadequate facilities, lack of training, and so on. This, in turn, brings about an apparent lack of progress in the health and welfare of the aged which helps to confirm the attitude that ageing is not a remediable condition, and that additional resources would make little or no difference. There is the added problem that many scientific and professional workers find ageing an unattractive area of employment. This helps to explain the prominence given to 'advocacy' of the aged even in the scientific literature of social and behavioural gerontology, and in geriatric medicine and nursing.

In special therapeutic settings, like residential homes and long-stay hospitals, the nurses, therapists, and other permanent staff play a key role in behavioural management (even when they are not aware of how their own behaviour influences that of the patients!). In order to be more effective, staff need to become aware of treatment goals as regards the behaviour and lifestyle of individual patients. They also need to move away from a passive paramedical role to an active therapeutic role, using their own behaviour as a therapeutic tool.

Behavioural assessment attempts to provide a functional analysis of the factors responsible for specific patterns of behaviour. It emphasizes the promotion of desirable forms of activity and the reduction or elimination of undesirable forms. In relation to ageing, this means promoting activities such as self-care and cooperation, and eliminating activities such as wandering, abuse, and apathetic withdrawal. It is important to identify *specific* sorts of behaviour, not just general psychological attributes.

Behavioural management in late life has a number of aims: first, to improve functional capacities that have been impaired by damage or disuse; second, to compensate for irreversible disabilities and to extend the individual's behavioural repertoire; third, to expand and enrich environmental opportunities and to remove unnecessary constraints on individual actions; fourth, to bring deviant behaviour back within the normal range of acceptability; fifth, to increase the person's ability to cope in ordinary environments.

We need not consider behavioural assessment in any detail, but can remind ourselves that we need to know what circumstances tend to elicit the behaviour, i.e. its antecedents, and what consequences follow from it. We also need to describe the behaviour itself accurately and in some detail in order to link it precisely with its antecedents and consequences. If our understanding of the behaviour is correct, then modifying the antecedents and/or the consequences, or enabling the patient to substitute other kinds of response, often produces the effects sought after. Behaviour modification of this sort is particularly useful in cases where the patient has little or no insight into his or her problematic behaviour, and where counselling, exhortation, or ordinary everyday sanctions are ineffective. Behaviour modification with the elderly mentally infirm is likely to be more difficult and less effective than with younger mentally intact patients, for obvious reasons. It may not be possible to reach the stage at which the patient is able to achieve 'self-control' in the ordinary sense of this term. Instead, the patient's behaviour may have to be continually 'managed' by means of reinforcement contingencies arranged by the care staff. References to 'behavioural' approaches to the management of the elderly include Davies (1981), Haley (1983), Hussian (1981), Leng (1985), Martin *et al.* (1986), Mintz *et al.* (1985), Pinkston and Linsk (1984), Riskind *et al.* (1985), Wisocki (1984).

Briefly, the aim of behavioural management is to identify the specific kinds and amounts of behaviour desired (or conversely *not* desired), and the contingencies of reinforcement likely to bring about the required effects. For example, in trying to get a patient to dress independently, or to soil herself less often, or to socialize more, the patient is positively reinforced for behaviour which moves in the required direction and negatively reinforced for behaviour which does not. If the patient understands the aim of the programme and cooperates with the therapist, then a certain amount of counselling is possible which should improve the patient's attitudes, set up appropriate levels of aspiration, and increase the therapist's understanding of the effects of the differential reinforcement.

The aim of behavioural management in relation to the elderly is to solve fairly specific problems of personal adjustment that have arisen as a consequence of the *interaction* between the person's disabilities, dispositions, attitudes, and actions on the one hand and the particular circumstances (medical, social, environmental) he or she encounters on the other. In some instances a satisfactory solution depends on modifying the individual's personal characteristics to suit the environment; in other instances, on changing the external circumstances. Usually, a combined solution is appropriate. Modifications to the environment might include, for example, easy and obvious access to toilets, floor and wall markings, velcro fasteners, safety locks, alarms, reminders, and specially designed domestic equipment—chairs, beds, bathrooms, and kitchen utensils.

It is as well to bear in mind that human behaviour can vary independently of the environment, and that not all outcomes are contingent on cues or responses of a certain kind. Variations in behaviour can arise for all sorts of reasons including, no doubt, the increasing unreliability of the central mechanisms responsible for the organization of behaviour as age increases. Hence there may be considerable uncertainty as to the effects of a treatment programme, especially in the longer term. It is commonly found that the benefits of a treatment programme for the elderly are relatively short-lived. Since the disabling condition is likely to recur or to become chronic, the treatment programme should try to ensure long-term support.

Some basic principles for managing the behaviour of the elderly mentally infirm can be taught to family members and care staff. In some cases it may be desirable to 'shape' their behaviour too, if ordinary advice and instruction prove ineffective. In the absence of proper training, care-givers may inadvertently reinforce undesirable forms of behaviour, for example by paying attention to or giving in to the patient in ways which are well-intentioned but misdirected.

Interventions intended to alter the characteristics of patients or their environment should be subsequently evaluated to see whether they have produced their intended effects.

Ageing is a process of change in the person and in his or her surroundings—the individual's motivations and abilities alter with the passage of time, as do the constraints and opportunities presented by the environment. The reinforcement contingencies which help to shape behaviour are also modified, sometimes quite markedly, for instance following bereavement, retirement, relocation, or ill-health. There is a strong tendency on the part of care-givers to reinforce dependent behaviour because it is often more convenient to do so, and because it seems harsh not to provide services that the elderly person could, perhaps with some difficulty, manage to provide for herself. However, as mentioned before, personal control of one's life is an important aspect of well-being. Loss of the sense of personal control is thought to give rise to depression and apathy.

Psychological functions which have fallen into disuse, for want of incentives and opportunities, need to be reinstated, as for example with physical activities, social interaction, and self-care. Sensory losses, particularly vision and hearing, need to be compensated for; technological advances may contribute significantly in these areas, and in the areas of 'communication-at-a-distance' and 'meta-cognition' (electronic devices which can be programmed to warn about, prompt, remind, and check individual behaviour).

Ideally, successful treatment has as its outcome the rehabilitation of the patient to the highest possible level of independent living in the best circumstances that can be arranged. In practice, of course, delays in referral, errors in diagnosis and treatment, lack of cooperation from patients and relatives, inadequate financial and environmental circumstances, mean that actual outcomes are sometimes far from ideal.

The difficulty with a behavioural approach to the management of elderly people or patients is not that they deliberately 'misbehave' but rather that they 'lose control', as in incontinence, disorientation, and antisocial conduct. These involuntary actions are not to be 'blamed' on the patient, because they are largely symptomatic of the mental or physical infirmity—rather as a limp is symptomatic of an injured leg. Re-establishing voluntary controls means enabling the patient to recognize and respond to appropriate cues, partly by increasing the number and salience of these cues and alerting the patient to them. The other approach is to 'engineer' the patient's physical and social environment so as to minimize the adverse effects of errors and lack of control. Surveillance and close supervision by staff, together with good physical facilities, continual involvement in satisfying activities, appropriate medication, regularization of sleep, and so on, will do much to bring disordered behaviour under control.

In non-institutional (community) settings, the same principles apply. Cues for behaviour have to be increased and amplified; the environment has to be reorganized in ways that support and encourage desirable forms of behaviour and inhibit undesirable forms. The elderly at risk should carry some form of identification which tells how to contact a relative, notices on exits from the house should carry reminders about keys and switches, elsewhere in the house visual or auditory reminders can automatically signal cues for medication, toileting, meals, visitors, and the like. Elderly people may need training and practice in the use of alarms and other devices.

Some of the behaviour modification techniques used with elderly patients were pioneered in the context of care of handicapped patients, as with dressing and undressing, feeding, toileting, washing, and so on. Patients are guided, prompted, and reinforced so that their behaviour is 'shaped' to the required pattern. Behaviour modification is most likely to be successful with those elderly patients whose basic skills have fallen into disuse through excess dependency in institutional care, or through neglect in the community.

An interventionist approach to the problems of ageing is based on the assumption that change and improvement are possible even in late life, and even for conditions and circumstances which have hitherto been regarded as intractable. The fact that interventions with the elderly may produce only small and short-term gains is not a sensible criticism of this approach. For example, psychological counselling or behaviour modification techniques, with or without accompanying measures, will almost certainly produce measurable effects on quality of life, use of facilities, life-satisfaction, social adjustment, and self-esteem. The appropriate questions in behavioural gerontology are those concerned with improving the effectiveness of the interventions by exploring and evaluating alternatives. A cost/benefit approach which makes reference to wider issues raises all kinds of difficult or insoluble ethical issues about the relative merits of different sorts of social investment in health and welfare, and goes well beyond the central concerns of behavioural gerontology.

Therapeutic environments

The extent of mental and physical disability in the elderly is considerable—see Figure 4.1. About one in 10 people over the age of 65 suffers from some degree of dementia; the proportion increases at older ages. Other conditions, such as stroke, arthritis, or depression, increase the proportion of handicapped and mentally impaired elderly people to about 20–25%. Naturally, these disabilities are found more frequently in patients in institutions—about 5% of the elderly. There is therefore a considerable amount of disability in the elderly population at large. There is in addition a great deal of unreported and untreated ill-health. Since some of the conditions are chronic, treatment may be unsatisfactory, and multiple disability is quite common.

In the period of adult life up to the point at which old age begins, i.e. when we become dependent upon others in carrying out the basic activities of daily living, the environment is generally regarded as providing opportunities for achievement, satisfaction, and the exercise of functional capacities—at work, in family relationships, and in leisure activities. In the dependency stage of old age, however, the environment offers fewer opportunities for action for persons who have suffered a decline in functional capacities. Furthermore, in order to ensure high levels of safety and security and physical well-being, environmental support—in the form of buildings, equipment, treatment programmes, and social welfare—needs to be provided. These may have the effect of restricting the behaviour of elderly people, in the sense that constraints, incentives, and sanctions are used by care-givers to discourage certain kinds of behaviour in a 'custodial' sense. This provides opportunities for neglect and abuse of the elderly infirm.

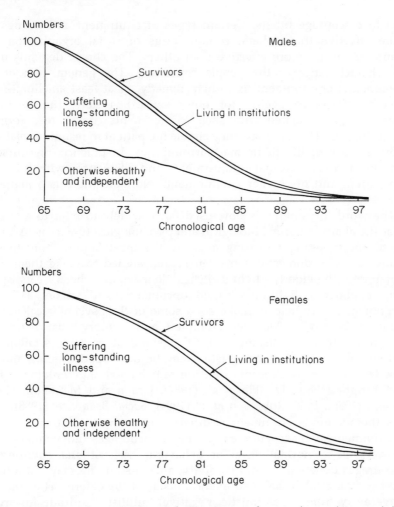

Figure 4.1 Status of survivors aged 65 years and over (assuming an initial population of 100 at age 65) separately for males and females in England and Wales, 1981–3. Based on *Social Trends*, no. 16, 1986. Central Statistical Office (1987)

The phrase 'therapeutic environments' has been used to refer to the sorts of environment which can be constructed in order to satisfy the needs of the physically or mentally impaired and to minimize the disadvantages of their disabilities—see Canter and Canter (1979), Lawton (1980), Lawton *et al.* (1982), Kettel and Chaisson-Stewart (1985). Such environments require careful architectural and social planning. The built environment can be so arranged as to encourage some behaviour patterns and to discourage others. Certain types of equipment and fittings are more effective than others; certain forms of social organization and management are more effective than others. The choice depends upon the characteristics of the people concerned. The general aim of the 'therapeutic environment' is to help remedy, or at least ameliorate, the adverse effects of ageing (or other causes). Ideally, the treatment programmes associated with such environments constitute a form of rehabilitation. That is to say, they enable the patient to resume a relatively 'normal' way of life in normal surroundings. In practice, of course, it may be necessary to make adjustments and allowances with regard to the patient and his or her environment. 'Normalization' is a matter of degree.

The word 'prosthetic' is now used fairly widely to refer to any kind of artificial aid to normal biological and psychological functions. Artificial teeth, spectacles, and hearing aids are the most familiar 'prostheses'. Many ordinary domestic items can be redesigned to make them more suitable for the elderly—light switches, door handles, beds, seats, stairs, taps, cupboards, lighting, printed documents, and so on. The new technologies may help to make good some of the psychological impairments of later life—electronic prompters and memory aids, devices for 'communicating-at-a-distance'; also drugs and other devices tailored to individual biological characteristics may be developed. Ageing and the new technologies is a recent extension of behavioural gerontology—Bray and Wright (1980), Dunkle et al. (1984), Grana and McCallum (1985), Plough (1986), P. K. Robinson et al. (1984), Social Behaviour (1988).

A therapeutic environment is different from the traditional custodial environment. A therapeutic environment encourages independence and recovery to a 'normal' level of behaviour. A custodial environment encourages dependency and passivity, and in so doing may fail to meet the psychological, social, and medical needs of the elderly. The aim is to move away from a pessimistic, negative, 'nihilistic' attitude towards a more optimistic, positive, 'therapeutic' attitude. The attitudes and practices of staff in the social environments of the elderly are important elements in fostering either a therapeutic or a custodial regime.

When one considers the range of differences between elderly individuals requiring support and treatment within one establishment, it can be seen that a therapeutic environment can have a number of goals: custodial (for the protection of patients and others), surveillance (for security, accident prevention, and effective treatment), rehabilitation (for restoring functional capacities), normalization (for reducing segregation), and enhancement (for making good the limitations of special environments). Obviously, such goals cannot be achieved without the use of trained and committed staff. In theory behavioural management in the context of a therapeutic environment implies extensive or even total control over the available contingencies of reinforcement, but practical control is usually limited by and dependent on the willingness and ability of staff to carry out the management policy. The treatment programme may need to take into account the circumstances that the patient will face when he or she leaves the therapeutic environment or when the treatment programme is finished. A behavioural management treatment programme is not likely to be perfectly successful, partly because we do not know enough about the processes underlying behaviour change, partly because of practical limitations such as human error in implementing the programme, insufficient resources, disruption of the programme because of the difficulty in achieving complete control over the environment.

The emphasis on 'control' in behavioural management should not be construed as a preference for external direction of patients' behaviour, but rather as a means of enabling patients to establish socially acceptable and personally satisfying lifestyles with the maximum degree of self-management. This is important to remember in circumstances where behavioural management forms part of a more comprehensive and permanent pattern of care, e.g. a geriatric hospital, a residential home for the elderly; otherwise it may degenerate into a repressive and stultifying form of routine care and control.

A comparison can be made between care for the elderly infirm and care for younger physically or mentally disabled people. Some of the major infirmities of late life are chronic rather than acute; treatments tend to be palliative rather than curative; the infirmities are multi-faceted, i.e. they have biomedical, psychological, social, and economic consequences; services for the elderly tend to cut across institutional boundaries.

A therapeutic attitude to ageing emphasizes privacy and individuality although, of course, one has to recognize that cultural and personality differences may affect reactions to lack of privacy and to collective living. The western democracies value privacy and individuality; one's sense of personal identity is closely tied in with one's personal possessions, social status, and territorial claims. These values continue to be expressed by elderly people in institutional settings, as for example in seating arrangements, the 'personalized' nature of rooms, and in social relationships.

A therapeutic attitude to ageing emphasizes activity and engagement. Engagement means becoming actively involved in some enterprise or other, usually but not necessarily with other people. In later life, continuing engagement in the activities of normal living, as in the exchange of services with friends and relatives or in leisure activities, is thought to contribute to a sense of well-being. However, one must not confuse 'quality' with 'quantity' of social interaction.

Activity and engagement call for patterns of behaviour which can be learned or unlearned, if necessary by resort to the sorts of contingency management procedures referred to earlier. Even lack of motivation may be a remediable condition. The essential ingredients in a treatment programme designed to increase activity and engagement are opportunities and incentives. Encouragement, guidance, demonstrations, copying or modelling, all these may be used to 'shape' patients' responses. Enjoyment, a sense of achievement, relief from unpleasant feelings, and other sorts of reward should reinforce successful participation and lead eventually to self-maintaining forms of activity and engagement.

This type of intervention makes considerable demands on staff time, patience, and skill. Moreover, the benefits may be short-lived if the treatment programme is not maintained and if patients are not periodically reinvigorated by staff interest and encouragement. Also, the turnover of patients may call for constant intervention to integrate newcomers into the existing framework of activities.

With patients who are severely impaired mentally, activity and engagement may never become self-maintaining. Even so, simple games and social activities under close supervision are thought to be preferable to sitting passively doing nothing. Such patients tend to lose their sense of time and identity, forget where they are, and fail to recognize close relatives. It has been argued that reality orientation therapy (Holden and Wood, 1982), should focus not only on immediate external realities (time, place, personnel, activities) but also and perhaps mainly on personal identity (the self, life-history, social relationships, current circumstances). This obviously calls for a more personalized form of treatment, possibly using reminiscence therapy—Coleman (1986), Kaminsky (1984).

Reality orientation has enjoyed considerable popularity amongst nursing and non-professional staff. It has good face validity and fits in well with the desire to provide a caring environment which does not encourage over-dependency. However, lasting benefits from reality orientation for elderly patients are not easily achieved, and reality orientation is probably best regarded as part of the normal environment to which an elderly dependent person is entitled. In an institutional environment the circumstances and events that normally keep an individual aware of his or her identity, whereabouts, and activities are likely to be less effective.

In the case of patients who are mentally alert, activity and engagement are best thought of as expressing self-fulfilment. Their actions are felt to be under their personal control, although there may be some anxiety or a sense of failure if the outcome is not satisfactory. An environment which is largely custodial, unchallenging, and highly routinized is thought to induce apathetic withdrawal. By contrast, an environment which fosters personal initiative and independence must be prepared to accept the increased risk that things may go wrong when people freely choose to engage in activities which push them close to the limits of their ability.

Normally, a sense of freedom and personal control is created by having freedom of choice over ordinary matters in daily life—sleeping, eating, social interaction, leisure activities. This is not possible in a custodial environment where standardized batch treatment is the preferred style of management. Personalized and private living space also contribute to a sense of being in control of one's own life.

Even within an institutional environment, differences between individual residents or patients are quite large. The recognition of such differences and a willingness to accept them and encourage individual lifestyles is what characterizes a 'therapeutic' environment.

Evaluation research

A great deal of what passes for satisfactory treatment and care of the elderly is based on current social attitudes and values rather than on demonstrable health and welfare benefits. One can, of course, point to individual cases of good and bad practice, but these are not usually collected in a systematic way, and so are illustrative but not probative. More detailed accounts have been based on surveys or on 'investigative' reporting. A great deal of the pressure for change comes from the advocates of improved care for the elderly infirm, who can point to objective indicators, such as staffing levels, safety conditions, mortality and morbidity rates. These and other indicators, including psychometric data from activity schedules and measures of life-satisfaction, can be used in a scientific way to evaluate institutions and their various activities. At present, references to evaluation research (as it is called) in ageing appear to be few—but see Anderson (1984), Glamser (1981), Litwin (1987), Smyer and Gatz (1983), Zepelin et al. (1981). It is a rigorous form of investigation which attempts to assess whether a programme, say a social or psychological intervention designed to improve the health or welfare of the elderly, is being carried out according to plan, and if so, to what extent it is producing the expected results. Exercises in evaluation research range from small-scale studies of particular treatments in particular settings to large-scale studies at a regional or national level. All sorts of factors, such as the layout of a building, interpersonal hostilities, patient-mix, material resources, local attitudes, may contribute to the effectiveness or otherwise of a health or welfare programme for the elderly. The aim is to test the validity of claims about the effects of policies and practices with a view to improving them and finding the most cost-effective solution. Evaluation research deals in real-world events, not closely controlled laboratory effects. For this reason the implementation of the research and the interpretation of the results are fused with political, economic, and personal considerations.

Psychological support

One can define old age as that period of life when the accumulated effects of ageing and disease render the person incapable of fulfilling the ordinary self-maintenance functions of everyday life without support from others. What sorts of psychological support are required?

First, help is needed to cope with sensory impairments. Deterioration of vision, hearing, balance, and so on creates needs for physical guidance and support and communication. Second, help is needed to cope with motor impairments—weakness, tremor, unsteadiness—similar to that for sensory losses. Third, help is needed to cope with the impairment of central (cognitive, affective, and motivational) processes, including the functions associated with personal identity. These central processes are concerned with the overall organization of behaviour, i.e. the individual's adjustment to his or her life-circumstances. We shall confine ourselves in this section to this third direct sort of psychological support. However, psychological support, of a similar if indirect sort, is often an integral part of the support given in relation to health, sensory impairment, and motor impairment, as in nursing, occupational and recreational therapy, and rehabilitation.

For various reasons the elderly have not been regarded as particularly suitable cases for psychological treatment, and much remains to be done: first, to develop techniques which are effective; second, to enable older people to benefit from them. The tendency has been to modify techniques developed for use with younger subjects, although one or two techniques have been developed specifically for the elderly. As yet, evaluation of these methods of psychological support is rudimentary.

Different approaches appear to be converging on a form of support which is relatively simple, i.e. easy for the subject to understand, and easy for the care-givers to administer. It aims at improved self-management by concentrating on short-term, limited behavioural objectives and on easily learned mental skills. For example, discussion with the subject might reveal undue anxiety about criminal assault. This would be dealt with by getting the subject to make a realistic appraisal of the risks, to take necessary precautions, and then to use techniques like desensitization, thought-stopping, or thought-switching to more agreeable matters.

Reminiscence and life-review are regarded as particularly useful techniques for engaging older people in personal disclosures, group discussion, and self-management. However, reminiscence and life-review appear to fulfil different functions in different people—see Chapter 6—so it would be unwise to generalize too widely. In either individual or group support situations use can be made of personal or archival materials—pictures, mementoes, diaries, letters, newspaper reports, and so on. These are useful in recovering memories and sharing experiences; in this way the individual's life-history can be reinforced, and possibly modified by reinterpretation of events and actions. Some organizations produce audiovisual presentations of historical periods. These appear to fulfil a similar function, and have good face validity as therapeutic devices.

Psychological interventions aimed at improving general adjustment (as opposed to eliminating specific symptoms) are notoriously difficult to validate. Provisional results based on improvements in anxiety and depression scores have been reported—see Chaisson-Stewart (1985a). However, few psychometric measures have been adequately standardized on elderly populations, so that quantitative data on the psychological effects of treatment may be fallible.

With mentally impaired patients, even relatively simple treatment procedures—physical contact, sensory stimulation, social interaction, and the like—seem to have therapeutic effects, if such patients have been living in an impoverished environment.

Positive and lasting improvements in mental health following specific forms of psychological intervention have been difficult to demonstrate. Indeed, it is commonly assumed that psychological intervention should be regarded as prosthetic, i.e. as a permanent form of support necessary for good adjustment, rather than as a treatment which cures a specific ailment.

Anxiety and depression in later life may arise as a consequence of intrinsic physiological changes, but environmental circumstances and interpersonal relationships are usually involved either as cause or consequence. Consider, for example, grief associated with bereavement, anxiety associated with financial and living conditions and health problems, depression and alienation associated with retirement, and guilt associated with interpersonal conflicts. A considerable amount of counselling, advice, and guidance may be needed by vulnerable individuals, over a long period of time. Limitations on resources constrain the sorts of psychological treatment that can be offered to the elderly. A major advantage is gained if treatments can be administered by nursing or non-professional staff who are in constant face-to-face contact with patients.

Unusual forms of therapy are likely to be rejected by the elderly who are more likely to prefer a relatively simple, structured treatment with good face validity. Group treatment may be acceptable and beneficial in some circumstances—for example, treatment designed to stimulate social interaction and to improve self-esteem through the use of reminiscence and life-review. Similarly, treatment designed to improve self-management and interpersonal relationships is likely to benefit from sharing experiences with others facing similar problems—see Yost and Corbishley (1985).

Research into the effectiveness of psychological intervention is likely to encounter a variety of obstacles which make it virtually impossible to carry out ideal experimental designs. However, quasi-experimental designs are feasible. Even here, data collection is a problem if it is to be derived from self-observations by elderly subjects.

Cognitive-behavioural therapy appears to offer some advantages in relation to the elderly—at least for those who are well enough to understand and follow its procedures. This calls for the identification of a set of personal problems and the means for their solution—a transaction between patient and therapist. There follows a period during which the patient tries out new strategies and tactics of adjustment, in relation to particular problems, and monitors their effectiveness in terms of shifting from less desirable to more desirable outcomes. Hence the need for clarity and objectivity in reporting outcomes, preferably by several independent informants.

Among the therapeutic techniques used are the following: (1) the reorganization of feelings and emotions, as in counselling; (2) the reorganization of motives and expectations, as in guidance and planning; (3)· contingency management, as in behaviour modification and environmental management; (4) social skills training; (5) self-control training; (6) training in specific procedures such as thought-stopping, rephrasing, imagery, problem-solving, desensitization, and so on. Depressed or withdrawn subjects may need to relearn how positive action can be instrumental in achieving desirable goals, or avoiding undesirable outcomes. The literature on psychological treatment is extensive and growing—see Church (1983), Cohen (1984), *Counseling Psychologist* (1984), Fozard and Popkin (1978), Knight (1986), Leszcz *et al.* (1985), Maddox (1985), Mintz *et al.* (1981), Ratna and Davis (1984), Sadavoy and Leszcz (1987), Yost and Corbishley (1985).

There are some indications that psychological intervention in depression can be as effective as drug therapy, at least in certain circumstances—see Chaisson-Stewart (1985b). The main problem is the relative complexity and individualized character of psychological treatment if it is to be effective.

Drugs are commonly used in the treatment of psychological disorders in later life. However, the relationship between the physiology of drug action and its psychological effects is not always clear, as for example in relation to dosage level, delayed action, and interactions between two or more drugs. Drug trials can be methodologically sophisticated, but of course if the investigator's main interest is in the psychological and behavioural effects of a drug, then the investigation can only be as good as the psychometric measures permit. There are numerous psychopharma-cological studies of ageing, including Levenson (1979), MacDonald and MacDonald (1982), Silverstone *et al.* (1986), Wheatley (1983).

In providing psychological support it is important to emphasize the person's ability to change (improve) and the opportunities that can be created to facilitate improvement. This may mean encouraging assertiveness and self-direction, and by contrast discouraging apathy, dependence, and passive acceptance of circumstances. The sorts of social support and example that can be found in group therapy may be as important as any other factor in promoting improvement. Behavioural models are particularly important. These can be presented in the form of real-life demonstrations and anecdotes, film or television programmes, fictional accounts, or clinical case-studies. They provide a sort of schema or script on the basis of which a patient may reorganize his or her behaviour. Without the help of such behavioural models a patient may be at a loss to know how to cope with life. Such models, presented via the mass media, may be important for normal community-dwelling elderly in promoting beneficial changes in attitudes and behaviour.

An elderly person who has become predisposed to depression, anxiety, or social withdrawal is likely to get caught in a vicious spiral of maladjustment because of the increased stresses and problems of later life. Poorer health, interpersonal difficulties, financial problems, slowness, forgetfulness, and so on, which might be shrugged off as unimportant or temporary difficulties in a younger person, may be experienced as more stressful. They may add to persisting sources of stress—such as family problems, past failures, and disappointments—and social change, and incline the individual towards defensive modes of adjustment—pessimism, lowered aspirations, dependence, apathy, and withdrawal.

The psychological interventions referred to above are designed to reverse such tendencies. Of course, some beneficial psychological effects may be obtained from interventions not specifically designed for that purpose. For example, occupational and recreational therapy may result in improved self-regard and interpersonal relationships even though no specific therapeutic effort has been directed to these ends. More usually, however, therapists of all kinds will be alert to the specific benefits that might be achieved through communication and cooperation in groups, through the exchange of experiences and practices, and through the familiar effects of example, leadership, and group pressure.

A sense of control over one's circumstances appears to be a self-evident psychological asset. Hence it is argued that elderly people and their supporters should be enabled and encouraged to participate in the management of the social organizations to which they belong. Democratic participation is cumbersome, slow-moving, and not always effective in solving problems. Nevertheless, even benign non-democratic regimes are likely to deteriorate in time to the disadvantage of the elderly patient or resident, whose welfare, after all, constitutes the prime function of such organizations. It is advisable, therefore, in the interests of democratic participation, for residents and patients to have access to information, to membership of committees, advisory groups, management, and so on, and for such provision to be written into the constitution of such organizations and periodically evaluated and reinforced. Democratic participation by the dependent elderly in the forms of social organization which affect their lives is a difficult problem since the individuals most capable of representing the interests of the dependent elderly are not themselves 'representative' of them. However, this state of affairs is by no means unusual in democratic practices in other age groups. The problem is to find people who will genuinely represent particular interest groups, 'advocates' in effect. There is obviously considerable scope for democratic participation and leadership among both institutional and community-living elderly. Consider, for example, group provision of recreation, security, the exchange of services, and voluntary effort.

Group meetings in the interests of democratic living are clearly different from groups specifically set up for therapeutic purposes. Nevertheless, there may be elements in common. In any event, those responsible for organizing such groups need to pay attention to basic matters such as the physical location of the meetings, their timing, travel arrangements, order of business, procedures, participation, and the like, all of which may pose special problems in groups of elderly people. The same principles apply to the organization of voluntary (charitable) bodies set up to help the elderly. We do not hear a great deal of debate about the rights of the elderly infirm, but it seems likely that the ethical and legal issues associated with late-life dependency will become increasingly important as a larger proportion of the population survives to experience such dependency—see Alexander (1981), Brocklehurst and Hanley (1976, pp. 247–50), Hellman (1985).

SUMMARY

The clinical area of behavioural gerontology deals with individual cases of psychological disorders in later life. These disorders are not easy to classify, there are differences between individuals in the way disorders are expressed, and they change over time. In a sense all the illnesses, injuries, and difficulties of later life have a psychological component. Although it is important not to lose sight of this fact, it is more convenient for us to concentrate on a limited number of late-life conditions, in particular depression, dementia, and the commoner problems of adjustment.

Estimates of the extent of psychiatric disorders in the general population in later life vary, depending upon the population studied and the criteria used in diagnosis. Tables summarizing the prevalence rates for various mental disorders in late life illustrate the diversity of estimates from various sources. It seems probable that there is a great deal of unreported psychiatric illness in later life. Conditions are not always correctly diagnosed or treated. There continues to be considerable uncertainty about the aetiology of the psychological disorders of later life. Genetic as well as environmental factors are involved, although their relative importance seems to vary from one condition to another and from one case to another.

The major psychopathologies of late life are depression and dementia. It is these conditions, amongst others, that lead to institutional care. Depression manifests itself variously in feelings of misery, worthlessness, and guilt; thoughts of death and suicide; loss of interest and pleasure in activities; loss of appetite; somatic complaints; weight loss; disturbed sleep and early waking; irritability; or slowed psychological reactions.

Depression of mild to moderate severity can accompany life-stresses or be associated with chronic bad health or poor living conditions. It can be brought on by relatively minor ailments, such as infection, poor nutrition, or inappropriate drug treatment. It is important to differentiate between the temporary reduction in cognitive performance associated with a major depressive episode and the permanent loss associated with dementia, since the initial effects of the two conditions are similar but the treatment possibilities are different. The points of contrast are that in depression the onset of symptoms is relatively more abrupt and cognitive performance improves if the depression lifts. In dementia, cognitive impairment is permanent and progressive.

Depression in late life can be treated by means of ECT or drugs. However, drug metabolism changes with age, in particular the metabolic products are retained longer in the body; so drug dosage levels need to be carefully monitored to minimize adverse side-effects. An elderly patient may be taking a variety of drugs for different ailments, or may fail to take the drugs as prescribed. For these reasons, complications may ensue. Psychotherapy and family therapy are also used to treat depression in later life. The condition may have a real foundation in unsatisfactory life-events, losses in personal relationships, and failure of aspirations. The patient's depression is bound to have an adverse effect on his or her care-givers, who may also need support and advice.

Depressive states of mind range from mild and temporary reactions to disappointments and losses in daily life to severe and lasting conditions which are psychologically disabling. Mild depression as a reaction to some of the adverse effects of ageing is hardly surprising, but adaptation to one's changed health and circumstances has the effect of moderating this sort of depression. Genetic predisposition and age-related physiological changes undoubtedly play a part in more severe depressive states, but the mechanisms are far from clear. Similarly, life-events dating back to childhood, as well as current life-stresses, play a part; but again, it is difficult to identify the common factors. An important feature of late-life depression is that it may be confused with dementia—this is the condition known as pseudodementia. A wrong diagnosis may have serious consequences. Severe depression may lead to suicide (paradoxically perhaps when the degree of depression has lessened slightly). Although depression is commoner among women than among men, men are more likely to commit suicide. Depression and suicide rates increase with age. Various signs and symptoms are regarded as indicative of depression, but none appear to be of critical diagnostic significance. Psychological and physiological theories of depression have been formulated, but none seems to provide a comprehensive account of this condition. It may be that depression can arise in a variety of ways and is susceptible to different modes of treatment. The psychological assessment of depression in the elderly relies on interviews, self-report measures, and symptom checklists. Psychiatric assessment includes physiological tests, reactions to medication, and the exclusion of other psychiatric conditions. In a small proportion of cases depression is connected with manic episodes, hence the phrase 'manic-depressive' psychosis. Manic episodes are thought to be found more often in early or middle adult life. Depressive tendencies may be expressed in different ways at different ages; this is because of changes in physical health and changes in life's circumstances. For example, they may interact with physical illnesses, sleep disturbances, hypochondriacal tendencies, retirement, and bereavement. The traditional forms of interviewing and testing are gradually being supplemented by more systematic computer-assisted methods of assessment, although the full benefit of such technology will not be felt until we have concepts and theories to account for the disorder.

Dementia is the term used to refer to the permanent impairment of higher mental functions—abstraction, generalization, reasoning, and memory. Temporary losses can occur in conditions of anoxia, depression, delirium, and fatigue. The loss is relative to the patient's pre-morbid level of intellectual functioning, but this may be difficult to assess. The current level can be assessed by psychometric methods as well as by direct and indirect observation of the patient's behaviour in the ordinary activities of daily life. The pre-morbid level can be inferred from the patient's performance on tasks which are thought to be resistant to the effects of ageing, as in the WAIS 'hold' tests or the NART. There may be life-history data available on the patient's previous activities, interests, education, occupation, and accomplishments, reference to which may provide an indication of the extent to which intellectual level has declined.

The functional consequences of dementia depend upon the demands of the individual's environment. In a simple, ordered, supportive environment the individual may be able to cope quite well. In a complex, shifting, demanding environment the individual can be expected to become confused and disturbed. Dementia or organic brain disease comprises two main categories: multi-infarct dementia (MID) and senile dementia of the Alzheimer type (SDAT). Multi-infarct dementia means that various areas of the brain have suffered cell death because of many small impairments in cerebral blood flow and the consequent loss of oxygen. The blood flow is impaired by a hardening and narrowing of the blood vessels. Although the onset may be sudden—with headaches, dizziness, and fatigue—the course of the disease is characteristically uneven, in the sense that the patient may be confused, impaired, and deviant at one time, and relatively lucid and well-behaved at another. MID is related to high blood pressure, and to the particular pattern of brain damage. Some aspects of behaviour may be affected but not others, although the condition worsens overall in an erratic, abrupt way, and impairs control of the person's thoughts, feelings, and desires, leading to deviant behaviour as well as to intellectual impairment. Treatment for MID attempts to improve cerebral blood flow. Obviously, preventive measures and early detection are of paramount importance. Other forms of therapy, recreation, protection, and social support may help relieve some of the adverse effects of the disorder on the patient and his or her care-givers.

Dementia of the Alzheimer type, SDAT, shows extensive degeneration of brain tissue not directly associated with cerebrovascular disorder. SDAT is only one form of dementia in later life, but may represent a characteristic or basic brain disease, especially after the age of 75 years.

Estimates of the extent of the disorder are difficult to make, partly because of the problem of defining dementia and distinguishing it from the 'normal' effects of ageing on intellectual functioning, and from other late-life mental disorders. In comparison with MID, SDAT has more gradual onset and a more even course. The more obvious symptoms are forgetfulness, mistakes in the use of words, and the impairment of mental skills. Anxiety about these symptoms may make matters worse. As the disease progresses, memory impairment becomes more pronounced, especially for recent events. There is a greater likelihood of confusion, lapses, and mistakes, and a general deterioration in the organization of behaviour. Disorientation for time, place, and person are likely to cause further complications such as suspicion and anger, as well as making life very difficult for family members.

Treatment for SDAT attempts to deal with the symptoms, e.g. drugs to calm the patient or to regulate the sleep/waking cycle. A variety of supportive therapies can be brought to bear—occupational and recreational therapy, reality orientation, reminiscence therapy, behaviour modification, family therapy, and so on. Care-givers may have difficulty in attributing the patient's behaviour to the disorder (they may assume it is deliberate and voluntary), because the normal and familiar methods of persuasion and influence do not work, or do not work for long. If the patient becomes a danger to self or others, or if there is a deterioration in personal habits—incontinence, sexual abnormality, for example—then institutional care may be the only option. However, many old people suffering from various degrees of dementia are looked after by their families at home, and can manage fairly well in familiar, simplified, routine environments.

In SDAT one finds, at autopsy, marked brain changes which include senile plaques (areas of pigmentation outside the nerve cells) and neurofibrillary tangles (the filamentous strands within the nerve process become twisted and tangled). It appears that, on average, the more extensive these conditions are the more intellectual deterioration the patient shows. The conditions are found to a lesser extent in the brains of normal patients at autopsy. Other changes in the brain include degeneration or loss of neurons, and enlargement of the ventricles. The hippocampus is one of the more affected areas, which may account for memory disorders in SDAT. The causes of SDAT have been variously attributed to immunological defect and to toxic substances. As one might expect, there is a genetic component, possibly related to chromosome 21 as in Down's syndrome. The relationship between SDAT and MID on the one hand, and normal ageing on the other, is not clear. There are many similarities as regards symptoms and post-mortem findings, and there are no doubt many borderline cases. Conditions which become severe enough to warrant medical and social intervention are diagnosed and defined as 'cases' and treated as such. The question is whether SDAT and MID are simply extreme forms of a normal dementing process, or severe forms which have exceeded some threshold value triggering abnormal effects, or disease processes in their own right separate from normal ageing. The conditions referred to as 'normal' and 'pathological' ageing need to be defined independently of each other.

Clinical assessment in behavioural gerontology uses a wide range of investigative procedures from direct observation of the patient's behaviour in his or her normal surroundings to precise quantitative measurements of the patient's performance on standardized tests administered under controlled conditions. In practice there is considerable reliance on tests and rating scales which may not be sufficiently reliable and valid for use with older people. Moreover, care staff may have insufficient time or training to collect the data needed for the purposes of research and evaluation.

Psychological treatment for disorders in late life could be said to begin with referral and assessment, since there is usually some measurable psychological benefit from knowing that help is available. At least this is usually the case with patients who are able to appreciate what is going on, i.e. the majority of patients with relatively mild disturbances. Recognition of the fact that the person needs professional help is often left to a concerned relative or friend who has to negotiate with service-providers and act as the patient's advocate. This is particularly so with elderly patients who are mentally impaired.

Depression and dementia are among the more serious psychological ailments of later life. Dementia proper cannot be cured, although some of the more distressing symptoms can be alleviated by drugs and nursing management. Depression in late life is likely to recur, so that periodic reassessment is necessary and treatment effects need to be kept under review. The tendency has been for the disorders of late life to be given low priority in terms of health and welfare resources, partly because of the belief that nothing could be done to cure or alleviate them. This tendency is much less marked today, and efforts are being made to improve the diagnosis and treatment of late-life disorders, and to improve the care of elderly patients who are suffering from chronic ailments in long-stay institutional environments. The clinical aspect of behavioural gerontology overlaps with the social aspect in relation to community care and institutional care of the elderly. There is also an ethical dimension to the issue of the health and welfare of the elderly.

Psychological treatments for the disorders of later life are quite varied. They include behaviour modification, especially for patients who are unable to benefit from ordinary forms of psychotherapy. Counselling is commonly used and may be practised by a wide variety of professional staff and voluntary workers. Psychological principles enter into the theory and practice of many professionals, so that psychologists have a role to play in professional education and training. Relatives and friends who function as care-givers may also need psychological support and advice for their own health and welfare, since caring for the elderly can be stressful, and there is widespread ignorance about mental health in later life.

Ideally, elderly patients with chronic disorders should be in 'therapeutic environments', i.e. in environments which minimize the adverse effects of their disabilities, normalize or maximize their opportunities for satisfying activities, and maintain a sense of personal control and social integration. Such environments have to be engineered in the sense of providing a suitably built and properly equipped physical environment and providing a properly managed, congenial human environment. Technological developments in computing and communications hold considerable promise of benefits for the elderly. Changes in the age structure of the population, changes in health and living standards in later life, and especially changes in social attitudes and values should eventually lead to much better arrangements for care of the elderly infirm.

There are many problem areas of later life where psychological support is likely to be of benefit. These areas include not only problems of adjustment which are largely or entirely psychological, but also problems where psychological reactions are secondary. Physical disabilities and illnesses have their psychological and social consequences. Social problems—for example, housing, finances, crime, family breakdown—have their psychological consequences, as do individual stressful life-events. Until recently the psychological problems of the elderly were virtually ignored, and even today psychological intervention operates on a small scale—relative to, say, drug therapy. The sorts of psychological treatments that are being explored include counselling and psychotherapy, reality orientation, reminiscence and life-review therapy, cognitive-behaviour therapy, group and recreational therapy. It is important that these treatments are properly evaluated.

Chapter 5

Adult Intelligence

INTRODUCTION

The term 'general intelligence' refers to a level of mental ability, relative to other people, measured in terms of performance on a variety of tests which 'sample' a wide range of cognitive functions without undue bias arising from individual differences in education (training and experience). Performances on different kinds of cognitive tests tend to be positively correlated, and the term 'g' refers to the hypothetical 'common factor' which underlies these correlations. However, the correlations between tests vary, depending on their content, format, difficulty level, and so on. This has led to a great deal of debate about the nature and measurement of intelligence. General intelligence is by no means a simple concept; but broadly it refers to the ability to organize complex patterns and sequences of information quickly and accurately, and to learn from experience how to improve performance on tasks of a recurrent kind.

The notion of general intelligence can be used to refer to a combination of two types of mental ability—fluid and crystallized. Fluid or unspecialized intelligence is thought of as a largely inborn biological capacity. It is assessed in terms of speed of mental processing, relational thinking, abstraction and generalization, and the management of large amounts of information over time. Crystallized or specialized intelligence, on the other hand, is thought of as an acquired capacity. It is assessed in terms of general knowledge, vocabulary, educational attainments, learned mental skills, and concepts. The distinction is brought out in part by contrasting intelligence with experience. The connection between fluid and crystallized intelligence is that fluid intelligence enables us to learn from experience, and experience enables us to use our fluid intelligence more effectively. A combination of organized experience and native intelligence accounts for the mental skills we see demonstrated in mathematics, chess, engineering, military decision-making, navigation, and even in cookery and gardening. Any performance which is not completely habitual or automatic and requires some thought combines intelligence and experience—fluid and crystallized abilities.

The ordinary activities of daily life are normally well within the limits of our mental ability, but from time to time, because of fatigue, anxiety, or pressure of events, we run up against these limits. In these circumstances we make mistakes—do the wrong thing or fail to do the right thing, perhaps even fail to notice that we have made a mistake. People with relatively low intelligence, by definition, are less able to cope with the cognitive demands of ordinary life.

If our mental abilities are tested to the limits by means of standardized tests of adult intelligence, such as the Wechsler subtests (Wechsler, 1986), it is possible to examine the level and spread of intelligence in a population, and to investigate the effects of ageing. What we find is that crystallized abilities tend to hold up with age, whereas fluid abilities tend to decline. This would correspond with other effects of ageing—the decline in fluid ability reflects the decline with age in physiological functions, especially cortical functions, whilst the maintenance of crystallized abilities reflects the continued exercise of these abilities in the ordinary activities of life—at work, at home, or at leisure. Failure to exercise acquired mental abilities leads to a loss of functions, which may be recoverable with renewed training and practice. At present the psychometric distinction between fluid and crystallized abilities is one of degree rather than kind.

Attempts have been made to subdivide general intelligence into a number of abilities such as memory, spatial reasoning, and verbal ability. So far these attempts have succeeded in showing that certain kinds of tests tend to correlate more highly with each other than they do with other kinds of tests. However, the special abilities thus far identified seem to have no special neurological significance and seem not to figure in current theories about cognition. It seems possible that the specific cognitive functions that make up what we call general intelligence will be more narrowly specialized, different from, and more numerous than the mental abilities proposed so far—see Gardner (1985).

As far as the effects of ageing are concerned, the differential effects on fluid and crystallized abilities seem to account for the results obtained using tests of primary mental abilities. Similarly, factor-analytic studies of changes with age in the structure of mental abilities seem to confirm the shift from fluid to crystallized ability—see Bilash and Zubek (1960), Horn and Cattell (1966), Schaie et al. (1989).

The effects of adult ageing on the intelligence of a particular individual depend upon a number of factors, including the effectiveness of the physiological mechanisms underlying cognitive functions and the extent to which the individual's training and experience can be applied to tasks requiring the exercise of intelligence. The individual's genetic endowment, his or her development during the juvenile years, and life-events and health in adult life, can all exert effects on intelligence.

Adult intelligence can be defined and measured reasonably well by standardized psychometric tests. Indeed, virtually all the evidence we have on adult intelligence is derived from such measures. But adult intelligence can also be defined in terms of the ability to deal with the information content of situations as they arise in daily life—this is referred to as 'practical intelligence'. The main differences are that practical intelligence tends to be exercised over longer periods of time and varies somewhat with personal and environmental circumstances. Thus interest, health, and mood might enhance or diminish a person's practical intelligence in a given situation.

The question is, 'What is the relationship between general intelligence, as measured by standardized psychometric tests, and practical intelligence as indicated by a person's ability to comprehend the situations faced in daily life?' If psychometric tests provided a good (reliable, valid) index of practical intelligence there would be no problem; indeed the evidence against the validity of psychometric measures of adult intelligence is not great. However, it does seem reasonable to argue that the way intelligence is exercised changes through adult life, as it does through the juvenile years. In this case, we need to know the practical criteria against which measures of intelligence are to be validated at successive stages of adult development and ageing. At present, tests of intelligence tend to be validated against other tests of intelligence, or against educational and some occupational attainments. They are constructed in the traditional forms derived from the study of juvenile intelligence.

Mental skills

An important and influential approach to the effects of age on cognitive functions has been that of Welford (1958, 1977). It is basically an information processing approach, although the term 'mental skills' is not inappropriate given the recent renewal of interest in the way intelligence is applied to real-world problems—see Sternberg and Wagner (1986). Information is received, processed, and used by human beings in situations calling for the acquisition of skills and the solving of problems. Intelligence can be regarded as a general capacity for acquiring and exercising mental skills and solving problems involving abstraction/ generalization, relational thinking, mental mapping, translation, and symbolism. In mental skills the sensory and motor aspects of behaviour are trivial in comparison with the complex central processing of information, as in playing chess. Normal ageing has adverse effects on mental skills because of the apparent deterioration of these central information-processing functions.

Psychology studies the *organization* of human behaviour. Some of the more complex and interesting forms of human behaviour require high-grade mental abilities such as abstraction and generalization, inductive and deductive reasoning, symbolic learning and remembering, and language. It is important to remember that mental abilities form only part of the psychological resources that human beings use in dealing with their everyday problems of adjustment. Reasoning, memory, and imagination function within the overall framework of our psychological make-up, and are affected by the context of the situation we are dealing with. Thus, in practice, our cognitive functions may be improved or worsened by relatively stable personal characteristics such as extraversion, energy or neuroticism, and by established habits and attitudes—Robinson, D. L. (1985, 1986). Cognitive functions may also be affected by temporary conditions such as fatigue, distraction, mental set, and unfamiliarity. If we are operating in a situation which is unfamiliar, changing rapidly, threatening, or otherwise unhelpful, we may be unable to exercise our mental abilities effectively—as for example with 'examination nerves'. Stress and disease obviously affect cognitive functions.

One source of difficulties in the investigation of adult intelligence is that psychometric measures developed to assess adult intelligence do not have a good theoretical basis and have been developed within two rather different contexts. On the one hand we have a test like the Wechsler Adult Intelligence Scale (WAIS) which has its roots in the mental testing movement (mainly concerned with educational selection and guidance) in the early part of this century, and in the massive selection procedures associated with the two world wars. On the other hand, we have a test like Raven's (1982) Progressive Matrices Test (RPMT), which has its origins in a reaction away from tests involving knowledge processing in an attempt to measure fundamental cognitive processes, namely, Spearman's principles of nöegenesis. However the RMPT was quickly applied to the same sorts of practical problems as the WAIS—including cognitive assessment in the context of clinical psychology. In other words, the intelligence testing movement has been driven mainly by the need for practical applications—in education, the armed forces, mental health, and industry, but partly by the desire to develop a basic theory of cognitive functions. The theoretical underpinnings of intelligence tests developed in the context of education—the main area of application—have been weak. They took the form of assumptions and working definitions, such as the idea that intelligence was the ability to profit from experience, in particular from education and training in mental skills, and the idea that intelligence measured a general capacity for adaptation to the environment. As psychometric measures of intelligence were developed in particular contexts—educational, clinical, military, industrial, and so on—they became more valid, more reliable, and more useful in their particular practical applications. So successful were they that through a sort of bootstrapping process they became better measures of intelligence than the criterion measures used to validate them. Intelligence came to be defined as 'What intelligence tests measure'; in particular, the common factor or factors measured by intelligence tests.

The psychometric and statistical problems associated with the study of intelligence dominated the theoretical debate for many years. Only recently, following the upsets associated with racial comparisons in intelligence and the discovery that Burt's data on twins were suspect (Hearnshaw, 1979) has the emphasis shifted away from the methodological issues of factor analysis and test construction. This shift coincided roughly with the advent of artificial intelligence and a renewed interest in the cognitive aspects of problem-solving. For views on changes in the concept of intelligence see *International Journal of Psychology* (1984, vol. 19, 4–5).

Hearnshaw's (1979) biography of Cyril Burt can be regarded as a contribution to the psychology of ageing in so far as he emphasizes the importance of some late-life events and circumstances affecting Burt's behaviour.

There have been some attempts to use a Piagetian framework in the study of adult intelligence, but so far these seem not to have given rise to any noticeable changes in the theory of adult intelligence or in practical applications. If one uses Piagetian tests—of, say, conservation—then adult age differences can be observed. As one might expect, the more 'difficult' the task, the poorer the performance of older subjects when task difficulty is assessed independently of adult age trends. The problem is that we have no way of translating scores on a test of adult intelligence into statements about a person's 'level' or 'stage' of cognitive development. A proportion of adults do not achieve what is called the stage of formal operational thought. Moreover, people may operate at different cognitive levels in different situations, depending upon the subject matter, their training and experience, and their state of mind.

The qualitative level of intelligence reached at the end of the juvenile period of development appears to be retained virtually unchanged for a large part of normal adult life, that is until the cumulative effects of ageing on brain functions in late life, or a dementing condition, bring about a qualitative shift to lower levels of cognitive operations. One would expect that older people would operate best in areas in which they had achieved their highest levels of performance and in areas in which they had continued to exercise their mental abilities. However, even in tasks which depend to some extent on knowledge and experience, fluid, i.e. natural or unspecialized, intelligence, together with mental speed, may be a major factor in successful performance.

The normal trend in intelligence in the adult years, say from the age of 20 to 75 years, is not easily described. It seems that we are not able to fully sustain the maximum level of competence that we reached in early adult life. The level at which we operate in a particular situation depends upon a variety of non-intellectual factors—motivation, temperament, momentary states of mind, habit, health, and so on. This is the distinction between competence and performance.

Differences in the intelligence of individuals arise because of specific abilities possessed by individuals—in speed of mental operations, in memory capacity, in processing visual or auditory information, in persistence, and in other psychological and physiological characteristics, including education and training (which increase the power of the intellect rather like coaching and practice improve our athletic prowess).

Individual differences in adult intelligence are clearly illustrated not only by the WAIS and RPMT but also by Thurstone's Primary Mental Abilities test (TPMAT). This test was developed out of the controversy over the interpretation of the correlations between different measures of intelligence. One interpretation was that there was a common or general factor of intelligence—called 'g'. The other was that there were several relatively independent or primary factors—visuospatial, verbal, memory, and so on. The normal effects of ageing on the TPMAT are probably best interpreted in the same way as for the WAIS. That is to say, those items which are more difficult (speeded, complex, effortful) *at any age* are proportionately more difficult for older subjects. In general, items which can be dealt with largely by means of 'crystallized abilities' (which hold up with age) are more likely to be solved than items which require 'fluid abilities' (which do not hold up with age).

Unfortunately it has not been possible, so far, to link the abilities identified as 'primary mental abilities' with other substantive work in psychology—in cognitive development for example, in psychopathology or neuropsychology, or in cognitive psychology generally. Similarly, Guilford's ambitious attempt to establish a comprehensive taxonomy of mental abilities—see Guilford and Hoepfner (1971)—has not so far been integrated with other substantive work in psychology, and little effort has been made to apply Guilford's concepts and methods to the study of age trends in adult intelligence.

In spite of the tremendous amount of work that has been done on factor analysis in relation to mental abilities, it is surprising to find no clear picture of the effects of normal ageing emerges—see also Reinert

(1970), Savage and Britton (1969). The mental abilities identified by means of factor analysis are affected by normal ageing in accordance with the extent to which they depend on fluid (unspecialized) and crystallized (specialized) intelligence. The abilities defined by factor analysis seem to have little or no relation with known brain functions—except perhaps visual–spatial ability—and seem to have little clinical significance in psychopathology. It is possible to suppose, however, that the so-called 'structure of mental abilities' changes with age both during the juvenile period and during adult life and old age. Unfortunately, the problems associated with research methodology, such as sampling and psychometric scaling, make it difficult to compare the 'structure of abilities' of samples differing widely in age and in the central tendency and spread of their scores on various tests. One could expect, however, that the structure of abilities of young adults would be maximally differentiated (and have a correspondingly smaller general or common factor) whereas the structure of abilities of older adults would be somewhat distorted, in comparison with young adults, by being de-differentiated as regards fluid abilities (those requiring mental speed, information processing, abstraction generalization, and relational thinking) but not as regards crystallized abilities (vocabulary, general knowledge, scholastic attainments).

The traditional psychometric approach possesses valuable technological merits but lacks the necessary theoretical underpinnings which would help advance our knowledge of cognition generally, and of adult intelligence in particular—see Rabbitt (1981). That seems to leave two possibilities for future work in adult intelligence. One possibility is that measures developed in the context of neuropsychological assessment (testing the cognitive effects of brain damage) will be sensitive to *normal* changes in intelligence even over relatively short periods of time in the adult years. There is in fact a long history of *ad hoc* attempts to link the cognitive changes found in normal ageing with those found in conditions of mental disease and brain injury. Until recently the psychometric technology that characterized the mental testing movement was not widely applied in neuropsychological assessment. One possible reason is that psychometric technology was developed mainly to establish normative standards for the practical purposes of selection and guidance affecting large numbers of subjects. Neuropsychological assessment, on the other hand, has tended to depend on the intensive study of individual cases and has more concern with brain/behaviour relationships in theory construction. It has demonstrated some unusual and presently inexplicable cognitive defects in brain-damaged patients in connection with tests like the Halstead–Reitan battery and the Luria–Nebraska battery, and in connection with memory functions and face recognition—Shallice (1979).

The WAIS, of course, has been used extensively in clinical settings as a diagnostic test. It even incorporates criteria for the assessment of dementia and other sorts of brain disorder. These criteria, however, are the result of empirical research which has made use of some convenient design features of the WAIS. The criteria were not part of any original theory of intellectual functioning when the test was first developed.

Another possibility for future work is that developments in the experimental psychology of cognition—studies of memory, problem-solving, and so on—may identify basic cognitive functions not hitherto recognized, and not adequately incorporated into traditional tests of intelligence. Allied to this possibility is the emergence of computer-assisted psychological assessment which promises to take much of the donkey work out of clinical diagnostic testing and to see much more standardization of procedures across clinics and research establishments (thereby increasing the size of samples and the opportunities for replication). Although computer-assisted psychometrics can provide a useful technology for investigations into adult intelligence (and the breakdown of intelligence in some disorders of late life), it cannot provide the theory necessary to direct the research.

Prevention and intervention

The idea that we can counteract and compensate for some of the adverse psychological effects of ageing is by no means new. It had a prominent place in Welford's (1958, 1977) classical work on skill and ageing. It is also implicit in the various biomedical and psychological treatments that have been developed for conditions such as stroke, depression, bereavement, sensory loss, and mental confusion. What is new in the psychology of ageing is not merely an increase in optimism about the prospects for intervention, but the proposal that intervention studies be regarded as a major method of research. The proposal is that we should concentrate more on testing practical applications than on theoretical and descriptive issues, using beneficial outcomes as the test of the theory on which the treatments are based. Like the Wright brothers, we need to get the 'plane to fly, and then worry about aerodynamics! There are arguments for and against such a proposal, and in any event we should not expect rapid or substantial progress even in applied research in ageing. It is possible, however, that developments in high technology—computerization and communications—will open up new prospects in the applied psychology of ageing.

Studies of the relationship between abilities and chronological age itself are of limited interest and usefulness. Chronological age is no more than a convenient time marker in terms of which the complex psychobiological causal pathways involved in human ageing can be compared and related.

Descriptive studies provide a starting point for the elaboration of questions and theories about ageing, which in turn give rise to questions, predictions, and useful applications. For example, to what extent do life-stresses lead to changes in mental abilities? Would regular physical or mental exercise retard intellectual decline or even reverse it? What effects do diet, drugs, or toxic substances have on adult intelligence? Can the precursors of psychopathology in late life be detected in everyday cognitive failures earlier in adult life?

Among the more interesting and potentially useful notions in the recent literature on the psychology of ageing are the following:

Excess disability

This refers to the tendency for behavioural and psychological impairment to be greater than that warranted by the person's physical condition and social circumstances. The general remedy for excess disability lies in an individualized assessment and treatment programme which attempts to carry out a detailed functional analysis of the person's adaptation to his or her circumstances. This is followed by intensive and prolonged efforts to recover abilities that have fallen into disuse, to make full use of residual capacities, to modify the person's behaviour to make it better-adapted to his or her surroundings, and to modify the person's environment so as to make it more supportive, less restricting and harmful, more manageable, and richer in opportunities for rewarding activities.

Disuse

The effects of irreversible mental deterioration brought about by physical damage must be distinguished from the reversible effects brought about by disuse of functions. It has been apparent for some time that educational attainments tend to decrease in the few years after leaving school if the person neglects to continue his or her education. Similarly, in adult life we frequently neglect to exercise certain mental skills such as a foreign language, mathematics, or chess, with the result that they fall into disuse and require a period of relearning and practice before they can be brought back to their previous level of competence. It does not seem to be unreasonable to suppose that basic mental abilities can become temporarily impaired through disuse, rather like muscular strength, coordination, and stamina become impaired if we neglect to engage in regular demanding physical exercise. Although studies in recovery from disuse, through programmes of mental exercise, are few in number and not altogether satisfactory in terms of method, it seems more likely than not that benefits comparable to those that have been demonstrated for programmes of physical exercise could be achieved—Plemons *et al.* (1978), Powell and Porndorf (1971), Labouvie-Vief (1985), Turner and Reese (1980). We should, perhaps, be encouraging middle-aged and older people away from spectatorship, whether live or on television, and towards participatory activities: physical exercise, games, hobbies, and other intellectually demanding cultural pursuits.

Obsolescence

Human knowledge and techniques are changing all the time, as may be seen by the changing contents of textbooks, technical catalogues, and job specifications. There is, however, a kind of inertia in human learning such that ideas and skills once acquired resist replacement by newer, more effective, ideas and skills. Thus we talk about conventional wisdom, and the conservatism of the older generation. The so-called generation gap is, in part, a gap between new fashions and old fashions in thinking and behaving. Nowadays, however, with a clearer recognition of the pace at which cultural and technological changes are taking place, schemes for retraining and continuing education are flourishing, for example in the medical profession in the USA and in industrial training in the UK. Howe (1977) reports on adult learning.

Older people whose ideas are obsolescent and whose mental abilities have diminished through disuse stand in need of advice and guidance on how to maintain and improve their psychobiological capacities and how to shape or change their environment so that it supports their changed physical and mental capacities—Hebb (1980), Skinner (1983). Studies on the effectiveness of methods of intervention to reduce the adverse effects of ageing are important from a theoretical as well as from a practical point of view. Intervention studies can be regarded as particularly important methods of scientific investigation because they require prior theorizing and subsequent evaluation. Training and regular practice in problem-solving could be regarded as remedial if their beneficial effects could be shown to generalize beyond the tasks used in training.

Although research evidence derived from prospective studies is still lacking, there are reasons for supposing that programmes of intervention, designed to retard the rate of deterioration or to improve the physical and mental well-being of people in middle age and later life, would be successful. Cognitive training might provide a preventive measure against the adverse effects of ageing. Cognitive retraining could include such procedures as: alerting people to the effects that ageing may have on their mental abilities; providing them with conceptual routines, e.g. aide-memoires, checklists, algorithms, for dealing with recurrent problems. Instruction and practice in the exercise of intelligence (problem solving) could easily be incorporated into adult education classes.

JUVENILE AND ADULT INTELLIGENCE

The concepts and methods used in the study of adult intelligence are, to a large extent, derived from the mental testing movement which had its main origins in the work of Alfred Binet in France and Charles Spearman in England, at the beginning of this century. The mental testing movement was mainly concerned with the measurement of individual differences in intelligence and attainments, and with their development during the years of childhood and adolescence. Many measures of intelligence were tried out, using verbal and non-verbal items, and a great deal of ingenuity and statistical sophistication was invested in the standardization and validation of tests such as the Stanford–Binet, Raven's Progressive Matrices, and Thurstone's Primary Mental Abilities.

During the First World War, American Army recruits were assessed by tests known as the Army Alpha and the Army Beta, which were derived from measures developed by Otis (Yerkes, 1921). Great consternation was caused in 1919 by publication of the discovery that the average mental age ($[MA/CA] \times 100 = IQ$) of these young adult recruits was about $13\frac{1}{2}$ years, substantially below the mental age of 16 years implied by the Stanford–Binet norms (Doll, 1919). Further consternation was caused when it became known that there were consistent decreases in the scores for successively older age groups on the Army Alpha test applied to several thousand US Army officers. There was, at the time, considerable reluctance on the part of investigators and commentators to interpret the evidence as indicating an actual decline with age in adult intelligence. Instead, it was argued that the tests were not adequate measures of adult intelligence, and that the age cohorts (samples) were not comparable.

In 1927 Spearman had concluded that general intelligence—or 'g' as it was referred to psychometrically—develops steadily during the juvenile years and reaches its maximum at about the age of 16 years, after which it is maintained at that level throughout adult life unless diminished by senility.

In 1939 the original Wechsler–Bellevue Scale for the measurement of adult intelligence was published. The concepts and methods on which it was based were those of the mental testing movement to which we have just referred. Several revisions have since been published and the test has been widely used for clinical and research purposes—see later.

Little is known about the effects of juvenile development on adult ageing. During childhood and adolescence a person's inborn capacities mature and develop in the context of the surrounding social and physical conditions. Nutrition shortly before and after birth, for example, will profoundly affect the developing brain of the foetus and infant; and it is possible that social and environmental stimulation at critical periods of development will affect the emergence of abilities such as spatial reasoning, mathematics, and the use of language. The resulting levels of cognitive development may, in later life, provide 'thresholds' for cognitive impairment. That is to say, the process of age-deterioration may undo the work of development, but people who have achieved higher levels of cognitive development have further to fall, as it were, before reaching the thresholds at which performance is regarded as impaired.

In normal circumstances, as the child develops, intelligence and experience grow hand in hand so that, within limits, acquired intellectual attainments, as measured by vocabulary, general knowledge, scholastic record, and so on, are indicative of inborn general intellectual ability. This hypothetical capacity—'g'—is useful in accounting for family resemblances in intelligence, concordance in twin studies, the intercorrelations between tests, and so on. During adult life, however, the relationship between ability and attainment, in normal conditions, is less close than in childhood; or rather, it is more difficult to establish such a relationship because adult achievements are much more diverse and more difficult to calibrate than juvenile scholastic achievements. There is a differential decline with age, such that intellectual attainments (crystallized abilities) tend to be preserved if practised, and are easily relearned, whereas intellectual capacity (fluid ability) tends to decline and, by definition, is not susceptible to modification.

The study of age changes in adult intelligence is more complicated than the study of changes in juvenile intelligence. There are several reasons for this state of affairs. First, it is administratively easier to obtain representative samples of subjects from well-defined populations during the juvenile years. Second, these subjects (children of school age) can be conveniently tested in large groups. Third, there are immediate practical benefits to be gained from the information obtained about a child's intelligence. Fourth, there are definite connections between chronological age and intelligence during the juvenile years. Fifth, there is considerable agreement as to how juvenile intelligence can be measured. None of these conditions applies in the study of adult intelligence.

In the study of juvenile intelligence there appear to be few or no discrepancies between the results obtained from cross-sectional and longitudinal research into age trends. Recently, however, there have been convincing reports of cohort effects for intelligence, see Flynn (1987a, b, c). Cohort effects are well established for height and age at menarche. In the study of adult intelligence the discrepancies between cross-sectional and longitudinal studies have been a major focus of attention and controversy—Schaie (1983). In addition, there has been considerable discussion about the nature of adult intelligence and its measurement.

The current view seems to be that 'adult' intelligence may have to be defined differently from 'juvenile' intelligence, at least as far as operational measures and practical applications are concerned. The argument is that adult intelligence is exercised in different ways and in relation to different sorts of problems from those characteristic of the juvenile years. In particular, some cognitive functions are trained and practised to such an extent that they have become routinized, fast, and efficient, and require little effort—Berg and Sternberg (1985), Sternberg (1985), Sternberg and Wagner (1986).

One question then is to what extent does a traditional type of intelligence test for adults correlate with the practical intelligence shown in the way people deal with the cognitive aspects of life's problems? A related question is to what extent can we develop standardized operational measures of adult intelligence which are ecologically valid? For studies in these areas, see Dixon and Baltes (1986), Rabbitt (1982b), Willis and Schaie (1986).

A further complication in the comparison between juvenile and adult intelligence is that during the juvenile years the various abilities which, overall, help to define intelligence, appear to develop at more or less the same rate. At least, no one so far appears to have demonstrated differential rates of growth for different mental abilities. This may be because of the way intelligence tests are constructed and standardized; they are relative, not absolute, measures. By contrast, during the adult years there is a well-established differential decline in mental abilities which shows up in both longitudinal and cross-sectional studies.

In practice, both intelligence tests and cognitive problems in daily life usually call for some admixture of fluid and crystallized abilities, i.e. of native or unspecialized intelligence on the one hand and acquired experience or specialized intelligence on the other.

At present, the way intelligence is defined in terms of mental performance means that one cannot separate out completely the knowledge base from the mental operations applied to the knowledge base. In order to test a person's intelligence we need to assess how well, relative to other people, that person can process information, using the term information in the broad sense of facts, sense data, and relationships. It does not necessarily follow that a person's ability to process information is constant over different sorts of information—visuospatial, numerical, verbal—or over different sorts of mental operation—memorization, transposition, implication, and so on—Gardner (1985), Salthouse (1985a, 1987).

The meaning of the word 'intelligence' is socially constructed. Defining it operationally in terms of performance on a psychometric test is simply one way of clarifying and coordinating our thinking about human cognition. We have no way of defining intelligence in absolute terms or by reference to any basic physiological functions, although it has been suggested that the speed of cortical processes, as measured by means of evoked potentials or inspection time, may provide one such index (Haier et al., 1983). The discovery of measurable physiological functions closely related to fluid abilities would do much to clarify the effects of ageing on intelligence. For related studies, see Hertzog et al. (1978), Kinsbourne (1974), Powell and Porndorf (1971), D. L. Robinson et al. (1984a, b, 1986), Vernon (1983a).

In the meantime we have to rely on fallible indirect indicators of adult intelligence. To the extent that the test materials themselves call for knowledge of facts and relationships which are historically conditioned, i.e. dependent upon the cultural circumstances operating at the time the materials were produced, there may well be cohort effects, and effects related to socioeconomic class, education, and race, all of which may obscure the effects of chronological age. For example, intelligence tests incorporate certain sorts of words and phrases, pictures and diagrams, and objects or materials to be manipulated. If the format of the test is not familiar or easy to adapt to because of a subject's age, education, or upbringing, then that subject will be at a disadvantage relative to other subjects. Consider too the use of a computer VDU to display the test items and a computer keyboard as the response panel. Obviously, younger subjects, relatively familiar with such stimulus–response arrangements, will have an initial advantage over older subjects.

Another issue is that later-born cohorts tend to enjoy higher standards of living—better health, better education. To the extent that test performance depends on health and education, these cohort effects may obscure the effects of ageing. Cohort effects related to stature and age at menarche are fairly well established; so it would be unwise to suppose that other biological and psychological characteristics—such as brain functions, temperament, intelligence—do not exhibit cohort effects. The measurement of adult intelligence is hindered by the many so-called 'methodological' problems referred to in Chapters 3 and 8.

Applications

The main area of application is that of clinical gerontology. Tests incorporating the assessment of intellectual abilities are used to assess the extent to which mental deterioration has taken place, to assess an elderly patient's current mental competence, and to monitor the effects of a treatment programme. Here, two kinds of information are useful: (1) how the patient compares with comparable normal subjects (this calls for normative data); and (2) how the patient performs now as compared with formerly (this calls for life-history data, repeated measures, or a measure of pre-morbid intelligence of the sort used in calculating deterioration quotients).

Psychometric research into intellectual deterioration dates back at least as far as Babcock (1930). Attempts were made to compare scores on functions which decline with age with scores on functions which do not decline, and to derive indices of deterioration. The Deterioration Quotient (DQ) based on WAIS subtest scores is a modern version of this idea. This kind of research is related to that which looked for similarities between normal ageing and psychopathology (brain damage, mental disease, senility) with regard to cognitive functions. It is not difficult to demonstrate that elderly 'normal' volunteer subjects show more 'abnormalities' in cognition than do young adults and middle-aged subjects. For example, they show more concreteness, confusion, egocentricity, failure to learn, poverty of ideas, repetition, and so on.

In recent years, following public and professional reactions against intelligence testing on the grounds of its supposed unfair discrimination against underprivileged minority groups, there have been attempts to widen the scope of the study of intelligence. Rather than thinking of intelligence as 'all-round, inborn, intellectual ability' and defining it operationally in terms of 'the general or common factor' in intelligence tests, the recent fashion has been to consider the *diversity* of intellectual functions, their development during childhood and adulthood, and the contexts within which intellectual activities take place. This modern approach lends itself to detailed descriptive accounts of specific sorts of intellectual activities, but it has not so far contributed much to the study of adult intelligence. The approach is considered in more detail in another section.

One of the negative aspects of the mental testing movement in relation to the assessment of adult intelligence has been the emphasis it has given to the intellectual *disabilities* of the elderly. More recent approaches, by contrast, have emphasized the maintenance or improvement of adult mental abilities following training, practice, and attention to health and welfare.

The other main area of application is in occupational testing for guidance and selection purposes. Intelligence tests and specialized 'aptitude' tests are widely used, but with little or no reference to the theory of adult intelligence.

ADULT INTELLIGENCE AND INTELLECTUAL DETERIORATION

The Wechsler tests

The Wechsler Adult Intelligence Scale (WAIS) is in the mainstream of the intelligence testing movement which commenced at about the turn of the century—see Frank (1983). In particular it has strong links with the US Army Alpha and Beta tests developed for selection purposes in the First World War, which in turn are linked with the Binet tests. Wechsler—see Matarazzo (1986)—hoped to assess a wide range of mental functions using tried and tested materials acceptable to adults. The raw scores were converted into scaled weighted points in relation to standards (norms) based on quasi-representative samples of adults at different chronological ages. The 11 subtests of the WAIS are as shown in Table 5.1.

It is not unusual for a subject to obtain somewhat different scores on these subtests. The resulting spread and profile of scores was thought to have implications for assessment. Patients with certain kinds of psychological disorder or brain injury might show characteristic score 'profiles' and 'scatters' different from those shown by comparison groups.

As with most measures of higher mental functions and complex psychological processes, it is not too difficult to find fault with the

Table 5.1 Subtests of the WAIS

Verbal	Performance
Vocabulary (word meaning)	Picture Completion (visual search, concept analysis)
Information (general knowledge)	Picture Arrangement (pictorial story logic)
Digit Span (memory span)	Block Design (spatial reasoning)
Comprehension (common sense)	Object Assembly (spatial reasoning)
Similarities (categorisation)	Digit Symbol Substitution (psychomotor speed)
Arithmetic (mental calculation)	

WAIS—in terms of item selection, standardization, validity, reliability, and so on. Frank (1983) shows that the correlations between different forms of the test, including the subtests, are by no means high or uniform, implying that these apparently parallel forms of the test and subtests are not necessarily measuring quite the same intellectual functions. It follows that attempts to use short (abbreviated) forms of the WAIS are not likely to produce reliable results, although the vocabulary subtest is probably the best single WAIS measure of general intelligence. Naturally, any *combination* of subtests is likely to correlate better with full-scale WAIS IQ than any single subtest. A neglected aspect of this issue is that where there are grounds for supposing that the subjects under investigation are themselves relatively unreliable (variable, inconsistent)— such as the elderly—then short forms of assessment are unlikely to be of much use. Such subjects may need to be tested repeatedly at different times and in different circumstances. The *aggregated* data should provide a more reliable indication of the level and spread of a subject's intellectual capabilities. The same principle applies in other areas of psychological assessment. Unfortunately the usual type of intelligence test is not suitable for repeated testing; it is primarily a single-occasion measure.

We have seen that scores on some intellectual functions 'hold up' with age whilst others 'don't hold'. Wechsler relied on this fact (the distinction between fluid and crystallized mental abilities) to calculate a deterioration quotient (DQ):

$$DQ = \frac{\text{Hold score} - \text{Don't hold score}}{\text{Hold score}} \times 100$$

The choice of 'hold' and 'don't hold' subtests can be varied, and more complex formulae for calculating a DQ have been developed.

Attempts to formulate a valid and useful index of intellectual deterioration by comparing test scores which 'hold up' with age with those that 'don't hold' have not been very successful as far as prediction and clinical diagnosis are concerned—but see Chapman and Chapman (1978), Eppinger *et al.* (1987), Klesges and Troster (1987), Ruddle and Bradshaw (1982).

Assessment procedures which employ difference-scores such as the WAIS DQ, or VIQ-PIQ, or change-scores in repeated measures using the same or parallel tests, are likely to be particularly unreliable, because of the psychometric and statistical limitations of difference-scores—see also Chapter 3.

One problem with the rationale of the WAIS DQ is that the assignment of subtests to the 'hold' and 'don't hold' categories, whilst maintaining a balance between verbal and performance subtests, brings about a situation in which some of the performance 'hold' subtests are subtests which decline more with age than some of the verbal 'don't hold' subtests.

The original assumption was that different kinds of brain injury and disease would produce at least some general intellectual impairment (as well as possibly some specific intellectual impairment because of focal damage) which might be detected by a DQ. The diagnostic uses to which the WAIS was put—using differential subtest performance as the key— were derived more from empirical generalizations than from theoretical expectations. Given our continuing ignorance of the relationships between brain states and behaviour this is perhaps not surprising.

In passing, we should remind ourselves that performance on an intelligence test is affected by what are called non-intellectual factors— motivation, personality, feelings. To the extent that such factors intrude in later life, as a consequence of normal ageing or of disease and disability, it follows that intelligence tests will be less valid as measures of intelligence alone.

The main features of the Wechsler tests (WB1, WB2, WAIS, and WAIS-R) are that they use verbal and performance (non-verbal) subtests, speeded and unspeeded subtests, and items arranged on a point scale within each of 11 subtests. The standardization and normative data are based mainly on fairly representative cross-sectional samples; the reliability and validity of the tests as measures of general intelligence are regarded as satisfactory.

Wechsler's results confirmed the differential decline in mental abilities during adult life referred to as crystallized or fluid abilities—see Horn and Cattell (1967). The distinction, however, is one of degree rather than one of kind. We know little about the brain processes that underlie these abilities or about the differential effects that ageing has on the human brain.

Variations in scoring procedure, such as changing the rules governing time limits and errors, would undoubtedly produce different effects. Hence the need for a *theory* of adult intelligence that would rationalize the procedures and help clarify the meaning of observed effects. At present it seems that neither the WAIS DQ nor other WAIS diagnostic formulae provide satisfactory means of discriminating validly and reliably between comparison groups of interest.

The problem with using the discrepancy between verbal and performance subtests scores as a measure of group differences is that, first, as we have seen, difference-scores are difficult to handle statistically. Also, the way in which the WAIS subtests were selected and standardized may have brought about built-in advantages or disadvantages to certain groups. A further problem, characteristic of attempts to generalize widely about individual differences in psychological characteristics, is that the various comparison groups used in research—young versus old, brain-damaged versus normal, schizophrenic versus non-schizophrenic—vary widely within themselves over time. Large quantities of data on relatively homogeneous groups need to be aggregated in order to establish clear-cut and replicable results. Without reliable comparative standards, diagnostic testing cannot succeed.

The Wechsler Adult Intelligence Scale has been revised. The revision is known as the WAIS-R and is based on American norms; an Anglicized version was published—Wechsler (1986), Psychological Corporation (1986). The subtests are basically the same as before, and there has been little or no attempt to develop the theory of adult intelligence, such as it is, on which it is based, or to modify the way test findings are interpreted. Recent reviews of the WAIS have been somewhat critical, arguing that short forms of the test are unreliable, and that it has little diagnostic usefulness in relation to brain damage or mental disease.

Effective differential diagnosis depends upon a number of consider-ations, including: adequate amounts of data on individual subjects; adequate standardization (norms, reliability, validity); adequate sensi-tivity (discrimination); and adequate preliminary screening of subjects (providing relatively homogeneous groups). Consider, for example, the task of trying to identify the characteristic diagnostic WAIS profiles of patients with 'diffuse' or 'focal' brain damage, and 'left' or 'right' hemisphere damage, even without the further complications associated with normal ageing, education, intellectual level, and personality factors. Frank (1983) reports that, in spite of such further complications, much of the research shows that left-hemisphere disorder brings about relatively greater impairment on WAIS verbal subtests, whilst right-hemisphere disorder brings about relatively greater impairment on WAIS performance subtests. This is in line with current views on the lateralization of brain function. The results for more localized lesions have not produced consistent patterns. We must remember that it is important for research results to be replicated and cross-validated if they are to be used as a basis for clinical diagnosis and treatment.

As far as normal ageing is concerned, the most consistent findings are that Vocabulary, Information and Comprehension 'hold up' with age, whereas Digit Symbol Substitution, Block Design, and Picture Arrange-ment 'don't hold'. The 'don't hold' subtests are timed, and it is well known that the speed of mental functions slows down with age. The difficulty is that normal ageing is often accompanied by a variety of other conditions which could affect performance on the WAIS—sensory and motor impairment, disuse of functions, physical and mental illness, and so on. Such factors can be expected to obscure the effects of normal ageing even supposing our current concepts and methods of measuring adult intelligence are correct.

Normal ageing is usually defined negatively, in terms of the absence of recognized pathologies and disabilities. Strictly speaking, however, 'normal' and 'pathological' ageing should be defined independently of each other, otherwise one risks a circular argument. Normal ageing is sometimes identified with the sort of ageing exhibited by the 'best specimens' of the elderly—the so-called 'ageing elite'. Their levels of health, performance, and well-being provide a convenient ideal standard against which progress in applied gerontology for the population at large can be assessed.

The usual practice of eliminating test items which favour one sex or the other means that we effectively prevent ourselves from studying possible sex differences in adult intelligence. For all we know, there may be quite considerable differences between the sexes in the *sorts* of intelligence they possess (as well as in the range and distribution of their intelligence). Ageing may affect male and female intelligence differently. For all we know, there may be built-in disadvantages for women because of the way tests were originally constructed (mainly by males for males).

It is interesting and somewhat puzzling that intelligence tests constructed on more theoretical principles, e.g. Thurstone's Primary Mental Abilities (PMA) test and Raven's Progressive Matrices (RPM) test, seem to have had even less success than the WAIS in relation to differential psychiatric and neuropsychological diagnosis and the study of adult intelligence. It remains to be seen whether tests more directly related to neuropsychological research, such as the Halstead–Reitan Battery or the Luria–Nebraska Battery, will prove more fruitful. Developments in cognitive psychology and artificial intelligence may give rise to new ways of assessing adult intelligence.

When the intercorrelations between WAIS subtests are factor-analysed, two main factors and one subsidiary factor are commonly found. The main factors are verbal or crystallized ability (defined by the verbal subtests) and spatial/speed or fluid ability (defined by the performance subtests). The subsidiary factor could be number/memory ability (defined by Digit Span and Arithmetic).

Attempts to examine the effects of ageing on the factorial structure of human abilities have been frustrated by a variety of conceptual and methodological difficulties. To begin with, there are the familiar problems associated with cross-sectional and longitudinal research designs in gerontology. Second, it is assumed that the items *within* a subtest are all measuring the same factor to about the same extent; if not, then subjects with different scores may be exercising rather different cognitive functions from those indexed by the factors. To make matters worse, the subtests may measure different combinations of psychological characteristics in different sorts of subjects. The items in some of the WAIS subtests are graded in difficulty, so that different items may tap different sorts and levels of ability. Third, factor-analytic studies reflect average effects in samples of subjects; such average effects are compatible with various combinations of individual effects; this is particularly so with heterogeneous samples of subjects. In factor-analytic studies of the WAIS across several age levels, the subtest composition of the factors is not consistent. In other words, it is not clear what the factors mean or how they change with age. Fourth, there is the problem of g, the general factor of intelligence. Performances on the WAIS subtests are all positively intercorrelated, although this is not very interesting nowadays from a theoretical point of view. Even so, they are not all equally indicative of general intelligence as indexed by the full-scale IQ or other measures of general intelligence, such as the Progressive Matrices test.

Close analysis of the WAIS subtests suggests that some of them might be testing more than one sort of ability, e.g. recall from long-term memory, logical reasoning, attention, verbal comprehension. This would apply to any test which comprises a wide range of items (usually thought necessary in tests of general intelligence). The process of test construction should classify and refine items by examining their intercorrelations and factorial composition. Naturally, face validity need not correspond with more objective measures of validity. For example, it is possible to regard the WAIS Picture Completion subtest as an exercise in conceptual analysis: you need to compare the pictures carefully with your images/concepts of the objects represented by the pictures; but how would one test this idea? Imagery and conceptual analysis are clearly within the cognitive domain, but difficult to investigate scientifically.

On the basis of the research evidence referenced by Frank (1983) it seems that the WAIS can provide limited information in clinical or applied settings. As an overall measure of general intelligence it is satisfactory, but differential assessment on the basis of subtest scores seems to be risky. It would be unwise to rely on the WAIS exclusively for assessing deterioration in late life, but it should be useful for counselling normal adults in relation to further education, and for vocational guidance and occupational selection.

Other approaches to adult intelligence and intellectual deterioration

Intellectual deterioration is the term used to refer to the irreversible decrease in intelligence consequent upon brain damage, mental disease, or ageing. Given the general and the specific psychological functions subserved by the cortex, one might expect that a particular pattern of brain damage would correlate with a particular pattern of psychological impairment. However, there are differences between individuals in brain anatomy and physiology, and differences between individuals in brain–behaviour relationships because of the way individual development has organized brain–behaviour relationships. Consequently, the adverse effects of mental disease and ageing could be obscured by these differences.

At least three other approaches to the estimation of pre-morbid intelligence have been attempted. One is to use a reading test containing familiar words with unusual spellings—ache, sign—on the assumption that correct pronunciation reveals a reading level commensurate with the patient's original ability—see Chapter 3. This avoids the problem of losses in higher levels of vocabulary through disuse or semantic failure, but depends on reading skill—see Cummings et al. (1986). The second approach is to use multiple regression equations based on the relationships between intelligence and demographic characteristics. For example, the WAIS-R standardization sample numbered nearly 2000, so that regression equations based on age, sex, race, education, occupation, and region could be used to estimate a 'normal' or 'pre-morbid' performance. Thirdly, other tests, such as the Halstead–Reitan and the Luria–Nebraska tests, have been used in attempts to estimate pre-morbid intelligence. The difference between present and pre-morbid intelligence should, in theory, help in differential diagnosis and give some indication of the locus and extent of the brain damage. Klesges and Troster (1987) report that, so far, progress has been limited, and they propose that future studies should concentrate more on investigating specific conditions in homogeneous groups.

The term 'intellectual deterioration' differs from the term 'thought disorder' in the sense that thought disorder refers not so much to loss of intellectual capacity as to a disorganization of mental processing—particularly the intrusion of emotionally disturbing or maladaptive thought processes. In late life, intellectual deterioration seems to render some individuals more prone to thought disorder, as in late paraphrenia, mental confusion, and concrete levels of thinking.

There is considerable evidence to support the view that, as age increases during adult life, and especially after early middle age, say 35–40 years, there are adverse changes in mental abilities. These adverse changes seem to be of two broad kinds. First, there are gradual but cumulative effects associated with normal physiological degeneration, and especially degeneration of the central nervous system. We think of the CNS as the physical basis for the organization of complex forms of behaviour.

Although their effects may not be immediately obvious in ordinary behaviour, these degenerative processes seem to lead to restrictions in the number of component mental processes that can be coordinated, to limitations on the serial organization of behaviour, to reductions in the speed of mental processes, and to a lowering of the level of abstraction and generality at which we are inclined to think about the task in hand. Second, there are intermittent but substantial effects associated with abnormal physiological damage, resulting perhaps from illness, injury, stress, or other causes. Such sudden and marked adverse changes in the CNS tend to have effects which are clearly observable clinically or in ordinary behaviour in everyday life—for example, marked slowing, confusion, disorientation, lack of concentration, disturbances of thought and language. For many years of adult life, however, the normal, gradual, cumulative effects are detectable only by means of careful quantitative measures carried out under controlled conditions, in laboratory or clinical settings.

One physical factor which may underlie both intelligence and psycho-motor speed is the supply of oxygen to the brain. It has been claimed that supplementary oxygen improves the mental performance of hemiplegic patients, and that inadequate oxygenation may account for part of the normal decline with age in mental functions. Physical and mental exercise can be expected to improve cerebral blood flow. Patients with cardiovascular disease affecting cerebral blood flow are found more often in older age groups. Such disease is thought to be associated with neuropsychological impairment, slower psychomotor performance, decreased CFF (critical flicker/fusion frequency), supposedly a measure of the discriminative capacity of the perceptual system, and lower maximum speed of tapping, supposedly a measure of the control capacity of the motor system. Cardiovascular disease and hypertension appear to have adverse effects also on more general aspects of intelligence— Hertzog *et al.* (1978).

This sort of evidence shows that care must be taken not to attribute deterioration in perception, intelligence, and psychomotor performance to 'ageing' when it might be more meaningfully attributed to specific disorders, physiological processes, life-events, demographic variables, genetic endowment, and so on. The cumulative nature of the processes we refer to as 'ageing' means that older age groups contain a much higher proportion of individuals with specific characteristics having adverse effects on behaviour. Hence, both cross-sectional and longitudinal comparisons over time can be expected to reveal an average, overall, deterioration even if there are no 'normal' effects of ageing, separable, that is, from identifiable pathological effects.

Cerebral blood flow is governed by variations in brain metabolism, and variations in cerebral oxygen are reflected in EEG frequency. Regional blood flow varies with behaviour. What is implied in a 'disuse' theory of ageing is that brain centres which are less active than they should be to maintain optimum efficiency, perhaps falling below some threshold value, will gradually atrophy—like little-used muscles. In circumstances where the total blood flow to the brain is barely adequate for normal activities, selective demand from 'active' regions of the brain may hasten atrophy in 'inactive' regions. On the other hand, quite independent factors may affect blood vessels in different regions of the brain, and lead to differential deterioration in behavioural characteristics, e.g. the differential decline of fluid and crystallized intellectual abilities.

Terminal decline

It can be demonstrated that older subjects whose cognitive performance declines tend to die earlier than subjects whose cognitive capacity declines less or not at all over the period in question—see Jarvik and Blum (1971), Siegler (1975), Steuer et al. (1981). Furthermore, cognitive capacity tends to be positively related to longevity. It is by no means clear, however, that the so-called 'critical loss' or 'terminal drop' in ability that heralds death is the same throughout adult life. Indeed, it would be surprising if this were so, considering the many and varied factors affecting longevity. Cognitive functions no doubt indicate something about the physiological efficiency of the human brain, but performance on cognitive tests can be influenced by a variety of factors—temporary states of mind, personality characteristics, and health. Life may continue for some considerable time in individuals whose cognitive capacities are seriously impaired. A decline in cognitive capacity in adult life or old age, therefore, has to be considered in the context of the individual's overall health and circumstances; only rarely if ever will a 'critical loss' in cognitive capacity be the only warning sign of impending death. Such loss is more likely to occur in the context of serious physical and/or mental disorder or, late in life, in the context of dementia associated with cortical atrophy or cerebral vascular disease.

Neuropsychological assessment

Research in neuropsychological assessment has given rise to a variety of clinical diagnostic procedures involving performances such as block-sorting, picture recognition, learning and remembering, spatial reasoning, and language. Initially, the norms and standards against which a patient's performance was judged were implicit in the clinical judgment. That is to say, an 'abnormal' or 'pathological' performance was thought to be clearly distinguishable from a normal performance. Eventually, however, some neuropsychological assessment procedures were enlarged, refined, and made more systematic, so that nowadays they are constructed, administered, and interpreted within the framework of psychometric theory and practice. So, for example, we have the Halstead–Reitan Battery—Incagnoli *et al.* (1985), Prigitano and Parsons (1976), and the Luria–Nebraska Neuropsychological Battery—Golden *et al.* (1980), Moses (1985), Spiers (1981, 1982), Vannieuwkirk and Galbraith (1985).

The Halstead–Reitan Neuropsychological Test Battery (HRNB) comprises measures of sensory and motor functions, verbal abilities, cognitive and memory functions. The Luria–Nebraska Neuropsychological Battery (LNNB) comprises a large number of items testing functions such as motor skill, rhythm, tactile recognition, receptive and expressive speech, reading and writing, arithmetic, cognition and memory. The test results are said to be indicative of brain impairment, left or right hemisphere impairment, relative to estimates of premorbid level of performance.

Another line of inquiry is based on experimental psychology, especially the experimental psychology of cognitive processes—problem-solving, mental skills, learning and remembering—see, for example, Charness (1985, 1985a), Craik and Trehub (1983), Kausler (1982), Salthouse (1982), Salthouse and Prill (1987), Welford (1985). Experimental investigations help to uncover the nature and extent of causal relationships in cognitive impairment, whether in the context of normal ageing, brain damage or disease, or functional psychiatric disorder.

The relationship between measures of adult intelligence and measures of neuropsychological functioning is illustrated in Moses (1985). When the Luria–Nebraska Neuropsychological Battery (LNNB) and the Wechsler Adult Intelligence Scale (WAIS) have been administered to a heterogeneous sample of subjects (normal and impaired), it can be shown that the two measures are correlated overall. A small number of WAIS subtests will account for a substantial proportion of the variance on each of the LNNB scales. However, the WAIS subtest scores appear to reflect overall performance level (presumably general intelligence combining verbal, spatial, and memory abilities). The WAIS subtests appear to account for only a small amount of the variance beyond that attributable to overall performance level.

It will be recalled that the WAIS subtests were derived from mainstream intelligence tests, i.e. those used earlier in educational and US Army selection settings. Any 'clinical' diagnostic value they may have had was, in a sense, coincidental. Similarly, the earlier neuropsychological tests were based on what was believed about brain–behaviour relationships, e.g. localization and lateralization. Any value they may have had as measures of general intelligence or special abilities was coincidental. As far as experimental studies of cognitive impairment are concerned, there has been surprisingly little effort, until recently, to link this work with either of the other two lines of inquiry—intelligence testing and neuropsychological assessment.

An example of how the experimental and neuropsychological approaches to cognitive impairment can be combined is described in Roth and Crosson (1985). They compared impaired and unimpaired subjects on several measures of memory. They observed, as one might expect, that subjects with brain damage (of various sorts) did less well on all memory tests than did the subjects without brain damage. However, the most sensitive measure of memory impairment proved to be delayed recall on the Wechsler Memory Scale (WMS). The addition of tests of immediate memory appeared to add little or nothing to the discriminating power of delayed recall on the WMS.

There is some indication that short-term memory for items which are more restricted in range, e.g. digits, is greater than for items which are less restricted, e.g. letters, words. However, differences in difficulty level between two measures do not make the more difficult of the two more discriminating in relation to diagnostic differences between particular groups. Such discrimination depends on the extent to which the tests measure particular cognitive levels or functions which are diagnostically relevant (over and above any general levels or functions). Diagnostic sensitivity also depends on various psychometric properties—the level and spread of scores, reliability, validity, floor and ceiling effects, item content, and so on. Roth and Crosson (1985) report that memory span tests made up of either verbal items or visuospatial items seem not to discriminate between neurologically impaired and unimpaired subjects. It is possible, however, that some other, more selective, comparison, say between left- and right-hemisphere damage, would demonstrate such differential memory impairment.

Memory impairment is not unique to the elderly or to those suffering from one or other of the psychological disorders of late life such as SDAT or MID. Memory impairment is found across a wide range of conditions affecting brain function, as well as in conditions where individuals are functionally disturbed. Stress and anxiety have adverse effects on attention and short-term memory in normal subjects. Consequently, the assessment of both short-term and long-term memory seems advisable for clinical and rehabilitative purposes.

Vannieuwkirk and Galbraith (1985) obtained results on the LNNB from normal subjects in three adult age groups. Their report indicates the continuing difficulty in establishing satisfactory comparison groups in cross-sectional studies of ageing because of selection effects, including attrition and volunteer effects, which tend to bias samples of older subjects towards higher ability and personal adjustment, even though their scores on cognitive tests are lower than those of younger samples. Many of the LNNB subtests show a decline with normal ageing, even when the effects of IQ and education are partialled out. In addition there is a differential decline with age on the LNNB as there is for the WAIS. In particular, performances on the motor, memory, and right-hemisphere subtests 'don't hold' relative to receptive speech, rhythm, and writing. Unfortunately, the relationships between test performance on the LNNB and neurological conditions are unclear; so the results of studies of the effects of normal ageing cannot, as yet, be related to information about age changes in the brain.

METHODOLOGICAL ISSUES AND COHORT EFFECTS

The main methodological difficulties of research into the effects of ageing on intelligence are covered in Chapters 3 and 8. The issues are reviewed by Horn and Donaldson (1980).

It is well known that a negative relationship between chronological age and score on an intelligence test could be the result of either a decline with age or a secular increase (successive cohorts achieving higher scores). The problem is more complicated than this, however, since there may be several age effects and several cohort effects interacting with each other, apart from effects of other kinds, e.g. period effects, measurement effects.

Parker (1986) examined the results of a number of normative and comparative studies of the Wechsler intelligence tests in order to see whether there had been any cohort effects on adult intelligence or any changes in the relationship between age and intelligence. Parker argues that there is a strong time-of-measurement effect, and that this is the result of an interaction between age and year of birth (cohort). In effect, the maximum level of intellectual development has been increasing and reaching the peak age later. He draws attention to changes in the age at which intelligence is at its maximum. Over a period of 62 years, from 1916 to 1978, the age of maximum performance has risen fairly steadily from 16 to 30 years. This could be the result of changes in the characteristics of the population and/or changes in the form and content of intelligence tests. The items and subtests that comprise a test of 'general' intelligence are deliberately diverse, and are intended to sample a wide array of cognitive functions. Clearly, one cannot argue sensibly about the effects of age or cohort on intelligence without distinguishing between the different functions that define intelligence, or at least between the two main sorts of abilities: fluid and crystallized. Parker's analysis confirms the shift in the peak years of maximum performance, but he points out that this shift accounts for only a small percentage of the variance in scores.

One possibility is that the average genetic potential for intellectual development has not been fully realized because of sub-optimal environmental conditions. Physical stature has shown a secular increase, and age at menarche a secular decrease. So there would be nothing extraordinary in finding a similar effect for intelligence—either fluid or crystallized or both.

Another possibility is that earlier intelligence tests have, for some reason, become easier for later generations, but not because of their increased intelligence. Education and test sophistication might bring about this effect; so too might biases in the way subjects are selected for inclusion in the samples used in standardization.

Parker estimates that over 41 years the average performance at a given adult age level has risen by about 10 points of IQ, as compared with a decline with age within cohorts of about 7.5 points. It is not suggested that the nature of intelligence, or the way it is measured, has changed. Moreover, the effects of age and cohort account for only a small percentage of the variance in IQ scores. These results raise questions about how intelligence is conceptualized and measured, and how tests are to be standardized and scored to take account of cohort and age effects.

Flynn (1987a) reports substantial secular gains in measures of intelligence in 14 nations during varying periods between 1936 and 1982. The gains ranged from 5 to 25 points of IQ in a single generation (30 years). The significance of Flynn's survey lies in the fact that the gains were not, as one might expect, gains in crystallized intelligence but gains in fluid intelligence. A measure of fluid intelligence means that test performance does not depend upon education or experience except for the minimum needed to cope with basic materials and instructions.

Flynn's further conclusions are also striking. He considers the existence of as yet unknown environmental factors that would account for much of the gain. He also considers that traditional measures of intelligence do not measure intelligence directly, but something weakly related to intelligence.

Flynn surveyed data on intelligence test scores made available from a number of countries. He attempted to use data-sets that met stringent criteria: the young adult samples were to be large and relatively unbiased; the tests used were to be the same from one year to another; the secular trends expressed in IQ points were to be estimated from differences in raw score from one year to the next. In his analyses, Flynn separates out various data-sets according to the extent to which these criteria are met.

Data from The Netherlands show that, over three decades from 1952 to 1982, there was a substantial increase from 31 to 82 in the percentage of men scoring over 24 out of 40 on a version of Raven's Progressive Matrices Test. This is equivalent to a gain of about 21 points of IQ, provided one makes certain statistical assumptions, and provided there has been no change in the way the samples were made available for testing—in this case 18-year-old male conscripts for military service, about 80% of the age group.

Data from Belgium show a gain of five or six points on Raven's Progressive Matrices test equal to about seven points of IQ over the 10-year period 1958–67. In this study, however, the later sample was more highly selected—77% of the age group as compared with 83%. Gains were also shown for tests of Arithmetic, Vocabulary and Shapes (spatial reasoning).

Data from France show a secular gain of 25 points of IQ over a period of 25 years from 1949. There were lesser gains in mathematics and verbal reasoning. The data from Norway are rather more complicated but indicate a secular gain of nearly nine points of IQ between 1954 and 1968, and nearly three points between 1968 and 1980. There were gains too for mathematical and verbal reasoning. Data from New Zealand show an average gain of nearly eight points of IQ based on the performance of large samples of children aged 10–13 years on the Otis Test, from 1936 to 1968. Data were obtained for Canada and the USA, but for various reasons the results are not as persuasive as those listed above. Nevertheless, they do indicate significant gains in IQ. Flynn (1987a) surveys data on secular trends in intelligence test scores for several other countries but again, for various reasons, regards the findings as less robust than for the countries cited above, even though IQ gains are found in every instance.

The trend for later generations of subjects to score more highly on Wechsler's tests of adult intelligence, and for the age at which peak performance is reached to move from the early 20s to the late 20s (Parker, 1986) is surprising, especially in relation to the performance subtests of the WAIS. One would have imagined that later generations of children would reach biological maturity earlier rather than later, and that the basic information needed to deal with most of the performance subtests would be acquired before reaching adulthood. In fact, the secular gains on performance subtests are greater than the gains on verbal subtests, not just in the USA but in several other countries.

Flynn's results are particularly important in relation to cross-sectional and longitudinal studies of the effects of ageing on intelligence. Such studies almost invariably reveal a differential decline, as between crystallized performances which hold up with age, and fluid performances which do not hold up. This differential decline has been a strong argument against the claim that the decline with age in adult intelligence is a myth and merely a reflection of a secular increase (cohort effect) in intelligence. The argument is that secular improvements would obviously affect intellectual attainments (crystallized abilities), and cross-sectional results would show either no differential decline or a differential decline greater for crystallized abilities, i.e. in the opposite direction from that observed. Flynn's argument, however, is that his results *confirm* the well-known differential decline because they show that secular gains in fluid ability have been greater than secular gains in crystallized ability.

Another way of interpreting Flynn's results is to say that either later generations are on average more intelligent than their forebears or else intelligence tests are not measuring intelligence. Another possibility, not easily tested, is that changes are taking place in the samples tested, in the tests, and/or in the way the tests are administered and scored. Flynn has attempted to eliminate this possibility. Another possibility, not considered by Flynn, is that a dramatic evolutionary selection process is at work in western industrial societies, assisted perhaps by selective immigration from the underdeveloped world. Paradoxically, it was only a generation or so ago that psychologists and educationalists were concerned about the apparent *decline* in national intelligence logically implied by social class differences in intelligence and fertility! (Maxwell, 1969). See Flynn (1987b) and Lynn (1987), for secular trends in Japanese intelligence.

We have considered the problem of validating psychometric tests of adult intelligence, and have found that it is not easy to demonstrate direct links with practical intelligence—intelligence applied to real-world problems. Flynn, however, appears to neglect family resemblances in intelligence, social class, and occupational differences; the use of intelligence tests in selection and training; and other indications, such as the speed and accuracy of mental processing, which seem to support the view that tests are valid measures of intelligence. The fact that correlations are sometimes low (rarely, if ever, zero or negative) may be attributable to range restriction or to other methodological constraints. To regard tests of fluid intelligence as measures of abstract problem-solving ability detached from the real world is difficult to accept. Flynn is not able to identify the environmental condition(s) responsible for massive secular gains in IQ. The more obvious contenders—test sophistication, education—seem to be insufficient.

It is possible that secular improvements in perinatal care, health, and nutrition lead to improvements in brain function. This could produce the differential cohort effects reported by Flynn, especially if educational practices have failed to register and adapt to such improvements. On the other hand, decreased emphasis on scholastic attainments and increased emphasis on self-expression (including discovery learning) and abstract problem-solving (test-taking) might also produce a differential cohort effect between fluid and crystallized abilities—see Raven (1977) for discussion of the relationship between education and intelligence.

MENTAL SPEED

The speed at which psychological functions can be carried out has obvious consequences for survival, effectiveness, and well-being. Speed of psychological functioning depends in part on the efficiency of the underlying physiological processes. It is well known that all physiological systems decline with age, some more rapidly than others. But their efficiency depends, in turn, on fundamental biological processes which are also affected by ageing—they are slower and more prone to error. Consider, for example, the conduction of nerve impulses, synaptic connections, and metabolism generally.

Botwinick (1984) provides a conveniently simple summary of the main kinds of slowing which can be expressed in mathematical form. As a task increases in difficulty, then, by definition, subjects take longer to deal with it. The question is how does the increased time that older people take compare with the increased time that younger people take to deal with an increase in task difficulty? The answer obviously depends upon the particular characteristics of the subjects, the nature of the tasks, and on contextual factors. The simplest kind of relationship would be for older subjects to slow down on more difficult tasks to the same extent as younger subjects, even if they are already slower on the baseline task. The next kind of relationship would be for older subjects to slow down by some proportional degree relative to younger subjects, say by two or three times the increase in time for younger subjects. The third kind of relationship would be for older subjects to slow down disproportionately, as it were, so that the increase in time required for a more difficult task is raised by some power, say the square or cube, of the increase required by younger subjects.

Botwinick (1984) expresses the response time of older subjects in terms of the response time of younger subjects. Thus, for an additive increase, $RT_{(old)}$ is equal to $RT_{(young)}$ plus a constant value. For a multiplicative (proportional) increase, $RT_{(old)}$ is equal to $RT_{(young)}$ multiplied by a constant value. For an exponential (disproportional) increase, $RT_{(old)}$ is equal to $RT_{(young)}$ exponentiated by a constant value. The response time for older subjects on difficult tasks may be considerably greater than that of younger subjects. Sometimes the difficulty level exceeds the capacity of the older subjects completely leading them to give up or to make an incorrect response.

Response times plotted against age level and task difficulty can be shown as a three-dimensional surface. Lashley (1929) demonstrated similar effects for different extents of brain lesion on maze running in rodents. Maze learning in humans follows a not dissimilar pattern.

Chronological age is accompanied by wide differences between individuals in response time, and its average effects can be obscured by other factors such as education, health, socioeconomic status, and so on. Longitudinal studies, adjusted where necessary for attrition, are needed in order to establish the most likely patterns of relationships between age, task difficulty, and response time. Even so, it seems likely that the observed trends and relationships would be specific to the particular sorts of subjects, age groups, and tasks used in the studies. The problem for the research gerontologist is to work out what a theory predicts given particular experimental arrangements. It would be surprising to find generalized trends and relationships of the sort described above.

Reaction time

Although speed of performance in relation to ageing has been extensively studied, Rabbitt (1980) points out that we do not have a good theory as to why these changes take place; furthermore, the data so far available do not enable us to answer some very obvious questions.

There is no doubt that speed of performance declines throughout adult life and old age. This can be demonstrated in a variety of ways: for example, by tests of simple or choice reaction time, by performance tasks involving speed and accuracy, by tests of attention and memory involving time constraints. Rabbitt considers one basic kind of task—choice reaction time—in which a subject has typically to select one of a number of responses in relation to one of a number of stimuli (variations include selecting a combination of responses in relation to a combination of stimuli). Each response is either right or wrong and requires a measurable amount of time (usually recorded in milliseconds). Normally, a subject's response is not a simple reflex but a decision process, involving complex sensori-motor and central nervous processes.

A typical choice reaction experiment in ageing involves subjects of different ages being given a number of familiarization trials on the task, say pressing one of two, or one of four, or one of eight keys in response to one of two, or one of four, or one of eight lights. This is followed by

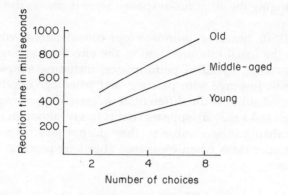

Figure 5.1 Hypothetical age differences in choice reaction time

a long series of trials, perhaps under varying conditions or instructions, such as stimulus-onset warning signals, or instructions to be fast or accurate.

The results of such a typical investigation usually show that as age increases, the choice reaction times of older subjects become longer, and disproportionately longer for difficult as compared with easy tasks. The results can be expressed in terms of Hick's Law, which states that choice reaction time is a function of the product of a constant b and the $\log_2$ of one plus the number of choices, plus a constant a representing a theoretical zero-choice time. Thus:

$$CRT = a + b \, (\log_2 N + 1)$$

where a can be represented by the intercept and b can be represented by the slope of a graph plotting the relationship of reaction time to N, the number of choices. Figure 5.1 provides a simple example.

Looked at in this relatively simple way, both constants a and b, intercept and slope respectively, tend to increase with age. The slope can be thought of as indicating the rate at which subjects can process information within certain limits of stimulus complexity; and this in turn can be thought of as reflecting some fairly basic neuropsychological process. The decline with age in mental speed then limits the subject's ability to deal with complex tasks.

The neuropsychological factors underlying choice reaction times of the sort referred to above are largely concerned with central processes, partly because peripheral processes (sensory and motor processes and nerve conduction times) may occupy only a fraction of the total reaction time, partly because it can be shown that complicating the decision process without changing the stimulus–response array increases the reaction time substantially.

Rabbitt (1980), however, points to four considerations which lead one to question the usual interpretation of the effects of ageing on speed of performance. First, speed of performance, including simple and choice reaction times, improve with practice, and when age effects are studied using practised subjects the differential increase in time required for the more difficult tasks may disappear. That is to say, although older subjects take longer than younger subjects, they do not take disproportionately longer on harder tasks when compared after long practice; the slopes of the equation

$$CRT = a + b (\log_2 N + 1)$$

are parallel rather than divergent.

It can be shown that practice on a choice reaction time task increases the speed and accuracy of a subject's performance until eventually an asymptote is reached. In situations where one wanted to test for discrimination between two stimulus arrays, the reliability of a subject's unpractised judgments, those occurring early in the series, would be less than that of practised judgments, those occurring later. Moreover, tasks which are at different levels of difficulty initially may, after long practice, become equal as regards speed and accuracy of performance. The unpractised subject is less discriminating than the practised subject—a not-unusual observation.

Second, in terms of signal detection theory (SDT), the overlap between the signal (S) and the signal-plus-noise (S + N) distributions would be greater (d' would be smaller) for the unpractised subject. However, it is not clear that the assumptions of SDT can be met in studies of the neuropsychological changes that occur with age.

Third, simple measures of speed and accuracy, and simple comparisons between unpractised subjects of different ages on tasks of different levels of difficulty, are not adequate to reveal the complex neuropsychological processes underlying even relatively simple performances. Such processes include those associated with attention, memory, decision-making, response control, and so on.

Fourth, the research data on the effects of ageing on choice reaction time are compatible with a variety of theoretical interpretations apart from any simple summation of delays occurring in the older central nervous system.

Rabbitt says that insufficient research data are available on the effects of sustained practice on the choice reaction times of older subjects. The expectation is that the slope (b) would decrease as it does for younger subjects, perhaps to zero. The same applies to some other kinds of performance, such as visual search and short-term recognition memory.

Rabbitt uses the notion of a trade-off between speed and error as a way of explaining how subjects establish a consistent manner of responding. Obviously, no trade-off can occur unless subjects are given knowledge of the results of their performance in terms of speed and accuracy (ignoring for the moment the problem of incentives or different types of error). Without additional evidence, age differences in speed and accuracy may be attributable to, say, greater cautiousness on the part of older subjects or to their inability to sustain fine control over their responses during the series or to failure of attention regarding feedback. Stable trade-offs can be achieved only after a considerable amount of practice.

One implication of all this is that comparisons of younger and older subjects at initial performance on a relatively novel laboratory performance task may be rather uninformative, simply because there are too many unknown and irrelevant factors affecting performance. By contrast, comparisons for stable performance on well-practised familiar tasks should simplify and magnify the effects of relevant and controllable variables, as well as generating data capable of more refined analysis.

The re-emergence of an interest in relatively simple mental functions such as reaction time and short-term memory has been one of the more surprising developments in the study of intelligence. It had originally been supposed that intelligence was best measured by tests of complex mental functions (hence the development of the Binet and the WAIS).

In relation to the study of adult intelligence, the general effects of age on speed of mental performance have been known more or less from the beginning. Simple reaction time, choice reaction time, writing speed, speed of mental arithmetic, speed of maze tracing, all slow down on average from early adult life. More complex effects have been demonstrated extensively in studies using the WAIS, and in experimental studies like those of Salthouse (1985b), Salthouse and Somberg (1982). A decline with age in the speed of mental processing is probably the most obvious and robust (replicable) finding in the psychological study of ageing—see also Cerella (1985).

Having said that, the question is: 'What precisely are the relationships between intelligence and the speed of mental processing?' Speed of mental performance can be measured in a variety of ways—for example, the following:

(1) Simple reaction time (the time taken to indicate awareness of a stimulus).

(2) Choice reaction time (the time taken to indicate discrimination between two or more stimuli).
(3) Encoding or inspection time (the time taken to indicate awareness of key features of stimuli, e.g. digit–symbol substitution, card-sorting).
(4) Short-term memory scanning (the time taken to indicate whether or not one or more items were present in a set of items previously registered).

Vernon (1983a) has shown that simple measures of speed of information processing are highly reliable, and consistent within subjects. (It would not be surprising to find that inter- and intra-individual differences are greater in older subjects than younger subjects.) Although Vernon found no relationship between speed and accuracy in a sample of young, above-average intelligence subjects, one usually finds that ageing brings about a decline in both speed and accuracy. In some situations it is possible and sensible to trade off speed and accuracy—as in handwriting, typing, driving, and cooking. In later life it is not uncommon to find older subjects trading off speed in favour of accuracy in laboratory tasks as a consequence of cautiousness (awareness of increased risk of error), possibly induced by their slower rate of mental processing.

The trade-off between speed and accuracy is an example of how ageing can change the way in which intelligence operates in solving problems. Another example is the liability to concrete forms of thought when abstract and general solutions cannot be formulated (as in proverb interpretation or object-sorting). The apparent decline with age in abstraction and generalization is difficult to explain, since it seems to be relatively independent of short-term memory and speed of mental functioning. It may indicate an early stage of a dementing process in a small proportion of otherwise normal subjects.

Simple speeded mental tests are highly reliable, and fairly highly intercorrelated, although simple and choice reaction times are less highly correlated with other measures, suggesting that a unitary source or set of sources should account for performance times. The analysis of reaction time data, however, is more complex than one might suppose (Rabbitt, 1980).

Naturally, the relationship between simple speeded mental functions and intelligence depends to some extent on the tests used to measure intelligence. If they incorporate the functions assessed by simple measures of speed of mental processing, as does the WAIS (and any intelligence tests which awards points for speed), then to that extent they will correlate with each other. Also, speed of mental processing is a limiting factor in certain kinds of task, such as tasks which present information serially or call for transformations of information held in short-term memory, as in making logical inferences or numerical calculations. Thus the efficiency, i.e. the speed and accuracy, with which individuals can process information, in combination with other genetic or acquired characteristics, helps to determine the higher levels of cognitive organization (concepts, rules, procedures, and so on) that determine their 'general intelligence'—a combination of fluid and crystallized abilities. Intellectual *competence* is a function of inborn ability acting on, or interacting with, experience, education, and training. It refers to what the person is capable of potentially. Hence the definition of intelligence as the ability to profit from experience. Intellectual *performance* depends on a host of contextual factors.

A reduction in the speed of central mental processes of the sort referred to above is not the only source of the overall decline in intellectual performance. Some decline is attributable to less efficient sensory and motor processes, e.g. visual and auditory discrimination, eye movements and hand–eye coordination (as in the digit–symbol subtest mentioned below). These effects, however, are thought to be small relative to central (cortical) processes in complex cognitive tasks. Also, especially at the higher levels of cognitive processes, the cumulative effect of slowing over numerous synaptic connections and metabolic processes in the brain must contribute to an overall impairment. The neuropsychological networks become weaker and more fragile.

It may be instructive to compare a subject's performance on one test with his or her performance on another. For example, the difference between the time taken to identify normal letters and the time taken to identify reversed or inverted letters can be construed as the time required to carry out the mental transposition, since all other features of the tasks are identical. Unfortunately, difference scores are notoriously unreliable, and validation may be a problem.

As Vernon (1983b) points out, the correlations between intelligence and speed of mental processing vary considerably depending upon the measures used. The WAIS and RPMT provide two well-standardized and widely used measures of intelligence. Some of the WAIS subtests incorporate a time element. The WAIS digit–symbol substitution subtest appears to be largely although not entirely a test of mental speed; performance on it declines with age more than for any other WAIS subtest. It is more usual however, to use laboratory-type tasks to measure mental speed. One example would be tachistoscopic or VDU stimuli presented very briefly to measure inspection time. Another example would be visual or auditory presentation of a list of digits followed by a probe-digit to test speed of matching against items in short-term memory. Other examples would include simple and choice reaction times, reading speed, retrieval time from general knowledge, and cortical evoked potentials.

In general, laboratory-type tests of mental speed are intercorrelated and share a substantial common factor. The correlations between fluid intelligence and independent measures of mental speed vary, depending upon which measures are used, although the relationship is usually positive. Vernon (1983b) points out that mental ability depends not only on the speed with which a person can carry out mental operations, but also on the consistency with which he or she can perform them. One could also suppose that there is a sort of 'resource-management' element in intelligence, in addition to speed and consistency.

General intelligence can be thought of either as a unitary ability, or as a small set of related abilities, which determines the speed and accuracy with which a person processes information. General intelligence enables a person to learn from experience, to build up knowledge and mental skills to deal with new or routine problems. Speed of mental processing should affect both the rate at which people can form new knowledge structures and the rate at which they can apply their knowledge. To some extent, mental speed and accuracy can be measured independently of the structure and contents of particular sorts of knowledge. But, of course, some knowledge structures may be organized through experience and practice in a way that maximizes speed and accuracy, e.g. the mental skills needed for the stock market, chess, or motorway driving.

Traditional measures of general intelligence correlate moderately well with a number of adult characteristics—educational level, occupational status, health, life-expectation, and leisure activities. As experience increases, tasks which were formerly novel become more familiar, knowledge and performances which had to be learned through training and experience become fairly automatic skills. Hence, the speed and accuracy (competence) of basic mental processing may decline with age without much, if any, decline in the performance of established mental skills.

In any event, it is only rare that new situations calling for speed and accuracy are encountered, and most routine problems do not test the individual's acquired skills to their limits.

The term 'metacognition' has been coined to refer to the way in which knowledge of mental processing is reflexive in the sense that it is knowledge which can be used to improve mental processing. For example, knowledge about the mental processes involved in driving and learning to drive could be used to improve driving performance. Knowledge of the psychology of problem-solving should improve problem-solving even in areas where specialized or technical information is also required. Knowledge about the factors affecting university examination performance should improve examination performance.

Mental processing takes place in the wider context of a person's characteristics and circumstances. So, for example, anxiety may disrupt new learning or even an established skill. High or low motivation may affect the degree and duration of attention to a task. Habit may prevent a person from recognizing or responding effectively to a situation which is unfamiliar but otherwise manageable. Physical and mental ill-health, and the normal physiological effects of ageing, can be expected to weaken the physical basis of mental processing.

Salthouse and Somberg (1982) argue that it is possible to demonstrate age deficits in speed of performance by examining the statistical interactions of age with stimulus encoding, central processing, and response organization. In this study, older subjects were disproportionately slower than younger subjects in all three aspects of a reaction time task. The task required subjects to identify an intact or degraded target stimulus consisting of a single digit, to compare it with a previous stimulus consisting of one or four digits, and then to respond in either a simple or a complex way depending upon the sequential stimulus pattern. The observed age differences could be expressed crudely in terms of a multiplier effect, the older subjects aged around 70 years took just over twice as long, on average, as younger subjects aged around 20 years for a given stimulus–response combination. Ageing appeared to affect all three stages of performance adversely. All three stages are interconnected, presumably by neural loops of considerable complexity. Ageing has a general slowing effect on neuropsychological processes apart from any specific effects that can be demonstrated.

The safest interpretation seems to be that reaction time increases in proportion to the difficulty of the task and in proportion to the age of the subject. Unfortunately this is somewhat vague, firstly because of the wide differences in functional capacity even between subjects of the same chronological age, and secondly because 'difficulty' is a psychological characteristic which can be operationally defined, but only in relation to a particular range of ability and context of use.

Even though an intelligence test may not incorporate items that call for specific sorts of mental speed, e.g. inspection, retrieval from long-term memory, short-term/long-term interaction, it may nevertheless correlate with tests of mental speed. Empirical studies are likely to be constrained by the nature of the sample, ceiling and floor effects in the distribution of scores, transformations applied to scores, and other methodological factors.

Perhaps the most problematic issue is showing that the same measures are *valid in the same sense* at different age levels. For example, does the digit–symbol subtest of the WAIS reflect intelligence *in the same way* at different chronological ages? Indeed, are we correct in supposing that intelligence can be defined in the same way at different ages? We are back to the point made earlier, that intelligence is a socially constructed concept. It does not refer (at present at least) to the sort of phenomenon that exists regardless of what scientists think about it—like the weather or electricity. It refers rather to the competence that people reveal in their performance on certain kinds of tests, which in turn relates broadly to a variety of other social indicators, such as educability and socioeconomic success. Attempts to develop related concepts, such as 'social intelligence' have not been particularly successful.

It remains to be seen whether there is any advantage, from a basic or an applied point of view, in defining and measuring intelligence differently at different adult ages. What has happened so far is that where intellectual functions are thought to be useful in diagnostic assessment, or in occupational selection, or in evaluating treatment intervention, procedures have been designed for specific purposes. These include: mental status questionnaires (to establish whether there is sufficient residual mental capacity to deal with the simple problems of daily living), measures of normal and high-grade intelligence, and measures of cognitive deficit and neuropsychological function (to establish more precisely the nature and extent of dementia or brain damage).

As the speed of mental processing declines, the older person's fluid abilities are reduced. On the other hand, experience and practice have the effect of maintaining crystallized abilities (although changes in the environment may render these abilities redundant and a hindrance to the acquisition of more effective skills and forms of knowledge). The 'resource management' aspect of general intelligence is related in part to what might be called the non-intellectual aspects of personality—attitude, interest, attention, flexibility, imagination, persistence—the psychological context within which basic intellectual functions are exercised.

What are these basic intellectual functions? They are the irreducible features of intelligent action—abstraction and generalization (induction), identifying classes and relationships, representing the real world with the symbols, operating with symbols independently of the real world, operating with systems of ideas (deduction), finding a *modus vivendi* between representation and reality without limiting the bounds of experience and imagination, thinking and acting quickly in order to stay alive and respond effectively, learning from experience and solving problems. The faster we can learn the more we can learn. The faster we can think the more problems we can solve. Speed is adaptive.

Intelligence construed as the ability to solve problems is not so much *applying* familiar solutions to *routine* problems but rather *finding* solutions to *novel* problems, i.e. fluid or unspecialized intelligence. This means thinking up possibilities for action, trying them out, and checking whether a solution is any nearer.

A new line of inquiry into adult intelligence would be to examine the changes that take place in the way subjects solve problems (not necessarily problems of the intelligence-test variety). This contrasts with the traditional approach which has been concerned mainly with quantitative differences in scores on intelligence tests of the WAIS, RPMT, and PMA variety. See Belmont (1983) for comments on the general issue of new ways of assessing intelligence.

Temporal integration

Belmont (1983) agrees that intelligence-as-problem-solving needs to be studied as a serial process of adaptation-solution perhaps occupying hours or even days, rather than the seconds or minutes required by traditional tests. The examples that come to mind, however, are the problems of coping with the real world—problems with people and things rather than problems with ideas. It is surely the capacity to organize *ideas* quickly and effectively that properly defines intelligence.

Complex real-life problem-solving processes may be sustained over long periods of time—several hours, days, weeks, or longer. This de-emphasizes the speed factor in favour of attention, memory and performance evaluation. Note that mental confusion in later life is defined in terms of disorientation for time, place, person, and activity—a failure to organize behaviour over time rather than a failure of speed of response.

The effects of ageing on learning and remembering are not easy to describe or explain—see Chapter 6. What seems to happen is that the processes of registration, retention, and recall are all adversely affected but to a greater or lesser extent depending upon concurrent contextual factors, such as the familiarity and meaningfulness of the stimulus materials, their rate of presentation, the sense modalities involved, the division of attention, interference, recognition, and cueing factors in recall.

Older subjects are likely to perform disproportionately less well than younger subjects on tasks which are unfamiliar or rapidly paced, on tasks which present unusual stimulus materials or information which cannot be easily organized and assimilated (understood), on tasks which call for divided attention, e.g. to a main and a subsidiary task, or for the 'translation' or reorganization of one system of ideas into another system, e.g. building a three-dimensional structure from a two-dimensional diagram.

The advantage of taking an information-processing approach to learning and remembering is that it suggests ways in which the adverse effects of ageing on a particular task can be minimized. In industrial retraining and adult education, for example, older subjects may benefit considerably from even simple improvements based on an analysis of the ways in which information is processed.

An information-processing approach to the study of mental abilities attempts to carry out a functional analysis of the mental operations required for different sorts of tasks. It is not primarily concerned with the standardization of psychometric tests or the assessment of differences between individuals. An information-processing approach promises to reveal the connections between intelligence and memory, or to dissolve the distinction between these concepts.

PROBLEM-SOLVING

Paradoxically perhaps, most recent psychological investigations into problem-solving have tended to concentrate on the *logical* operations required to solve the problem, rather than on the *psychological* characteristics of the problem-solving process. This contrasts with earlier work in problem-solving which was based more on subjective reports and psychological analyses of what is involved in thinking through a problem. Recent attempts to set up computer models of reasoning and problem-solving have reinforced the emphasis on the process of logical inference (formal or deductive logic). The so-called 'expert systems' do not claim to demonstrate how expert problem-solvers actually operate, but rather incorporate their findings, questions, and procedures, where these can be made explicit, so that the less expert problem-solver can be guided by them.

Among the approaches to the study of problem-solving in adult life and old age are those that employ abstraction and generalization, sorting and categorization, logical reasoning, Piaget-type studies, creativity, and flexibility. These approaches fall under the general heading of concept formation. In general, concept formation is closely correlated with fluid intelligence and declines with age.

Intellectual faculties such as attention and memory obviously play a role in problem-solving, as do other psychological characteristics such as motivation, persistence, and imagination. To some extent, problem-solving is a skill. This is obvious when one considers particular sorts of problem-solving, for example, in chess, card playing, motor vehicle maintenance, or cooking. The question is to what extent can problem-solving ability be *generalized* by training.

There are two rather distinct issues concerning problem-solving in later life. The first is that of transfer of training. Is it possible to improve the ability of adults to solve problems in general (or are the effects of training always fairly specific)? The second is that of counteracting the effects of disuse of function. To what extent can abilities and performance in later life be reinstated, maintained, or improved? A related issue is the extent to which the physical and social environment of the older person can play a supportive role in relation to the improvement and maintenance of abilities. The new technologies hold promise in this connection because they could provide information, instructions, and cues useful in instigating and guiding performance, for example in the activities of daily living and productive work.

Failures in problem-solving in later life are likely to occur because of faults at each stage of the process of problem-solving: identifying the problem in the first place; working out what additional information is required; putting together what is known and looking at it in relation to the problem; reformulating the problem; setting up hypotheses about its solution; breaking the main problem down into subsidiary problems; setting criteria for testing solutions; and verifying the correct or best solution. Successful problem-solving requires the systematic application of intelligence, experience, and imagination; it involves not only logical reasoning but also a variety of personal qualities. Hence the recent interest in the *diversity* of intellectual functions.

A neglected aspect of problem-solving is that many forms of argument which constitute explanations of or solutions to real-life problems do not lend themselves to analysis in terms of formal or deductive logic. Problems in the real world, in the world of empirical facts as opposed to the world of normative rules, are open-ended and context-dependent. The relationships and effects we deal with in the real world are by no means wholly susceptible to formal logical analysis. But this does not mean that we cannot solve problems or make sense of situations. Obviously we can, and do. Different areas of life, different fields of endeavour, impose their own terms of reference as far as problem-solving is concerned. Consider, for example, problems in human relationships, history, architectural design, warfare, and social policy. Although one cannot legitimately break the rules of deductive logic, deductive logic alone will not usually provide solutions to problems which are not purely formal.

The above digression is intended to do no more than make the reader aware of the limitations of recent approaches to the study of adult intelligence and problem-solving, and to encourage an awareness of the complexity and diversity of human psychological functions (Charness, 1985b; Cornelius and Caspi, 1987; Poon et al., 1989).

Another area of interest which is likely, sooner or later, to affect the study of adult intelligence and problem-solving is that of biases and heuristics or social cognition—Nisbett and Ross (1980). It can be shown that human thinking in its ordinary forms is liable to a variety of misconceptions, errors, and biases. The question is whether these liabilities change with age, and if so, how and to what extent. For example, there appears to be an increased tendency for older people to revert to primitive and concrete modes of thinking. Does this mean, for example, that the availability heuristic (the tendency to rely on vivid personal recollections rather than objective knowledge) becomes more pronounced as age increases? Or is metaphorical thinking more pronounced?

The decreased ability of older people to engage in effortful intellectual activities suggests that when unable to cope with a demanding mental task they tend to revert to simpler cognitive strategies—strategies which are more natural and less effortful than the sophisticated procedures acquired through training and experience. Failures of attention, memory, and imagination show up as errors, omissions, delays, repetitions, confusions, and so on.

Such failures are easily demonstrated by testing subjects to the limits of their intellectual capacities. These limits are reduced as age advances, at least in relation to the sorts of tests used in research. On the other hand, performance on familiar, well-practised tasks can be maintained well, even if the tasks themselves are relatively difficult, for example operating complex equipment. There are obviously limits to how well intellectual performance can be maintained in the face of age-related disabilities.

Intellectual efficiency appears to decline with age, but if one controls for *general* intelligence, for example by matching different age groups, then many *specific* aspects of cognition will also differ little or not at all across the different age levels—deductive reasoning, for example, or creative thinking. The effects of ageing on deductive reasoning, apart from the usual slowing and reduced capacity for holding information, appear to be partly a function of failures in cognitive control processes. Older subjects tends to pay attention to irrelevant information, to miss or forget the point of the exercise, to let personal experience substitute for logical reasoning. The effects of ageing on creative thinking are largely accounted for by mental slowing and diminished persistence, which reduce total output and particularly reduce the number of original responses (which are produced late in a series)—Bromley (1967).

Intellectual creativity

Creative productivity in the arts and the sciences has been a significant area of research for many years. It was, in fact, one of the earliest areas of interest in the psychology of ageing, following Dorland's research in 1908. It appears that Lehman's (1953) substantial research findings were stimulated in part by this early work. We need not review Lehman's work in detail (see Chapter 8), but his work is important in so far as it provides a kind of independent real-world account of the relationship between chronological age and high-grade intellectual productivity. Lehman (1953, 1962) demonstrated that in samples of scientists, writers, and others, there was a fairly consistent relationship between chronological age and the rate of intellectual achievement. Thus, for a wide range of intellectual endeavours—in mathematics, medicine, chemistry, technology, psychology, poetry, and other literature—the rate of intellectual output rose rapidly from about zero in the late teens or early 20s to a peak rate in the mid-30s, followed by a steady decline to zero or near zero late in life.

Creative work is produced by people of all ages but tends to be concentrated around its maximum rate in the mid-30s. Half the total output is achieved after the age of about 40 years. If only very high-grade intellectual achievements are considered, these age trends are even more pronounced. In general, quantity and quality of output are correlated—the more productive people tend also to produce the best work—but quantity of output is less adversely affected by ageing than is quality of output.

For various reasons there are differences between areas of intellectual endeavour. For example, the distribution by age of the production of short stories is not exactly the same as that for discoveries in mathematics, chemistry, or medicine; similarly writings in military history, poetry, or novels differ somewhat from each other in the way output is distributed by age. The reason for such variations is, presumably, that these different sorts of achievement require a different mix of general intelligence, special aptitudes, education and experience, motivation and other personality characteristics, opportunities, tools and materials, and so on. The surprising thing is that, given the wide range of circumstances affecting intellectual creativity, the age trends should be so consistent, regular, and similar.

Lehman devoted most of his energies to the compilation of data for different sorts of achievement, and to the refinement of methods for collecting and analysing these data—see also Dennis (1956, 1958). He listed some of the social and psychological factors which might help to explain the age distributions for achievement that he obtained, but he was unwilling to admit that the decline with age in adult intelligence was important in this connection. Nevertheless, the contrast we have drawn between fluid (unspecialized) and crystallized (specialized) abilities, together with our knowledge of the differential decline with age in mental abilities and the effects of age on mental speed, seems to go a long way to explain both the general similarity between the distributions by age of intellectual achievement and their differences—see Bromley (1974a, pp. 211–29). In general, those achievements which tend to occur *later* in adult life seem to depend more on crystallized ability, i.e. on education, experience, and special training or technical skills, as for example writing history or novels. Those achievements which tend to occur earlier in adult life seem to depend more on fluid ability, i.e. on abstraction, generalization, relational thinking, and insight, as for example in mathematics or solving problems in chess. An analogous contrast can be seen in the effects of age on various sorts of athletic achievement.

Examples can be found of findings which seem to run counter to those of Lehman. These illustrate some of the problems that arise when we try to generalize widely about the effects of ageing on human performance. As noted elsewhere, many findings depend heavily upon the context in which research is carried out—sampling, age distribution, method of data collection, and so on—Cole (1979), van Heeringen and Dijkwel (1987a, b). With regard to ageing and creativity, the effect of age at death has been a source of confusion.

Laboratory studies of intellectual creativity in relation to ageing have been rather few in number—see Kausler (1982, pp. 541–5). Psychometric tests which provide measures of the quantity and quality of creative intellectual output can be used to demonstrate effects compatible with those discovered by Lehman.

The lower limit for the sorts of intellectual creativity studied by Lehman is about 20 years. The peak years for rate of output are the mid-30s. This strongly suggests that crystallized abilities (educational attainments, experience, special scientific or literary skills) are a major factor in creative achievement in real life. However, after the mid-30s the rate of output declines on average, and output of higher quality declines faster than output of lesser quality, i.e. 'quantity' of output is maintained relatively better than 'quality' of output. This seems to support the view that even though crystallized ability may be maintained or even improved in middle life, it does not compensate fully for the decline with age in fluid ability, assuming that fluid ability is the main determinant of creative thinking. Fluid ability may have less effect on some sorts of 'intellectual' creativity than on others. Thus loss of motivation and mental speed are not responsible for the decline in quality of output but loss of performance evaluation might be.

Psychometric research on the decline with age in creative intellectual output has been criticized on the grounds that the tests have only face validity, and are too formal and abstract. One issue is that of discriminant validity, i.e. the extent to which tests of intellectual creativity measure something different from general intelligence. However, there has been no satisfactory demonstration that tests with such discriminant validity can be constructed. Creative, divergent, thinking in relation to cognitive tasks is closely related to general intelligence and to convergent thinking.

Reasoning by analogy from the test performances of volunteer subjects to the real-world achievements of outstanding innovators in western science and culture is obviously risky. The aim of psychometric studies, however, is not to test the *validity* of Lehman's work but rather to explore, under relatively controlled conditions, some of the ideas and assumptions associated with Lehman's research. In the light of research on mental abilities in adult life, Lehman's rejection of the effects of a decline in intelligence on intellectual achievements in adult life cannot be justified.

Language and cognition

Verbal behaviour and language comprehension, in so far as they do not involve fluid abilities—i.e. mental speed, complexity of control, or large amounts of information—are generally regarded as resistant to the normal effects of ageing, although they are susceptible to focal brain damage associated with injury or disease. Vocabulary, in particular, appears to increase up to the 30s or 40s and then to remain fairly constant until late life. This holds whether vocabulary is being tested for comprehension or as an aspect of language production—see Light and Burke (1988) for reports on language, memory, and ageing in normal and impaired subjects.

Surprisingly little research work seems to have been done on language functions other than vocabulary (except coincidentally when employing verbal materials for experimental convenience), and most of what has been done concerns language comprehension (input) rather than language production (output)—but see Flicker *et al.* (1987), S. Kemper (1986, 1987), Kemper *et al.* (1989), Kemper and Rash (1988), Schmitt and McCroskey (1981), Spilich (1985), Ulatowska *et al.* (1986), Zabrucky *et al.* (1987). Studies of language comprehension have used both printed and spoken language. For example, sentences are presented and the subject may have to answer questions about the text—see Belmore (1981). Apparently, older subjects are similar to younger subjects in their ability to discriminate what was actually presented from what could be inferred, provided the task is not demanding, although, in conversations, older subjects are more likely to forget or be confused about who said what.

There is a considerable and growing literature on the neuropsychological assessment of patients with SDAT. The references given here and elsewhere only hint at what is available given present-day automated library search methods—Bondareff (1981), Bondareff *et al.* (1987), McLean (1987a, b), Morris (1987). Cognitive and linguistic functions in normal subjects and patients with SDAT have been a particular focus of attention recently—Hart (1988), Hier *et al.* (1985), Obler and Albert (1980), Spinnler *et al.* (1988), Stevens (1985). Many studies of depression have been cited in the text—see also Cole (1983); any linguistic emphasis is usually on the 'content' of utterances.

It is not obvious that the study of language in relation to brain damage and mental diseases of late onset has clarified our understanding of normal age-changes—see Oyer and Oyer (1976, pp. 155–74). Cross-sectional and longitudinal research findings indicate relatively little if any decline until very late in life in mental abilities such as vocabulary, general knowledge, and the sorts of information that are commonly used in everyday life. These include the language skills used in occupational performance, i.e. the production and comprehension of language expressing technical concepts. These language functions, however, are relatively simple, well-practised, and largely reproductive (rather than creative). What happens to the ability to use language in more complex ways—for example at higher levels of generality and abstraction or in more complex logical relationships, as in legal reasoning? What happens to language which is creative or exploratory—in the sense of being productive and original rather than stereotyped, as in poetry or revolutionary scientific ideas? What happens to the cognitive and linguistic abilities needed for fast, accurate cognitive processing, as in technical emergencies? There seems to be little or no research on the effects of ageing on these higher forms of language ability.

Little attention seems to be paid to the confusing or misleading effects that the language used in test instructions may have on the psychometric performance of older adults. Test instructions need to be clear and simple, otherwise they are likely to affect the results. Some test items may present problems of comprehension, especially if they are long and impose a load on working memory. In personality testing, test items may carry a different meaning for older as compared with younger subjects. The content as well as the form of cognitive test items may very well affect age comparisons.

In so far as language is used to comprehend or reproduce familiar information at an undemanding pace, it can be regarded as calling on 'crystallized' ability. But in so far as language is used to interpret or to formulate new or unfamiliar information, especially if the information has to be processed quickly, or in large amounts, then it can be regarded as calling on 'fluid' ability. Obviously language functions of the second sort are more adversely affected by ageing than are abilities of the first sort.

Language is important in a wide range of human activities and not least in cognitive functions, such as problem-solving. Problem-solving may involve the description in language of facts and relationships, conceptual analysis, speculation and reasoning, critical thinking, and so on. The study of language—its processes and products—might tell us a great deal about these mental abilities.

S. Kemper (1986) found age-related changes in syntactic complexity in diary entries. The older the subject, the fewer embedded constructions. Sentence length, however, did not decline. The effects of age on written language production were different in some respects from the effects of age on spoken language.

It seems unlikely that the effects which can be demonstrated experimentally have much practical significance in the ordinary activities of daily life. But they may play a part in more demanding tasks, and may yield clues about language disorders in later life.

THEORY AND PRACTICE

At present we do not have anything that could reasonably be called a 'theory' of adult intelligence. What we have is a collection of loosely related ideas drawn from several areas of psychological interest which together indicate the nature and scope of the area referred to as 'adult intelligence'. The nearest approach to a theory is that of Berg and Sternberg (1985).

Current psychometric measures of adult intelligence have come to be regarded as inadequate for two reasons. First, as single-occasion tests they may fail to uncover the adult's intellectual competence (or potential) which would be more effectively revealed by performances following training and practice. Second, because of the content and organization of test items, intelligence tests do not necessarily enable older adults to demonstrate their intellectual abilities. This second reason implies that tests of adult intelligence lack the external validity that characterizes tests of juvenile intelligence. In the absence of such criteria, test constructors have been obliged to rely on traditional forms of assessment: analogies, series completion, spatial and verbal reasoning, memory, numerical operations, common sense, mental speed, and so on.

Berg and Sternberg (1985) have proposed a triarchic theory of intelligence applicable to adults. The first element in this theory is that intelligence serves adaptational functions—we modify our ideas in response to changes in our environment and we modify our environment to bring it into line with our ideas. These functions are not very different from Piaget's notions of assimilation and accommodation. Indeed, several attempts have been made to examine the effects of adult ageing on test performances of the sort used in connection with Piaget's ideas—see Labouvie-Vief (1985). Berg and Sternberg's argument is that during adult life we accumulate a vast amount of experience which enables us to organize our behaviour economically, quickly, and effectively across a wide range of situations. Consequently, older adults are inclined to resort to well-established cognitive schemata when faced with a problem. They naturally rely on experience—crystallized abilities—which is relatively quick and effortless. By contrast, the younger adult, lacking experience and conceptual routines, must engage in effortful problem-solving using fluid abilities.

The second element in the theory is more difficult to deal with, since it concerns the very structures and processes of cognition—the central problem in the study of intelligence. To be intelligent is to be alert to the possibilities implicit in the situations we encounter; it is the ability to plan and implement appropriate courses of action, to make strategic plans and tactical adjustments as required. It is the ability to monitor the progress of events and to evaluate outcomes in relation to future contingencies.

The third element in Berg and Sternberg's triarchic theory is that behaviour is modified through learning and experience. Hence, after repeated experience of coping with a particular sort of situation that was initially a problem to be solved by the exercise of intelligence, the relevant cognitive processes are transformed into a relatively automatic response schema. Consideration of this third element in the theory means two things. First, a task may involve more or less native intelligence—fluid ability, and more or less experience—crystallized ability, depending upon the individual's resources. Second, intelligence test items, like problem situations, may be dealt with in different ways by different subjects; the more familiar the content of a test item or problem situation, the more likely it is that the subject will resort to well-practised forms of reasoning. Hence the need for care in the design and administration of tests of adult intelligence, and incidentally more care in arguing from test results to competence in daily life.

Berg and Sternberg argue that intelligence is most clearly manifested in situations which are relatively novel and where the relevant mental processes are gradually becoming automatic or habitual. Thus, older adults faced with a completely new situation are likely to be disadvantaged relative to young persons because they will be inclined to interpret and to react to that situation in terms of mental habits acquired through training and experience, whereas young persons lacking this experience are obliged to think the problem through, and in the process arrive at an intelligent solution rather than one based on preformed notions. Similarly, young persons lacking training or experience in a given area will be disadvantaged relative to older adults because intelligence as such may be unable to make up for their lack of experience.

Berg and Sternberg offer an interesting summary of how people ordinarily attribute intelligence to others. The behaviour characteristics they refer to change somewhat according to the age group they have in mind—30-, 50-, or 70-year-olds, but include the ability to solve problems, competence in daily life, coping with disastrous situations, curiosity, and being well-informed. It remains to be seen whether the implicit criteria they list can be transformed into operational psychometric measures.

The tendency to define intelligence in terms of the ability to adjust well to one's environment is unfortunate, because it neglects the many and various personal characteristics that affect one's adjustment—emotionality, interests, values, health, social factors, and so on. The whole point of the intelligence testing movement was to define and assess intelligence as a distinct characteristic, separate from other social, psychological, and physical characteristics affecting educability. If educability is defined as the ability to improve with training and practice, then obviously intelligence is an important, but certainly not the only, factor affecting it.

We must therefore be clear about what we mean by adult intelligence. Do we mean the ability of adults to cope with life's situations, as judged by their actual performance? Or do we mean the ability of adults to improve their mental performance (in standardized, representative ways) following training, experience, and practice? Or do we mean the ability to 'process information' (for lack of a better expression) reflecting some, as yet undetermined, set of brain processes? These three questions are successively more reductionist in their formulation of the problem. Investigations into the relationship between intelligence and the speed of cortical functions show that the third question is legitimate. The answer to the first question seems to be negative. That leaves the second question as the one that opens up the most promising lines of inquiry for psychology. The lines of inquiry opened up by the third question lead mainly into neurophysiology, whilst leaving the problem of defining intelligence to psychology. It is likely that, in the end, a reductionist approach will lead to a redefinition of the term 'intelligence'. In the meantime, there are many practical problems associated with the study of intelligence—in particular how to maintain it effectively in adult life and how to assess it for the purposes of counselling, diagnosis, and treatment.

The proposal that adult intelligence means the ability of adults to improve mental performance in standardized, representative ways, implies two things. First, that the single-occasion intelligence test is not a satisfactory measure of adult intelligence (and may not be a satisfactory measure of juvenile intelligence). Second, that the 'ways' in which mental performance should be assessed might vary from one age level to another.

Changes with age in the physical fabric of the body, and in life-circumstances, lead one to question whether the same indices can be used to measure intelligence at different adult ages. (We use somewhat different indices to measure the intelligence of children at different ages.) This does not mean that measures of adult intelligence need be radically different from one age to the next, since intelligence at one age must somehow shade into intelligence at a later age. A theory of adult intelligence should also explain how normal intelligence breaks down in conditions of mental impairment.

We must not confuse intelligence, which is one sort of *competence*, with adjustment, which is a *performance* characteristic. Adjustment or adaptation depends on a variety of personal and situational factors, one personal factor being intelligence. Just as it would be unfair to judge an elderly person's intelligence without taking account of his or her sensory and motor disabilities, so it would be unfair to assume that his or her adjustment to bereavement or retirement is largely a reflection of intelligence. Indeed, one would normally avoid using behaviour with a strong emotional component as an index of intelligence. We would be more likely to consider the long-term adjustments—made in a more settled frame of mind—as indicative of intelligence (taking account of the circumstances surrounding such adjustment). We would look at changes in the behaviour of the person, and at the changes he or she had made to the environment. For example, a voluntary change of residence might or might not be seen as a sensible, i.e. intelligent, decision.

Assuming that there is a set of abilities for mental processing which together make up what we mean by fluid intelligence, then there is no reason to suppose that ageing brings into play a different set of abilities. Intelligence has a biological basis in the structures and functions of the brain, and the main issue is how the effects of ageing on these brain structures and functions bring about changes in mental processing. The fact that older people face problems of adjustment different from those of younger people is a separate issue. Even the fact that older people combine their intelligence and experience in different ways to deal with these problems is a secondary issue, albeit one with important implications as regards the theory of adult intelligence, and practical applications affecting adult intellectual performance.

Berg and Sternberg (1985) propose six metacomponents or stages in adult cognition: formulating the problem, marshalling relevant experience and skills, selecting preferred mental techniques (strategies), applying these techniques to the particular problem, making tactical adjustments or changes of strategy in response to progress in dealing with the problem, evaluating solutions in relation to solving the problem. They argue that each component or stage may be affected in one way or another by ageing. For example, older adults may have a well-established routine for dealing with a particular type of problem; they may be slow to switch from a well-tried strategy which is proving ineffective, and so on.

Some of the components in mental processing were referred to in connection with the issue of mental speed—for example, inspection time, rehearsal time, rate of retrieval from long-term memory. These components can be broadly classified as input components, central components, and output components. The bulk of the evidence suggests that it is the central components that define intelligence, although input (sensory) and output (motor) stages may well affect actual performance. However, such is the complexity of mental processing that the interfaces between sensory and central, and central and motor, processes are not well-defined psychometrically, and apparently minor changes in a task can bring about substantial changes in performance.

The fact that language abilities are extensively developed and practised seems to help maintain mental processing. It is possible that the age decline in some abilities is attributable to insufficient development and/or insufficient practice (disuse), but the fact that some mental functions can be improved with training and practice seems to give more support to the latter view.

Performance self-evaluation is a relatively neglected aspect of the assessment of adult intelligence. It refers to the ability to monitor one's performance against internalized standards or external performance indicators. For example, if the task is to describe something, performance evaluation would involve checking one's description for choice of words, spelling, sentence construction, and relevance, whilst maintaining a check on external criteria—the passage of time, discourse rules, and so on.

Virtually every child and adult has experienced the development of skills involving some degree of thinking (problem-solving, reasoning), and the change from being a beginner to acquiring some degree of proficiency. The sorts of skills in question are varied, and range from highly symbolic activities such as calculating, playing chess, and composing a report, to more concrete activities such as those involved in social relationships, house repairs, or driving an automobile. Through the processes of reasoning, learning, and remembering we gradually build up cognitive systems, schemata, by means of which our behaviour becomes more efficiently organized in relation to recurrent situations of the same sort—chess, driving, or whatever. As we become more proficient, more skilled, our behaviour becomes less effortful, faster, smoother, more accurate, and generally better adapted to that sort of situation.

Intelligence is a necessary component, but not the only component, in this transition from novice to expert. In the early stages of acquiring a specialized mental skill, a person is relatively ignorant of the terms of reference within which problems are identified and decisions about appropriate actions are taken. Consider, for example, the novice's approach to learning word-processing, meteorology, or flying. In these and in other areas there are basic facts and rules to be learned, one has to become familiar with certain materials and equipment, and with the wider context within which the skill is to be exercised. In addition, there are many things to learn about the meanings of symbols and ways of operating with symbols.

In time, with training and practice, and with the exercise of intelligence and other personal attributes, the individual achieves some degree of mastery over that part of his or her environment defined by the terms of reference. In the process, situations which were earlier seen as problems, or of no particular significance, become meaningful and familiar. They are dealt with as matters of routine. The individual acquires a variety of drills and strategies for solving problems that are likely to arise—how to cope with a change of type-face in word-processing, what to expect from a particular set of data in meteorology, how to cope with an engine failure in flying. The aim is to solve such problems quickly and easily, and to operate the system efficiently so as to achieve the desired results.

It is easy to see that, where complex cognitive processes are called for, mistakes are likely to happen. Hence part of the skill lies in anticipating errors, monitoring performance, and evaluating the results. There is also the possibility that new problems will arise—problems for which there is no ready-made solution. It can be argued that intelligence reveals itself most clearly in the initial stages of learning a cognitive skill, in particular in the rate at which the individual gains mastery, and the level reached after a period of training and experience. Intelligence also reveals itself in the extent to which the individual can solve problems not previously encountered, since this involves not merely the application of routine solutions (which may sometimes be maladaptive) but the production of new ideas which may provide solutions to the new problems.

Intelligence is basically the set of cognitive processes involved in proposing solutions for problems. Of course, translating a proposed solution into effective actions is another matter, since the solution may require resources and characteristics not available to a particular individual, e.g. tools, time, patience, opportunity, support from others. This sort of situation then poses these further problems as far as the exercise of intelligence is concerned. We note in passing that the exercise of intelligence in the context of certain personal and situational characteristics can be maladaptive, even catastrophic, in its consequences, as for example when intelligence is exercised in the context of false beliefs, criminal intent, or psychiatric disorder.

The knowledge base on which our intelligence operates is structured, not only in the sense that we can retrieve existing information quickly and in an orderly, controlled, way, but also in the sense that we can work out new patterns and relationships by implication from existing information. However, there is still much that we do not understand about the relationship between intelligence and experience. For example, we do not necessarily, or even usually, develop new ideas through a conscious deliberate process of logical reasoning. Rather, we seem to use guesswork and heuristics to arrive at possible solutions or hypotheses which then have to be tested to see whether they are logically or empirically acceptable. It is as if the schemata that comprise the 'knowledge base' have a natural logic of their own which the 'human operator' simply acknowledges. This might go some way to account for creative thinking, in which ideas seem to come unbidden into consciousness. It is certainly the case that where individuals have become experts in a particular area of intellectual life, they are often able to generate new intellectual products—music, poetry, scientific theory, inventions, formulae—but cannot give an account of the production process. Recent work in cognitive heuristics and biases seems to confirm the distinction between 'natural' and 'sophisticated' forms of reasoning (Kahneman *et al.*, 1982). The effect of ageing on heuristics and biases seems to be an unexplored area.

The comments on practical intelligence are intended to draw attention to the limitations of the traditional psychometric approach, and at the same time to show that we still have a lot to learn about cognitive processes in adult life. Intelligence is not clearly expressed in the ordinary activities of daily living, because the activities of daily living do not normally make heavy demands upon our cognitive capacities (as do intelligence tests). On the other hand, one could argue that certain sorts of failures in coping with the activities of daily living may index the lower levels of practical intelligence. These would have to be 'cognitive' failures, i.e. failures in learning, remembering, information processing, and problem-solving. Such failures can be indexed by direct observation and by questionnaires, although the methodological limitations are fairly obvious.

The emphasis on 'practical intelligence' is not intended to belittle psychometric measurement, since it seems likely that psychometric measurement will continue to be the preferred approach to the assessment of cognitive functions in clinical and research settings. Nevertheless, more attention should be paid to the ways in which ageing affects natural forms of cognition in the ordinary circumstances of daily life.

SUMMARY

The concept of adult intelligence is derived from the notion of general intelligence, first studied in relation to juvenile development and operationally defined in terms of performance on psychometric tests. Intelligence was shown to predict scholastic attainment reasonably well. Efforts were made to produce tests of intelligence which did not inadvertently measure educational or cultural advantages. Little effort was made to discover how intelligence and experience were combined during juvenile development.

The study of adult intelligence has been dominated by the psychometric approach. This has resulted in a number of claims, about which there is still a certain amount of debate. For example, performance on measures of fluid or unspecialized intelligence shows an age-related decline whereas performance on measures of crystallized or specialized intelligence shows less or no decline. Performance on tests involving speed of mental processing also declines with age. However, longitudinal studies of adult intelligence and studies of secular trends in intelligence support counter-claims, to the effect that age-related changes have been overestimated in cross-sectional studies, and that the decline with age in intelligence tends to occur relatively late in life.

Further criticism of the psychometric approach to adult intelligence comes from those who claim that adult test performance does not necessarily correspond to the ability to solve the cognitive problems encountered in adult life, including problems extended in time.

A weakness of the psychometric approach to intelligence is that it has little to offer in the way of a theory of intelligence. Hence, it is not at all clear how intelligence enables us to profit from experience or how experience enables us to use our intelligence more profitably. Adults develop their cognitive capacities in all sorts of ways, and acquire many kinds of skills calling for various kinds and amounts of cognitive capacity—whether in cooking, knitting, playing golf, computing, flying, investing, or whatever. Abilities involving training and experience are referred to as crystallized abilities, and they seem to be maintained reasonably well provided they are exercised regularly in a moderately demanding way.

Surprisingly, perhaps, the special or primary abilities identified in factor-analytic studies of psychometric intelligence have not proved to be of much significance in relation to the normal effects of ageing, or in relation to dementia or other sorts of brain disorder. It is possible that the primary cognitive abilities are more specific and more numerous than those so far identified in the context of intelligence testing. Even neuropsychological test batteries have not been particularly useful in clarifying the normal effects of ageing on cognitive functions. At present, the study of adult intelligence is hampered by our ignorance of the component cognitive functions and their physical counterparts in brain activities. However, this does not prevent us from looking more closely at what is called 'practical intelligence'—the way intelligence is exercised in the ordinary activities of daily life at home, at work, and at leisure. Cognitive functions are central to the organization of behaviour, especially in situations which are new or where the individual is in the process of learning how to cope effectively with recurrent situations of a particular sort—as in learning any skill involving the exercise of intelligence.

A person's intelligence is only one of many factors that affect the ability to adapt to his or her surroundings; so we must be careful not to define even 'practical adult intelligence' as the ability to adapt. Practical intelligence needs to be defined operationally in terms of that combination of intelligence and experience which makes the individual 'competent' in a given area of reasoning, even if his or her 'performance' is impaired by extraneous conditions such as anxiety or ill-health.

The notion of practical intelligence is particularly important in behavioural gerontology because of the need to maximize cognitive capacity to offset the deleterious effects of ageing which might otherwise lead to excess disability, i.e. to a degree of dependency greater than that warranted by the individual's residual cognitive capacities. The idea is to find ways of counteracting and compensating for the adverse effects of normal ageing and late-life disorders. The assumption is that training and practice in relevant mental skills will transfer to performance in the activities of daily life. So, for example, people might be trained to learn and remember more effectively, to solve everyday problems, and to use their time and their opportunities more effectively.

Mental skills that are not exercised regularly tend to fall into disuse. However, they can usually be relearned without too much difficulty, presumably because substantial 'memory traces' of the original learning still remain. Some mental skills are acquired in a particular cultural or technological context; the danger is that such skills may become obsolete. Consider, for example how the skills involved in using a slide rule, or in valve technology, or in typewriting, have been replaced by skills in computing, integrated circuit technology, and word-processing. Thus, the study of adult intelligence, at least as far as practical applications are concerned, should lead to ways of offsetting the effects of disuse and finding effective ways of retraining adults in new skills.

The Wechsler tests have been used extensively in the study of adult intelligence. They provide a reasonably reliable and valid index of intelligence as it is presently understood, and demonstrate the differential decline with age in fluid and crystallized abilities. The method of calculating a deterioration quotient (DQ), reflecting the extent to which an individual's intelligence had declined from its young adult maximum, seems not to have lived up to its early promise, but the basic idea is worth pursuing because of the diagnostic value a valid DQ would have.

Other measures of adult intelligence have been developed, e.g. Raven's Progressive Matrices test. Neuropsychological test batteries have much in common with measures of fluid intelligence. Laboratory measures of learning, remembering, problem-solving, and creativity also tend to correlate with measures of adult intelligence. Indeed, general intelligence accounts for a substantial proportion of the variance in specialized tests of cognitive function.

One serious objection to the assessment of cognitive functions in adults is that first-time, single-occasion measures fail to reveal the full potential of older adults. Training and practice usually lead to substantial improvements, although younger adults too show improvements. The argument is that a well-practised function constitutes a more reliable, consistent index of a cognitive capacity and this index is therefore more useful for making comparisons.

Technological advances in computing and communications may permit more direct access to brain activity and provide more effective measures of cognitive functions.

Methodological obstacles in the study of intelligence include all those traditionally associated with behavioural gerontology. In particular, there are the problems of theorizing and measurement. Recent studies have revealed substantial secular gains in measured intelligence, especially in fluid ability. These studies call into question the definition and measurement of adult intelligence. There appears to have been a secular increase in measured intelligence and in the age at which intellectual development reaches its maximum. This raises the question of the relationship between intelligence and experience, as well as the relationship between juvenile and adult intelligence.

Mental speed can be shown to be highly correlated with intelligence as generally measured. There are also indications that mental speed and the speed at which cortical activities take place are closely related. Mental speed declines with age, except where the person is responding to a familiar situation and exercising a well-practised skill in relatively undemanding conditions. Broadly speaking, the time required to respond depends upon the complexity (difficulty) of the task. Older subjects tend to show a disproportionate increase in time to respond as the difficulty of a task increases, especially on tasks which are close to the limits of their working memory.

Problem-solving in daily life requires a combination of intelligence and experience. Intelligence test items, by contrast, minimize the relevance of experience and present what appear to be examples of context-free problems. To the extent that component cognitive functions are pre-adapted to deal with certain kinds of experience, we may find that existing tests of adult intelligence do not take sufficient account of the way intelligence is exercised in practice. It has been assumed that the inclusion of verbal, spatial, numerical, memory, and other subtests provides a reasonable 'sample' of the component cognitive functions.

Creative thinking, in the context of cognition (as contrasted with artistic and expressive activities), seems to be closely connected with fluid abilities in experimental investigations, but obviously depends upon crystallized abilities in the circumstances of real life. The effects of age on context-free tests of creativity are to reduce total output, and as a necessary consequence to reduce the output of original responses.

Language and cognition are closely related. Everyday language functions are little affected by ageing but, as one might expect, when tested to the limits, some language functions decline with age.

Recent theoretical developments have been directed mainly towards understanding the practical applications of intelligence.

Chapter Six

Learning, Knowing, and Forgetting

INTRODUCTION

The effects of ageing on memory have been of interest to behavioural gerontologists from the beginning and have been investigated with considerable rigour and in considerable detail—see Poon *et al.* (1980). Much of the work done so far has been directed towards finding out which of several psychophysiological functions in remembering are most adversely affected by ageing. In general, the results indicate that the time factor is important no matter which particular function is being tested. Thus, older subjects given longer to register brief stimuli will perform more like younger subjects (and, given the opportunity, usually take more time than they actually need). Similarly, older subjects given longer to learn material, or to recall it, or to recognize it, will perform at levels nearer to those of younger subjects, although in some circumstances they underestimate how much time they need.

It is difficult to separate out the effects of ageing on different memory functions. Controlling for time spent learning, for example, affects the amount learned, which may affect the structure or pattern of what is learned and therefore how well the material is recalled or recognized. Similarly, controlling for level of learning usually means increasing the time spent learning by older subjects, which affects trials, interest, interference, and so on. A useful practical approach to the problem of learning and remembering in later life is to assume that *all* memory functions are impaired to a greater or lesser extent, and that there is a cumulative effect. Examining the ways in which the performance might be improved (or its loss reduced or deferred) means considering each and every aspect of the performance—its acquisition, retention of it over time, and the contexts in which it is reproduced. Thus, for example, if we find that ageing is accompanied by an apparent reduction in the ability to keep track of the events portrayed in a novel or a film, or to follow an instruction booklet, then what we need to do is to examine *all* aspects of the processes which give rise—in the end—to such comprehension of the events as subjects can achieve, with a view to optimizing each of the component processes—see Owens (1987).

Let us consider in more detail the task of keeping track of the events portrayed in a novel, or film, and ask what adverse effects ageing might have on the processes involved and how such adverse effects might be minimized. For convenience we shall adopt a semi-technical information-processing approach.

Registration (encoding)

Information about the characters, relationships, objects, circumstances, and events in a story can be portrayed in various ways—in words or pictures—and by means of different material features. Thus clarity of sound track, printed word or diagram, sentence length, the amount of detail presented, the sequential order of the material, and so on, are likely to affect the ease with which the information can be registered in the first place. Material which is not properly registered in the first place, or not adequately reinforced subsequently, obviously will not be learned and recalled well. Therefore, material presented to older subjects should compensate for the known or likely effects of ageing. For example: the layout of a page of print can be improved in all sorts of ways to aid faster reading and more effective registration; choice of vocabulary and syntax also determines what is registered, as does the order and logic or the material. In a film, the choice of 'shots'; their pace and duration; the order of presentation; the content, pace, and quality of the dialogue; and so on, will affect the extent to which the information is registered in the first place. One would expect that the 'design features' in printed or filmed material for the elderly would benefit other sorts of subject with similar disabilities in learning and remembering—see Hartley and Burnhill (1977) with reference to printed material.

Retention (storage)

Information, once registered, may be lost through interference or confusion with similar material, or possibly through decay (fading) because of lack of use (non-rehearsal) over time. Information which, for one reason or another, is difficult to retain, e.g. computer skills, needs to be used, rehearsed, or otherwise reinforced early and fairly frequently. Thus, in a book of instructions, certain technical terms may need to be defined on the first few occasions of use; in a novel, important facts may have to be referred to more than once; in a film, reminders of one sort or another may have to be shown—by flashbacks or repetitions. The adverse effects of interference and disuse on memories accumulate over time and so are more obvious in later life. The measures to counteract these effects have to be correspondingly more thorough, for example by reducing the amount of collateral information to be retained. The time and effort required to register and retain the information is greater for older people. Also the costs in time, money, and effort required to produce the material in a form better suited for use by older people is greater. Whether the overall cost/benefit ratio is acceptable is a matter which can be settled only with reference to particular cases. Thus, an instruction booklet on services for the elderly should be designed to facilitate comprehension by the elderly, whereas a film intended for general release might be spoiled by design features to help the elderly viewer. There is much that can be done by professional workers to communicate more effectively with older persons.

Recall and recognition (retrieval)

Information which has been registered and 'stored' in some way for possible later use is more (or less) accessible, depending upon a variety of factors. For example, the meaning of a later sentence may depend on subjects having understood and remembered some earlier material. A film would not make much sense if we could not recognize certain characters from their earlier appearance.

What can be done to improve the capacity of older people to recall the information they need or to recognize it when they encounter it? One very general way would be to educate people about the basic mechanisms of learning and remembering. This could take the form of health, welfare, and safety education through the media, and include a variety of practical illustrations about improving learning and remembering. Recall can usually be improved by increasing the amount of time and the degree of personal involvement in the learning process, including subsequent rehearsal and integration with other relevant information. Recall can also be improved by the use of retrieval cues such as checklists, mnemonics, prompts, and reminders, and in some instances by heuristics such as mentally replaying sequences of thoughts or actions closely associated with the required material, e.g. a person's name, the location of an object. Information is more easily and more effectively learned and remembered if it can be organized in a meaningful way, i.e. if the different elements can stand in some patterned relationship with each other, as for example the points of a story, the parts of a machine, the symbols of an equation, the lines of a diagram. A great deal of practical action is governed by plans and scripts by means of which we coordinate our intentions with external circumstances and events.

Recognition can be improved by arranging for more or better cues to retrieval, such as priming, associating, and attending. Person recognition is easier for younger and older people alike when other people are distinctive in appearance and are encountered in the same setting.

Some strategies in learning and remembering are commonly used by younger people. An older person whose learning and memory capacities have been reduced needs less demanding conditions, or has to make correspondingly greater effort, if he or she is to function at a level which enables that person to respond as quickly and as correctly as a younger person. It seems that older adults tend to neglect to use these natural strategies.

Relearning

Relearning can be used experimentally to measure the extent to which material has been forgotten. In daily life, however, there are many circumstances in which, for practical purposes, it is necessary to relearn material partially forgotten—a foreign language, computer programming, driving a car, woodwork, needlework, and so on. A distinction must be made between 'relearning' and 'retraining'. The former term is most conveniently used to refer to the renewal of original material—information or skill; the latter term usually refers to the learning of a *new* skill—perhaps based on or related to earlier learning, but more often not. Relearning is essentially a process of refreshing information that has lost its previous clarity and organization through disuse and interference. A common response to relearning by an older person is to underestimate the time and practice required to relearn the material or skill, just as he or she may underestimate how much time was originally spent learning the material or skill.

Some conditions favour learning and some do not. For example, interest and simplicity favour rapid error-free learning while fatigue and irrelevant context do not. It follows that teaching and learning with the elderly need to get closer to the ideal conditions in order to compensate for the overall impairment in learning ability. Younger subjects often cope with less than optimum conditions for learning, but such departure from optimality becomes increasingly disadvantageous as age increases. Factors which do not affect younger subjects much may affect older subjects markedly—for example time constraints, stimulus complexity, irrelevant context. Briefly, ideal conditions for learning include the following:

stimulus simplicity, response simplicity, information processing which is simple and of short duration, and maintenance of direct and immediate contact with changes in the situation, e.g. minimum reliance on delayed or weak signals regarding the onset of a stimulus or the outcome of a response. Other ideal conditions include: high levels of well-maintained and focused interest and attention (provided they do not exclude relevant peripheral information), comprehension of and familiarity with the task (provided they do not induce proactive interference), and self-paced organization of behaviour. These considerations are important in adult education and occupational training—see Dixon (1983), and Lumsden (1985).

The reduction with age in speed of mental functioning means that any measures of learning and memory calling for fast reactions or complex information processing are likely to show older people at a disadvantage. It follows that education and training for older people should be designed to minimize this disadvantage. For example, self-paced, distributed learning with small increments in task difficulty and ample knowledge of results is a standard recommendation.

Educational technology can provide ways of optimizing the learning environments of older people. Educational technology deals with the design of the curriculum, with learning objectives, with the content and presentation of information, and with evaluation of the results of training. The problem is to identify those particular features of adult learning and remembering that educational technology can make use of; for example, rehearsal and branching in programmed learning, the use of different stimulus and response modalities.

There are some elementary procedures that can be used to facilitate learning and remembering—mnemonics, self-instructions, problem-solving procedures, checklists. These contribute to the efficient organization of cognitive processes and to a reduction in mental effort.

Disuse of function and tasks which push the individual to the limits of his or her ability are likely to lead to errors and confusion. Procedures designed to facilitate learning and remembering in the elderly must arrange that the level of difficulty of the material is well within the limits of the learner's ability, that the rate of presentation is similarly manageable, that the amount to be learned at any one time does not induce fatigue, and so on. These principles are really no different from those appropriate at younger ages.

The relationship between learning and relearning can be understood in part as a process of transfer of training. If an individual has retained many of the basic principles and elements of a skill or a system of ideas, then transfer to the relearning situation is likely to be considerable, particularly if the conditions and methods used in relearning are identical with the originals. In most instances of relearning in later life, however, the target performance is likely to be somewhat different from the original performance, and the conditions and methods used in relearning are also likely to be different. Even with activities as basic as domestic work, tools and materials change, and so do working methods. Typing, driving, dancing, and craftwork similarly change with the times; so that one may find both positive and negative transfer from the original to the new learning—positive transfer in so far as basic principles and individual elements are the same, negative transfer in so far as the originals are incompatible with the new. In later life, negative transfer is more likely to be noticed and remarked upon because its adverse effects are more noticeable.

There is a considerable literature on the effects of interference on recall and recognition—on proactive and retroactive inhibition, for example. The general finding is, as one might expect, that older subjects become more susceptible to interference. For example, working closer to the limits of their capacity, their performance is more likely to suffer if distractions occur. Older people seem less able to ignore irrelevant (distracting) information. They find it more difficult to switch their attention or to perform two or more mental operations in parallel. It follows, therefore, that the best conditions for learning and remembering for older people are those that minimize the effects of interference—whether from environmental or internal sources. This can be achieved by paying attention to things like task instructions, the layout of materials, procedures for efficient learning, timing, correction of errors, and explicit self-instructions.

An advantage of relearning is that one can usually recall or recognize where the original difficulties lay and how they can be overcome. Also, one has usually profited from later learning experiences so that one is better at learning generally than one was before. Otherwise, relearning is much the same as learning, and is probably best undertaken in the same way, e.g. by distributed (spaced) practice, by early rehearsal, by more frequent rehearsal of more difficult (more easily forgotten) material, by avoidance of errors (close monitoring of performance), by reinforcement of correct responses, by 'chunking', and so on. Repetition without interest, knowledge of results, personal involvement, or meaningfulness is largely a waste of time.

Learning and remembering constitute a complex set of interrelated sequential processes. Information arising in the outside world has to be registered by one or more of the special senses. It has to be held momentarily at least, and either screened out or inhibited, or else rehearsed to prevent its being lost by fading or interference from other materials. Subvocal, subgestural, and imaginal activities are commonly used to retain information in immediate awareness—as, for example, in dialling telephone numbers, and listening to route instructions or messages. Other sorts of information may be assimilated into well-established frames of reference with little or no rehearsal, especially if there is no need to remember certain features of the item (where it came from or the precise form it took)—for example, information about consumer goods or social history. On the other hand, it may be that the time and effort spent assimilating new material into an existing framework of ideas is reflected in the extent to which that material can be remembered. This is the so-called 'levels of processing' theory of memory—Craik (1984).

Information previously acquired is subject to a variety of influences. The physical basis of memory may change and decay through the accumulation of random errors over a period of time. The memory trace may be interfered with by more substantial physiological change—induced by illness, stress, exhaustion, or whatever. The memory trace may be interfered with by other traces competing for the same physical basis.

In addition to simple loss through decay or interference, information previously acquired may be transformed—information may be transposed, distorted, added to, and so on. This comes about because much of the information we acquire is interconnected, and there are strong tendencies to establish consistency of belief and action in the interests of satisfactory adaptation.

A further complication is that information may be retrievable on some occasions but not others. For example, sometimes we can remember a name, sometimes not. Familiarity through recent acts of recall or recognition of an item of information is probably an important factor in the retrievability of that item. Retrievability is also likely to be a function of the importance of the information in relation to the individual's life-history, self-concept, and current pattern of adjustment—information has psychological significance, emotional overtones, and functional utility. Thus, if ageing brings about some disengagement from the mainstream of social life and productive employment many sorts of information will become redundant and fall into disuse.

A decline with age in the physical basis of memory makes it more difficult for new information to be acquired and retained. By contrast, well-established information, i.e. acquired relatively early in life and central to the individual's self-concept and modes of adjustment, should persist relatively unchanged except in conditions of serious mental disturbance, when the individual may well lose his or her sense of time, place, person, and purpose.

In view of the complexities of the processes involved in learning and remembering, especially over long periods of time, it is not surprising that the effects of ageing on the various components have not been determined with any precision. A further obstacle to understanding is that the anatomical and physiological bases of memory are not well understood; so that although we know that the ageing brain suffers a variety of adverse changes, including changes in its biochemistry, it is not at all clear how these changes affect or are related to age changes in learning and remembering. Additionally, if important background factors—health, well-being, and environmental conditions—are adverse they can seriously impair performance through fatigue, disuse, loss of interest, loss of confidence, anxiety, depression, and the like.

In later adult life, especially perhaps in retirement, we may lose some of the self-discipline we needed to manage our working life. We may no longer have the sorts of long-range incentives needed for sustained and concentrated effort in a particular course of action—learning a language or completing some other project, for example. The external sanctions and supports associated with employment or full social engagement may no longer exist. A worsening of physical and mental health may further impair the background conditions that foster effective learning and remembering.

Although the maladies may be clear enough, the remedies are less obvious. The recommended strategy for dealing with these background factors in learning and remembering in later life is to assume that improvements in each of them will increase the likelihood of improvements in performance. Indeed, it could be argued that just as very simple changes in the critical features of a task, such as the size of stimuli or better pacing, may bring about substantial improvements in the performance of older subjects, so simple changes in the critical background factors, such as alleviating a specific symptom or disability, modifying an attitude or communicating more effectively, may remove a barrier to improved performance.

MEMORY FUNCTIONS

Some of the current issues in the study of the effects of ageing on remembering are dealt with by Craik (1984). Traditionally, memory has been conceptualized as a system of stores (sensory, short-term, long-term) together with mechanisms for the registration (encoding), storage, transfer, and retrieval of information. Memory has been seen as closely integrated with other aspects of cognition, for example, language and reasoning, and strong efforts have been made to develop a computational account of cognition and memory, i.e. an account which can be simulated by programming a computer.

The effects of age on remembering vary with the conditions of the task. Typically, both registration and retrieval processes slow down, especially if the performance is not familiar or well-practised. So, for example, retrieving the meaning of a given word is faster and less effortful than retrieving the word for a given meaning. Retrieving a list of items in the reverse order of presentation is slower and more effortful than retrieving the items in the order presented. In general, memory functions are well retained provided the person can employ well-established methods for the retrieval of familiar material, as for example, in the ordinary activities of daily life, where recognition rather than recall is often possible, and where many cues are available to prompt recall. Also, some aspects of a stimulus situation seem to be remembered with relatively little effort, e.g. spatial position, order of occurrence, whereas other aspects have to be attended to more closely, e.g. associated name, relative frequency. A good deal of the apparent reduction in memory in later life is probably attributable to failures at the registration (encoding) stage because of mental slowing, attentional deficits, inappropriate strategies of learning, and so on. However, the retrieval of material well-learned in the first place is not unduly affected by normal ageing.

Experiences of a routine sort are not likely to be well-remembered, although they may contribute to a sort of generic memory for experiences of that sort, e.g. work experiences, daily activities. A salient memory is salient because the experience to which it refers was different in some way from other, more routine, experiences. That is to say, the experience is important, distinctive, unusual.

Although some long-term memories appear to be easily retrieved and stable as items of personal knowledge or experience, other memories have to be reconstructed or searched for. It is not at all clear how we form impressions of our experience of events, although it is clear that such impressions can undergo various changes or fade entirely. Normally, we distinguish between the process of remembering and the process of perception, just as we normally distinguish between dreaming and waking experiences. In some disorders, however, the distinction breaks down. In dementia, for example, a patient may confuse his or her present surroundings and social relationships with those of earlier life.

One example of semi-automatic information processing can be found in playing chess, where a skilled player can recall much more of a 'game pattern' of chess pieces than of a 'random pattern'. Non-players perform about equally well on both types of pattern. Further research by Charness (1981) indicates that when chess players of equal skill are compared, older players are less accurate in their immediate recall of visually displayed chess patterns. After a delay with interference, however, it appears that accuracy is decreased and retrieval time increased equally for young and old. Charness claims that ageing diminishes encoding rather than retrieval of information in short-term visual tasks—the median time required to recall the first chess piece was similar for young and old subjects.

Generalizing to other aspects of life, we can expect experts or professionals in a given area to remember things better than beginners. To the extent that the experience accumulated by older people takes on the character of expertness—in occupational, domestic, or leisure activities—it should result in more effective encoding and therefore more effective retention, recall, and recognition. This should apply to both short-term and long-term memory.

Craik (1984) distinguishes between primary memory and working memory. Primary memory is a matter of forming and reproducing an impression almost immediately without having to modify it in any way. So, for example, one might retain an impression of a face, musical phrase, or sentence momentarily and recognize or reproduce it immediately. Working memory is a matter of retaining an impression whilst carrying out some other mental activity. For example, one might retain an impression of a face or melody whilst trying to put a name to it; or one might have to engage in a completely different task for a time before having to recall or recognize the face or melody. Age appears to have adverse effects on working memory; primary memory is less adversely affected. Craik distinguishes between semantic memory and episodic memory. Semantic memory refers to the general knowledge or factual information available to a person. Episodic memory refers to information about events and circumstances which form part of the person's life-experience, in the sense of referring to a particular occasion (time, place) of occurrence. A relatively new perspective on memory—autobiographical memory—is being developed—see the section 3 entitled 'Autobiographical memory'. Its name implies a close relationship with episodic memory, but semantic memory is involved too because a great deal of information which is relevant to personal identity, the self-concept, and one's life-history knowledge, is not episodic.

According to Craik, the effects of age on semantic and episodic memory depend on the demands of the task. So, for example, simple measures of vocabulary and general knowledge hold up with age, as in the Wechsler Adult Intelligence Scale. Similarly, it is assumed that memory for familiar recent life-events holds up reasonably well. However, when the task is made more difficult, by introducing constraints on time or on the form of a response, then older subjects are likely to do less well than younger subjects.

Research studies following Hasher and Zacks (1979) demonstrate that older people as well as younger people perform less well on tasks that require more 'mental effort' and are less familiar. Tasks which cannot be handled automatically are experienced as more effortful, and require more attention and initiative. The cognitive resources needed to process information appear to decline with age, as indicated by the effects of age on performance on a subsidiary task or tasks in parallel. The effects of age on cognition and memory, however, are far from simple. Variations in the acquisition phase, the sorts of information involved, familiarity, test instructions, subject characteristics, and so on are likely to affect age differences in performance. It is not just that measures of cognition and memory are not robust (insensitive to minor variations in conditions), but rather that cognition and memory functions themselves are context-dependent—see Craik *et al.* (1987).

The memory performance of older subjects can be improved by training and practice. Various strategies, cues, prompts, and 'aides-memoire' can be used to improve recall in the activities of daily living. It is unlikely that such training will have a generalized effect, i.e. lead to improvement in activities not directly related to the training.

A neglected aspect of memory in adult life is that some experiences are difficult to forget, no matter how hard we try to avoid thinking about them. Such salient memories almost certainly plays a formative role in personal identity and adjustment. Consider, for example experiences of parental preference for a sibling, or peer ridicule, or betrayal.

Depth of processing

It is possible to describe learning and remembering in terms of the extent to which information is organized and assimilated by the individual, i.e. in terms of what is called 'depth of processing'. Some of the effects we experience in daily life lie on the fringe of conscious awareness. They may be hardly noticed, and yet be recalled as 'incidental memories' given an appropriate cue for recall. Of course many other, presumably most, experiences of this sort are quickly and completely forgotten. Indeed, a vast amount of personal experience remains lost to voluntary recall, as shown by those occasions when circumstances provide reminders. For example, an acquaintance says, 'Do you remember when . . .'. We have seen that errors, inventions, omissions, and distortions can occur in recall and recognition. Learning and remembering are active processes of assimilation and reconstruction, not passive processes of recording and replaying.

The 'depth of processing' approach is based on the assumption that the extent to which information is assimilated (learned, understood, incorporated into existing knowledge structures) determines its retrievability in conditions of recall or recognition. Thus, an item of information, say the name of a person or a plant, is more likely to be remembered if it is attended to and thought about in relation to some wider context of personal knowledge, such as the person's relationships with other people, or the position that the plant will have in the garden. Simply hearing the name without further consideration of its meaning and implications is likely to lead to promptly forgetting it.

In experimental investigations, different instructions can be used to achieve different 'depths' of processing. For example, one might present a series of faces as stimuli. Under one set of instructions (shallow) the subjects would simply study the faces, under another set of instructions (deep) they would select descriptive terms or identify a similar face belonging to a well-known person. Under these more active conditions of study (deep processing) one would expect the faces to be recognized more readily after an interval of time or subsequent to distraction or interference.

It appears that although deeper processing leads to greater retrievability for both younger and older subjects, older subjects appear to be relatively more impaired than younger subjects under the conditions of deeper processing. This is probably because deeper processing is more difficult, more effortful. Also, younger subjects are more inclined than older subjects to adopt a systematic approach to learning, i.e. a deliberate strategy, even when the experimental instructions do not prompt it.

Even without the benefit of formal training in the processes of learning and remembering, most people behave 'as if' they understood something about the factors affecting learning and remembering. The ability to make use of this sort of knowledge is called 'metamemory'. Thus, using mnemonics, checklists, and reminders illustrates how memory performance can be improved by the exercise of meta-memory. Older subjects seem not to take sufficient account of the extent to which age has diminished their capacity to learn and remember. It is thought that the exercise of 'metamemory' could help compensate for this effect. Thus, older people should take more time, concentrate more, and arrange better conditions for assimilation, rehearsal, recall, and recognition.

Most adults are familiar with the risk of quickly forgetting the name of a person to whom they have been introduced, especially if two or three introductions follow in quick succession. One's awareness of this risk of forgetting is an aspect of 'metamemory' in so far as it tends to condition our behaviour in that kind of situation. For example, we are inclined to ask to have the name repeated, to rehearse the name, to associate the name with a cue (or mediating idea) which will help us to retrieve the name when needed. These techniques are memory strategies.

In another situation, say trying to remember some factual details and the drift of an argument in a scientific report, we become aware that the concepts and methods described are not as familiar as we expected, that they need closer examination and more time to be grasped than we had thought, that they need to be translated into our own words and fitted into our own pre-existing framework of ideas. The processes of metamemory therefore constitute a kind of psychological context within which learning and remembering take place, and involve motivational as well as cognitive functions. Thus, in this second example, our interest gives rise to increased attention, lengthened study time, selection and assimilation of the information, translation into familiar terms, and rehearsal.

Some elderly subjects who perform quite well on laboratory tasks may yet complain about memory failures in everyday life. The complaints are probably complaints about their performance now as compared with the past, rather than about their performance relative to other people. In everyday life, we usually acquire knowledge and skills gradually over long periods of time and in a way that enables us to make a response quickly and accurately. These sorts of performance are usually acquired in a wider, longer, and more complex context than is characteristic of laboratory experiments. The problem is how to investigate this kind of learning and remembering in a systematic way, and how to separate out the more obvious 'age-related' factors, such as health, experience and intelligence, from those which are less obvious; so that, eventually, we can account completely for the observed effects of 'ageing'.

It is possible that the familiar complaint of old people—that their memory is not what it used to be—actually refers to two related changes. First, there is a worsening of memory in the narrow sense—the capacity to record, retain, recognize, and recall. Second, there is a worsening of the psychological context within which memory and other basic functions operate—less awareness of one's powers and limitations, less recognition of the need to mobilize and redirect one's psychological resources, and to adjust one's aspirations, standards, and conditions of performance.

Murphy et al. (1981) showed that whereas younger subjects tended to underestimate their memory span for line drawings older subjects overestimated theirs. Incidentally, Murphy et al. found a substantial age difference in mean score, although age differences in the standard digit-span test are usually negligible. More significantly, they found that younger subjects increased the amount of time spent on learning as the difficulty of the tasks increased, whereas older subjects did not. In a follow-up study they showed that if older subjects were obliged to spend as much time on learning as the younger subjects, then their relative standing on the more difficult tasks was the same as that of the younger subjects. This strategy, i.e. increased obligatory time spent on learning, was superior to training in the strategy of chunking and rehearsal, and both were superior to the strategy of emphasizing accuracy (no time limits imposed).

This finding confirms the familiar but casual observation that older adults tend to underestimate the time they need to spend learning a new skill, e.g. learning a foreign language or learning to drive. Also underestimated, probably, is the rate at which knowledge and skill fall into disuse in adult life if not used or rehearsed.

Thus, although there is really no question but that speed of performance, working memory, and other 'fluid' cognitive capacities normally decline in adult life and old age, yet the above considerations suggest two possibilities. First, awareness of these adverse psychological changes in ourselves is an important factor in enabling us to compensate for them. The maxim 'know thyself' remains good throughout life apparently! Second, behaviour change through self-monitoring and the use of new or modified strategies of adjustment continues to be a sensible way of coping with environmental conditions which are difficult, or impossible in themselves, to modify. Naturally, the complementary strategy is to seek out or create environments suited to one's diminished functional capacities and changed aspirations.

The process by means of which certain mental functions operate in an automatic or semi-automatic mode seems to have its main effect on working memory—on the mechanism which enables sensory and other information to be assimilated in a meaningful and functional way, as in the immediate comprehension of a familiar word or short sentence. Working memory refers to control functions such as selective attention, simple encoding, short-term storage, rehearsal, and retrieval. An unfamiliar difficult task calls for a concentrated and careful performance because little or nothing can be assigned to the automatic mode; only after training and practice can some of the elements of the performance be so assigned, namely those parts which can be simplified, routinized, and managed with little or no call for voluntary effort and close attention.

What we have called 'voluntary effort and close attention' is limited and susceptible to fatigue and distraction. So, for various reasons, we can expect older subjects to be less good at tasks making such demands on performance, as can be seen in tasks calling for divided attention or complex mental operations.

Using these tasks one can demonstrate, in younger subjects, decrements in performance analogous to those ordinarily found in older subjects. It seems likely that the decline with age in incidental learning can be explained in a similar way. Incidental learning occurs when we are able to recall information which was not deliberately attended to or intentionally learned.

Long-term memory

Long-term memories are derived from experiences which have a relatively strong initial impact (because of their personal importance and the emotional reaction they provoke) or from experiences which, for one reason or another, are frequently rehearsed (mentally or behaviourally). Experiences which are highly distinctive, perhaps because of their surprise value or their rarity, are also more likely to be retained as long-term memories. By contrast, experiences which have weak initial impact, little or no personal relevance, provoke no particular feelings, are not rehearsed, or have no distinctive attributes, may be retained in working memory only briefly—for as long as is necessary to deal with the task in hand—and are promptly forgotten when the task has been completed. To the extent that much of our daily behaviour in later life becomes routinized we can expect to pay less attention to ordinary events and therefore to be less able to recall them at a later date.

Long-term episodic memories make up the contents of our self-concept and life-story, and are organized into patterns of meaning or competence called schemata. The behaviour we exhibit when finding our way about, interacting with other people, working at our job, engaging in leisure-time activities such as playing chess, and so on, can be thought of as being organized by, or based on, such schemata. Thus the 'mental map' which one 'consults' in order to move one from one spatial location to another, or in order to give directions to another person, is one sort of schema. 'Plans', 'scripts' and other patterns of meaning or competence enable us to fulfil our social roles, exercise skills of various sorts and generally adapt to our environment—Schank and Abelson (1977). Only in severe conditions, such as senile confusion, would we expect such routinized forms of behaviour to be disturbed.

By the time we reach later life we have normally accumulated a vast store of long-term memories organized in terms of the sorts of schema referred to above. At the same time, we have forgotten many of the specific experiences we have had. Other experiences are retained at varying levels of accessibility and in varying states of organization. Disuse and interference, in other words, will have taken their toll of previous learning and experience.

Not surprisingly, in view of what we know about remembering, it is possible to regenerate a great deal of information, experience, and skill that one has not had access to for a long time. As we have seen, relearning a skill or a system of ideas usually shows some benefit, transfer, or saving, from previous learning. Also, through a process of life-review— systematic reminiscence (with or without the assistance of a counsellor)— we can recover memories which have lain dormant for a long time. The technique is simply that of constructive, detailed association and cueing; so that memories evoke other memories, until quite often they come flooding back with little or no effort. Unfortunately, distortion in remembering may bring about errors even in what seem to be clear recollections. In a situation in which one wishes to recall a particular piece of information (information which one knows one once had), it usually pays off to associate systematically to those other sorts of information to which the required piece is known to be related. So, for example, to help recall the name of a person, we recall associated information in the hope that this will cue or trigger the name.

The processes of acquisition (registration or encoding) can be studied by measuring the amount of time and the number of trials required to learn material to a given level of performance accuracy. Kausler (1982) argues that ageing has little effect on the retention of well-learned material. However, the problem is whether equivalent performance, e.g. three accurate recalls, means the same thing for subjects who take a longer time and more trials than for subjects who take less time and fewer trials to learn. Some of the technicalities in research on long-term learning and remembering in adult life are dealt with by Howe and Hunter (1985, 1986).

One complication is that our imagination operates on the same stores of information as does our memory, so that it is possible to confuse the products of imagination with those of memory. The consequences can be serious if ageing is accompanied by a breakdown in reasoning processes and by loss of inhibitory control over emotions and behaviour. In such circumstances the individual may become thoroughly confused and deluded, as in dementia or paranoia. Another complication is that there are grounds for supposing that certain kinds of experiences, ideas, and feelings are excluded from conscious awareness by inhibitory controls which are themselves outside awareness, but nevertheless give rise to feelings of tension—anxiety, hostility, guilt—which lead to maladjusted behaviour. If the degenerative effects of ageing lead to a weakening of the inhibitory controls, then it is possible that all sorts of ideas, feelings, and desires may emerge to influence behaviour. These ideas, feelings and desires will at first seem to be 'foreign' to the person involved, and to his or her family and friends, and give rise to hostility, sexual or homosexual inclinations, vulgarity, and other distressing forms of behaviour. As the condition deteriorates, the patient loses the feelings of guilt and anxiety for these 'foreign' elements in his or her make-up.

So, whereas previously counselling might have helped to control the undesirable behaviour (by establishing insight and rational forms of control), when the condition has deteriorated, more basic forms of behaviour modification (contingency management) are required.

AUTOBIOGRAPHICAL MEMORY

The phrase 'autobiographical memory' is not well defined. It is therefore helpful to list some of the issues that have been regarded as falling within this broad category of interest. Obviously, oral or written accounts self-presented as autobiographies, life-histories, reminiscences, or life-events are included. Similarly, personal accounts elicited with help from biographers, historians, counsellors, and research psychologists are included. Studies investigating long-term memory as such can be included, but with less confidence, unless the studies are concerned with memories that have some personal significance. For example, I can recall that (know that) Clement Attlee headed the Labour Government in the UK in 1945. But is this personally relevant in the way that my recollection of the first motor vehicle I owned is relevant? Childhood memories (after the age of five years) seem to play an important part in personal identity, giving a sense of continuity through change. Public memories, memories that are shared by a large number of people, as with the example above, can be used to make comparisons between individuals with regard to memory functions. For example: How does recall vary with the length of time that has elapsed since the event? To what extent do people differ in the sorts of events they can recall? How do people retrieve or reconstruct information about events in the distant past? How do people identify 'when', 'how', 'where', 'why', and 'in what order' events occurred?

The importance of autobiographical memory in human ageing can scarcely be exaggerated. The destruction of autobiographical memory through dementia in late life, leading to disorientation for time, place, and person, and to the loss of a sense of personal identity, is a prospect that would frighten anyone. The core of autobiographical memory is knowledge of personal identity, which entails awareness of key elements in one's life-history, existing social relationships and circumstances. Failure to keep track of calendar time is likely to be a sign of breakdown in autobiographical memory in dementia; failure to organize one's activities appropriately given the surrounding circumstances signifies a more serious disorientation for place and activity; finally, loss of self-identity and loss of recognition of previously familiar people marks the virtual extinction of autobiographical memory.

For the majority of old people whose long-term memories are not seriously affected, the increased opportunity for recollection and reflection can provide an important source of emotional satisfaction. For those who are maladjusted, counselling which involves working through autobiographical memories may provide beneficial therapy (Malde, 1988).

One problem in the study of long-term memory is how to verify that what is recalled is recalled correctly, and that the temporal or ordinal position is accurate. For example, I can recall the purchase of my first motor car easily as a fairly distinct set of images, but if I am asked to give a date or say whether it occurred before or after certain other events then I have to think more systematically and try to work out the answer logically. This is the reconstructive aspect of memory. Memories for public events are obviously easier to verify than memories for personal events. However, the distinction between public and personal events is one of degree rather than kind. In other words, some parts of our autobiographical memory are concerned with completely private matters, other parts are shared with one or a few others, other parts still are shared with a much wider public. These distinctions probably correspond with what we have called the personal relevance of memories.

Episodic memory is concerned with particular events or circumstances—for example the memory of first meeting one's future wife/husband. Semantic memory is concerned with meaning and knowledge generally—for example, recalling or knowing how to get from one place to another, or that one has relatives not seen for a long time. Thus one could, if necessary, distinguish between autobiographical knowledge (my height, weight, where I was born) and autobiographical episodes (entering military service, buying a car, meeting my wife).

Some of the research into autobiographical memory is reviewed in Rubin (1986). I draw attention to it for the reasons given above, namely, its importance in relation to personal identity and adjustment in later life. It can be argued that the correspondence of autobiographical memories with the facts is less important than their internal coherence. Internal coherence will certainly maintain a sense of personal identity, but only so long as the person is not confronted with contradictory evidence. Such confrontation may be relatively infrequent, especially in later life, so one could expect a considerable amount of reconstruction to take place in the interests of establishing a coherent self-concept.

The contents of autobiographical memory can be accessed in various ways depending upon the requirements of the situation. For example, in answer to the question 'Do you remember when we first met?', one may experience instant recall, or one may have to reconstruct the occasion by working out the implications of other information available in memory about times, places, persons, circumstances, and events related to the occasion in question. To the extent that such reconstruction takes time and effort we might expect older people to be less good at it than younger people.

Undoubtedly, some periods of life are more interesting or more memorable than others. Hence we should not expect the contents of autobiographical memory to be evenly spread day by day and year by year over the lifespan. On the other hand, it could be argued, public events are fairly evenly spread because of the way the mass media of communication cover the many and varied world events of public interest.

One problem with research using memories of public events is that people differ widely in the extent to which they attend to such events and subsequently rehearse them. Another problem is that such events may be more, or less, psychologically significant for one person as compared with another.

One's recollections from childhood are likely to be of the personal variety with little awareness of events in the wider world. In adult life there is likely to be a shift away from involvement in purely personal matters towards matters of public interest, especially if one is fully engaged in central roles in society. Disengagement releases time and effort for more personal matters. To the extent that adult life becomes routinized, events become less memorable, so that it becomes remarkably difficult to recall what happened or what one was doing, in say 1967 or 1973, unless something distinctive or personally important happened at that time.

Autobiographical memory should not be regarded simply as a collection of items which is added to day by day. It is rather a cognitive system by means of which we map our life-events in the context of a wider knowledge base. We can, as it were, examine sections of the map in some detail and trace a chronology of events. We can, to some extent, redraw the map and adjust the chronology as more information becomes available. Appropriate stimulation, effort, and practice will almost certainly revive memories which have lain dormant for a long time. Counselling should help a person to reorganize his or her life-story, by removing doubts, resolving conflicts, and diminishing guilt and anxiety, and to make a more effective adjustment.

Some areas of autobiographical memory are better organized than others, for various reasons. For example, salient episodes of deep emotional significance are likely to have been the focus of considerable reflection over a long period of time, e.g. episodes involving success or failure, great happiness or unhappiness, danger or excitement. Memories of this sort are likely to become organized into schema, in ways which permit ready access and the production of systematic and detailed accounts of the events in question. Sometimes, such schema become somewhat stereotyped, in the sense that the person tends to mull over the same ideas and to produce near-identical accounts from one occasion to the next, as if the organization of the ideas had become resistant to change. Such stereotyped accounts are by no means confined to the elderly. One can find them in situations where people are called upon repeatedly to give some account of themselves—politicians for example, or people whose personal affairs are being investigated for one reason or another. Frequent rehearsal has the effect of standardizing the account.

People who have kept diaries may experience a contrasting effect, that is of failing to remember, or perhaps not even recognizing, events or experiences to which the diary refers, and of seeming to remember things which can be shown to be not the case. Our inability to recall the details of life-activities in the not-so-distant past means not only that much information is forgotten, but also that much of what goes on in life is not adequately registered (noticed, attended to) in the first place, or perhaps not subsequently rehearsed.

Discussions between people who have shared experience of the same situation sometimes reveal disagreements about what happened or when it happened. Such disagreements may be attributable to differences in interest, attention, and so on, but it seems likely that such differences may also arise as a consequence of the way life-experiences are transformed as they are assimilated into long-term autobiographical memory—Howe and Hunter (1986), Reiser et al. (1985). There are good reasons for believing that such assimilation takes place through selection, deletion, emphasis, de-emphasis, transposition, distortion, and invention. Such assimilation is adaptive, as we have seen, if it results in greater simplicity, coherence, and efficiency of response, but not if it is constantly invalidated by external realities.

Age differences in autobiographical memory can be investigated in a number of ways. One can use a stimulus word or phrase to elicit recall of personal experiences, perhaps in association with a particular year, age, or public event. The test instructions and the nature of the stimulus are likely to be critical factors. For example some aspects of autobiographical memory can be expected to hold up with age, others not. Allowance needs to be made for the cognitive slowing characteristic of later life, for this reduces the number of memories recalled in a given period of time. The analysis of responses to a test of autobiographical memory also presents problems, since the test is likely to elicit different sorts of memories from different subjects. The order of appearance of the memories is likely to be of interest. Content analysis of the responses raises problems of inter-observer reliability.

Another way of investigating age differences in autobiographical memory is to ask subjects to report significant life-events, i.e. formative or stressful or important life-events—see Chapter 2. One can then compare the type and frequency of memories at different periods of life for people of different ages.

If one tests for long-term memory of public events, one can plot the extent to which such recall is reduced through the combined effects of ageing and the passage of time. For example, if subjects at ages 30, 50, and 70 years are tested in 1990 on their memory for public events in 1980, then specific memories would be 10 years old. For public events in 1985, specific memories would be five years old. The question is how ageing affects the recall of events which vary in time-since-acquisition. Alternatively, one could test a given age group for recall of public events in each year from, say, 1975 to 1984, to determine the shape of the curve of forgetting. The problem, however, is that results seem to vary a great deal depending upon the precise conditions of the investigation and the way in which the data are analysed—see Brown *et al.* (1985), Conway (1987), Conway and Bekerian (1987), Rubin (1986).

The availability of cues to recall—either self-generated or provided externally as in reminiscence therapy—can increase the amount of material recalled. Recognition tests provide another way of investigating memory, as in the recognition of famous names, faces, and events.

Various strategies can be used to facilitate the recall of autobiographical and other long-term memories. The type of strategy used depends on the purpose to be served by accessing such memories. Clearly, if speed is not important, then one could prepare written lists and gradually fill in more detail as one memory associates with another. One could use a chart or a list of headings to remind one of the different areas of memory to be accessed. For any item recalled, one could ask questions like, 'What happened before?', 'What else was happening at the time?', 'What happened afterwards?', 'Who was there?', 'What did they do?' and so on. These questions stimulate recall of associated memories.

Some autobiographical memories are spontaneous, in that they occur for no apparent reason in the course of an unrelated activity. Some can be persistently intrusive, as in ruminating about matters which, for some reason, have not been resolved—for example, a broken friendship, a serious mistake, a victimization. In some cases of depression, autobiographical memory seems to be biased towards recall of mood-consonant events—failures, losses, and the like. Treatment to counteract this tendency may have a beneficial effect.

When autobiographical memories are made explicit, as in a written or spoken account, they often take the form of stories or instalments of a story; that is to say, they have a sort of 'story-grammar' in which a plot gives structure and significance to a narrative of events. The central character is usually the person doing the remembering, the circumstances are those that the subject 'seems to remember', the outcome closes off that particular episode. It is this structure that helps the subject to retrieve the details systematically and coherently.

Autobiographical memories can be arranged in an orderly chronological way, as for example in published autobiographies or clinical life-histories. However, this does not mean that they are necessarily accessed according to their chronological order, only that most people have a sense of the chronological order of events in their life (except perhaps for events which occurred closely together). It is sometimes the case that memories are used to establish ordinal and temporal relationships. In other cases the sense of time or sequence is used to retrieve memories. The salience and durability of public memories appears to be affected by the lapse of time, but in rather complex ways—see Rubin (1986, pp. 191–272). Relatively few memories can be retrieved for the first five years of life. Thereafter, there is a fairly steady increase in the amount of material recalled, although the distribution of autobiographical memories across the lifespan seems to vary with the method of investigation used.

Memory can be affected by various sorts of disease and brain damage, as with disorientation for time, place, or person in dementia, confabulation in Korsakoff patients, amnesia in brain injury. The physical effects of normal ageing are such as to bring about a variety of cognitive defects of greater or lesser severity, some of which will adversely affect autobiographical and long-term memory. The familiar complaint, as far as long-term memory is concerned, is being unable to remember names and other information of peripheral interest. But this may be more a matter of initial interest and attention, and subsequent rehearsal, than of retrieval. It is not at all clear how the brain operates in relation to learning and remembering. Some brain injury cases show quite peculiar patterns of long-term memory deficit—see Shallice (1979) and Rubin (1986, pp. 225–52).

The chapter on intelligence considered the tendency for older people to operate at a more literal, concrete level than younger people of a comparable sort. Older people are less able to abstract and generalize. The ability to abstract, classify, and generalize, the ability to make logical inferences and to solve problems involving the use of symbols enables us to learn and remember all sorts of things that would be impossible if we were restricted to simple forms of imagery and association by similarity and contiguity. Where it is necessary to reconstruct a particular system of ideas and experiences, the control processes in recall may well employ the abstract classes and the logical relationships of the system to prompt recall or recognition of the appropriate ideas and experiences. Consider, for example, an old soldier recalling his experiences of a war many years ago. If the framework of his ideas is systematic and logical—

that is to say, if it is orderly in terms of main and subsidiary issues, relationships between people, and sequences of events—then, with a little effort he can organize his particular recollections according to this general framework. If, however, he has lost the ability to operate at an abstract general level, then his recollections will be disorderly—one memory will trigger another but for reasons which are peculiar to the features of the stimulus memory—its affective quality, and coincidental associations. This point reminds us of how difficult it is to deal with psychological processes in isolation from each other. Our ability to learn and remember something depends, to a greater or lesser extent, on our intelligence and other personal qualities.

Wagenaar (1986) studied his own memory for 2402 life-events spread fairly evenly over a six-year period. He systematically recorded selected events in terms of what an event consisted of, who was involved, where it happened, and when it happened. Each event was rated in terms of frequency of occurrence for events of that sort, emotional involvement, and pleasantness. In addition, a critical detail was noted; this was to serve as a criterion for complete recall. The items of information: *who, what, where,* and *when* were treated as variables in cued recall. Special features of the investigation included a one-year pre-test period and a one-year post-test period, and a special record of events that occurred on the same day. Wagenaar attempted to recall events, drawn at random from two one-year and one four-year periods, after being given a cue.

He found, among other things, that overall correctness of recall under these conditions fell by about 15–20% in the first half-year and by decreasingly smaller amounts thereafter. The retention curve can be described mathematically by a simple power function. After a five-year period about 20% accuracy was achieved (assuming 10% accuracy by guessing). Similarly, about 20% of the information recorded could not be retrieved without further help, although this does not mean that no trace whatsoever remained.

Wagenaar argues that the power curve of retention does not describe a property of memory, but is rather an effect of the way adult life is structured. Spontaneous rehearsals and reminders have the effect of strengthening memory traces, especially of autobiographical memories since these are likely to be associated with circumstances and activities which are relatively important and long-lasting (unlike items in a laboratory task).

In trying to date events, Wagenaar reports that errors were about equally divided between overestimates and underestimates of time-since-occurrence, although his Table 3 (p. 237) seems to show a tendency to overestimate the time since more recent events occurred.

As one might expect, Wagenaar found that recall was more effective throughout the retention period for events of the sort that were more infrequent, i.e. more salient. Similarly, events with higher emotional involvement were remembered better. Very pleasant events were remembered well, unpleasant events were less well remembered, at least for a year or two after their occurrence.

The most effective cue for recall was what the event was, i.e. what activity occurred—see also Reiser *et al.* (1985). The cues for person (who) and place (where) were about half as effective. Multiple cues were more effective than single cues (other than time cues). The time cue (when) was almost completely ineffective, suggesting that information about times is encoded and/or retrieved differently from other sorts of information. Perhaps key times or periods are clearly registered and used as markers for inferring the times of other events. See Brown *et al.* (1985) for a study of the dating of events in long-term memory.

We must not neglect the way in which the emotional features of information and experience affect their 'memorability'. Events which are surprising, striking, frightening, enjoyable, and so on, are more distinctive, more clearly registered and more effectively integrated with previous experience. This fact is particularly important because it influences the way we recall our experience in situations calling for judgment and action—see Nisbett and Ross (1980). To the extent that emotional reactions are brought under greater cognitive control in later life, we might expect a reduction in affective learning and remembering, but there seems to be little or no research on this topic.

Spontaneous recall, reminiscence, in later life can be a valuable way in which an individual, with or without the help of a counsellor, can reconstruct his or her life experiences in the interests of effective personal adjustment. When we reflect on the events in our lives and on the things we have learned or experienced, such recollections are imbued with feelings of one sort or another. These feelings signal the value and significance of these events as components in our self-concept and life-history; the stronger the feelings, possibly, the more salient the recollections. As the individual's life develops these emotionally significant—memorable—events constitute focal points in the organization of the individual's life-experiences and 'life-story'.

The process of reconstruction in recall is obvious in reminiscence and life-review in later life. This process affects recall and recognition in a variety of ways. The meaning, the psychological significance, of events may change as the years go by. One realizes one's mistakes and missed opportunities, one learns that events were not what one had supposed; one sees many things differently in the light of experience and new knowledge. Reminiscence and life-review are not peculiar to later life, they are natural processes of reflection and readjustment essential to adaptive behaviour throughout life. However, because of the normal reduction in the scope of behavioural opportunities in later life, the accumulation of experience and the relevance of much of this experience to current behaviour, it is not surprising that reminiscing and life-review are relatively more salient activities then. If the individual, because of physical or environmental limitations, has no pressing problems of adjustment, then more time is likely to be spent in reverie. However, some older people apparently do not spend much time reminiscing; the tendency to reminisce is probably more of a personality characteristic than an age characteristic—see the section entitled 'Reminiscence', p. 241–8.

The process of reconstruction in the recall of experience is by no means entirely rational. Generally speaking our reinterpretations and revaluations are determined to some extent by self-interest, by long-standing beliefs and values, and by the demand characteristics of the current situation. Consequently, it may be difficult for an interviewer to separate out fact from fiction in an older person's account of his or her life-history. The apparent salience and clarity of a recollection is no guarantee of its validity, especially after a long time interval.

Knowledge structures

The notion of an individual 'knowledge structure'—see Reiser *et al.* (1985)—is useful in the study of autobiographical memory because it suggests that both personal knowledge (knowing how and knowing that) and impersonal (general, public) knowledge can be integrated in a common framework. The notion also suggests that this knowledge base can be accessed in various ways and for different purposes. In relating an anecdote from one's personal experience, for example, one accesses words and images, facts and relationships, beliefs and values, feelings and expectations. Some of this information is utilized on other occasions in different contexts.

It is not possible to give a complete account of how knowledge is organized subjectively or how knowledge acquisition, storage, and retrieval operate. It is obvious that we can retrieve some items of information at will and with little or no effort. Other items of information are more difficult to recall or even recognize. Our confidence in our cognitive and memory functions depends upon our continuing ability to remember the information we want at the time when we need it, and to use it effectively. Sometimes the information is very specific, at other times not—for example, I know where the tea-bags are kept, I also know how to review a book—but these are rather different sorts of knowledge.

During adult life we acquire a great deal of knowledge, much of it of ephemeral interest—derived from newspaper reports, television programmes, daily activities. Knowledge which is important in relation to personal adjustment is rehearsed fairly frequently and reinforced when used effectively. Information of little importance will tend to fade through disuse. Consequently, the time and the mental effort required to recall or recognize familiar material is less than that required to recall material which has been referred to less often. It may be necessary to search, in the sense of trying to find clues to the item of information in question— the name of the person, the title of a book, the date of an event. The fact that retrieval sometimes fails at first, and succeeds later—a common experience—suggests that retrieval is more of a problem that storage (retention), at least for information we expect to retain (intentional learning).

Exactly how this information is retained is something of a puzzle. It is likely that different sorts of knowledge are organized in different sorts of ways. For example, a pilot's knowledge of pre-flight checks takes the form of a series of items conveniently organized as a drill which combines rote-reproduction with prompts from the cockpit environment, at least for elementary flying. The pilot's knowledge of meteorology or navigation, however, is a more abstract form of knowledge, although in practice it may require only the application of a small number of rules and procedures. A written examination in meteorology or navigation would call on a much wider range of information and a deeper conceptual understanding. We rely on scripts or drills, procedures, for the organization of our behaviour in the more informal routine activities of daily life. We are not often called upon to explain or justify such behaviour. Consequently, the background information, e.g. the justification for a belief, may fall into disuse and be difficult to retrieve.

In situations where we are trying to remember something from our personal experience, a useful strategy is to focus on the activity—what was I doing? What was going on?—see Reiser et al. (1985), Wagenaar (1986). This seems to help reinstate the script or schema by means of which the experience is represented. In situations where we are trying to access knowledge of a more general sort—say the geographical position of the states in the USA—retrieval is likely to depend on how the information was originally acquired, e.g. casually through visits, newspaper reports, and so on, or more systematically, through school geography lessons.

Labouvie-Vief (1980) argues that whereas younger subjects tend to recall considerable detail and produce accurate summaries of stories, older subjects recall fewer details but more generalities. The nature of these generalities perhaps deserves closer examination.

REMINISCENCE

Reminiscence and autobiographical memory are closely related (Hyland and Ackerman, 1988). Until recently, the natural tendency for older people to talk about their life-experiences tended to be regarded at best as tiresome and at worst as indicative of a worsening psychological condition. This negative attitude was probably the result of confusing ordinary reminiscence with the repetitiveness and mind-wandering associated with failing memory. A contributory cause might have been neglect of the fact that people of all ages reminisce, since reminiscing is simply giving an account of something remembered. Moreover, older people obviously have more experience to be reflected on and talked about.

The word 'reminisce' has a possible emotional tone in that it tends to imply the recall of pleasurable events. That is to say, it implies not so much a brief factual recollection, but rather a more extended account emphasizing one's personal involvement in the events recalled. The possession of mementos—photographs, souvenirs—provides clues as to the matters dwelt on when people reminisce or are absorbed in reverie.

Reminiscence as a normal psychological process must be distinguished from that morbid preoccupation with unpleasant memories sometimes referred to as ruminating, i.e. going over and over the same experiences without altering their psychological significance. This kind of thought-process seems to be indicative of unresolved emotional disturbances. Chapter 7 will argue that secondary reflective adjustments to emotional upsets may be spread over long periods of time, or may never be satisfactorily settled.

Diaries and other written records tend to reflect the observations and interpretations of a small number of relatively detached, literate persons; reminiscence, by contrast, gives access to the experiences of the majority. Coincidentally perhaps, the status of reminiscence has improved as a consequence of the increased interest in oral history—the history of ordinary people's experience of life through historical time.

Closely associated with the notion of reminiscence is the notion of 'life-review'—Butler (1963). Life-review refers to the systematic use of reminiscence in constructing an account of one's life so far. It is well known that memory is an active process of reconstruction, not simply passive recording. Later experiences may significantly alter the interpretation one places on life-events and consequently alter their emotional significance and their long-term behavioural consequences. As we review our personal history we are inclined to impose on it some sort of pattern and consistency, although it is by no means rare for individuals to recognize marked discontinuities in their life, and contradictions (conflicts) in their own psychological make-up.

In late life the prospects for a radical reappraisal of one's personal history become vanishingly small. What is more, one will have had years in which to reflect on and reconsider the formative, critical and culminative experiences that constitute one's psychological life-history. The questions therefore are: 'What psychological functions does reminiscence fulfil in later life?', 'Are these functions different from those of earlier life?' (Thornton and Brotchie, 1987).

It seems reasonable to assume that reminiscence fulfils an adaptive function. In pre-literate societies this would be clearly demonstrable by virtue of the elders constituting a repository of knowledge for the community and being assigned higher status as a consequence. In modern society, however, as the interest in oral history shows, the life-experiences of older people may have *only* historical value to the community at large. The experiences of ordinary people are likely to have much in common, so the historical interest is likely to be satisfied by small-scale representative sampling.

Our knowledge of the processes of personal adjustment tells us that we tend to structure our experience in such a way as to fulfil our aspirations, deal with conflicts and stresses, and achieve consistency in our behaviour and experience—see Maddi (1980). Any life-event which is psychologically significant is associated with a variety of motivations, emotions, and thought processes. But later events have to be assimilated into an evolving system of beliefs, attitudes, values, expectations, and aspirations. In so far as the individual is normal and lives in a relatively stable environment, such internal dispositions and mental states tend to stabilize, to become internally consistent, and to be adaptive.

Reminiscence in the form of internal reverie can fulfil a number of functions: reliving past enjoyments, rethinking what might have been, rehearsing possible future actions, reinterpreting the meaning of events. Reminiscence in the form of talking to or with others can also fulfil a number of functions: abreaction (expressing pent-up emotions); explaining or justifying one's past behaviour; sharing common experiences; asserting a point of view. Reminiscence, like opinion-giving, can fulfil a variety of functions. It can be used to show solidarity or set oneself apart, it can be an outlet for anger or a plea for sympathy, it can be used to entertain or instruct or solve a problem. Reminiscence is central to psychotherapy, since the aim of therapy is to improve the person's adjustment to his or her environment by helping the person to reorganize his or her thoughts, feelings, desires, and actions. It is possible, of course, that the sorts of issues typically dealt with in psychotherapy with younger adults (sex, aggression, social and family relationships) may be somewhat different from those dealt with in older adults (bereavement, social isolation, dependency, loss of interest in life).

Reminiscence seen simply as a process of actively reviewing one's experience of significant life-events then is by no means confined to later life. As a concept in gerontological psychology it provides an important link between juvenile development on the one hand and adult development and ageing on the other, and so helps to make sense of the so-called 'lifespan' approach to psychological processes. The reason for this is that many formative life-events are experienced during the juvenile years and retain a prominent place in the individual's self-concept and subjective life-history. Typical of such events are those associated with family relationships, school, and adolescence. Reminiscence, therefore, has a contribution to make to the 'ontogenesis' of adult behaviour and experience—see Chapter 2.

An interesting aspect of adjustment in late life is that many of the external psychological imperatives of adult life—sex, work, family, status, loyalties—are reduced or removed, and not replaced. Instead, the individual is inclined and encouraged to attend more to matters of personal health and comfort. For a time the older person is, to some extent, free to develop a lifestyle geared to personal predilections. However, the habits of a lifetime, together with the constraints on opportunities and resources, are likely to restrict choice for most people. Reminiscence can be expected to play a part in the way people moving towards retirement (disengagement) revalue their activities and circumstances. Naturally, a reduction in preoccupation with central social activities (employment, parenting) leaves more time available for personal reflection. Reminiscence then becomes a more systematic 'life-review', by means of which (and not for the first time) the individual tries to make sense of his or her life so far and to anticipate life yet to be lived. Social norms, values, and attitudes, and social comparisons (adjusting one's ideas and inclinations in relation to other people's behaviour and circumstances) play a part in this process of revaluation.

The realization that one's further expectation of life is now much reduced, and that one's personal history cannot be rewritten or substantially redirected, has implications for self-appraisal and for personal adjustment in later life. Ideally, old age should be accompanied by a sense of integrity. This means accepting one's past life without undue regret, understanding how and why things happened in the way they did, facing up to the future realistically, and accepting the inevitability of death without fear. This ideal sense of integrity follows the achievement of a sense of 'identity' and of 'generativity' (concern for the younger generation) earlier in adult life.

Unfortunately, human lives are far from perfect—we make mistakes, live to regret them, persist in our ignorance of the real facts, neglect other people's interests, and fail to live up to ideal standards of conduct. It may therefore be quite difficult to achieve the sense of integrity referred to above. This may contribute to feelings of depression in later life. Reminiscence may simply reinforce our misconceptions or sense of moral failure; the contradictions, discontinuities, and unresolved problems in our life may never be fully accepted. In any event, the habit of rational reflection and personal questioning seems to be far from universal, and no doubt some people make little use of reminiscence or life-review, relying instead on a relatively simple or stereotyped view of life, such as might be expressed in religious belief or conventional wisdom.

Reminiscence in the form of rational reflection may be one way of coping with a problem of adjustment, as for example when we reflect on how we have dealt with similar problems in the past or when we recognize how a personal failing may have been responsible for lack of achievement in a particular area. On the other hand, reminiscence may fulfil a defensive function, protecting us from the guilt, anxiety, or anger we would feel if we admitted our faults and mistakes.

Coleman (1986) describes how *avoidance* of reminiscing may also fulfil an adaptive or defensive function in later life. For example, feelings of grief, anger, or guilt evoked by certain memories may be made less disturbing simply by engaging in reminiscence less often, and by becoming more fully engaged in other activities. By contrast, some individuals who have led satisfying lives and are reasonably well adjusted may not need to dwell on the past.

Coleman summarizes the main features of reminiscence and illustrates its psychological functions in late life by presenting, in some detail, a number of case-studies. His main questions are whether reminiscence is an effective way of coping with loss, or justifying one's existence, or enjoying life, or reappraising oneself. He also raises questions about the relative absence of reminiscence on the part of some elderly people—see Table 6.1.

Thus, the tendency of people to reminisce or not is not, in itself, particularly important. What is important is the way the individual deals with past experiences in the context of present circumstances. For example, failure to come to terms with aspects of one's earlier life may result in feelings of anger or depression which interfere with current problems of adjustment. The shock of betrayal by a loved person may inhibit the formation of close attachments later on. Failure to appreciate how one's behaviour was perceived by others, such as family members, may give rise to interpersonal conflicts when such behaviour is criticized later in life.

Coleman (1986) collected large quantities of reminiscence, but this was partly the result of the 'demand characteristics' of the situation—subjects

Table 6.1 The relationship between reminiscence and life satisfaction

	Higher present life satisfaction (morale)	Lower present life satisfaction (morale)
Greater tendency to reminisce	Many pleasant memories compatible with current interests	Many troubled memories interfere with current life or aggravate current difficulties
Lesser tendency to reminisce	Involvement with current interests reduces need for reminiscing	Avoidance of reminiscence because of contrast with present adversity

Note: Coleman (1986) concludes that assistance with the process of life-review has much to offer those people who are dissatisfied with their past life. He offers a four-fold classification of attitudes to reminiscence (p. 37), on which this table is based. Lack of current interests is likely to lead to reminiscence, even when memories are painful. In particular, unsolved problems, unresolved emotions, and incomplete or failed aspirations are likely to intrude.

were encouraged to talk about the things that interested them. Even so, some subjects were reluctant to engage in reminiscing once they had provided life-history information.

To the extent that insight into one's psychological make-up and life-circumstances is necessary for good adjustment, reminiscence in the sense of rational reflection (not just passive reverie) also seems necessary, and is of course made use of in self-analysis and psychotherapy at all ages. This is not to say that 'reminiscence therapy' is always desirable (since it might be counter-productive in some cases), but only that it may be appropriate and should be seriously considered.

The case for supporting the process of reminiscence as a natural process (not simply a useful psychotherapeutic aid) in later life can be made out as follows. First, each individual life has worth, and people should be encouraged and enabled to review it. Second, many lives have much in common, and a sense of community may be strengthened by sharing common life-experiences. Third, reminiscence provides a way of reinterpreting events in the light of historical knowledge, i.e. with the benefit of hindsight.

The precise character and function of reminiscence varies from person to person, and changes as the person progresses through life. For example, we like to remember our achievements, we puzzle over outcomes we do not understand, we remind ourselves not to repeat earlier mistakes, we reassert our own views, blame others, or wonder if we could have been mistaken. These, and other sorts of reflections, form part of a continuing process of appraisal—of oneself, of others, and of the world generally. The extent to which such reflections are egocentric depends in part upon whether the individual is able to share them with other people and get the benefit of their experience and opinions.

Reminiscence seems to go wrong in cases where a person is maladjusted—anxious, depressed, or angry. The person may be preoccupied with events which were stressful—losses, failures, injuries, ill-health, and so on—and be unable to compensate for them by reflecting on happier events or unable to disattend in favour of current interests. In a sense, the psychological condition and the preoccupation reinforce each other.

As one might expect, a person's current state of mind may well affect the sorts of memories recalled, as for example a depressed state giving rise to memories of loss and disappointment. By contrast, anxiety or anger about current problems may, in some cases, go hand-in-hand with satisfaction with earlier life-events.

The general tendency seems to be for people to adapt to their life-circumstances, and to achieve a fairly stable level of life-satisfaction. Hence, expressions of dissatisfaction with one's life as a whole would probably indicate serious maladjustment. Expressions of satisfaction, however, may not stand up to close examination. In cases of this kind we could expect people to avoid reminiscing, or at least to be selective in their recollections. It seems reasonable to suppose that the tendency to reminisce, whether covertly, or overtly in conversation, is a fairly stable personal characteristic along which people differ, and that the tendency is consistent, at least for situations of a given sort, e.g. conversations with old friends, or reviewing family relationships. Generally speaking, one would expect level of satisfaction with the past to be associated with current level of satisfaction, since both are influenced by personal characteristics, such as optimism or anxiety. In addition, current circumstances are likely to be seen as the result, in part, of past circumstances.

Reminiscence seems not to be closely correlated with life-satisfaction or well-being. Its psychological significance lies in the way its presence (or absence) helps to reveal the way people react to circumstances, especially circumstances which have a bearing on their self-appraisal—see Table 6.1.

As one might expect, there are methodological difficulties in the assessment of reminiscence, and especially in the assessment of 'reverie' (silent reminiscing). Questionnaires, interviews, and direct observation of social reminiscing are among the more obvious techniques of investigation. Consequently, the views expressed in this section are at best tentative. A difficulty with research into reminiscence is that one is restricted to volunteer subjects, and even to subjects capable of average to good speech fluency. Moreover, some subjects will not disclose matters of emotional significance, except in an extended therapeutic relationship. Consequently, one is confined to reminiscences which are socially acceptable. A third difficulty is that a subject's reminiscences are selected and adapted, or reconstructed, in accordance with the subject's psychological make-up, so that one cannot easily assess the truth or the importance of what is being said. A fourth difficulty is that often the opinions expressed in reminiscences are relatively simple, stereotyped, or conventional statements picked up from the media or in social exchange. They may or may not fulfil important psychological functions. If they are widely shared among older people, and different from the opinions expressed by other age groups, then one might detect an interesting social psychological function, as for example in relation to the defence of an outmoded value system—see Hazan (1983, 1984). Finally, a sixth difficulty is that of separating out reminiscences from other psychological functions based on personal experience, such as giving advice or offering opinions.

A common feature of reminiscence in late life is making unfavourable comparisons between the way things are now and the way they used to be, and between older and younger generations. This has its counterpart in the social prejudice of younger adults towards their elders. Distancing oneself from changed principles and practices is a way of defending a way of life to which one has been dedicated, and in which one has an emotional investment. It may also reflect a 'sour grapes' attitude and resentment, in the sense of denying the value of benefits enjoyed by the younger generation—shorter working hours, better living conditions, sexual freedom.

Reminiscence seems to be just one factor, and possibly a minor factor at that, affecting an older person's adjustment. It hardly compares with factors such as physical health, financial security, family support. Nevertheless, it is an interesting psychological phenomenon with diagnostic and therapeutic implications.

One possible danger in reminiscence is that it tends to impose a pattern of meaning on events which are essentially unconnected or coincidental. We seem to be reluctant to accept that the life we have led is partly the result of chance events, and yet there is ample evidence of this. Obviously, the important events psychologically ought to be those over which we had some control. Nevertheless, we may be inclined to take the blame for, or feel aggrieved about, adverse events, just as we are inclined to take the credit for, and feel happy about, favourable events. Thus chance events (fate, misfortune) can be written in to our life-history as attributable either to our psychological make-up or to our circumstances. Psychological counselling may be needed to help people rethink their life-story and to make more sensible connections, and to adopt a more realistic perspective.

Failure to construct a meaningful pattern may be disturbing. One's life may be viewed as senseless or worthless. Evidence about reminiscence then becomes useful as an indicator of contradictions and discontinuities in self-experience over the lifespan. It may help, in an individual case, by enabling a counsellor to suggest patterns of meaning not otherwise available to the person concerned. Individuals fortunate enough to have a stable and coherent view of themselves may not feel the need to rehearse and re-examine their own life-history. Some individuals may not attempt to construct a coherent life-story and remain content with a few fragments of personal experience. Written self-appraisals are usually quite short in fact, and few people embark on extended accounts.

One would expect to find a clear connection between reminiscence and the emotional importance of life-events, as in love relationships, comradeship, danger, achievement, and so on. These are the formative, critical, or culminative episodes in a person's life, i.e. the episodes that would figure in a professional biography. Reminiscence provides the 'inside story' of a person's life, even if the story is incomplete and fictional in parts.

MEMORY FAILURES

Among the more common complaints about memory in later life are that one is less able to recall the names of people, and that even faces are not recognized if they appear in an unfamiliar context. Such complaints, however, are made by younger people too, so the memory faults are not age-specific. Also, it may be the case that older people are more sensitive to errors like these, and are more likely to see them as symptoms of a more generalized memory loss. Another, less obvious, type of failure— less obvious perhaps because it is not so readily detected—is that of not keeping track of events over time—as when watching a film, reading a book, taking part in a conversation. The first sign of ageing probably shows up as increased effort as we are pushed closer to the limits of our diminished capacities by the demands of the task; we respond by becoming more selective—and perhaps lose interest if we cannot make sense of what is going on. Eventually, we may withdraw attention altogether and blame the material for being poor, rather than ourselves for not being able to follow it.

Yet another type of memory failure commonly thought of as being typical of older people is absent-mindedness. Forgetting, for example, to switch off lights or electrical appliances, forgetting what one had gone into a room to get, mislaying things, forgetting items of shopping—these are typical instances of absent-mindedness. For the most part such lapses are minor—scarcely noticed in fact—but even a minor lapse in the wrong place at the wrong time can lead to serious consequences—a traffic accident, a fire, a strained relationship. When these minor lapses are studied closely it is possible to identify the factors responsible for them—for example, the running together of two closely related patterns of activity—putting tea in the pot instead of coffee, taking the wrong book back to the library (or to the wrong library!), confusing the identities of two casual acquaintances—see Broadbent *et al.* (1982), Reason (1977).

The remedy for such behavioural lapses is the same as that already indicated—more time and effort spent on planning or learning the required pattern of behaviour, more effective distribution of attention over the activity in order to monitor the critical events, better control of the activity by simplifying the task, making it more distinctive, and eliminating irrelevant distracting elements.

Understanding how we learn and remember is necessary in order to develop general-purpose strategies to reduce memory lapses and to facilitate learning. It is possible to deal with specific regular forms of absent-mindedness in the sorts of ways already indicated: keeping the coffee and the coffee pot separate and distant from the tea and the tea pot, use labelled bookmarkers to identify the library and whether the book is 'in use' or 'due for return', make one's impression of casual acquaintances more distinctive by emphasizing their unique features.

Memory dysfunctions are found in a variety of conditions which adversely affect the brain, and not merely in conditions associated with late life and its disorders. The frontal lobes and the reticular formation appear to be associated with the processes of attention and registration. The frontal lobes and the limbic system appear to be involved in the processes of planning and intention. Of course, the sensory cortex and the motor cortex are necessarily involved in any task involving learning and remembering. The association areas, the hippocampus, the mammillary bodies, the frontal lobes, and the medial thalamus are involved in the processes of analysis and integration, and in relationships with pre-existing neuropsychological states and functions, e.g. long-term memories, attitudes, and coping strategies. Lateralization means that the left and right hemispheres fulfil somewhat different functions in relation, for example, to the processing of verbal and visuospatial information. It follows, therefore, that the effects of normal ageing and the disorders of late life on neuropsychobiological functions are likely to be extremely complicated and obscured by wide differences between individuals.

There are certain kinds of psychopathology in later life which seriously affect learning and remembering, and cognitive functions generally. These conditions may occur before the person would normally be regarded as 'old', i.e. before the normal age of retirement, but they become increasingly common afterwards, so that a substantial proportion of people aged 80 or older suffer from one or more sorts of psychopathology. The most widespread is senile dementia of the Alzheimer type (SDAT); sometimes dementia in late life is referred to as brain failure or chronic brain syndrome (CBS). Dementia is a state of generalized cognitive impairment in which the person is no longer rationally oriented with regard to his or her physical surroundings, the people he or she comes into contact with, or with regard to the passage of time. Patients may, for a while, experience periods of insight and rationality, and not unnaturally get distressed about their condition. As the condition worsens, however, the confusion increases and patients may fail to recognize even close family and friends. Not surprisingly, they forget most of what they had once known or learned. As we have seen, it is possible that patients may lose their sense of personal identity, i.e. not know who they are, their name, address, or personal history. Hence the importance of including 'sense of personal identity' in attempts to maintain patients' orientation to reality.

Next, there is the question of what occasions are thought of as lapses of memory, and the extent to which one's behaviour and the circumstances in which it occurs are arranged to minimize memory lapses. In many situations, for example, one is prevented from forgetting—by spouse, secretary, diary entries, notebooks, calendars, and frequent repetition of behaviour routines. It may be that, in later life, the environment is less supportive of performance, and that standards of performance evaluation are less demanding, consequently errors of memory and failures of planning increase.

Unfortunately, we are inclined to regard memory lapses in later life as inevitable. We may not hold ourselves entirely responsible for such lapses, and so make little effort to improve our memory functions. By contrast, if we do take full responsibility for our actions we may feel anxious and guilty, not realizing the extent to which we have become more liable to such lapses.

It is possible to study the effects of ageing on memory in everyday life. One can construct questionnaires, ask subjects to keep diaries, carry out spot checks, and introduce 'natural' things-to-be-remembered into a subject's ordinary life and test recall or recognition later. Surprisingly few studies of this sort have been carried out, perhaps because of the methodological problem of establishing the sorts of investigative controls necessary to draw reasonable conclusions from naturalistic observations.

There appears to have been little research on memory as it affects actions taken in anticipation of future events. For example, planning a holiday may involve purchasing tickets in advance, getting the car serviced, tidying up the garden, making arrangements with neighbours. In a situation like this we have a mental map or schema which represents the aims and activities of 'going away on holiday'. The more experience we have of going on holiday the more likely it is that we can access such a map or schema, and make use of it in anticipating routine events, such as those mentioned above.

A mental map or schema is a kind of general plan or strategy designed to cope with a situation. Not infrequently, however, the situation that arises is different in some respects from the situation that was anticipated. This gives rise to a need for tactical adjustments to the general strategy; such tactical adjustments are, in effect, exercises in problem-solving. One might expect older people to take the necessary anticipatory actions in dealing with familiar routine situations, provided the complexities and time-pressures are not too demanding. Older people, however, might experience difficulty in anticipating unusual eventualities and in making tactical moves to deal with them when they arise. Consider, for example, the different abilities involved in planning a holiday as compared with coping with an accident whilst on holiday. Good planning consists in catering for eventualities which are reasonably foreseeable. The difficulty for older people comes in planning for situations that they are not familiar with, or situations that they have not 'rehearsed' for a long time. In dementia in late life we find a breakdown in foresight and planning such that the person fails to carry out activities essential to safety, security, and well-being in daily life. Sometimes errors and accidents—the unplanned outcomes of actions—occur because of discrepancies between the mental map and the situation it is supposed to represent, or because one plan gets confused with another, or because elements in the plan are forgotten, transposed or distorted—see Table 6.2. Such errors are commonplace and not restricted to later life—Reason (1977). The issue is how to identify the particular problems that ageing brings as regards foresight and planning and the associated mechanisms in memory, imagination, creative thinking, and problem-solving.

There is evidence that when older people (and young children) are enabled and encouraged to use appropriate strategies of learning and remembering, then their performance tends to improve. The obvious explanation seems to be that older persons sometimes neglect to use the most effective cognitive strategies. This may arise as a consequence of disuse, or it may arise as a consequence of a reduction in the cognitive resources needed to employ such strategies.

Table 6.2 General recommendations for reducing the adverse effects of absent-mindedness in later life. The classification of errors is based on Reason (1977)

Type of error	Possible safeguards against absent-mindedness
Failing to detect error	Arrange prompts and reminders and knowledge of results
Forgetting short-term intentions	Arrange for cues (prompts and reminders) to remain in field of attention
Forgetting what consummatory action to take	Review possible consummatory actions at that point, or return to start of action
Failing to verify transition points in behaviour	Reduce competing claims on attention, i.e. run fewer actions in parallel
Misunderstanding the situation	Ditto
Habit persistence	Establish separate and distinct patterns for 'confusable' actions
Premature onset of action	Allow more time; more serial and fewer parallel actions
Premature completion of action	Allow more time; more serial and fewer parallel actions; better knowledge of results
Insertion of wrong action	Rehearsal of action pattern under conditions of close attention
Omission of correct action	Ditto

Note: these safeguards are important in connection with errors which are frequent or dangerous, or otherwise maladaptive.

Attempts have been made to study the effects of ageing on memory and cognition in everyday life using questionnaire methods—see Broadbent *et al.* (1982) and Martin (1986).

Questionnaire methods of investigation seem to be of limited value in this area. For example, questions like: 'How often do you forget what it was you intended to do?' or 'How often do you find yourself trying to remember a word (or face, or name)?' are based on the assumption that subjects are comparable with regard to their everyday circumstances and activities, that they can remember memory lapses, and estimate their relative frequency (often, sometimes, rarely). In order to justify this assumption one would have to demonstrate that questionnaire items were equally representative and relevant for subjects of different ages. However, even if questionnaire methods are not altogether valid as measures of ability, they may at least reveal the beliefs people have about their cognitive and memory capacities. It seems reasonable to assume that such beliefs affect the associated behaviour.

Since younger people and older people tend to have different interests, lifestyles, and priorities, it is not surprising that their attention is distributed differently across their daily activities and that memory lapses, when they occur, affect them in different ways. One may become aware of a memory lapse spontaneously, but perhaps more often one becomes aware of it because the omission has consequences which serve as reminders. This must be an important aspect of self-awareness as regards cognitive and memory functions, and must play a part in long-term and autobiographical memory. Self-report methods can reveal adult age differences in cognitive and memory performance, but the problem is how to separate out age differences in situational factors (life-circumstances) from the age differences in ability. This seems to be another example of the need to distinguish between performance and competence.

Questionnaire methods are used because of the obvious difficulty of using direct observation and measurement on learning and remembering in daily life. It has been shown that self-reports of personality traits which are regarded by the subject as characteristic of self or consistent across occasions are likely to be more valid than self-reports of traits regarded as less characteristic or less consistent. It may be that the same effect can be shown for self-reports of cognitive and memory performance. For example, I rarely mislay anything but I frequently fail to recall (or register) names. The terms 'rarely' and 'frequently', in this context, imply characteristic or consistent forms of behaviour. According to the above argument, independent observation should confirm this self-report. Unfortunately, this does not overcome the difficulty of establishing that the two self-report statements have the same meaning for different subjects, or that different subjects are equivalent with regard to the number of opportunities they have to 'mislay anything' or 'fail to recall names'.

Guttentag (1985) draws attention to the similarities between memory performance in young children and memory performance in older people. Both groups tend to perform less well than adolescents and younger adults. Part of the reason for this is that young children and older adults make less effective use of rehearsal and of ways of grouping or organizing the material to be remembered. Apparently this deficiency arises not so much from an inability to rehearse and organize material, but rather from a neglect to do so, unless prompted. Similarly younger children and older adults seem to engage in a less thorough semantic processing of the material to be learned, unless prompted. Guttentag sees the deficit in attention in younger children and older adults as responsible for their relatively poorer memory performance. The mental effort necessary to operate effective strategies of learning and remembering is too demanding, so they resort to less effortful but also less effective means of coping with the task. Self-evaluation of performance may also be less effective.

It has been difficult to assess cognitive capacity independently of speed of mental processing. The use of tests without time limits does not necessarily separate one from the other. To the extent that they can be separately assessed they seem to be fairly closely correlated. Tasks involving learning and remembering make demands on cognitive capacity, i.e. the capacity to sustain attention, to attend to a range of stimuli, to hold and process information, to make decisions, to monitor and evaluate performance. A 'difficult' task is one which is close to the limits of the individual's cognitive capacity. It follows that if ageing has the effect of reducing cognitive capacity, then tasks that were easy become more difficult, and tasks that were 'difficult' become impossible. The difficulty of a task is subjectively experienced as mental effort, reflecting the extent to which the individual's cognitive capacity is occupied by the demands of the task. 'Cognitive capacity' can be thought of not as a single function but as a set of interrelated functions. In this case performance might depend not on the average effectiveness of the functions involved but on the effectiveness of the least effective function, i.e. the weakest link in the chain. To some extent cognitive capacity can be distributed, in parallel, across two or more concurrent activities, as in driving, talking, and listening to the radio. In well-practised performances this may not be difficult. However, if the complexity or pace of the task increases and approaches the limits of the person's capacity to cope, then errors are likely. In later life, as performance capabilities decrease, errors are likely to occur in tasks with which the person could previously cope. Experimental tasks calling for divided attention are used to separate out different components of cognition and memory, and to demonstrate the differential effects of normal ageing and pathology. For example, a task which requires subjects to *both* trace a path with a stylus *and* monitor or remember auditory signals will produce interference and poorer performance if subjects are working close to capacity. But depending upon test instructions and other contextual factors, the effects may be selective in so far as they depend on particular cognitive or memory functions, e.g. slower decision processes, shorter auditory span, disrupted rehearsal, less effective performance evaluation, and so on.

In general, then, a reduction with age in cognitive capacity, including a reduction in the range and depth of our attention as well as a reduction in the speed at which we can switch attention and manipulate and transfer information, leads to an increase with age in the difficulty of tasks and so to an increase in mental effort if performance is to be maintained. Those aspects of performance which are relatively automatic and effortless will not be affected to the same extent—Hasher and Zacks (1979).

EXPERIMENTAL STUDIES

It is not necessary to review in detail the experimental investigations that have been carried out in attempts to identify the precise character of normal age changes on the one hand—see Kausler (1982), Poon (1985, 1987)—or of pathological changes in age-related disorders such as dementia on the other. For the most part these investigations have been in the mainstream of research into memory and have employed mainstream methods, e.g. delayed recall, divided attention, interference, together with one or other of the various research designs—cross-sectional, longitudinal, or mixed. There are therefore three sorts of critical evaluation that can be made of such studies. The first has to do with the 'logic' of the investigation, i.e. does the argument make sense? The second has to do with methods and materials, i.e. was this a good way to collect the evidence? The third has to do with research issues peculiar to ageing, namely, are the age comparisons legitimate? Or are the results artefacts of a method which fails to account for or control the many diverse factors that affect performance in later life? Such factors include health, education, sensory acuity, instructions, attitude, and motivation.

Although reduced motivation is rarely an important factor in the experimental study of ageing (because of reliance on volunteer subjects), it may well be important in relation to the way older people react to the opportunities and constraints of daily life. Even in laboratory studies, tasks may push older subjects close to the limits of their patience and interest.

In educational settings, older subjects have to be prepared to devote the necessary time and effort required to master the task. Where possible the task should be broken down into subsidiary tasks to be learned separately, so that a sense of progress towards the final goal of mastering the complete task can be induced. Self-paced, exploratory learning appears to have advantages. The problems of adult learning and industrial training seem set to re-emerge as a consequence of changes in the age structure of western industrial societies.

Selective reminding technique

One general method of investigating memory processes is to present a list of items to be learned (usually words selected according to their frequency or imagery effects) under standardized conditions. The technique of selective reminding involves asking subjects to recall as many items as possible on each of a series of trials; but before each successive trial they are reminded of (presented with) only those items not recalled on the previous trial. The assumptions underlying the selective reminding technique are as follows: (1) that on each trial the subject retains some presented items in short-term memory (STM) and retrieves other items (presented on earlier trials) from long-term memory (LTM); (2) that items may enter LTM and be stored but not be retrievable.

Ober *et al.* (1985) have used the selective reminding technique to compare memory functions in patients with mild and moderate SDAT and normal controls. They also used a 20-minute delayed recall test which showed a loss of 25% for the normal controls, but a loss of 80% for the mildly impaired and 96% for the moderately impaired patients. Their results with the selective reminding technique are best interpreted and summarized in terms of the way subjects attempt to cope with the task, given their limited cognitive capacities, and in terms of the sorts of comparisons one can make with psychometric data obtained in this way. Thus, apart from the question of how well the patients, particularly, understood and followed the test instructions, there is the question of possible experimental artefacts. Ober *et al.* (1985) report that mildly impaired patients concentrated on recalling presented items (neglecting items previously presented); the more severely impaired patients, on the other hand, seemed less able to discriminate between just-presented and previously presented items. This suggests an interesting lead into the study of mental confusion, since the inability to separate out recent from not-so-recent events, and to retain a sense of the consecutive nature and frequency of events, is characteristic of confusion. This aspect of memory failure is different from that which reveals an apparent persistence of remote long-term memories, e.g. childhood events, in parallel with a failure of recent memory in patients with SDAT.

The poorer performance of patients with SDAT on relatively difficult cognitive and memory tasks might also be accounted for in terms of a tendency to deploy their limited attention and intellectual resources in relation to those aspects of the task they feel they can manage, neglecting other aspects. Some types of 'concrete thinking' might be interpreted in this way—the patient cannot understand or remember the formal context and abstract features of a task, and concentrates instead on its more tangible, familiar features. Thus, instead of sorting blocks into categories as instructed, the patient builds with them; instead of working out the logic of an argument, the patient offers a personal opinion.

The component processes in memory are closely interrelated and difficult to disentangle, even without the complications arising from ageing. The question, for example, of whether information of a visual nature is remembered relatively better in later life, i.e. declines less rapidly, than similar information of a verbal nature requires the investigator to construct tasks which are identical except for modality, or at least to use representative samples of verbal and visual tasks of comparable difficulty. Consider, for example, whether a largely diagrammatic account of a set of events is more likely to sustain retention of information than a largely verbal account, assuming both accounts were equally effective and equally difficult as regards initial level of learning at several age levels. It is easy to see that subsequent recall, recognition, and relearning could be affected by a variety of age-related factors and experimental artefacts, e.g. differential effects on lateralization, learning strategies, rehearsal effects, interference, conditions of recall, and so on. Even if these factors can be controlled in experimental conditions, it does not follow that those special conditions bear much resemblance to the real world (although, presumably, they would be of considerable theoretical interest).

PRACTICAL APPLICATIONS

Learning and remembering can be facilitated by organizing information into a systematic frame of reference (schema). It might be thought that mnemonic strategies would enable older people to remember more effectively, but mnemonics are of limited usefulness—suitable perhaps if they are fairly universal and frequently used or rehearsed, but otherwise helpful only as temporary devices for assisting recall until the material is assimilated well into long-term memory and can be recalled with little or no effort, e.g. drills, procedure, lists, and so on, of the sort used in medicine, sport, or industry.

In order to illustrate the diversity of ways in which learning and remembering in late life can be improved, it is worth listing some of the concrete, practical measures that have been suggested, many of which are in widespread use anyway by people of all ages. First of all, ignore or discard irrelevant information, concentrate on the essential or key items in the system of ideas and skills to be acquired. Second, make use of permanent records (lists, diagrams, filing cards, and so on) unless this pushes the demands of the task too close to the limits of one's capacity. Such records serve as useful prompts and reminders, for example with regard to the routine activities of daily or weekly life, shopping, maintenance jobs, household chores, and special occasions, such as Christmas arrangements, or holidays. These files or records should be as short and as simple as possible, i.e. easy to check. Third, make use of the various commercially available aids to planning and self-management—write-on calendars, diaries, year-planners, memo-pads, timers, and alarms (for short-term activities). These are a great improvement on knots in handkerchiefs or objects placed as reminders, and save the effort of having to continually rehearse the proposed course of action. Fourth, eliminate time-wasting activities to make more time for planning, learning and doing the more important things in life. Fifth, simplify and clarify the environment and associated behavioural activities to help achieve the same end. These measures can also be employed to reduce the likelihood of making mistakes. We have seen that even apparently minor lapses and errors can lead to unpleasant consequences. Increase safety precautions by using alarms, checklists, and other drills or procedures. Sixth, cooperate with other people in mutual monitoring of performance— for example with regard to car driving. Seventh, make use of what is known about the psychology of learning and remembering—for example, be prepared to spend the necessary time and effort on the task, make use of cues to retrieval including the powerful effects of environmental context and state-of-mind (state-dependent recall).

SUMMARY

The normal effects of ageing on learning and memory constitute a major area of basic research in behavioural gerontology. Serious cognitive and memory impairment is associated with a number of clinical conditions, for example dementia and focal brain damage.

The neurophysiological basis of learning and memory is not well understood, neither are the relationships between the different functions underlying learning and memory performance. A useful practical assumption is that all learning and memory functions are impaired by ageing to a greater or lesser degree, but that steps can be taken to minimize these effects.

Looked at sequentially, a performance moves from acquisition (registration, encoding, learning), through retention (storage), to retrieval (recall, recognition). The information or skill that is being acquired is liable to the effects of rehearsal or practice on the one hand, or to those of fading or interference on the other. Considerable effort has been devoted to disentangling the effects of ageing on these interrelated memory functions.

It seems likely that some of the cognitive functions underlying learning and remembering are natural or instinctive, or at least acquired and exercised with relatively little effort. These natural abilities can be supplemented by more deliberate, acquired techniques or strategies used in connection with specialized areas of interest, such as mastering academic knowledge, occupational and domestic skills, and leisure activities. These natural and acquired cognitive functions are exercised in circumstances which either facilitate or hinder learning and remembering. Consider, for example, the differential effects of self-pacing versus external pacing, distributed versus massed practice, single versus multiple tasks, and explicit versus implicit structure in the material or skill to be learned. Any psychological analysis of the effects of ageing on learning and remembering must take account of the characteristics of the person, the characteristics of the situation, and possible person–situation interactions. So, for example, older subjects may resort to inefficient procedures because they are easy to use, or fail to make full use of the time available for learning because of a fall in standards of performance evaluation.

In the event that some body of knowledge or degree of skill cannot be reproduced at will, this does not necessarily mean that the memory traces are entirely lost. Faint or incomplete memories may be reinstated if the necessary cues and associations can be made available. Knowledge and skills which are relearned may reveal, through the rate at which relearning takes place, how much of the original learning has been retained. The availability (strength) of a memory is partly a function of time and usage. Older people are likely to have acquired a great deal of knowledge and many sorts of skills which have deteriorated through disuse, interference, and the passage of time. The important point is that such knowledge and skill can often be relearned without much difficulty, provided the underlying cognitive capacities are still adequate. The maintenance or re-establishment of the knowledge and skills needed for independence in the activities of daily living is desirable since it promotes self-esteem and a sense of personal control as well as easing the burden of care on others.

Changes in the age structure of the population and changes in employment opportunities have produced an increase in the need for continuing education (post-professional training, job retraining, pre-retirement education, health education). The effects of ageing on learning and memory need to be taken into account if continuing education is to be fully effective. Much of what we have learned becomes outdated or redundant with the passage of time. The danger here is that old skills and forms of knowledge will hinder the acquisition of new. Much depends on the extent to which the earlier learning transfers positively to, or interferes with, later learning. The tendency is for older people to exercise familiar skills and forms of knowledge in familiar contexts and for younger people to acquire new skills for new contexts, as for example in the use of industrial equipment.

A number of basic concepts have been developed to account for the diverse phenomena of learning and remembering. They include primary or short-term memory, working memory, long-term memory, episodic memory, semantic memory. In addition, basic concepts such as encoding, storage, transfer, and retrieval have been introduced in an attempt to explain how memory works. Ageing seems to bring about several significant changes. A reduction in mental speed has adverse effects on the extent to which information can be effectively processed, i.e. attended to, encoded, rehearsed. A reduction in cognitive capacity has adverse effects on the extent to which attention and mental effort can be allocated according to the demands of the situation. By contrast, well-established forms of knowledge and well-practised skills make it possible for an older, more experienced, person to react quickly and efficiently in familiar situations. Knowledge of how we learn and remember can be used to improve learning and remembering. Such knowledge—metamemory— seems not to be normally used to full advantage in later life.

The study of long-term memory and autobiographical memory is relatively recent, but particularly important in relation to ageing. Autobiographical memory provides the knowledge base for personal identity, and hence for many sorts of interpersonal relationships. Some elements of autobiographical memory are normally rehearsed and updated, but in dementia in late life the system may break down, so that a patient becomes disoriented not only for time and place, but also for person. There is a tendency for memories to fade and change over time, so that what is recalled is more in the nature of a reconstruction of the original experience, rather than a reinstatement of it.

Memories tend to be organized into knowledge structures. Familiarity with a structure makes it easier to retrieve individual items of information. However, experiences which are not distinctive are likely to be forgotten. Some features of an experience are more likely to be remembered than others. Although a few episodes can be dated accurately, and act as time markers, most episodes are difficult to date accurately, and then by reasoning rather than direct recall.

Reminiscence reveals autobiographical memory. Its significance for behavioural gerontology is that ideally elderly individuals have ample time to review the main episodes in their life-history, to make sense of what happened, and to consolidate their sense of personal identity. This is particularly important given the diminishing opportunities to add to the sum total of one's life achievements. In practice, of course, people may not be so fortunate: they may not be able to reconcile themselves to the events in their lives, they may have no opportunity to 'talk things out' with a confidant(e) or counsellor, and the stresses of late life may deny people the opportunity for calm reflection. Reminiscence therapy makes use of the tendency to recall psychologically significant life-events to help the patient to reinterpret those events and to see them from other perspectives, with the result that their meaning and significance are changed in the interests of greater emotional stability and current life-satisfaction. As with other psychological characteristics there are wide differences between individuals in the extent to which they reminisce and in the way reminiscence functions in relation to personal adjustment. Some elderly individuals do not reminisce to any great extent.

The experiences that are thought of as part of long-term memory do not necessarily correspond with the episodes or facts to which they refer. This is because memories tend to be actively reconstructed rather than passively recollected. This presents a difficulty in experimental or life-event research, but this can be overcome to some extent by using public events or recent personal events which can be accurately dated.

As far as practical applications are concerned, the important issue may be not the external validity of personal memories, but their internal coherence and psychological significance. In other words, one may make up a satisfying and effective life-story which contains substantial elements of fiction. The danger is that even in late life we may have to face up to questions and realities which threaten the self-concept we have developed over the years.

Memory failures are popularly regarded as characteristic of the elderly. This partly explains the prominence of memory research in behavioural gerontology. Memory failures, as the name implies, are assumed to be failures of retrieval (recall, recognition), because it is at the retrieval stage that we become aware of a failure. However, the fault may lie less with retrieval than with registration (encoding) and retention (storage). These three basic functions in learning and remembering are closely interrelated, and it is difficult to separate out the effects of ageing on one from the effects of ageing on the others.

Age changes in the brain mechanisms serving learning and memory are likely to be varied and complicated. Although some distinctive memory disturbances can be diagnosed, as in the Korsakoff condition and in dementia of the Alzheimer type, it seems that specific neurological conditions can produce specific memory disabilities in the context of a more general pattern of disease, injury or normal ageing. A reduction in the speed of mental processing and in cognitive capacities generally helps to explain some aspects of normal memory failure.

There is some evidence that learning and memory performance in later life can be improved. This is not altogether surprising when one considers that normally we do not need to operate close to the limits of our cognitive capacities. It seems reasonable to assume that some cognitive functions decline through disuse, and that these same cognitive functions will respond to training and exercise by increasing in efficiency. The problem is to identify which cognitive functions can be retrained, and then to develop acceptable and effective retraining methods. Ideally, one should retrain basic, general-purpose, cognitive functions rather than specific cognitive skills, so as to achieve transfer of training to a wide range of performances—for example, techniques for planning and for the self-evaluation of performance. However, training in specific skills is justifiable if those skills are useful to the elderly in daily life.

Direct methods of observation in the study of memory failures is difficult, and there are limitations and disadvantages in using diaries and questionnaires. Experimental studies of the effects of ageing on learning and remembering have been concerned not so much to establish the overall rate and degree of impairment as to discover the differential effects of ageing on registration, storage, and retrieval processes. This has not been easy because these processes are interconnected, and because ageing is not the only factor affecting learning and remembering. As explained elsewhere, ageing itself is not a causal factor; we need to know what age-related factors actually account for the observed changes in performance. Recently, there has been increased emphasis on experimental studies of the effects of retraining cognitive functions in the elderly. There are many sensible practical steps that older people can take to improve their learning and remembering in the ordinary activities of daily life.

Chapter Seven

Motivation and Emotion

INTRODUCTION AND TERMINOLOGY

The following account offers a description and explanation of motivation and emotion in later adult life and old age. It provides a broad theoretical and conceptual analysis with illustrations from clinical reports, empirical research, and common knowledge. Basic terms are defined as they are introduced, and the main area of interest is considered first independently of ageing. In the absence of substantial evidence in the form of systematic empirical data, suggestions are made about the prospects for psychological research in this area.

In ordinary usage the term *feeling* refers to a mode or quality of awareness, sometimes associated with specific sensory and somatic experiences, as in feeling pain, feeling sick, feeling giddy or faint, feeling hot or cold. A related but somewhat different usage is associated with an awareness of the emotional quality of an experience independent of specific sensory or somatic components, as in feeling lonely, sorry, happy, relaxed, fond, jealous, suspicious, or uncertain. When the term *feeling* is used, or terms referring to feeling, the syntax and context will generally make clear which of these two main categories of awareness is being indicated, although the precise state of mind may be unclear, even to the individual experiencing the feeling.

The term *emotion* does not refer to specific forms of sensory or somatic awareness, and is normally used to refer to a mode or quality of experience which is more intense or disturbed than a feeling. However, the terms *emotion* and *feeling* are to some extent interchangeable in the sense that either form may be used to refer to certain modes or qualities of awareness. Not much is known about the language of feelings and emotions, or the non-verbal aspects of emotional expression, in relation to ageing. Grammatical constraints on the use of words expressing feelings and emotions, however, are of interest to psychologists because they illustrate the extent to which such states of mind are culturally defined and acquired. For general background on feelings and emotions see Denzin (1984), T. D. Kemper (1987), Norman (1984), Strongman (1987), and for a detailed psychological description and theory see Frijda (1986).

Feelings and emotions are *temporary states* of mind and expressive reactions usually evoked by or associated with specific sorts of stimulus conditions related to the individual's motivational concerns. The term *mood*, by contrast, refers to a more enduring state or disposition. It refers to an inclination to experience certain kinds of feelings and emotions rather than others. So, for example, to be in a bad mood is to be disposed to become angry. It may be difficult at times to distinguish between a mood and an emotion, as in depression. A 'moody' person is someone who is inclined, without obvious cause, to shift from a relatively neutral to a depressed or hostile frame of mind. One can think of moods as states of mind in which there is a lowered threshold for the elicitation of certain types of feelings and emotions. A mood may be attributed variously to conditions within the person or to events in the external environment; the individual may be unaware of the factors which induce the mood. Moods as short-lived dispositions or 'states' (of mind) must be distinguished from 'traits', particularly constitutional traits associated with temperament and acquired traits of personality, which are thought to be virtually permanent characteristics.

The term *temperament* has a somewhat old-fashioned look, and is indeed historically associated with the classical division of mankind into four types of humor (sanguine, choleric, melancholic and phlegmatic)— a typology which survives still in modern dress—see Eysenck and Eysenck (1969); see also Eysenck (1987).

The term *sentiment* is useful in relation to feelings and emotions in later life because as the years go by we build up stable, complex, enduring attitudes and values in relation to key features of our environment and personal history—towards ourselves, towards the persons and objects with which we are involved, our possessions, and the events we regard as central to our experience of life. In order to adapt well we need to continually review the systems of feelings and desires that govern our reactions.

The term *motivation* refers to a psychobiological condition in which the individual is oriented towards, and tries to achieve, some kind of fulfilment. Words like want, desire, aim, need, drive, wish, motive, are used to refer to such goal-directed behaviour. Motivational states can be active or dormant, simple or complex; they can be inhibited and redirected. Some motivational states like hunger and thirst are essential to survival. Other motivational states are connected with cultural upbringing and individual life-histories.

There appears to have been little research on age-related changes in motivation. However, given age changes in anatomical and physiological characteristics, in abilities and experience, and in personal circumstances, it seems inevitable that motivation changes throughout adult life. The most obvious examples are changes in sexual motivation, leisure interests, physical effort, and risk. Motivational states are usually accompanied by feelings and emotions, e.g. loving, hating, curiosity, fear.

Feelings and emotions can be said to have 'meanings' in so far as they reflect the interpretations that the individual may make of the situations he or she encounters. Such interpretations require some kind of cognitive appraisal based on beliefs, values, and expectations. Thus anger or sadness are typical affective responses to events which 'mean' that a desire is being frustrated or something treasured has been lost. Feelings and emotions as states of mind often pervade those mental functions referred to as perceiving, wanting, thinking, learning, remembering, and imagining.

A useful way to cope with the fact that mental states are multifaceted, i.e. involve feelings, thoughts, and motives, is to think in terms of 'attitudes'. An *attitude* may be defined as an overall affective, motivational, and cognitive orientation to a situation which predisposes the person to act in certain ways, e.g. being hostile predisposes us to attack, being jealous predisposes us to be watchful and possessive.

So far, we have briefly considered seven related psychological concepts—feeling, emotion, mood, temperament, sentiment, motivation, and attitude. These concepts fall under the general heading of *affect*, an important but poorly understood area of psychology. The effects of ageing on human affective states (and dispositions) have not been studied to anything like the same extent as, say, cognitive functions or sensorimotor performance or basic biomedical processes. The reasons for this will become clearer as we go along.

One of the possibly misleading consequences of the language of human emotions is that it inclines us to think of motives and emotions as simple, discrete, all-or-none states, for example, angry, fearful, pleased, relaxed. However, these states are multifaceted and vary widely for all sorts of reasons; each such experience has a temporal pattern. In short, no two affective states are identical, although they may be similar.

The language we use to describe human emotions also obscures the great complexity of culturally acquired feelings and emotions such as remorse, grief, depression, and jealousy. In these sorts of affective states we find cognitive and learning factors playing a considerable part, in contrast to the simpler emotions which make their appearance early in life, find expression in largely inborn patterns of behaviour, bear a close relationship to the emotions in higher animals, and probably have a more identifiable physiological basis, e.g. fear, anger, pleasure, pain, surprise (startle).

One might suppose that these simpler reactions were relatively fast, brief and involuntary—elicited by specific, concrete situations; and that complex reactions, like remorse, grief, depression, and jealousy were relatively slow, controlled and persistent—elicited by circumstances of a more abstract, general sort. Such a neat distinction, however, is merely a convenient fiction. The distinction depends on the relative balance of biological and cultural determinants, and on the extent to which cognitive factors—memory, thinking, and higher forms of learning—modulate and regulate the affective reaction. Individuals differ widely in their affective characteristics as in all other characteristics.

In spite of the fact that feelings and emotions are familiar in everyday life and readily described in ordinary language, they are *not* self-evident. That is to say, other people's emotional expressions are not always what they seem to be, and individuals may even attach the wrong label to their own feelings and emotions, e.g. confusing depression with anger, or affection with dependency.

We attribute feelings and emotions to ourselves or to other people partly on the basis of our expectations and preconceptions. This may have the effect of leading us to impose an incorrect pattern of meaning on the actual evidence available to us. In any event, it is not usually just a standard facial expression or pattern of behaviour that leads us to believe that a person is angry, anxious, or depressed, but rather an array of behavioural signals distributed over time in a situational context interpreted by means of a complex judgmental process largely outside of awareness.

This brief introduction to the psychology of motivation and emotion has dealt with only the most elementary concepts, and yet we can already begin to see the problems we face in trying to describe and analyse changes in affective states in adult life.

Motivations, emotions, moods, and temperament have a developmental history. They are culturally acquired and closely interlocked with other psychological processes—cognition and perception—in development. It follows that affective reactions later in life will be conditioned, in the general sense of that term, by affective reactions earlier in life. Consider, for example, our feelings about work and leisure activities, our feelings about other people, our emotional reactions to illness, or to other life-events.

Losses with age in sensory and motor capacities must change the person's responsiveness to emotional stimuli, just as losses in the CNS must change the cognitive contents and controls in affective reactions.

As we grow older, our behavioural options are reduced because of restrictions on physiological and psychological functions, and because of reductions in opportunities for action. As we shall see, there are other reasons for supposing that, at later ages, feelings and emotions probably become less complex generally, less intense and of shorter duration. In psychopathological conditions associated with depression or dementia, however, feelings and emotions are likely to become less well-controlled, less well-expressed, less sensitive (i.e. to other people's emotional reactions and behaviour), even though the basic temperament remains recognizably the same. Ageing is likely to increase moderate chronic moods reflecting more clearly the older person's basic temperament, and the effects of stresses and decreased capacities (especially moods of depression, anger, and anxiety).

Some alternative ideas have been put forward by Schulz (1982). Schulz points out that human emotions have been little studied from the developmental perspective of adult life and old age, and that they cannot be properly understood without reference to a variety of disparate disciplines—psychology, biology, sociology, and so on. His review offers a number of conclusions: the intensity of emotions in later life is not reduced; their duration may be longer and their variability less; although there is a general drift towards negative emotions such as depression, anger, and anxiety, older people's expectations and control over events may minimize their effects; since emotional experiences leave psychological traces which influence the character of later experiences, it is not unreasonable to suppose that similarly named emotional reactions to similar events, e.g. disappointment or pleasure in relation to friends' actions, will be different in later life as compared with middle age or early adult life—perhaps by becoming more familiar, i.e. less intense; finally, Schulz concludes that the sorts of circumstances and events which elicit emotions change during the adult lifetime, together with the individuals' expectations and emotional reactivity. Schulz's treatment of the problem provides a useful if tentative map of the area, including a number of suggestions about how this relatively unknown territory might be more thoroughly explored.

In so far as the individual's capacity to cope with his or her environment diminishes with age, especially in late life, because of physical and mental infirmity, or because of deterioration in social and economic circumstances, there will be an increase in the frequency of unsatisfactory life-events, i.e. events likely to evoke feelings of sadness, anxiety, bitterness, and guilt. Chronic states of frustration may take the form of depressive illness or apathy or aggressive self-centredness.

Schulz (1976) and Schulz and Hanusa (1980) report that if older people can be enabled—by behavioural and environmental modification—to achieve greater control over personally important outcomes, then this seems to have the effect, as one would expect, of improving their sense of well-being and reducing their feelings of depression.

It goes almost without saying that some forms of emotional experience are characteristic of different ages (or stages in the lifespan)—separation anxiety, romantic love, parental attachment, occupational stress, certain vicarious enjoyments, bereavement, grief, and so on. A moment's reflection, however, reveals that all we are doing is focusing on specific situational factors, and so perhaps neglecting the basic qualities common to different sorts of experiences. In other words, there are family resemblances between emotional experiences which enable us to distinguish between them or to regard them as similar—depending upon our purpose and the language available to us. Thus the term 'grief' can be used to refer to the emotional reaction to object loss in infancy, to the breaking off of a romantic attachment in early adult life or similar attachments later, to the death of a spouse (or other close companion) in later life, or to the loss of familiar surroundings.

MOTIVATION AND EMOTION

Feelings and emotions are normally associated with motivational processes: drives, desires, appetites, intentions, wishes, and the like. The association is complicated by the ways in which emotional reactions can be shaped by experience, by the inhibitions and controls imposed by higher-level cognitive functions, and by repressions and distortions induced by involuntary (unconscious, non-verbal) psychological defences.

The term *arousal* is used widely in psychology, although not always with the same meaning. It can be roughly translated as the degree of interest or excitement shown by a person in response to a given set of circumstances; it can be operationally defined in terms of physiological measures—skin conductance, EEG, free fatty acids, for example. By definition, strong feelings and emotions are associated with high levels of arousal, at least with regard to fear, anger, and excitement. The association between depression and arousal, however, is less obvious.

Although one might expect the overall effect of ageing to bring about a reduction in the standing level of arousal (and thereby diminish the intensity of emotional expression and experience), yet a contrary view has been that autonomic *over-arousal*, as indicated by free fatty acid (FFA) level, may contribute to the decline in performance on psychologically demanding tasks.

For the purposes of simplicity and convenience, motivational states can be divided into desires and aversions—the former leading to approach behaviour, the latter to avoidance. This simple view, however, has to be modified to take account of cultural learning which may teach that certain natural desires are bad and should be avoided, whereas certain natural aversions must be overcome. This has the effect of generating motivational states which are ambivalent (mixed and conflicting), usually with adverse effects on performance, as in vacillation, anxiety, and remorse.

In situations where the natural desire is culturally acceptable, arousal is normally accompanied by pleasurable anticipation and excitement (hope or acceptance). In the event that the desire is fulfilled, the associated consummatory activity (feeding, sex, companionship) is also pleasurable, i.e. enjoyable, happy, satisfying. Arousal in the event of an aversion is normally accompanied by dislike and discomfort (fear or revulsion). In the event that the aversion can be avoided, the associated consummatory activity (withdrawal, rejection) is also pleasurable, e.g. relief from discomfort. By contrast, if the desire is not fulfilled, i.e. is frustrated, the emotional reactions are unpleasant, e.g. disappointment, anger, depression. The behavioural responses to frustration and stress include persistence in the same line of action, variations in behaviour (problem-solving), or displacement activity. If the aversive situation cannot be dealt with satisfactorily this will provoke anxiety, anger, or disappointment.

Thus the four basic emotional reactions are hope and longing that go with desire, fear or anxiety that go with aversion, satisfaction and relief if the outcome is positive, disappointment and pain, or discomfort if the outcome is negative.

In terms of this simplified framework of behaviour one could expect the effects of ageing to lead to certain consequences. As we have seen, ageing, at least in later life, is accompanied by restrictions in the range of behavioural opportunities, brought about by changes in psychobiological capacities and in the circumstances of later life. Many of these restrictions are restrictions on the fulfilment of desire, e.g. those associated with sex and work. As long as the desires persist and are not adequately fulfilled, we can expect them to engender negative feelings and emotions. However, we tend to adapt to permanent changes in circumstances, so that loss of opportunities for need-fulfilment should lead gradually to a relative decline in the intensity of that need (excluding, of course, biologically essential needs). Also, in time, deterioration and disuse, and concern with more primary needs, can be expected to diminish the strength of secondary desires—sex, ambition, companionship—and to diminish the negative effects of non-fulfilment. Thus the emotional and motivational precursors of action are diminished and finally extinguished.

The effects of cumulative and repeated experience on learning and understanding are likely to lead to a more effective integration of desires and aversions into the overall organization of behaviour. This comes about partly by damping or moderating their intensity through the use of inhibitory controls, displacement and compensatory activities, and habituation. Experience may also have the effect of elaborating and redirecting desires and aversions through cultural norms and rituals— consider, for example, romantic love, national pride, racial prejudice. Much of this learning occurs as a developmental process in the juvenile period and in early adult life, but continues into old age.

When desires and aversions are mixed in relation to the consummatory outcome, age and experience can be expected to lead to a resolution of the conflict one way or the other or to some other kind of stable pattern of adjustment. Thus, for example, ambivalent marital relationships tend to get resolved, as do ambivalent attitudes towards work or towards a type of food. Conflict resolution is basic to human nature—see Maddi (1980). This is not to say that age and experience always have the effect of damping desires and aversions, and of resolving ambivalent attitudes. In some respects emotions and appetites may increase as a function of time and lack of consummation. Later retrospective estimates of the intensity of emotional experiences tend to be lower than earlier estimates.

The feelings and emotions that accompany the onset of desires and aversions and the subsequent goal-directed behaviour are different from those that accompany the consummatory actions. Consummatory experiences connected with basic biological drives are fairly intense and short-lived and have a characteristic sensory or somatic component, e.g. sex, aggression, hunger, thirst, excretion. Consummatory experiences connected with culturally acquired desires are psychologically more complex, in that they signify mastery and achievement, or reinforce the goal-directed behaviour that made them possible. Consider, for example, scientific work, business, home-making, and the arts.

It is likely that adult ageing, whilst bringing about a systematic reduction in biologically based consummations will, for a time at least, until middle age or later, bring about a systematic increase in culturally based satisfactions.

THE EXPRESSION OF AFFECT

Motivation and emotion have an outward and visible expression as well as an inner psychological meaning and physiological basis. For example, our feelings of anger, love, excitement, or depression can be seen in our postures, gestures, facial expressions, and vocalizations. Some of these forms of expressive behaviour are natural in the sense of being unlearned and apparently universal—smiling, crying, for example; others are culturally acquired or elaborated—gestures of hostility, contempt, or affection, for example. Feelings and emotions can be expressed in paralinguistic ways as well as in the actual choice of words and phrases.

Degrees of emotional intensity are likely to be expressed in several ways: more relevant signals, signals of greater amplitude, and signals of longer duration. Under resting or neutral conditions some people can be said to 'look' sad, angry, anxious, and so on. This is because their facial expression and posture exhibit features which typically signal those emotions, e.g. as in sadness—inner corners of eyebrows raised, corners of the mouth drawn downward, lowered head. It would not be surprising to find that older people were more likely to exhibit some set expressions because of a combination of factors—well-established moods, age changes in facial skin and musculature, age changes in posture—see Figure 7.1. The resulting 'expressions', of course, may be quite misleading as clues to mental state. Certain sorts of emotions are obviously more difficult to identify than others, especially in the absence of knowledge of the circumstances surrounding an expression of emotion. Where such knowledge is available, on the other hand, the observer is inclined to attribute an 'appropriate' emotion to the person concerned. Social stereotypes of the elderly as 'sad' or 'bitter' may interfere with judgments of their mood or emotional state.

Any framework for the description and analysis of emotions must include a number of basic concepts such as those adapted from Ekman (1982), Schulz (1982, 1985). Aspects of emotional expression and skill in relation to ageing are reported in Malatesta et al. (1987a, b).

(1) *Affective stimuli.* These are features of the environment (or of the person) whose occurrence tends to be relevant to the person's needs and desires and to elicit emotions of one sort or another fairly promptly.

(2) *Orientation and interpretation.* These are psychophysiological processes which direct the person's interest and attention selectively to the environment (or to aspects of the person's own existence) and impose some pattern of meaning on the events and stimuli perceived. This enables relevant motivational and affective stimuli to instigate a particular sort of emotional response (not necessarily the most appropriate or effective response, because people can easily misinterpret situations).

(3) *Motivational and affective controls.* These are psychophysiological processes which organize and direct patterns of emotional responsiveness.

(4) *Normative social rules.* These are widely accepted social prescriptions for expressing emotions in particular settings, and help to shape an emotional response.

Figure 7.1 Posture, gesture, and facial expression in an institutional setting in later life. Note the increased reliance on close physical proximity, the effects of restricted mobility, sensory loss, and fatigue. Schematic drawings based on photographs of real-life behaviour

(5) *Secondary or reflective adjustments.* These are subsequent reactions by the person to his or her primary (habitual or unthinking) emotional response.

Cultural training enables us to perceive other people's feelings and emotions, and to express our own appropriately. The patterns of behaviour which spontaneously express feelings and emotions can be simulated. That is to say, behaviour which seems to be involuntary and emotionally expressive may be largely instrumental and deliberate. Not only are we obliged to learn how to simulate, we must also learn how to detect simulation in others. Dissembling is characteristically human and probably learned early in life. Dissembling, of course, may not always be reprehensible. A person may hide his or her feelings in order not to embarrass or alarm others, or in order not to impose on their sympathy. The main point, however, is that powerful cognitive controls can be imposed on the experience and expression of feelings and emotions.

Our powers of emotional expression increase, especially during the juvenile period. Subsequently, in adult life it seems likely that we become even better acquainted with the wide diversity of human feelings and emotions simply because it takes time to experience them or to become vicariously acquainted with them. At the same time, experience will usually teach us at least some of the clues that enable us to detect dissembling in others, as well as how to dissemble more effectively ourselves. Emotional expression is one of the more difficult aspects of human behaviour to examine—see Ekman (1982). Feelings and emotions can be expressed in a variety of ways, as we have seen. Many of the components are brief and not at all obvious—for example, a flicker of a smile, an eyebrow flash or a glance, occupy a few milliseconds in a complex changing behaviour pattern.

The effects of ageing on emotionally expressive behaviour must be examined from two points of view: first, the production of such behaviour; second, the perception of such behaviour. One of the normal effects of ageing is to slow down the rate of mental and behavioural processes, another is to restrict the range of a response. Thus we could expect emotional expressions involving components such as brow raise, smile, stare, grimace, to have a delayed onset, slower course, and reduced definition as age increases, especially in later life when the voluntary muscles are weaker and less fully innervated than before. We would expect such expressions to be more difficult for an observer to identify. Emotional expression in adults may be fragmented (some components are present but not others), blended (components from different emotions are present), and miniaturized (the intensity and duration of the expression are reduced).

The involuntary autonomic reactions which are visible to the observer—blushing or pallor, dilatation of the pupils—are probably also less marked in older people, as are associated reactions—pulse rate, perspiration, blood pressure. These associated reactions may not be noticed by an outside observer, but the subject himself or herself may very well be influenced by them (not necessarily consciously) in identifying his or her mental state as embarrassment, jealousy, or anxiety, for example. The overall reduction in the amplitude of these reactions, their slower onset, retarded progress, and shorter duration in later life makes it likely that older people will be less accurate in identifying their own affective states when the contextual factors are obscure.

More often than not, however, we identify our motives and emotions in relation to what is personally appropriate in a given situation, and the accompanying physiological processes may play only a small part. Hence, for most kinds of affective reactions in everyday life the older person's familiarity with and habitual response to situations of emotional significance should enable him or her to respond promptly and effectively. By analogy with the effects of age on mental abilities, therefore, we could contrast 'fluid' affective reactions (indicating the person's basic ability to identify and respond to novel emotional stimuli with new forms of emotional experience and expression) with 'crystallized' affective reactions (indicating the person's ability to identify and respond to routine affective stimuli in established, familiar ways).

The most important aspect of this issue, however, is that the speed, subtlety, and complexity of emotional expression in younger people may be greater than older people can effectively monitor, simply because even moderate or mild cognitive deficit means that they can no longer monitor and process the information fast enough.

An added complication with the institutionalized elderly is that loss of opportunity to exhibit emotional expressions and to interpret emotional expressions in others may lead to disuse of function which further aggravates the losses referred to above.

The reduction in emotional expressiveness on the part of the elderly means that younger people may misunderstand their state of mind. Their 'fixed' expression may be misinterpreted; their relative lack of expression may be mistaken for lack of feeling and emotion. Conversely, the failure of the old person to register the younger person's faster emotional expressions may lead to lack of appreciation. The state is therefore set for mutual misunderstanding between older and younger people—see Bromley (1978). Matters may be made worse by the so-called 'generation gap' which diminishes the mutual ground of life-experiences, common interests, shared values, language, and lifestyle.

THE DETERMINANTS OF EMOTION

Affective behaviour is the result of a variety of causes and conditions which are still poorly understood. Apart from the influence of adult ageing and experience, we can deal with them only in a general way— as contextual factors of indirect interest only. To begin with, there are obviously genetic and constitutional factors which give rise to the anatomical and physiological basis of the individual's temperament, i.e. his or her basic disposition to experience and express feelings, emotions, and moods of a characteristic kind (characteristic in the sense that we tend to attribute them to the person rather than to the environment). In practice, however, we realize that behaviour, whether emotional or not, is always the joint product of stable psychobiological factors (dispositions or traits) within the person, temporary attitudes (states of mind), habits or learned response tendencies, and the surrounding circumstances (stimulus conditions).

Learning, especially social learning, and outside influences like social norms and prescriptions, moderate and elaborate the individual's repertoire of motives and emotional reactions in the course of juvenile development, leading to more finely differentiated reactions, to the inhibition and redirection of socially unacceptable desires and emotions, to the development of cultural feelings far removed from their biological origins but nevertheless imbued with strong affect, e.g. loyalties, aesthetic appreciations, interests.

Adult development and ageing, by definition, sees the continuation of some of these social and developmental processes as well as the diminution or discontinuation of others. For example, family life, employment, and the use of leisure time, provide plenty of scope for the emergence of new motives and emotions and for the further development of pre-existing affective characteristics. At the same time they give rise to changes in and constraints on emotional reactions which may lead, for example, to loss of affection, waning interest, and the replacement of love by hate. It is, however, extremely difficult to define and record this aspect of human life. As we have seen, retrospective accounts of real-life experiences are not necessarily valid, and concurrent accounts interfere with the experiences and expression they try to capture.

Bühler's early work on subjective emotional reactions to events in adult life used numerous case-history records (Bühler and Massarik, 1968). Subsequent research, however, has used standardized, objective methods to quantify stressful life events and their effects; see also Chapter 2.

There seems to be little doubt that for most people later life brings diminishing returns in terms of subjective life-satisfaction. In terms of achievement or most enjoyable events and conditions, youth, early adult life, and early middle age are more rewarding. This alone may explain some part of the increased depression associated with later life, especially if life-events lead individuals to feel that they are losing control over their life because of increasing dependence on others.

That feelings and emotions are reactions which persist, though not without change, to the end of life at first seems unsurprising when we consider the anatomical and physiological basis of feelings and emotions (van Toller, 1979). As we have seen, the ANS and the endocrine system do undergo changes with age, but not in ways that we can easily relate to changes in temperamental characteristics and motivational states. Adverse changes in the CNS might also contribute to mood shifts, decreased control of desires and emotional expression, and changes in the intensity and 'meaning' of emotional experiences.

It would not be surprising to find that the adverse effects of adult ageing on the endocrine system disturbed its normal checks and balances and made it less responsive to the normal demands of psychological adjustment. The normal effects of ageing on the endocrine system, as on other bodily systems, tend to be cumulative, so that even small effects accumulated over many years may eventually reach threshold values which lead to major consequences, as with the menopause and loss of sexual potency. In addition, the effects of ageing include an increased liability to diseases and injuries of many kinds, including those affecting the endocrine system.

In relation to depression, it has been argued that central norepinephrine levels are decreased, whereas in the manic state levels are increased, as indicated for example in catecholamine excretion and response to particular sorts of drug—antidepressants and tranquillizers. Such is the complexity of the whole problem, however, that no firm conclusions can yet be reached regarding the psychopharmacology of psychiatric conditions in later life. This is not to say that there are no effective drug therapies for the many major and minor psychological disorders associated with later life.

Pathological motives and emotions may be a consequence of mental disease, brain damage, or of other deterioration associated with ageing. Thus, schizophrenia and manic-depressive psychoses are accompanied by, indeed partly defined by, disturbances of affect; injuries to certain areas of the brain such as the thalamus may bring about disturbances of affect. Affective disturbances may accompany dementia and cerebral arteriosclerosis. Since ageing is accompanied by an increase in the number of pathologies, it follows that there is an increasing risk of abnormal emotional reactions, apart from any cumulative effects arising from adult experiences within the normal range, disuse of functions, and change in circumstances.

AGE EFFECTS ON THE TIME-COURSE OF AN EMOTION

Emotional reactions have a time-course which can, for convenience, be thought of as having five stages—see Table 7.1. In the first stage there are the initial conditions and affective stimuli which engage the individual's attention—either through their peculiar intensity or through the individual's special sensitivity. In the second stage the individual adopts what seems to be an appropriate attitude or orientation to the stimulus conditions and interprets the meaning of the situation as best he or she can. In between the first and second stages there may take place a brief instinctive or involuntary reaction, as for example in startle

Table 7.1 The time-course of emotion

1.	Onset—initial stimulus
2.	Pattern of meaning
3.	Emotional experience Emotional expression Physiological reactions
4.	Secondary reflective reactions Social conformity
5.	Tertiary, long-term reflective adjustments Self-image

or surprise or alerting. In the third stage a relatively organized pattern or programme of actions takes place, this is normally goal-directed and emotionally expressive. Internally, motivational and affective processes may be inhibited or otherwise regulated. Thus an outburst of anger or a controlled expression of pride have both external manifestations and internal indications. In the fourth stage internalized normative rules (socially prescribed and acquired through cultural learning) and secondary reflective adjustments contribute to the overall control and manner of expression of the emotional reaction to the immediate situation. Finally, in the fifth stage, tertiary reflective adjustments, occupying seconds or minutes or recurring at intervals weeks or months later, exert assimilatory and accommodatory effects in an attempt on the part of the individual to learn from the experience and to come to terms with it.

Ageing affects each stage of the time-course of an emotion. First, older individuals have poorer sensory and cognitive capacities, so they are likely to be slower and less able to detect the sorts of conditions and stimuli which, if they could, would lead them to react emotionally. In other words, because of failing eyesight, hearing, attention, and memory, they miss some of the briefer and more subtle cues that would trigger an emotional reaction in a younger person. This is not to say that older people do not have certain sensitivities which make them more liable to emotional reactions than younger people, e.g. lowered thresholds for anxiety regarding health and personal security.

Second, the ability of older people to process information is reduced in that they are mentally slower and less able to deal with complex, abstract, and unfamiliar situations. Thus, their initial reaction to emotionally provoking stimulus conditions, i.e. their initial attitude, is likely to be slower and based on those features of the situation that are familiar, concrete, and comprehensible, rather than on those features which are critical to understanding and truly representative of the actual situation.

If this is the case, then their initial orientation to, and interpretation of, the situation may be inaccurate and maladaptive—as for example in reacting negatively to a new fashion in clothing or to relocation, or misinterpreting another person's actions through false assumptions.

Third, the cumulative effects of ageing on the ANS and the endocrine system will have altered to a greater or lesser extent the physiological basis of feelings, emotions, moods and temperament—see Frolkis (1977). In addition, the cumulative effects of ageing on the CNS will have altered the cognitive controls and programmes governing the organization of emotional expression and experience. The loss of inhibitory controls is likely to be the most obvious effect; less obvious perhaps will be the flattening of affect produced by gradual cumulative loss in ANS/endocrine responsiveness and by familiarity. Any loss of central control will lead to somewhat unpredictable shifts in emotional reaction. Reductions in psychophysiological 'reserves' will lead to persistent (chronic) low levels of negative affect because of the associated increase in stress.

Fourth, in relation to the normative social rules which govern emotional expression, two contrasting effects of ageing may be observed. On the one hand, the older person's internalized rules may be obsolete in relation to the changed fashion of the times, as for example in the use of bad language or violence or deference. On the other hand, the same rules govern an older person's interpretation of the emotional behaviour of other people; so he or she, unaware or forgetful of the changes in social fashion, misinterprets that behaviour—judging people to be more aggressive, vulgar, or impudent than they really are.

To put the matter another way, older persons' frames of reference for judging emotional reactions, their own and other people's, are built up gradually during the juvenile period and early adult life; these frames of reference may become outmoded by cultural changes, including changes in social relationships, changes in norms and rules, such as those associated with gender and race, with the democratization of society, and with economic and technological changes. The effect of the increasing obsolescence of the older adult's internalized social norms is to engender what is called a 'generation gap', unless the older adult, through association with younger people and through a continuing interest in current affairs, is able to accommodate his or her ideas and sentiments to the changing fashions of the times. The 'generation gap' represents a difference in beliefs, values, sentiments, and standards of behaviour between people in the same community separated by substantial differences in age and life experience. The emotional investment that older people have in certain cultural forms—political structures, religion, social segregation, standards of dress and behaviour—may not be shared by younger people. This may lead to misunderstandings and conflicts because of the failure of each 'generation' to appreciate the other's point of view—see Bengston and Black (1973).

Consideration of social norms and expectations for the elderly leads one to suppose that he or she shares with the rest of society the relatively high valuation put on activity, expressiveness, and optimism—youth-oriented values basically. The contrasting values of reflection, quiescence, and realism also are acknowledged as appropriate, but as solitary, rather than communal, activities. These latter values and forms of emotional expression sometimes lead to a certain uneasiness on the part of observers, who feel more secure in the presence of the dominant social values. On the other hand, attempts by older people to conform to age-inappropriate norms and expectations can sometimes lead to behaviour which verges on the absurd. One of the more important tasks in applied social and behavioural gerontology is to identify, develop, and foster age-appropriate forms of behaviour for older people, whose role in present-day society is decidedly ambiguous.

Fifth, the effect of ageing on those secondary reflective adjustments which occur in the fourth stage of the time-course of an emotion is probably to diminish their importance as modifiers of behaviour. With accumulating experience of life the individual normally makes smaller incremental adjustments to his or her interpretation of and reaction to emotionally significant events. In time, therefore, the individual should establish fairly stable emotional reactions to recurrent situations, and should have little cause to rethink and modify his or her behaviour. There is some risk, perhaps, that emotional reactions will become ultra-stable (over-crystallized), in the sense that the person is insensitive to the maladaptive nature of an emotional reaction or incapable of modifying a lifelong emotional habit. Also, the older adult's self-concept and lifestyle are likely to be ultra-stable and resistant to the readjustments called for by changes in the person and the environment. It is a common experience of older people that the 'felt-self' is young relative to the bodily and social self.

Figure 7.2 summarises the conceptual framework within which the effects of ageing are discussed.

SEVEN ASPECTS OF EMOTIONAL ADJUSTMENT IN LATER LIFE

In this section we consider some of the basic problems of emotional adjustment that can be expected as part of the normal course of later life. The problems are listed in Table 7.2. Butler and Lewis (1982), Malatesta and Izard (1984), and Sheehy (1976) provide further sources of information.

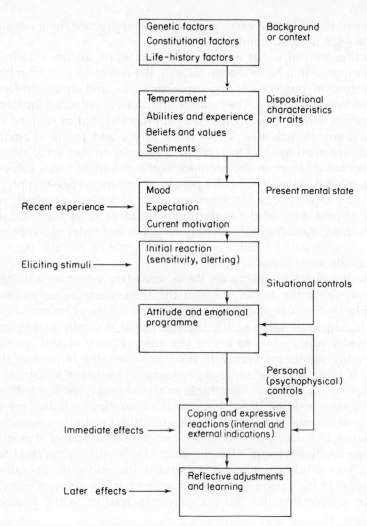

Figure 7.2 A conceptual framework for the study of affect in later life

The reappearance of basic reactions

The middle stage of adult life is normally thought of as fairly stable; and many individuals experience relatively few occasions on which a significant emotional reaction is evoked. Those that are evoked tend to be culturally elaborated and subject to considerable social and personal controls. With the onset of old age, however, the person becomes incapable of carrying out the ordinary activities of daily living without

Table 7.2 Further adverse effects of ageing on emotional adjustment

1. Reappearance of basic emotional reactions
2. Diminished coping
3. Diminished emotional controls
4. Age-related stresses
5. Maladaptive temperaments
6. Maladaptive sentiments
7. Emotional exhaustion (shock)

support from others, and becomes prey to the many maladies of later life. The individual experiences increasing numbers of physical and psychological stresses, some of them severe—physical disease and injury, bereavement, insecurity, relocation, social isolation, dying. Such stresses can be expected to elicit feelings and emotions at a level of intensity which the individual has not experienced for many years—pain, grief, fear, loneliness, anger. The reappearance of such basic reactions may come as something of a shock, with the individual unprepared for their intensity, and perhaps unable to cope effectively for the reasons referred to in earlier sections.

Among the more obvious forms of help for older people with emotional problems are: preparation through education and counselling; full and repeated explanations and guidance during the period of stress; social support, preferably from familiar trusted care-givers; and management of all the contextual factors—health, welfare, housing, and so on—that contribute to well-being.

Diminished coping

The process of adjustment in later life is partly that of coping with the irreversible effects of ageing, disability, and disease. It is also partly that of selecting and modifying the environments to which one has to adjust— the physical environments as well as the social and institutional environments. Perhaps because of people's optimism, or unwillingness to face up to realities, or because of the inadequacies of our health, education, and welfare provisions for old age, there is often a gap between the functional competence of the older person and the demands arising from their environments. The typical outcome is that of diminished coping—such as reduced mobility in relation to distance and stairs;

accidents associated with poorer vision, hearing, and balance; self-neglect through ignorance and poverty; and strained or broken social relationships because of unbalanced costs and benefits or disturbances in emotional adjustment.

The diminished coping of older people may lead to increased frustration and failure with regard to ordinary needs and desires, giving rise to associated negative feelings and emotions—anger, resentment, disappointment, anxiety, unhappiness. It would not be surprising, therefore, to find that old age was accompanied by low chronic levels of anxiety and depression reflecting persisting stresses to which the person has partly habituated but nevertheless continues to anticipate in the interests of self-protection—consider, for example, moderate hypochondriasis, fear of strangers or crime, excessive dependence, worry over money.

The emphasis so far in this section has been on the negative aspects of feelings and emotions in later life, for the simple reason that these are the more obvious and troublesome problems that call for investigation and intervention. The positive aspects are dealt with on pp. 302–6.

Diminished emotional controls

The loss of normal control over emotional expression can be observed in certain pathological conditions in later life—in dementia, late paraphrenia, and cerebral arteriosclerosis. The consequential disturbances in behaviour present serious problems of behavioural management. One possibility is that this is a consequence of adverse changes in the ANS and endocrine system which cannot be handled by the normal cortical controls. Another possibility is that the normal cortical and subcortical controls have been weakened or destroyed because of the cumulative and selective loss of neurons arising from disease, injury, and 'normal' ageing. Some combination of these two possibilities might occur.

It seems reasonable to suppose that 'normal' ageing, even in the absence of disability or disease, is accompanied by the same sorts of effects but to a much lesser extent. If so, then ignoring adverse changes in sensory and perceptual processes, we could expect thresholds for the elicitation of certain emotional reactions to be lower in later life; the reactions themselves would be simpler, more basic; their after-effects would be shorter; and there would be less resort to secondary reflective adjustments. The pattern of emotional reactions would depend to some extent on the nature, size, and location of the diffuse and focal damage to the CNS, the ANS, and the endocrine system.

Age-related stresses

I referred above to the ways in which diminished coping in later life would tend to elicit negative feelings and emotions—the same sorts of negative reactions experienced earlier in life when we failed or were frustrated. In addition to the stresses that are common to most age groups, however, there are stresses which are more characteristic of later life—retirement, disability, bereavement, isolation, general infirmity, loss of psychological capacities, insecurity. Unlike the younger person, the older person does not have the same ability or opportunity to escape from or to compensate for these unwanted circumstances. The overall effect of these age-related stresses is to aggravate the negative feelings and emotions already referred to.

A contrasting effect, however, may come about because of reductions in responsibilities and demands placed on older people. To the extent that such responsibilities and demands are self-imposed, it will be up to the older person himself or herself to weigh up their advantages and disadvantages and to make sensible and realistic adjustments in lifestyle. The process of disengagement is a sort of mutual readjustment between the person and society, the success of which is reflected in the emotional adjustment of the individual person (degree of satisfaction, morale, well-being, and so on).

It has been argued that the stresses of later adult life are greater than the stresses of earlier adult life, so we can expect older people to exhibit more anxiety. However, it is not at all clear that late-life stresses as such are greater than those of earlier adult life, even when the events constituting the stress seem to correspond, e.g. loss of spouse, physical illness, financial loss, interpersonal conflict. The stress experienced is perhaps more a function of the older person's reduced physical and psychological resources. Many life-stresses are closely associated with a particular age period, e.g. the menopause, retirement, first marriage, the onset of parenthood, departure of the last child, certain age-related physical disorders, bereavement, and dying; so it is difficult to compare emotional reactions to these sorts of stresses with those that are less age-specific. Also, age-related life-stresses can be anticipated and prepared for to some extent as normal life-events, and the individual can often 'share' his or her experience with others in the same age or occupational group, e.g. marital and family problems, widowhood, redundancy. Life-events which are unexpected for one's age or social position are likely to be more stressful than they would otherwise be, if only because, being rare and unexpected, they are less well prepared for and less easily shared with others.

As life goes on, and individuals are exposed to events of various sorts, their experiences must come to stand in some order of importance or salience. The emotional intensity of an experience must be a major determinant of its lasting psychological significance. Thus, although the intensity of the emotional experience itself will fade with time, its psychological significance relative to other emotional experiences will gradually become more firmly established. In this way the individual structures his or her life experiences and may be influenced by them when responding to current problems of adjustment. In the process of reminiscence and life-review—see Chapter 6—the individual identifies and integrates these salient, psychologically significant life-events and the experiences associated with them. The process, of course, is not necessarily one of passive recollection but rather of active reconstruction; nevertheless, it seems likely that the degree of affect experienced at the time will be one main determinant of the availability of a memory—see Nisbett and Ross (1980).

Maladaptive temperaments and personality types

It is obvious that some varieties of temperament are well-suited to the adjustments people try to make to their environments, whereas others are ill-suited—otherwise it would be even more difficult than it is to explain why some people succeed whereas others fail, why some people enjoy life whereas others suffer psychologically.

Unfortunately, it is not easy to categorize human beings into distinct temperamental 'strains' or 'types'. Attempts have been made to devise theoretical schemes which indicate some of the possible varieties, based on data from young adults. Since we know all too little about the effects of ageing on temperament, we cannot say whether or not the typologies so far developed would apply equally well to older people.

A modern typology of temperament with historical roots in Greek and Roman medicine is shown in Figure 7.3. One can, without too much difficulty, think of individual cases who exemplify one or other of the four categories very well. One can also think of cases which do not seem to fit any one category, or cut across two adjacent categories. Nevertheless, we need some kind of conceptual framework to deal in an orderly and systematic way with the feelings and emotions of later life. The scheme illustrated in Figure 7.3. suggests that the temperament best suited to adjustment in later life is the same as that in earlier life, i.e. an emotional disposition which is stable (not given to wide fluctuations in mood or to inappropriate reactions). Individuals whose circumstances generate demands for social interaction will presumably be better off with an

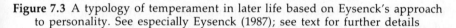

Unstable (neurotic)

Melancholic

Predisposed to strong
negative affect: anxious,
serious, unhappy,
suspicious

Choleric

Predisposed to strong
positive and negative
affect: egocentric,
active, excitable,
histrionic, deviant

Introverted ———————————————— Extraverted

Predisposed to weak
positive and negative
affect: reasonable,
controlled, calm,
persistent

Predisposed to strong
positive affect:
hopeful, easygoing,
sociable, contented

Phlegmatic

Sanguine

Stable (normal)

Figure 7.3 A typology of temperament in later life based on Eysenck's approach to personality. See especially Eysenck (1987); see text for further details

extroverted nature. Individuals without such demands will be better off with an introverted nature. In between these extremes, some fusion of introvert and extrovert characteristics would be appropriate.

In later life, circumstances change somewhat unpredictably; and such is the range of differences between individuals that it is impossible to predict with any accuracy how well-suited temperamentally the individual will be to his or her circumstances in later life. To some extent, individuals choose the environments they wish to operate in, and no doubt temperamental qualities play an important part in determining what sorts of environment are sought after or avoided. Hence, given reasonable choice and control over their lifestyles, we would expect older people to move into the sorts of environment, and engage in the sorts of activities, best suited to their temperaments and abilities—see Quattrochitubin and Jason (1983).

What happens when older people are unable to find a suitable niche? Presumably they become dissatisfied and frustrated and react accordingly. In due course, if their emotional reactions are unsuccessful in dealing with the environment, then experience, habituation, and secondary reflective adjustments will have the effect of moderating their depression, anger, and fear. There could be a shift from an acute level of emotional reaction (in response to the immediate situation) to a low chronic level (largely independent of circumstances). In other words, we usually learn to live with environments we cannot change, but at some continuing cost.

If this analysis is correct we could expect motivation and emotion in later life to appear more unstable (neurotic), not because of any basic change in temperament (emotional disposition) but because older people are less able to meet the demands imposed on them by their environments (unless these demands can be reduced). Furthermore, because of the diminution in abilities, in power and resources of other kinds, and in their social value to others, older people are less able to utilize active outgoing forms of emotional expression in seeking to achieve their ends. That is to say, exhibitions of extreme anger, hilarity, recklessness, agitation, self-injury, independence, and expressions of a 'choleric' (unstable, extroverted) temperament are not as convincing or as effective as they were earlier in life, because the older person can no longer follow through, and other people know this.

Another side to this issue is the cultural expectation that older people should be emotionally less intense and less expressive than younger people. This almost certainly imposes a real constraint. Displays of emotion in the elderly therefore will often be met with only a semblance of appreciation and compliance—this is known as 'humouring'.

This leaves 'melancholic' feelings and emotions as the ones most likely to be experienced and expressed in later life. Again, not necessarily because the emotional disposition changes, but because these feelings express the typical reactions of many people to the difficulties of later life, and fit in with social expectations.

Within the so-called 'unstable' categories of temperament, two types of emotional reaction can be picked out for special mention in relation to old age. The first is social assertiveness, i.e. aggressiveness, demandingness, and selfishness, which can be effective in situations where competition for scarce resources prevails—for attention, care, seating space, and other goods and services. The second is anxiety, at a low or moderate level, which keeps the individual alert to hazards and threats to well-being—ill-health, insecurity, isolation. Hostility, demandingness, and anxiety, provided they are not excessive, can thus contribute to self-interest in later life, especially where social support is in short supply.

There have been several attempts to devise typologies of personality and adjustment in later life, the best-known of which are those of Reichard et al. (1962) and Neugarten et al. in Neugarten (1968); see also Gaber (1983). The value of a typology is that it provides a useful administrative device for assessment and treatment in relation to the provision of health and welfare resources. It avoids, at the one extreme, the sort of blanket or block treatment that fails to distinguish properly between individuals and, at the other extreme, the costly forms of individualized assessment and treatment that cannot be applied to more than a small proportion of the elderly—the wealthy, or those fortunate enough to benefit from the resources of an exceptionally well-endowed local facility.

If we now list a number of distinguishable types of personality (or, better, strategies of adjustment) in late life, we can see their likely relationship with the sorts of temperamental dispositions illustrated in Figure 7.3:

(1) The *mature/constructive* type is basically stable, and inclined towards phlegmatic characteristics in that he or she is realistic, patient, and determined to maximize self-help.
(2) The *passive/dependent* type is also basically stable, but inclined towards sanguine characteristics in that he or she is more optimistic, satisfied, and looks more to others for support.
(3) The *selfish/assertive* type is slightly unstable and extroverted (choleric)—active and dominant in a self-seeking way, which may be advantageous in some sorts of environment.
(4) The *angry/hostile* type is much more unstable and extroverted (choleric) in that he or she has failed to come to terms with the adverse changes of later life. Such a person is likely to blame others, to be resentful, and to show poor emotional control.
(5) The *armoured/defensive* type is introverted and not as stable as the mature/constructive type. The main strategy of adjustment is that of withdrawal, denial and self-protection rather than selfish-assertion.
(6) The *pessimistic/self-hating* type is even more introverted and unstable (melancholic), given to depression, self-blame and social withdrawal.
(7) The *apathetic/exhausted* or *disorganized* type represents an extreme sort of 'adaptation' to persistent lack of control in adverse conditions and no-solution situations, analogous in a way to 'shock' or 'freezing' or to random efforts to escape. It seems reasonable to suppose that persons exhibiting such strategies of adjustment are using a different sort of mechanism for coping with negative affect—see 'Emotional exhaustion', below.

Self-reports suggest that older subjects use much the same sorts of coping mechanisms as younger subjects, except that they are selected 'survivors', face different sorts of stress, and may perhaps exhibit less hostility and escapist phantasy.

Maladaptive sentiments

We have defined a sentiment as a complex, enduring system of ideas and feelings about some object, person, event, or circumstances or about some aspect of the self—one's appearance, status, or achievements. The function of sentiments is to provide stability and consistency in the long-term organization of behaviour. Sentiments reflect, in a sense, the psychological values which inform the individual of the personal importance of the issues being faced. Sentiments develop throughout life and are affected, as we have seen, by life-history events, temperamental qualities, social norms, and no doubt many other factors. The problem then is: what happens when a long-standing sentiment has outlived its usefulness, or needs to be modified in the interests of realistic adjustment because of changed circumstances?

Sentiments can endure and give satisfaction even when the things they refer to no longer exist. That is to say, one can maintain an attitude towards and valuation of something in memory—a former friend, some personal accomplishment or failure, a political event, a bygone fashion. Such attitudinal memories are an important part of one's psychological make-up—the sorts of content found in reminiscence, life-history reports, biographical and autobiographical writings. Sentiments, however, can be maladaptive. They may hinder or prevent the person from establishing new and more rewarding patterns of behaviour—as for example being unwilling to move from a treasured, familiar home that has become quite inappropriate to the older person's reduced circumstances and abilities. A deep sentimental attachment to particular people, to daily routines, to former lifestyles, may hinder the formation of new social relationships, new activities of daily living, and new sources of satisfaction.

Sentiments, in a way, function as psychological capital or ballast accumulated over many years, so it is not surprising that in helping to organize and stabilize the individual's adjustment they also increase the individual's resistance to change. The appropriate modes of intervention here are ones which enable the older person to engage in new relationships, new activities, and to experience rewarding feelings and emotions without destroying or devaluing aspects of the individual's personal history, i.e. long-held values and attitudes (sentiments). Some reconstruction of the life-history and the self-concept may be possible through counselling and behavioural management, with ample time for preparation, explanation, and follow-up support. Rational–emotive therapy would seem to offer a useful way of disconnecting outmoded sentiments from current problems of adjustment without diminishing their value in the individual's life-history.

Emotional exhaustion (shock)

There is a long history of research in psychology dealing with the emotional and behavioural consequences of chronic conflict and frustration. Psychoanalysis, and psychodynamic psychology generally, provide one line of inquiry. Research with animals, of the sort carried out by Seligman and Elder (1986), on reactions to situations which offer no control, or no solution without adverse effects, provides another. The reactions of people and animals to these sorts of stressful situations vary. Aggression, self-injurious behaviour, apathy, depression, and schizoid withdrawal appear to be the most common.

An analogy has been drawn between the depressed/apathetic/with-drawn elderly person and an animal in a state of shock/freezing in the face of extreme threat, say from a predator. Jarvik and Russell (1979) draw attention to this relatively neglected aspect of emotion which they refer to as 'freezing' and the 'third emergency reaction' (the other two being fight and flight). They draw an analogy between 'freezing' (as exhibited by some animals under threat) and the way in which some people under chronic or acute stress inhibit emotional responsiveness, partly to forestall any increase in stress, partly to gain time and conserve resources. The tendency to 'block' emotional reactions, to go into emotional 'shock', as it were, rather than react more overtly by becoming angry or fearful, could be simply one aspect of the range of differences in temperament between individuals—differences brought about by the combined effects of genetic endowment and life experiences.

With low or moderate levels of stress, emotional 'inhibition' rather than 'shock' would be more appropriate. The question, therefore, is whether the overall effects of ageing—biological as well as psychological, together with the effects of social and environmental factors—are likely to increase the likelihood of emotional inhibition or 'blocking'. Jarvik and Russell (1979) argue that such a reaction would be adaptive in the face of the numerous, largely unavoidable losses and frustrations of later life. They also argue that the older person's loss of resources brings about a shift from active mastery to passive mastery.

In the case of excessive emotional stress, e.g. chronic lack of control or a persistent no-solution situation, such as one might find in late life associated with bereavement, institutionalization, relocation, and so on, the adverse consequences may be subjectively felt and outwardly expressed in anger, depression, withdrawal, apathy. The passive reactions mimic emotional 'shock' or 'freezing' so as to avoid further adverse consequences. It is quite a normal reaction for humans in a hostile environment to 'keep their heads down' or to 'surrender' their personal control so as not to draw attention to themselves.

Emotional exhaustion taking the form of apathy or depression could arise from two contrasting causes. First, the effects of old age and deprived living conditions could easily exceed an old person's level of stress tolerance and capacity for coping. Second, an environment which is actually inimical—crowded, hostile, lacking resources, controlled by unsympathetic untrained people—could generate a classical 'no-solution' situation, with apathetic withdrawal or depression as one option and outbursts of rage as another. Or, at a more rational level, it could lead to meekness and submission to the regime as the most sensible strategy of adjustment.

OBSERVATION AND MEASUREMENT

This section considers the various ways in which motivation and emotion can be observed, recorded, and assessed. Casual observation and interpretation are needed in the ordinary activities of life; more systematic observation, recording, measurement, and theorizing are needed for basic research and applications.

In considering the effects of ageing on motivation and emotion, one must bear in mind that samples of community residents are affected by the selective effects of morbidity and mortality; residents are also, usually, volunteers. Older community residents possess the characteristics of survivors more so than do younger residents. It would not be surprising to find that emotional stability, control of affect, and the communication of feelings were negatively associated with physical illness, mental disorder, and relatively early death—thus removing the individuals so affected from the wider community and from the volunteer sample. If this were so, it would not be surprising to observe relatively little in the way of cross-sectional age differences in feelings and emotions among normal community residents. In addition, there are broad social and economic determinants of the quality of later life, such as health and living standards, reflected in feelings of satisfaction and well-being or in feelings of dissatisfaction and resentment. These may well obscure individual differences and age-related changes in emotional behaviour.

It is not clear that much is to be gained by trying to establish generalized normal age trends in emotional behaviour. Given the range of individual differences and the complexity of the contextual factors affecting emotion, we might be better advised to concentrate on particular sorts of people, in well-defined circumstances, preferably over a relatively narrow span of years. Such a piecemeal approach would enable us to build up, in time, a comprehensive and useful map of emotional behaviour during adult life and old age. The same argument applies equally well to other areas of research in social and behavioural gerontology—to intellectual functions, personality, social behaviour, and so on. Such a gradual piecemeal approach would obviate many of the severe methodological problems encountered in gerontology. It could also provide an immediate pay-off in terms of more effective practical applications.

Lay judgments

At the lowest level of sophistication, casual observation can take note of postures, gestures, facial expressions, and other expressive features of behaviour. When taken in context, i.e. with knowledge of the person and the situation, such observations are interpreted fairly automatically, without much reflection, as indicating pleasure, anger, remorse, or some other state of mind—simply because the observer has learned through common experience and ordinary language how to attribute mental states to people and how to interpret their behaviour—Schwarz and Clore (1983). The rules we use in attribution and interpretation are normally implicit in judgment, but can be made explicit (sometimes as rationalizations) when the observer is asked to 'account for' his or her judgments. Individuals can be assessed and, if necessary, trained to a higher level of competence in the exercise of such rules and skills. Training in the relevant social skills for staff working with the elderly might be particularly beneficial.

Clinical appraisals

If we want assessments of a more objective sort, we are obliged to standardize the conditions of observation and to establish inter-observer agreement on what is actually recorded. This requires observers to have a common language and a common conceptual framework. Professional clinical assessments of emotional states are based on training and experience during which clinicians acquire concepts and procedures for interpreting what they observe. It does not follow that all such professional methods are valid, reliable, or useful.

Clinical modes of assessment can be formalized, i.e. they can be separated from the subjective personal characteristics of clinicians. So, for example, we can construct standardized measures of anxiety, hostility, depression, morale, well-being, and so on. Such measures are extremely useful in basic and applied research because they enable investigators to determine the reliability and validity of the assessments they are making, which in turn makes it more likely that findings can be replicated and put to good use. Plutchik (1980) describes a variety of instruments for measuring emotions, none specifically designed for the study of emotions in late life, but see Kane and Kane (1981), McNair et al. (1982), Mangen and Peterson (1982a, b), and Schuessler (1982).

Adjective checklists

A simple example of an operational measure of feeling, mood, or emotion is an adjective checklist. Observers use an agreed list of words (preferably defined and exemplified in prior training) and simply check whether or not a word corresponds with what is observed, e.g. tired, anxious, or resentful behaviour. Such checklists can be used by subjects themselves to identify their own states of mind.

It is important to recall that common-sense and ordinary language enable us to use words and phrases denoting affective states with considerable fluency, but not necessarily with much degree of validity. It can be demonstrated that contextual factors affect our judgment of people's emotions and that they are normally simple and stereotyped. Thus, although adjective checklists may yield reliable results, the results themselves may be more a function of social expectations than real events and therefore not completely valid.

It is obvious that the words chosen for inclusion in a checklist greatly affect the results. For this reason, adjective checklists should be based on systematic studies of the questions at issue, so that the words fairly represent the proper range of emotional reactions under investigation.

The importance of adult ageing on those aspects of observation and measurement so far considered are as follows. First, there is likely to be a considerable age difference and 'generation gap' between the observer and the person being assessed. As we have seen, the observer probably judges the emotional state of the older person without allowing for age changes in expressive behaviour, communication, and information processing. Second, there are few or no satisfactory norms and standards for the psychological assessment of the elderly. Consequently, there is a tendency for investigators to rely on the face validity of clinical impressions or on objective tests standardized, if at all, only on younger subjects. Third, it may be that investigators lack the words and phrases most appropriate for labelling the affective states of elderly people, simply because no one has systematically investigated them.

Content analysis

Content analysis is a method of systematically classifying the parts or elements of a total set, e.g. the different sorts of words and phrases in a report, the different facial features in expressions, the responses to projective tests. The importance of content analysis in the study of feelings and emotions is that it is more or less the first step in the task of systematically describing and classifying feelings and emotions. There has been a considerable amount of research work investigating patterns of emotional expression in animals and man, and investigating the language, mainly the vocabulary, we use to refer to feelings and emotions—see T. D. Kemper (1987) and Plutchik (1980). Such studies have led to quite ingenious systems of classification, many of which are based on the metaphor of the spectrum. Few if any investigations have studied the content and organization of feelings, emotions, and moods in later life (but see Orford et al., 1987). None appears to have studied the language of affect in later life either from the observer's viewpoint or that of the subject. The Orford et al. (1987) study suggests that feelings of dominance, hostility, and protectiveness were prominent in the caring relatives of dementia patients. However, although subject to negative actions by the person cared for, they were able to express compassion, understanding and humour.

Experimental induction

One method used to study emotional expression and sensitivity is through experimental induction. Subjects are asked to recall and express their reactions to certain kinds of situation they have experienced, or to enact a role. From the data thus generated, it is possible to identify some of the elements in emotional expression. Using cross-sectional or longitudinal methods it would be possible to investigate the effects of ageing on emotional expression and on sensitivity to emotional expression. However, the study of emotional communication is complex and technical. For example, it is difficult to distinguish between different emotional states, individuals vary in the way they express their feelings; video-recording is necessary to capture and analyse rapid subtle expressions. The induction of emotions under laboratory conditions may not correspond with emotional behaviour in daily life.

Rating scales

From a psychometric point of view, rating scales are an improvement on adjective checklists and clinical judgments because they provide a method of quantifying observations (if only in a crude way). Several aspects of a phenomenon can be assessed by using different rating scales. There are other sorts of dichotomous or ordinal scales which are not technically 'rating' scales but have much in common with them—magnitude scales, Thurstone scales, Q-sorts and point scales. We need not enter into detailed discussion about measurement issues—see Ghiselli et al. (1981).

The main point to remember is that some scales for the psychological measurement of affect are more appropriate than others for work with the elderly. In particular, as well as being reliable and valid, they should be acceptable and meaningful to the elderly and standardized in a way that makes the results truly representative of emotional reactions in later life.

Questionnaires

Questionnaires dealing with affect are obviously constrained by the language available for reporting. Answers to questions are likely to be fairly simple because most people are not used to disclosing their motives and emotions to others in this way, and do not have the vocabulary and phraseology needed to describe and analyse complex states of mind. Moreover, ignorance and psychological defences may prevent the individual from appreciating the true nature of his or her feelings. The contents of people's 'accounts'—self-reports—of how they feel cannot be taken at face value.

Questionnaires administered to or self-administered by the elderly should meet the usual requirements for effective testing—the materials should be meaningful, interesting, fully explained, adapted to the abilities of the persons concerned, and so on. Questionnaires which deal with simple straightforward topics such as leisure activities or household arrangements are likely to give more valid data than questionnaires which deal with complex, emotionally sensitive issues such as interpersonal relationships, sexual behaviour, or stressful life-events.

Malatesta and Culver (1984) report a 19-year longitudinal study of feelings in women college graduates as assessed by TAT cards, questionnaires, and depression and anxiety scales. Methodological difficulties—changes in the methods of assessment, subject attrition, uncertain reliability and validity—render the findings somewhat uncertain. However, their results at least give indications for future research. Among the more frequent sorts of feelings and emotions experienced by these women were: affiliation with people; lack or loss of affiliation; anger and aggression; fear and anxiety; depression and unhappiness; success and recognition; disappointment. People experience feelings and emotions in relation to all kinds of things—their work, social relationships, material possessions, leisure activities, life-history events, and so on; so emotional reactions are, in an important sense, unique to the individual. Malatesta and Culver, however, attempt to show that certain feelings and emotions can be identified at different stages of adult life. The problem is to identify the affective states that people report, together with the circumstances that give rise to them, and to work out how they change over adult life.

Lawton (1984) describes some of the difficulties in constructing scales to measure affect in older people—for example, separating out the 'interior' and 'exterior' components of subjective well-being. He shows how the causal influences leading to positive or negative affect can be represented diagrammatically.

Physiological measures

Most, if not all, physiological measures of affect have been pioneered on animals and young adults—skin conductance, blood pressure, heart rate, respiration, pupillary response, salivary response, metabolic rate, analysis of blood and urine, EEG. It is not known to what extent the criteria used in diagnosing significant changes in affect by these means are applicable in later life. In any event there appear to be no standard physiological patterns corresponding to psychologically definable feelings and emotions. Even if such correspondences could be demonstrated in younger people there is no guarantee that they would not be different in later life, given the comprehensive but somewhat unpredictable effects of ageing on the different organs and systems of the body.

OTHER ADVERSE EMOTIONAL REACTIONS

There appear to be few if any indications that any of the clearly identifiable emotions or moods change systematically as age advances, with the possible exception of despondency resulting from the effects of poorer physical health, lower living standards, disengagement from familiar activities and people, and bereavement. These effects would also be sufficient to account for an increased inwardness or introversion in later life as the person has more time, opportunity and inclination to think about his or her present circumstances and past history.

The effects of ageing on feelings and emotions are likely to be seen most clearly in relation to maladjustment. Maladjustment can occur in relation to physical ill-health or disability, acute or chronic environmental stress, endogenous psychiatric disorder, or some combination of these. Among the more characteristic emotional reactions to these conditions would be anxiety, depression, rage, and shock. Where the emotion is associated with psychological conflict, defensive reactions may occur, such as denial, conversion (into physical symptoms), hypochondriasis, social withdrawal, displacement, or projection. In other words, the

Table 7.3 Further adverse emotional reactions in later life

1. Apathy
2. Depression
3. Grief
4. Reactions to dying
5. Hypochondriasis
6. Paranoid suspicion
7. Anger
8. Transient disturbance
9. Chronic moderate anxiety

person's true state of mind may be masked by these secondary reactions, and it may be difficult to diagnose and remedy the condition.

The special features of ageing—reductions in many sorts of capacities and increases in life-stress—lead, as we have seen, to a greater likelihood of failure and frustration as the individual operates close to the limits of his or her capacities. In addition, there are many stresses which are more characteristic of late life than of other periods; some of these stresses are intense and prolonged. However, we must not forget the part played by inborn and stable dispositional characteristics in determining the individual's response to such stresses, and the part played by adaptation (habituation) to new conditions, including continuing difficulties.

It would not be surprising to see some emotional reactions become pathological, i.e. outside the normal limits of ordinary experience and management. Some common emotional reactions in later life are listed in Table 7.3.

Common adverse emotions

(1) *Apathy* has already been described and discussed as a serious risk, especially among the less able elderly living in chronically stressful or unrewarding environments. Lack of control or ineffectiveness leads to feelings of helplessness—see Baltes and Baltes (1986), Rodin (1983), Rodin *et al.* (1985), Rodin and Langer (1977), Seligman and Elder (1986).

(2) *Depression* is a common reaction to the stresses characteristic of later life—loss of loved persons, objects, and familiar surroundings; loss of control over one's life; loss of the prospect of a worthwhile future. By contrast with acute anxiety, depression appears to increase with age. Indeed, in later life, when the unavoidable stresses of physical ill-health, retirement, and so on multiply, it might be difficult to distinguish a low

level of chronic anxiety from a low level of persisting depression. Thus low levels of emotionality—whether anxiety, depression, anger, or agitation—could all be regarded as natural long-term adaptations to the stresses of life, particularly in circumstances where the adaptive utility of high levels of expressed emotion has been reduced, i.e. high levels of expressed emotion may be much less effective than they were at younger ages. Recent references to depression and ageing include Baldwin and Jolley (1986), Brasted and Callahan (1984), Chaisson-Stewart (1985b), Magni *et al.* (1985), Sartorius and Ban (1986).

(3) *Grief* is a sort of temporary spasmodic depressed state of mind typically consequent upon the loss of a loved person, associated with feelings of isolation or desolation. There is a sort of suppressed grief in situations where the loss is anticipated. Bereavement may be accompanied by a variety of emotional reactions—commonly anxiety, anger, guilt, relief—see Jacobs *et al.* (1986), Lofland (1985), Rando (1986) and Shuchter (1986). Unless personal or situational factors interfere, the grief gradually reduces in intensity. The sentiment built up in relation to the lost object or person continues as a relatively static system of ideas and feelings available to consciousness and forming part of the individual's psychological make-up. References to the management of grief include Alexy (1982), Kalish (1985) and Parkes (1986).

(4) *Reactions to dying.* Terminal illness, together with an awareness of the much-reduced further expectation of life, is more characteristic of late life than of any other part of the lifespan. It can be regarded as an identifiable stage in the normal human life-path—Bromley (1988b). It therefore warrants special attention in relation to the issue of motivation and emotion.

As with all other aspects of ageing, differences between individuals in their emotional reactions to the prospect of dying are likely to be wide and somewhat unpredictable. These differences arise for reasons we have already referred to: temperament, life-history experiences, biomedical factors, concomitant circumstances (including the emotional reactions of other people), social expectations, and so on. Variations in mood and emotional reaction occur during the terminal condition because of fluctuations in the individual's physical state, and in the surrounding circumstances.

Several types of emotional reaction can be identified. At one extreme we find a calm acceptance of the prospect coupled with a controlled sadness and concern for those to be left bereaved. Alternatively, we find a grim determination to fight the process by resisting its encroachments on behavioural competence. At the other extreme we find severe depression or, alternatively, angry denial. Between these extremes we find various degrees of anxiety and confusion, especially if the dying person is unable to make good sense of what is happening. Apathy or panic may ensue as the individual fails to find any adequate way to deal with what seems to be an adverse no-solution situation.

(5) *Hypochondriasis* was referred to earlier as an example of the way in which moderate chronic anxiety might serve an adaptive function by keeping the individual alert and ready to react to small signals threatening his or her well-being, and to justify claims to dependency on others. The decrease in health and fitness as age advances can be expected to reinforce any dispositional tendency the individual has towards anxiety of this sort. References to hypochondriasis and ageing include Costa and McCrae (1985).

(6) *Paranoid suspicion* in later life is a rare pathological condition, possibly with organic involvement. Alternatively it could be seen as a type of reaction characteristic of the unstable introvert (melancholic) type of old person, especially if cognitive failure leads to confusion—mistakes, lapses, losses—easily blamed on others.

(7) *Anger* in later life presumably is likely to be associated with an unstable extroverted (choleric) type of temperament. Since anger cannot be sustained indefinitely, and may be ineffective or unconvincing in an older person, it must eventually give way to some other reaction—exhaustion, apathy, sadness, depression. Assertiveness, however, continues to be an important factor in situations where passivity would lead to relative neglect or deprivation.

(8) *Transient situational disturbances* in later life may be attributable to some accidental coincidence of psychophysiological conditions and environmental stresses. They are more obvious among patients who are confused or psychotic and where environmental management is inadequate. So, for example, social intrusiveness, wandering, sexual misbehaviour, resistance to reasonable persuasion, agitation, aggression, withdrawal, or other inappropriate behaviour, are commonly observed in dementing patients lacking adequate medical and welfare arrangements.

(9) *Chronic moderate anxiety* may find expression not only in morbid concern with one's health; it may lead to social withdrawal, inappropriate diet and medication, as the individual adopts an excessively self-protective attitude. One difficulty in establishing the relationship between normal ageing and anxiety is that of establishing measures of anxiety that are valid for various age levels and for various sorts of subject. The same difficulty is encountered in the study of emotions other than anxiety (and indeed of psychological characteristics generally). The indications, such as they are, suggest that acute anxiety becomes less common as age advances, although a low level of chronic anxiety becomes more common. This age trend, if it could be confirmed, might reflect a sort of generalized adaptation. The individual learns, in effect, that most life-stresses have

to be coped with in one way or another, and that high levels of anxiety do not pay off. A low level of chronic anxiety could reflect a residual alertness for danger signals by means of which the individual avoids, or prepares more adequately for, stressful life events.

TECHNIQUES OF INTERVENTION

Recent developments in psychology have produced a variety of means for counteracting the adverse effects of ageing on affective behaviour.

Environmental improvement

Environmental improvement refers to the many sorts of changes that can be made to the environments of older people so as to make them easier to adapt to. Under this broad heading we can include 'therapeutic environments' specially designed for the particular needs and disabilities of the elderly—see Chapter 4. Built environments, designed for the average user, provide many examples of unnecessary defects—stair risers, lighting, furnishings, routing, signs, layout—which limit mobility, increase the likelihood of accidents, add to confusion, and militate against social interaction and self-management.

Together with the 'built' environment we can consider the technological environment—transport, equipment, communication, materials. Work on technological aids for the disabled, including recent advances in computing and communication, illustrates the kinds of applications possible. To some extent we can compensate for failing sensory and motor capacities, but not yet for failing affective and cognitive capacities.

More important in some respects than the built environment is the social environment. The social environment includes not only those people with whom the individual has face-to-face contact, and those others whose behaviour affects the local 'social climate', but also the wider society with its institutions, social attitudes, and norms. There is a 'climate or opinion' about old age—a framework of beliefs, values, and social prescriptions—which influences the behaviour of old people. We must recognize, however, the plurality that exists in large democratic societies.

The social interventions needed have to do with the selection and training of care-givers (voluntary and professional), with policy changes at national and local government level, with improvements in education and welfare generally. Changes in these areas need skilled and persistent advocacy. Such environmental interventions should help older people generally to cope more effectively, to achieve greater fulfilment, to suffer less stress, and so lead to greater satisfaction, i.e. to a sense of well-being and to more positive feelings and emotions. Quite often, improved subjective well-being is an important index of the effectiveness of an intervention, although it does not necessarily correlate well with objective indices—see Fillenbaum (1984), Flanagan (1982), Larson (1978), Palmore and Kivett (1977).

Counselling

This is a general term referring to a collection of psychotherapeutic techniques all of which depend largely on systematic verbal interaction between client and counsellor. They aim to reorganize the client's personal qualities, mental states, and behaviour so as to reduce or eliminate frustration and failure and to increase achievement and adjustment. Rational–emotive therapy provides a good example of a general-purpose method of counselling suitable for older people who are mentally intact. It aims to restructure the way the client thinks and feels about himself or herself and the circumstances he or she is in, making considerable alterations in the language the client uses to identify and express feelings.

Behaviour modification

Behaviour modification through contingency management is effective in a wide range of situations, and obviously a possibility with elderly patients who are not mentally intact. It may prove valuable in changing the way patients express their emotions, for example, by becoming less apathetic or less aggressive. See Hussian (1981) for a description of behavioural techniques in the management of geriatric patients.

Behavioural management in the natural environment refers to an arrangement whereby the people who are most frequently in contact with, and exert most influence on, an individual—by making promises and threats and giving or withholding rewards and punishments—are enabled to agree on a common aim and a coherent pattern of treatment. The 'enabling' is done by professionals, trained and experienced in behaviour modification, who instruct the intermediaries and monitor their behaviour. They, in turn, structure the patient's environmental contingencies and shape his or her behaviour towards the desired pattern, e.g. more socializing, less aggression, more recreational activity, more independence and personal control.

Behavioural shaping is clearly at work in rational emotive-therapy in so far as the person's use of emotional language is gradually modified by the counsellor's consistent and systematic reinforcement of appropriate labels, interpretations, and responses. With mentally intact patients there is in addition a cognitive process at work, leading to increased insight and better understanding of their situation.

Social skills training

Social skills training has not so far been applied to any great extent to the elderly. It is most appropriate for deprived or handicapped individuals who have never been adequately socialized in the first place, or to individuals needing to acquire special social skills, e.g. receptionists, general practitioners, personnel officers, the police. The desocialization that may accompany ageing usually comes about because of intrinsic psychobiological changes which have deleterious effects on motivation, cognition, and memory, and on affective reactions which then disrupt social relationships and social behaviour previously well-established. Loss of social adjustment is characteristic of senile dementia.

One sort of social skills training with the elderly then shades into behaviour modification aimed at eliminating antisocial or unsocial behaviour. Another, more positive, sort is that which aims to develop the residual abilities of the aged, especially where these have fallen into disuse because of social isolation and poor environmental conditions, whether in the community or in institutional settings. Among the more obvious examples are recreational and group activities such as games and outings, and interpersonal relationships developed through conversations and mutual help.

We must not neglect the sorts of social skills training that might benefit the not-so-old adult—the person made redundant or prematurely retired who needs to make a fairly drastic shift from one lifestyle to another. Such a shift entails dealing with different people in other settings for other reasons than before. For example, a person may decide to move from an industrial occupation and a suburban home to a smallholding in the country, or from a military career to shopwork, hotel management, or catering.

A major element in all these different kinds and levels of social skill is the management of affect—skill in promptly identifying emotionally significant situations, skill in adopting an appropriate initial attitude, skill in organizing the necessary pattern of expression and coping behaviour, skill in reflecting upon the experience and learning from it.

Medication and surgery

Medication and surgery as techniques of intervention in relation to the management of affect are numerous and diverse, but not directly relevant to our inquiry, which is concerned largely with the psychology of motivation and emotion. Nevertheless, psychological considerations become directly relevant in the evaluation of the effects and side-effects of drugs and surgery. For example, drugs and operations designed to change moods or to remove disabling emotional reactions should be assessed objectively, preferably by means of standardized measures before and after treatment. See also Chapters 3 and 4.

POSITIVE ASPECTS OF AFFECT IN LATER LIFE

Our analysis so far has concentrated on the negative aspects of feelings and emotions, for a number of reasons. First, negative effects have been subjected to closer and more extensive investigation than positive affects. Second, the available methods of assessment and treatment are naturally concerned with attempts to reduce negative affects. Third, the cumulative effects of ageing increase rather than decrease the likelihood of negative affects.

What aspects of ageing might lead to positive affects? The answers to this question are even more speculative than those offered to earlier questions. We do not have sufficient good research data to support a convincing account, and we need to be careful about accepting common-sense notions at face value.

Popular wisdom has it that as age advances there is a diminution in the intensity of drives and desires—especially those associated with intense consummatory emotions. The most obvious example is that of sex; the research evidence indicates a substantial reduction in frequency of sexual intercourse, although this reduction is not entirely accounted for in terms of reduced drive. Other sexually related activities may continue to provide emotional satisfaction—Starr (1985). Research into sexual behaviour is obviously difficult, and findings are open to a variety of criticisms related to sampling and methodology—Adams and Turner (1985), Ludeman (1981), Weg (1983), Wharton (1981).

Comparable surveys might also indicate reductions with age in various other activities associated with intense feelings. For example, older people are less inclined to engage in hazardous activities which generate 'thrills' and stresses—rock climbing, parachuting, hooliganism. The affective and motivational involvement in parenting could also be expected to diminish as the children become more independent.

If there is some diminution with age in basic urges like sex, curiosity, and activity, then the negative emotions associated with non-consummation will also diminish (as of course will the positive emotions associated with fulfilment). The overall effect is supposed to be more emotional quiescence. Unfortunately for this line of argument, other drives and desires seem not to diminish and may even increase in salience. Typical of these would be the needs for physical security and bodily comforts. In so far as these needs can be met in ways that fit the individual's expectations, they will engender satisfaction and positive affect.

Social (particularly occupational) disengagement removes the individual from a range of situations which engender a variety of feelings and emotions (Mottaz, 1987). The common expectation is that the individual will benefit emotionally, at least in the longer term, because the satisfactions associated with the voluntary activities of retirement may more than compensate for the satisfactions associated with employment. At the same time, the individual is relieved of the stresses of employment. So disengagement too can be expected to foster emotional quiescence and well-being since most of the activities engaged in in retirement are optional and personal, yet somehow not emotionally intense (O'Brien, 1981). Disengagement permits individuals to pursue their self-interests more fully and relieves them of many obligations. The increased time available for the activities of daily living should foster a calmer more detached, reflective outlook. Some professional interests and achievements continue well into 'retirement' (Dorfman, 1985; Rowe, 1989).

By the age of retirement most individuals will have built up a stable system of attitudes based on the beliefs, values, and modes of conduct, built up through experience. We are, of course, talking about the great majority, say 75%, of community residents who are free from major mental and physical disabilities. They can also be expected to have come to terms with their now greatly reduced further expectation of life, which will reinforce a sense of relative detachment from the issues about which younger people feel strongly.

The processes of reminiscence and life-review help to resolve emotional conflicts and increase the overall consistency of the individual's thoughts and feelings. Ideally, this should result in a sense of fulfilment and satisfaction with one's life.

One must not forget those very obvious factors that improve the quality of late life and sense of well-being—good health, financial security, satisfying occupational or recreational activities, social support from family and friends.

Fifteen factors commonly affecting, in a positive or negative way, the quality of life and the sense of well-being of elderly people have been described by Flanagan (1982) following a national survey of 70-year-olds. As one might expect, physical health and material well-being were the most important, followed in rough order of importance by marital condition, children, friendships, recreation, and work. These same factors were also felt by the 70-year-olds to have been important *throughout* life.

Table 7.4 A short list of the more frequently mentioned positive and negative contributions for males and females separately to (A) 'Excellent quality' of life, and (B) 'Fair or poor' quality of life, at age 70

Positive contributions (A)		Negative contributions (A)	
Male	*Female*	*Male*	*Female*
Spouse	Friends	Health	Health
Friends	Children	Spouse	Material well-being
Material well-being	Socializing	Material well-being	Spouse
Children	Passive recreation	Work	Children
Active recreation	Material well-being	Children	Work
Socializing	Creativity	Learning	Relatives
Health	Health	Socializing	Learning
Positive contributions (B)		Negative contributions (B)	
Spouse	Passive recreation	Health	Health
Passive recreation	Children	Material well-being	Material well-being
Children	Friends	Spouse	Spouse
Friends	Socializing	Work	Friends
Socializing	Helping	Learning	Work
Helping	Understanding self	Children	Children
Relatives	Creativity	Friends	Socializing
Understanding self	Relatives	Active recreation	Helping

The contributions are arranged in order of higher to lower frequency of mention. Based on data from Flanagan (1982).

The more obvious sex differences were the relatively greater importance of contact with their children, and other people generally, for the women, and the fact that women were more often widowed than men. Consequently, the women appeared to be deriving relatively more life-satisfaction from non-marital areas of activity—education, involvement in local and national government, passive recreation, contact with relatives and friends, and so on. Flanagan concludes that much more could be done to improve the sense of well-being and life-satisfaction (the 'affective' response to quality of life) by better provision of health and social services, through improved health education and preventive medicine, and through environmental improvements in relation to safety, security, transport, and communication. Table 7.4 summarizes the positive and negative contributions to the quality of later life.

Larson (1978) in an extensive review reported that the most important determinants of subjective well-being in later life were, in order of importance: physical health, socioeconomic status, social interaction, marital status, housing, and transport. James *et al.* (1986) have examined some of the psychometric aspects of life satisfaction.

Investigators have used large sets of data and complex factor-analytic methods to establish that several aspects of subjective well-being can be regarded as common to adults in the age range 25–75 years. These are the economic, health, residential, and interpersonal–leisure aspects. The relative importance of these factors, however, and their interrelationships, vary from one age group to another.

The condition of 'well-being' can be looked at subjectively in terms of inner satisfaction and objectively in terms of normative external criteria. It appears that negative feelings and emotions are more closely associated with inner psychological processes (including functional capacity in relation to daily life) than with normative criteria. Conversely, positive feelings and emotions appear to be more closely associated with external objective factors, such as social interaction and opportunities for action, than with dispositional and functional characteristics.

Straightforward self-report measures of subjective well-being reveal little or no change with age in spite of quite obvious changes in health and circumstances. This is probably because we tend to adapt to changes and to judge our own circumstances relative to others. As we have seen, life-satisfaction and well-being in later life tend to be associated with the sorts of conditions that make for happiness at any age—health, socioeconomic status, social relationships, and so on.

Chronological age itself seems to account for only a small proportion of the variance in measures of well-being, but of course the proportion of variance accounted for depends upon the nature of the sample. Socioeconomic status, sex, and education are similar in this respect. Under certain sampling circumstances, therefore, personality characteristics such as extroversion and neuroticism may appear to be important factors in well-being, especially if there is any overlap in (confounding of) the criteria used in assessing personality and well-being. Old people are a small and unrepresentative sample of the cohort to which they belong, and those who adjust well are an even smaller, highly selected sample. One must conclude, therefore, that the popular image of the old person as calm, contented, detached, reflective, and emotionally quiescent is one face of the stereotype, the other face of which, equally over-simplified, is that of the older person as anxious, dependent, depressed, selfish, withdrawn, or cantankerous.

Perhaps the most important idea to bear in mind is that the human affective system is to some extent modifiable and trainable. It remains to be seen just how and to what extent we can improve the system's adaptability to the internal and external changes of adult life and old age. The satisfactions associated with certain kinds of feelings and emotions, such as affection, sexuality, wonder, amusement, can certainly be anticipated and deliberately sought after. Even if the feelings themselves cannot be directly induced, the circumstances and actions which precede them can. Similarly, we learn to avoid those circumstances and actions associated with the onset of unpleasant feelings and emotions, although for example, anger and depression, as in sulking, may be 'induced' because they are instrumental in achieving a more remote goal—influencing another person, perhaps. Lack of emotional control could hardly be adaptive, and yet spontaneous feelings, like spontaneous thoughts, come into awareness without conscious deliberation. Good emotional adjustment, like good problem-solving, requires a combination of freedom and control (generativity and selectivity). Ageing probably leads to a reduction in both of these aspects of emotion.

In situations where emotions are instrumental (rather than merely expressive), it may be that older people have more to gain from a passive–avoidance strategy of coping with stress, whereas younger people have more to gain from an active–approach strategy. For example, in coping with the stress of illness and hospitalization the consequences of being in a no-control or poor-control situation may be less acceptable to younger than older subjects because younger subjects have more to lose and are facing a relatively unexpected event. Surprisingly, there is evidence that a passive–avoidance strategy in a no-control situation may be more adaptive than an active–approach (resistance) strategy. Note the implications for general strategies of adjustment in later life, i.e. the advantages of passive–dependency in those areas of life where mastery is low or uncertain.

MOTIVATION AND EMOTION IN THE LIFE-HISTORY

The adult's life-story, expressed in reminiscence and life-review data, crystallizes around significant life-events which, by definition, are associated with relatively intense and definite motivations and emotions. Consider, for example, life-events such as those associated with one's education, marriage, employment, or military service. As age increases, together with life-experience, earlier life-events shape our reactions to later events, which are in turn reorganized (reconstructed, revalued) as life-experiences. For example, a failed marriage may induce caution and pessimism regarding relationships with the opposite sex, and a second marriage may induce a change of attitude towards the first marriage. Thus emotional reactions are normally adaptive. Maladaptive emotional reactions may arise from conflict between desires or because of barriers to need-satisfaction. They may hinder the development of the individual's potentialities, and the integration of behaviour and experience.

Motivations and emotions in later life must be strongly influenced by the long-range effects of childhood experiences and socialization, not forgetting that these in turn depend in part on the child's genetic and constitutional make-up. The socialization of emotional experience and expression during the juvenile years fulfils a variety of needs that we must perhaps take for granted. First, control over one's personal reactions in the interests of the community (being brave, showing sympathy or solidarity). Second, control over one's personal reactions in one's own personal interest (concealing disappointment, being deceitful). Third, inhibiting or regulating one's desires (moral attitudes, persistence in the face of fatigue). Fourth, making life simpler (habitual reactions, token responses, warning signals).

Normally, by the time we reach early adult life, we have experienced a variety of desires and emotions in all sorts of contexts, we have learned how to express and inhibit our feelings and drives and how to simulate them. We have also, to some extent, learned how to read, induce, and control other people's feelings and how to detect the feelings they are trying to hide. To the extent that we have had many opportunities to experience particular kinds of life-event we tend to develop a sort of routine or standardized emotional reaction to them. Hence, older people are generally regarded as wiser and calmer in the sense of not letting feelings and emotions disrupt rational appraisal of a situation. Having 'seen it before' they tend to be in a better position to know how to react. Emotional reactions are often psychologically costly, in the sense of being upsetting, tiring, and distracting. Age and experience normally bring a reduction in the intensity of emotional response and an increase in rational control over feelings and emotions.

Among the changes that take place in emotional reactions during development, there are three that are particularly relevant to the study of adult life and old age.

(1) One we have already referred to, namely, inhibition or emotional control. This is the process whereby we learn to restrain or block the outward expression of feelings and desires, particularly those that are socially disruptive or personally disadvantageous. We also learn to simulate feelings and emotions, i.e. to 'dissimulate', for the same reasons. This is sometimes called 'masking' ('There's no art to find the mind's construction in the face').

(2) Another change is the differentiation and integration of basic reactions to achieve more complex and blended forms of emotional expression and experience. Consider, for example, adult feelings of parental pride or disappointment, lover's jealousy or professional contempt.

(3) A third sort of change is the acquisition of skill or efficiency in emotional expression and sensitivity to others' emotions. This calls for economy of effort and speed of response, which means that

emotional expression tends to be restricted to key features (those most effective in response terms), and that emotional sensitivity increases in the sense of detecting early and faint signals of impending emotional reactions. Thus: a child becomes sensitive to degrees of parental opposition to a request; in relationships between the sexes there are subtle signals indicating attraction or 'cooling off'; in marital relationships husbands and wives usually become expert at reading the other's state of mind from small, brief signals (facial expressions, tones of voice, pauses, bodily movements) that other observers could not even detect, much less interpret. The term 'miniaturization' has been used to refer to the way in which emotional expression in adults is compressed in time and in extent (brief glances, eyebrow flashes, lip tightening, occupying only milliseconds—and so presenting problems of perception in later life)—see Malatesta and Izard (1984, pp. 253–73).

We tend to assume that emotional expressiveness and sensitivity to the expression of emotions in others are relatively independent of each other. Doubtless, both have a basis in genetic endowment and family upbringing. It is possible to argue that persons brought up in emotionally expressive families are themselves more emotionally expressive than persons brought up in families which are less expressive. However, families have a genetic as well as a social influence on offspring. Persons brought up in families which are less emotionally expressive appear to be relatively more sensitive to emotional expression in others—having had to learn to detect less obvious, more subtle, cues. Emotional behaviour in humans is difficult to study under controlled, laboratory conditions, although unobtrusive audio- and video-recording can provide useful data. Orford *et al.* (1987) report on expressed emotion in family response to dementia.

Longitudinal studies provide one way of examining age changes (as opposed to age differences), provided there is little or no attrition or effects from repeated measures—see Malatesta and Culver (1984). It would not be surprising to find that some kinds of events and some kinds of emotional reaction occurred more often or affected a larger proportion of the subjects than others. But these events and reactions might not be the same from one age to the next; although one would expect some consistency within a homogeneous sample. As we have seen, there is a considerable amount of stability in behaviour in adult life produced by (a) relatively stable environmental conditions, (b) genetic and constitutional factors and (c) ultra-stable psychological characteristics (values, traits, abilities, sentiments, and habits).

Longitudinal psychometric studies seem to confirm the stability of basic personality characteristics over many years of adult life. So one can expect the young extrovert to continue to be outgoing, sociable, and expressive in later life; one can expect the young neurotic to continue to be emotionally unstable, anxious or depressed, or withdrawn in later life. Some individuals will be predisposed to react to life-events, such as ill-health, relocation, bereavement, or retirement, in these characteristic ways. Because life-events are interpreted and reacted to in terms of the person's predispositions, the predispositions would seem, if anything, to become even more influential with the passage of time.

Among the emotions most commonly studied in relation to ageing are the following: life-satisfaction and well-being, anxiety, depression, cautiousness, dependency. In very late life, in conditions of physical and mental infirmity, we can expect to see a lessening or breakdown in emotional control because of intrinsic losses in inhibitory processes, increased discomfort, stress and psychological loss, and decreased social conformity.

There are, in a sense, no standard patterns of emotional response (expression and experience) in adult life because the various classes of response to which we can give names can take many forms, depending upon circumstances. For example, my anger can express itself in shouting, fighting, phantasy, silence, withdrawal, displacement activities, sleeplessness, inability to concentrate, and so on. The problem for the observer is to work out—from observations of the subject's behaviour, self-reports and circumstances—how best to characterize his or her emotional response. This may be achieved not necessarily by assigning one of the familiar emotional terms—anger, jealousy, or whatever—but possibly by giving as full an account of the affective state as is required—see Frijda (1986). Subjective accounts—found in autobiographies or in counselling—incorporate a variety of contextual material so as to justify or 'make sense' of the reaction. The observer may choose to edit this account in the light of more objective knowledge.

The study of particular sorts of life-transitions, especially those lived through by particular sorts of people, is likely to be more rewarding than the study of average patterns of adjustment for all kinds of people over the adult part of the lifespan. Moreover, chronological age itself, within limits, may be a relatively minor variable, and could in any event be reduced in importance by appropriate subject selection. Consider transitions like first and subsequent employment, marriage, relocation, military service, parenthood, divorce, serious illness, bereavement. The adult life of an individual consists of a series of overlapping, interconnected sequences of behaviour patterns or episodes, as described in Chapter 2. A considerable amount of sheer chance helps to determine the way the individual's life develops. There is no necessary 'direction', 'pattern', or 'shape' to it. In retrospect, of course, a biography or autobiography may impose a pattern, but this is not a scientific inference or discovery, but rather a convenient conceptual framework for making sense of the person's life.

RESEARCH PROSPECTS

The relationships between the three major facets of affect—the somatic, the behavioural, and the experiential—are still not well understood even without the complications associated with ageing. It seems unlikely, therefore, that much progress will be made in understanding these basic processes, and their relationships, by studying the apparent effects of ageing. As with other areas of psychological inquiry, the complexity and unpredictability of ageing, together with the well-known methodological difficulties of research, make gerontology an unpromising area for basic research into the psychobiological processes of motivation and emotion.

What then remains? Primarily research into ways of preventing or ameliorating maladaptive 'negative' emotional reactions in later life, and into ways of optimizing motivational fulfilment. Interventions of this kind, if well designed and carried out, might take us some way towards basic forms of understanding, even if it proves impossible to set up the necessary controls and procedures that would satisfy the 'pure' experimenter. For example, single-case-studies using detailed clinical appraisals and carefully monitored treatment effects provide one sort of approach. Experimental and quasi-experimental designs—Cook and Campbell (1979), Kausler (1982)—provide another. Small surveys should go some way towards identifying the important contextual and subject factors, such as social relationships, life-history, and physiological functions. Statistical estimates of the magnitude of the observed effects should help decide whether the benefits likely to be obtained by intervention are worth the effort.

Even research into the effectiveness of interventions, however, depends on the availability of methods of observation and measurement which are reliable and valid—Kane and Kane (1981), Mangen and Peterson (1982a, b), Schuessler (1982). Much remains to be done to develop methods for the study of affect in later life. Research into research methods is therefore inescapable, and really the first priority. How might such methods be developed? First, one should resist the temptation to rely on single-occasion, single-instrument assessments. It is most important in the study of ageing to engage in longitudinal studies using multiple methods and diverse samples on several occasions. In this way, by 'aggregating' data—Epstein (1983)—one can obtain results which are robust in the real sense of being capable of replication. Otherwise, one may finish up with an effect which is statistically significant but otherwise uninteresting and not generalizable to slightly different samples and conditions.

Some lines of inquiry have been referred to in passing. One possibility would be to use content analysis to study the descriptions that people offer for their own and for other people's needs, emotional states, and expressive behaviour. One might find that the 'language' of emotional experience and emotional expression changes with age. Also, if one could obtain more satisfactory physiological and behavioural measures, one might be able to test whether the underlying 'character' of felt and expressed emotion changes with age. Another possibility would be to examine emotionality at critical periods in adult life, to see what changes if any occur. Studies of the menopause, departure of children, retirement, and bereavement have been made but usually without reference to differences in emotionality before, during, and after these events. In other words it may not be the average effects of ageing in general that we should be looking for, but rather the specific effects of significant life-changes that produce stepwise (even if temporary) alterations in emotionality.

If one is prepared to rely on self-report measures it should not be difficult to study age differences in the relative and absolute frequencies of linguistic references obtained, for example, from adjective checklists, mood rating scales, or free descriptions. This would give us some idea of the effects of ageing on emotional experience. By all accounts, feelings of anxiety and sadness increase, as do responses associated with introversion.

Experimental studies using film/video would quickly test the view that older subjects are less able to monitor another person's emotional expression. The use of 'expanded' and 'acted' film sequences would enable one to see what was required in the way of emotional expression (its pace, intensity, etc.) to bring older subjects up to the level of younger subjects responding to 'normal' emotional expression. Film/video could also be used to record and analyse age differences in emotional expression in response to standard instructions or stimuli. Such material, if it confirmed the view argued in this chapter, could be used to train younger people to 'read' the expressive behaviour of older people more accurately.

Study of the effects of ageing on sentiments seems to demand longitudinal studies. It seems likely that ageing will be accompanied by systematic changes in value/belief systems. Retrospective self-reports are unlikely to provide conclusive evidence. Long-term trends in attitudes and values are administratively difficult to investigate; but such studies would be of interest in relation to the so-called 'generation gap'.

The immediate prospects for progress in the neuroendocrine basis of affective ageing look poor, given the additional methodological obstacles to research in this area. However, one would expect continuing progress in the study of distinct psychopathologies with disorders of affect. One would expect such advances to throw light on the normal effects of ageing.

As a counterweight to the concern with negative emotions in later life, research is needed to discover what can be done to build up positive emotional reactions in older people. Hitherto, this has been done by surveying sources of satisfaction and dissatisfaction, and by examining morale and well-being. The results of such surveys have confirmed common-sense views about the determinants of happiness, in particular the importance of things like physical health, housing, income, family support, personal control, security, and mobility. Surveys of interests and leisure activities and of consumer preferences among the elderly provide indices of motivation. They indicate a wide range of possibilities for increased life-satisfaction. Research into effective education and counselling would help develop the means to encourage an active positive outlook, meaning an outlook in which internal locus of control is high and an active search is maintained for rewarding environments.

More research is needed into the nature of loss of control of affective reactions, possibly by more systematic clinical studies and surveys. Ideally, prospective epidemiological research is needed into those disorders of later life in which disturbances of affect are prominent. This would help reveal the natural history of such disturbances.

As far as 'normal ageing' is concerned, we need substantial longitudinal studies of motivation and emotion. These studies would record, in qualitative and quantitative detail, age effects in a wide range of feelings associated with the self, the environment, and life-events. They would record the more intense positive and negative emotional reactions, keep track of periodic and episodic changes in mood, and examine age-effects in temperament (affective dispositions) and motivational priorities. This assumes the necessary psychometric measures could be made available. Studies like these should enable us to see whether there are systematic effects in adult life and old age analogous to those observed during juvenile development, and whether the proposed distinction between 'fluid' and 'crystallized' affective reactions is valid.

The phenomenon of dissembling is likely to prove difficult to study, but may be related to age changes in emotional control, disengagement, and belief/value systems.

One of the more interesting and promising areas of research would be on the idea that late life sees a trend towards lowered thresholds for negative moods and emotional reactions, e.g. anxiety, anger, sadness, as a sort of increased alertness to threats to well-being (to compensate for reductions in competence and 'reserves'). How could such research be carried out? Surveys of reactions to minor threats to well-being, e.g. slight changes in health, surroundings, or social relationships, might show that older people were more inclined to respond in ways indicative of anxiety, anger, and sadness, in situations where younger people would be inclined not to react, or to react in a more positive way. The ability to 'wait and see' what happens and to withhold an emotional response might be reduced in later life as inhibitory control is weakened. On the other hand, increased affective 'quiescence' might strengthen such control.

There is a growing interest in therapies for the emotional problems of later life. Psychotherapeutic and behavioural intervention presents its own problems as far as research evaluation is concerned. The problems associated with remission, placebo effects, selective samples, drop-out, control groups, observation and measurement, and so on, are likely to be even more pronounced in studies of the effectiveness of therapeutic interventions with the elderly. The same principles apply to other sorts of interventions, such as physical exercise, cognitive training, reality orientation, and drug therapy.

One task of applied social and behavioural gerontology is to rid the environment of adverse conditions which lead to negative (unhelpful) emotional reactions in older people. Another task is to enable and encourage older people to react more appropriately to those adverse conditions which cannot be eliminated or ameliorated further.

SUMMARY

Among the basic concepts in the psychology of affect are the following: feeling, emotion, mood, sentiment, motivation, and attitude. Understanding the corresponding psychobiological phenomena requires reference to cultural and linguistic considerations and to the physical basis of affect. The effects of adult life and old age can be seen to be partly a consequence of biomedical changes, partly a consequence of individual experiences and social learning.

Feelings and emotions are an integral part of the motivational process. In particular, they are related to levels of arousal, to the contrasting behavioural consequences of desires and aversions, to appetitive and consummatory activities, and to whether outcomes are satisfying or not. Changes in behavioural capacities and environmental conditions with age bring about complex effects on motives, actions, and outcomes, and hence on affective states.

Motivations, emotions, and moods are accompanied by internal and external indicators which play a part in determining how a person reacts and what an observer reports. The complexity and speed of affective expression would seem to put the older person at a disadvantage in terms of controlling and monitoring the process. This aggravates the 'generation gap' which hinders communication between young and old.

The determinants of emotional reactions are complicated. Genetic and constitutional factors, juvenile social development, life-events and experience during the adult period, normal ageing, and pathology, all play a part in determining the individual's affective dispositions and in shaping his or her affective reactions.

Ageing has effects in relation to each stage of the time-course of an emotional reaction: sensitivity to the stimulus conditions; adequacy of initial orientation; speed and effectiveness of the programme of expressive and coping behaviour; conformity to normative prescriptions; and the longer-term effects of secondary reflective reactions.

A number of basic emotional problems can be predicted in the normal course of adult development and ageing: the reappearance of basic emotions like pain and fear; other negative reactions to diminished coping; reductions in voluntary control, especially in the event of psychopathology; negative reactions to age-related stresses; increasing difficulty in finding environments suitable for certain types of tempera-ment and personality characteristics; increasing difficulty because of sentiments unsuited to changed personal circumstances; a greater likelihood of emotional exhaustion as a consequence of persisting stress.

A variety of observational and measurement techniques have been developed to assess affective states and traits, including lay judgments, clinical appraisals, adjective checklists, projective tests, content analysis, rating scales, questionnaires, and physiological measures. It remains to be seen whether affective states can be effectively investigated by these means. The problems of validity, reliability, and utility in relation to the description and measurement of emotions in adult life and old age constitute serious obstacles to research.

There are a number of emotional reactions in later life which are serious, yet fall within the normal range of experience. They include the following: apathy, depression, grief, reactions to dying, hypochondriasis, paranoid suspicion, anger, transient situational disturbances, and chronic moderate anxiety. Such troublesome conditions may be helped by one or another kind of intervention—environmental change, psychological counselling, behaviour modification, social skills training, medication, and surgery. For obvious reasons the negative aspects of affect in later life have been our main interest. A case can be made out for the emergence of some positive emotional reactions.

Unfortunately, there has been relatively little scientific research into the 'normal' effects of ageing on motivation and emotion. Research efforts in behavioural gerontology should be directed towards evaluating the effectiveness of interventions designed to optimize motivational fulfilment and emotional adjustment in later adult life and during the period of dependency in old age.

Chapter Eight

Methodology

INTRODUCTION

Scientific method has a prominent place in the academic education and professional training of psychologists. Not surprisingly, then, psychologists have the reputation of being knowledgeable about research methodology and are often consulted by workers in related fields who wish to carry out research involving psychological issues. Partly as a consequence, research methodology has occupied a prominent place in the literature on the psychological effects of ageing; but, additionally, scientific investigations in this area face many difficult obstacles.

In this chapter I emphasize and advocate diverse methods of research, especially small-scale qualitative research. The reasons for this approach are (1) that the traditional problems have been discussed *ad nauseam*, and (2) that ideal, large-scale, prospective studies incorporating representative cohorts and age groups followed up over intervals of several years are likely to be few and far between, since they require substantial funding and administrative arrangements approaching a national scale. In order to appreciate the value of small-scale research methods, however, it is essential to know something about the traditional approach to research methodology in gerontology, and to consider what scientific method means in the context of behavioural gerontology. The methodological problems encountered in large-scale research in ageing (those concerned with separating age, cohort, and period effects) are dealt with more fully later in this chapter—see also Berger (1986), Birren and Renner (1977), Hoyer *et al.* (1984), Kausler (1982), Nesselroade and Harkins (1980), Palmore (1978), Paykel (1983), Plewis (1985), Schaie (1983), Wasserman (1987), Zimmerman (1983).

If one studies subjects who are broadly comparable but who differ in chronological age—say several generations of families drawn from the same cultural and socioeconomic background—one can observe a variety of differences. There are age differences in physical appearance, in health

317

and physiological functions, in psychological capacities, in social attitudes, personal qualities, behaviour, and performance on tests. Further inquiry will reveal age differences in lifestyle and surrounding circumstances. In addition, obviously, if one divides these subjects into several age bands from, say, the 20s to the 80s, then one may suspect differences arising as 'cohort effects', i.e. the effects of being born in a particular year or decade, and 'period effects', i.e. the effects of having experienced circumstances of one sort or another over a particular period of time. Separating cohort, period, and age effects has been a methodological preoccupation with behavioural gerontologists.

Chronological age

Chronological age is measured by the passage of time (years since birth) and conceptualized as a single independent subject variable. This means regarding it as an attribute of the person, but not one over which the investigator has experimental control. Investigators can *select* subjects *from* different age groups but cannot *allocate* subjects *to* different age groups. This limits the extent to which chronological age can be manipulated in experiments and surveys; and it means that chronological age itself cannot be a dependent variable, i.e. age cannot be the outcome of an experimental manipulation, except in the limiting case of 'age at death'. Age at death in animals can be experimentally modified, for example, by treatments involving exposure to radiation, dietary restrictions, or selective breeding of forebears.

If chronological age is regarded simply as an index measuring the passage of time since birth it can carry no causal efficacy. That is to say, the number of years one has lived cannot, of itself, produce any biological or other effect. It is obvious then that what produces the ageing effects we are interested in must be the various biomedical, psychological, social, and environmental processes and sequences that *occupy* time and produce effects that accumulate and interact *over* time. So, for example, we can observe the cumulative changes with age in the circulatory system, the lens of the eye, and in the brain; we can observe the differential decline in intellectual abilities, changes in leisure activities and in experience; we can observe changes in social relationships, social position, and status; we can observe changes in the demographic distributions of people as they grow older, changes in their residential accommodation, and in their response to stress and hazard.

The processes and sequences of ageing converge on a final common path that ends with death. But the various processes and sequences are not necessarily closely correlated during the adult years. We shall not consider the problem of ageing in the juvenile phase, even though one of its aspects—the decline of the thymus gland—may be important in understanding adult ageing of the immune system. Some processes show substantial and continuous decline—the reduction in speed of mental performance, for example, and the decline in respiratory efficiency. Other processes decline little if at all, e.g. language production or pain perception. Some effects, those associated with illness and injury such as cancer, brain disorder, or stress reactions, may be abrupt and substantial. On the other hand, some recovery of function is possible through the natural processes of healing and through treatment, training, and practice.

If we were able to study individual cases continuously and in detail we could expect to see the unfolding of complex patterns and sequences of effects associated with the passage of time. Unfortunately, we are usually restricted to making a small number of observations on a small sample of subjects spread over a limited period of time. When we average these observations, this may have the effect of *smoothing* the age trends and masking the differences between individuals. We may be unable to clarify the causal connections between the variables of interest, and we may miss *stepwise* changes (substantial changes over a relatively short interval of time) because we do not know what analytical procedures might identify such stepwise changes, except in the presence of such obvious time-markers as the menopause, retirement, illness, bereavement, and so on.

Obviously, chronological age is related to numerous variables of interest. The question, however, is how to explain these relationships. Many of them disappear or change if one takes account of moderating variables. For example, the apparent relationship between intelligence test score and chronological age varies, depending upon whether the health and educational status of the subjects in the various age groups is allowed to vary naturally or is standardized. The relationship may be accounted for in part by cohort effects. Statistical methods make it possible to separate out the effects of variables singly or in combination, without necessarily resorting to selection and matching.

In addition to chronological age (measured in years since birth), one can refer to biological age (measured relative to physiological age norms) and functional age (measured relative to age norms of performance). Society too has its age norms, namely the ages at which people are expected to occupy particular positions, engage in particular activities, and so on.

We need not employ a cross-sectional method of the sort described later (where we look for *differences* between people of different ages). Instead, we could take a sample of people of a given age, say 40 years, and observe them at five-year intervals over a period of time, say 30 years. We would not necessarily find that the age relationships in this longitudinal study (where we look for *changes* in people at different ages) were the same as those observed for the comparable cross-sectional study. In this event we would have the problem of explaining the discrepancies between the two sets of results.

Another possibility is to compare an older age group tested at an earlier date with a similar age group tested at a later date, so that the period between the times of testing matches the interval between the two cohorts. Thus, a comparison between subjects born in 1910 and tested in 1970 (at age 60) and subjects born in 1930 and tested in 1990 (at age 60) provides a simple *time-lag* or time-sequential comparison.

Notice that even if we could be reasonably sure that an observed difference in behaviour was attributable to age (rather than to cohort or to period), we have still not identified the causal mechanism(s), since chronological age is merely a time-marker. Many diverse factors have age-related effects.

In practice the problems multiply. The samples used in cross-sectional studies belong to different cohorts, with all that that implies in the way of life-history effects; the older subjects represent survivors, not the original cohort. The sample used in a longitudinal study belongs to one cohort which may be different from adjacent cohorts. At successively later stages in the follow-up the sample suffers attrition through death, relocation, ill-health, withdrawal, and so on. The subjects available at the later stages are not comparable with the original sample because the losses are not random; on average the subjects who remain are more able, healthier, and better adjusted.

The effects attributable to cohort (time of birth) and period (the interval of time under consideration) and ageing (intrinsic maturational and senescent processes) cannot be easily separated from each other or from the effects attributable to the particular occasion(s) of assessment (time(s) of testing). The difference between cohort effects and time of measurement effects is that cohort effects are usually regarded as the overall result of secular changes in genetic and environmental conditions which bring about differences between successive generations of people, whereas time of measurement effects are more specifically related to the occasion(s) of observation, and the period(s) in between. Thus observations carried out during a period of unusually hot or cold weather, or during a period of social unrest or economic upheaval, might be affected by those particular circumstances. In practice, time of measurement effects are regarded as artefacts—as unavoidable conditions which may be relevant and so have to be reported. The resulting interpretation thus usually depends on *post-hoc* reasoning.

Of course, cohort effects, time-lag effects, and effects arising from occasions of measurement, may be considerable for particular groups of people, e.g. minority groups, or for particular sorts of function, e.g. attitudes and opinions. Changes in dietary habits, physical exercise, employment, social attitudes, and so on can be expected to obscure the normal effects of ageing, especially in connection with studies of obesity, physiological functions, and lifestyle.

Elaborate experimental designs comparing subjects born at various times and tested at various times at different ages (using either repeated measures or comparable independent samples) can go some way to indicate the effects of cohort, age, and time of measurement, but do not seem to provide a formal proof of these effects—see pp. 336–52.

SCIENTIFIC METHODS

There are many genuine attempts to use scientific procedures in behavioural gerontology, the findings of which fail to find acceptance because the procedures do not, on close examination, measure up to the required standards. It is relatively easy to find flaws in the methods and arguments described in the published research. This section raises some issues which, if taken further, would lead us too far into the philosophy of behavioural science, i.e. the wider context of behavioural gerontology—see Table 1.4.

The standards of what is scientifically acceptable in behavioural gerontology are, in principle, no different from the standards in any other scientific enterprise. Each such enterprise has its own special requirements, of course, and to that extent they are all different—as meteorology differs from archaeology and as genetics differs from social psychology. The closer one gets to the frontiers of research in these and other disciplines the more obvious these conceptual and methodological requirements become.

What scientific enterprises have in common is the use of rational argument and empirical evidence to further our understanding of Nature (including human nature) and a willingness, even an obligation, to subject claims to knowledge to critical inquiry. Scientific knowledge is not so much the accumulation of observations as the continual evolution of conceptual systems which provide us with improved understanding, control, and prediction of Nature.

It is important to hold fast to this root idea of scientific method as a combination of rational argument and empirical evidence. First, because by this means we can consider a much wider range of inquiries, some of which may appear to have little in common and may fall outside the traditional forms of scientific inquiry. Second, because behavioural gerontology as a multidisciplinary area covers a wide range of topics anyway, it must remain free to use concepts and methods derived from other disciplines, and free to develop its own wherever necessary. The main reason, however, for holding fast to the root idea of scientific method is that no one method, no single inquiry, is likely to provide a clear (much less irrefutable) conclusion about the topic under investigation. Scientific claims to knowledge are always provisional and approximate, never final and exact. The best way to proceed, scientifically, is to use a multiplicity of relatively independent rational approaches and empirical methods in the expectation that these will eventually converge on one conclusion rather than another. Other ways of proceeding are to replicate studies, to aggregate data so that findings are robust, i.e. do not vary unduly across minor variations in conditions, and to combine the results of independent investigations in meta-analyses.

It follows that, although there may be a small number of methodological considerations which are peculiar to behavioural gerontology as a 'scientific' discipline, it will nevertheless be capable of pursuing its inquiries by means of a wide variety of scientifically acceptable methods. Indeed, we have an obligation to test our claims to knowledge in different ways. Our account of the appropriate methods, therefore, will cover a wide range of techniques at a relatively elementary level, simply to show the diversity of approaches; those methodological considerations which are peculiar to the area will be dealt with in rather more detail.

Scientific inquiry begins with curiosity and puzzlement, followed by a desire to satisfy that curiosity, solve the problem, and understand the phenomenon of interest. This sort of research is said to be 'curiosity-led'. For example, it would be interesting to know why women, on average, live longer than men, and why some cognitive functions decline with age more rapidly than others. Another sort of research is that which attempts to solve a practical problem. For example, it would be useful to be able to measure the social benefits and financial costs of community care of the elderly infirm, and to construct hearing aids tuned to individual hearing losses.

Ordinary everyday experience, or experience gained in the laboratory or field of professional inquiry, provides investigators with vaguely formulated expectations and beliefs about matters which puzzle them. They may wonder, for example, why one recently widowed woman should grieve deeply and for a long time, whilst another, whose initial grief seemed just as deep, should recover from her bereavement in a relatively short time. Again, they may wonder whether a fixed retirement age, with its apparent neglect of individual differences in occupational demands and personal characteristics, might be abolished in favour of a flexible retirement age. Most of us, when we observe the adverse effects of ageing on physical and mental capacities, wonder what might be done to prevent, retard, or alleviate these infirmities of later life.

In order to pursue our initial interest in a topic we obviously need time, ability, and resources. Their availability helps to determine the extent to which we can formulate the problem more fully, generate ideas as to possible solutions, collect relevant evidence, and demonstrate a reasonable answer. Accordingly, scientific methods vary in rigorousness from casual observation and *ad-hoc* reasoning to systematic observation and integrated theorizing.

Casual observations and ordinary explanations are familiar in 'common-sense' approaches to ageing and may seem, at first glance, to be the antithesis of scientific inquiry. It is a mistake, however, to reject casual observation and common-sense accounts of behaviour and experience, because they can sometimes provide suggestions for more rigorous scientific inquiries. They can also constitute formidable 'facts' which a scientific account must somehow dissolve or come to terms with. Moreover, ordinary explanations are interesting in their own right and may well have a part to play in behavioural gerontology, e.g. in relation to self-reports of health and performance. We need not describe the various scientific methods in any sort of detail, but simply note that clinical observation and individual case-studies play an important role, as do experiments, surveys and field-studies—see Bromley (1986), Kerlinger (1986).

The life-history method

Biographical and autobiographical studies have played a relatively small part in psychological research generally, but see Runyan (1982). They have been seen mainly as contributions to the study of history—hence the term 'psychohistory' which is used to refer to attempts to use psychological theory, and especially psychoanalysis, to interpret the behaviour of important historical figures. The lives of some well-known people—artists, scientists, criminals, businessmen, politicians, soldiers— may be of interest to us as psychologists.

It is easy to see that the study of lives, with its emphasis on the psychological and social factors in behaviour and its concern with the context and consequences of that behaviour, is an important research strategy in social gerontology. Its emphasis would have to shift somewhat from the earlier to the later stages of adult life, and the theoretical (explanatory) approach would have to be scientifically acceptable. Its techniques of inquiry would remain essentially the same as those of historical research, although the scope of an inquiry might be broadened in view of psychology's theoretical input. Biographical and autobiographical research need not be confined to the study of important and well-known people. The method can be used to study quite ordinary lives. The disadvantage here is the relative paucity of information and the difficulty of tracing records and informants. Reminiscence and life-review are natural and acceptable to older people—see Chapters 4 and 6. However, such self-reports need to be guided, checked for internal consistency, and where possible corroborated by reference to external testimony, public and private records, and so on.

What contribution could biographical and autobiographical research make to our knowledge of ageing? First, it could illustrate the more frequent sorts of life-histories as well as the wide variety of possible life-paths—see Herbst (1970) and Runyan (1984). Second, it could show cohort effects in the sorts of lives people lead. Third, it could concentrate on the study of the later stages of lives with particular reference to successful ageing. This third possibility would tie in with the case-study approach, since a case-study is simply a detailed inquiry into one segment of, or major episode in, the life-course. A case-study concentrates on the more immediate, proximal, factors in behaviour, without unnecessary reference to life-history data. A life-history, on the other hand, tries to identify long-term patterns of behaviour, continuities, and discontinuities in the life-course. So for example the case-study method might seek to describe and explain an elderly person's adjustment to residential care in terms of the factors operating at the time, and with little reference to the person's previous life. The life-history method, by contrast, would seek to describe and explain the elderly person's adjustment in the context of that individual's personal history—to see it as a natural consequence or as a characteristic reaction, or possibly as a clear discontinuity brought about by unusual circumstances such as stress or mental breakdown.

Intensive clinical observation leading to the conceptualization of 'model cases', and to comparisons and contrasts between subsets of cases, has affinities with the survey method. There are procedures, such as cluster analysis, which, when applied to data sets from relatively large samples, enable one to group together cases which 'belong together' as a statistical subset because of the relative similarity of their characteristics and to separate such subsets from each other because of the relative dissimilarity of their characteristics. The now classical work on strategies of adjustment in later life (see Reichard et al., 1962) made use of cluster analysis in identifying several distinct personality types or strategies of adjustment: constructiveness, dependence, denial, anger, and self-hate. Even though these distinctions between personality types are only provisional, they may be of considerable practical value because they provide a way of conceptualizing and dealing with different sorts of elderly people.

The difference between the intensive (clinical) method and the extensive (survey) method is that the former is essentially small-scale, open, exploratory, sequential, and recursive (i.e. it progressively revises its descriptions and taxonomy), whereas the latter generally operates on a large scale and depends upon some pre-existing theory to guide the procedure by means of which the data are collected and analysed. Naturally, the results of an extensive survey can be used to develop revisions of the theory and method for the next occasion of research.

The survey method is also too well known to warrant detailed description here. However, there are a number of points to be made about the survey method in the context of social and behavioural gerontology. First, survey respondents are usually volunteers, and often the response rate in social surveys is less than satisfactory. This applies particularly to surveys of a personal nature (sexual behaviour, spending habits, and so on), and to surveys which require time and effort (psychometric surveys, longitudinal surveys, lengthy questionnaires, and so on). For various reasons—health, mobility, accessibility—older subjects are less likely to be approached, and less likely to volunteer if they are approached. Hence, the 'representativeness' of samples of older subjects is easily called into question.

Todd et al. (1984) were able to compare the characteristics of volunteers and non-volunteers by obtaining access to information about people eligible to volunteer in three organizations. Middle-aged white subjects were more likely to volunteer than younger or older subjects. Younger women and middle-aged women volunteered more readily than men, although older women did not. There are other factors affecting willingness to volunteer. Hence, investigators wishing to draw a quasi-representative sample from a given population cannot rely on volunteers, unless they make a special effort to recruit subjects who would otherwise not volunteer.

Second, survey interviewers are usually relatively young; so there is a risk of distortion arising because of the age discrepancy between young interviewers and old respondents. Third, self-completed questionnaires may be designed and printed without regard to the ability of respondents to understand the instructions and statements on the form. The size of print may be too small, the layout of text may hinder comprehension. Personality questionnaires and social attitude scales designed for young adults may not be entirely appropriate (valid) for older age groups. Fourth, older subjects may be prone to response biases different from those known to affect younger respondents.

In practice, research subjects are usually not selected in a representative way; they are often not drawn from a well-defined population (although medical registers may provide a good approximation). They cannot be randomly allocated to important conditions because variables such as age, education, health, socioeconomic status, and ability, operate as 'subject variables', which means that they are characteristics of the subject and cannot be distributed as the investigator would wish. Attempts to set up 'matched' or 'contrasting' groups entails considerable waste of subjects and assumes prior knowledge of related effects. Furthermore, unless great care is taken with regard to the circumstances of testing—environment, instructions, materials, and so on—there may be differential effects on the various age groups. Hoinville (1983) describes a considerable number of problems encountered in sampling and interviewing the elderly in the context of social survey research.

Conclusions reached on the basis of experimental studies may or may not generalize to behaviour in real-life situations outside the laboratory. The extent to which findings can be generalized or shown to have 'ecological' validity has to be established empirically. Much human behaviour is context-dependent. Even apparently small variations in the circumstances surrounding an action may influence its course. So, for example, an improvement in performance following training in a laboratory may disappear when the subject is observed in his or her natural surroundings. Similarly a sex difference found in an experimental study of learning may have no implications for sex differences in behaviour outside the laboratory.

Change-scores and time-series

Another problem is the use of change-scores to measure the effects of ageing—see Goldstein (1979), Harris (1967), Plewis (1985). If the effects of ageing are relatively small but cumulative the investigator has to make comparisons over, say, a five- or 10-year interval at least to be reasonably sure of detecting a significant effect. Furthermore, change-scores are particularly unreliable (because they compound the unreliability of each of the test scores from which they are derived). The changes may be associated with initial levels of performance. For example, there may be a regression effect whereby high initial scores are associated with losses, and low initial scores with gains. Statistical methods are available to overcome some of these difficulties—for example, covariance analysis, but see George and Okun (1976).

A time-series analysis is one in which observations (measurements) on a few persons are made on many occasions over a given period of time. This contrasts with the traditional longitudinal method in which observations on many persons are made on a few, usually two or three, widely separated occasions. Serial measurements show interdependency, i.e. measurements which are near to each other in time are more closely related than measurements distant from each other. The problem is how to assess and explain the serial dependencies observed in adult life characteristics, e.g. successive measures of personality, intelligence, work output, social attitudes, self-concept, and so on. Consider, for example, a situation in which social activity or physical exercise is a 'treatment' designed to improve well-being or relevant performance. Repeated measures over the treatment period would show either improvement, decline, or no change (or conceivably a nonlinear change). The problem is to determine whether a true time-series effect is present, and if so, its magnitude and causes.

It is possible that changes over time may occur even though the underlying determinants remain stable. Similarly, the underlying determinants may change without obvious observable effects. For example, there may be age-changes in the speed and accuracy of a perceptual-motor performance, such as maze-tracing, even though the underlying cognitive strategy remains the same. Similarly, a person may maintain a given level of performance, say in work output or golf or in terms of expenditure of money, and yet do so in different ways at later ages. What the investigator needs to do is to examine not just the numbers, as it were, but also the relationships between the numbers. For example, although there may be a complex pattern of changes in the scores over time on an intelligence test or personality test, the underlying factor structure may remain stable. By contrast, if the tests are sampling somewhat different characteristics at successive ages, i.e. if the factor-structure varies across different age groups, then the test scores may not change much because people of different ages are dealing with the items in different ways.

A distinction can be made between 'stability' and 'temporal invariance': stability means that the scores do not change over time; temporal invariance means that the relationships between scores do not change over time. The standard practice for assessing the stability of psychological characteristics is to calculate the test–retest correlation (one sort of autocorrelation). But the test–retest correlation is affected not only by the reliability of the test, but also by the stability of the characteristic the test is designed to measure. Thus a low autocorrelation value might mean either low reliability, low stability, or both. As mentioned above, the factorial composition of a test does not necessarily remain constant over successive age levels (or indeed over other variations in the characteristics of samples); so this too may reduce a test–retest correlation. There are various ways in which an autocorrelation can be corrected for the unreliability of the test. Note that whereas unreliability reduces the test–retest correlation, the use of the same or a very similar test on both occasions will tend to increase it (because of shared method variance). The use of more than one measure—multiple indicators—should help to reduce measurement error.

The statistical technique called 'path analysis' (Salthouse et al., 1988) may clarify the causal connections between several variables, e.g. age, sex, education, health, friendships, and an outcome measure such as social adjustment, cognitive performance, functional capacity, or well-being.

The limitations imposed by psychometric measurement, non-normal distributions and nonlinear relationships add to the methodological complications already referred to. As if this were not enough, there is no guarantee that a test which is valid for one age group is equally valid for another.

Surveys report unacceptably high levels of methodological and statistical errors in the published literature of psychology and psychiatry—see Davies et al. (1987). In view of the additional methodological and statistical complications encountered in research in the psychology of ageing, the need for extra care is obvious (Overall, 1987; Scialfa and Games, 1987). Replications and the use of diverse approaches to a problem should lead to improvements in the general level of confidence in the results of research in behavioural gerontology.

Experimental investigations, like any other kind of scientific investigations, must therefore be treated with considerable caution and scepticism because in psychological gerontology particularly the complexities of the phenomena are considerable—a multiplicity of interacting variables, wide differences between individual persons, relatively unstable individual characteristics, poorly standardized methods of measurement, cohort effects, selective death rates, volunteer effects, drop-out effects, and so on.

Readers should now appreciate why methodology is a 'central topic' in behavioural gerontology. Given that a problem is interesting enough, with reference to its theoretical or practical significance, how can investigators decide what scientific methods of inquiry to employ? There is no easy answer to this question. In the first place their choice is limited by time, money, and other resources, such as the availability of skilled manpower. In the second place their choice depends upon the state of scientific knowledge in the particular area of inquiry. Consider, for example, a proposal to study the effects of ageing on adult intelligence. Investigators have to take account of the concepts, methods, and findings that constitute the present state of knowledge, admittedly confused, about adult intelligence, and cognition generally. This might incline them to believe that a series of overlapping short-term longitudinal surveys using specially designed and properly standardized psychometric tests would be the best way to proceed, except that they would need something like 50 person-years of research time and £2m (two to three million dollars) to carry out the investigation. Alternatively, they might consider the intensive cognitive assessment of specially selected cases matched at different age levels (a cross-sectional and clinical approach), in an attempt to correlate findings from a wide array of psychometric, clinical, and laboratory measures of cognitive function with findings from detailed neurological investigations using the most modern electronic and computing technology.

Scientific research is something of a gamble, at least as regards the extent to which an investigator is successful in making a significant and lasting contribution to scientific knowledge. As in war, scientific victory often goes to the big battalions, i.e. to well-endowed research teams, but in many areas of scientific research there are no big spenders, yet a solitary investigator, or perhaps two or three colleagues working together, without much in the way of support services, can sometimes generate ideas and methods with revolutionary consequences, and often produce worthwhile contributions.

Scientific method is mainly about testing ideas against the relevant evidence, but the ideas themselves are the products of experience, imagination, ingenuity, and problem-solving. Consider an extremely apt illustration in this connection—the work of Lehman (1953) on the effects of age on intellectual creativity. Lehman's starting point was the question of whether the rate at which people were making significant contributions to art, science, literature, and technology was related to chronological age. In particular, did it decline after age 40? Lehman's effort lay clearly in the tradition of scientific discovery—10% inspiration, 90% perspiration. He saw that history books and source books (or other archival data) in a particular field of intellectual endeavour would cite significant and lasting contributions by particular people; that the birth date and age at death of these individuals would be available, and that by combining comparable fields of endeavour, or splitting them, as appropriate, he would be able to plot frequency distributions or show the rates at which people at different chronological ages were making significant contributions to their field of endeavour. As is well known, the age distribution for many kinds of scientific and intellectual endeavour rises from near zero at age 20 to a peak at age 30–35, and then declines steadily throughout the remainder of the lifespan. Scientific work, however, does not end with a systematic description of the observations made. These observations have to be interpreted in some kind of conceptual or explanatory framework. Lehman's findings have been the subject of critical examination and have stimulated various kinds of related research—see McLeish (1981), Simonton (1977), van Heeringen and Dijkwel (1987a, b) and Zusné (1976). Some critics have objected to the methods used in collecting the data, others have objected to the sorts of explanation Lehman has put forward to account for his findings. There are, of course, other ways of investigating the relation between age and intellectual achievement. In passing, we should note that archival data— information recorded and stored for possible future use—must play an increasingly important role in behavioural gerontology because the long periods of time over which age-related effects accumulate tend to exceed the working lives of researchers, and can only be handled effectively by organizations, such as institutes of gerontology.

Non-reactive methods of observation

Some aspects of adult life and old age lend themselves to systematic, non-reactive methods of observation. An obvious example would be pedestrian behaviour in relation to motor vehicles; other examples could be found in the ordinary activities of daily life—domestic and leisure activities. Pedestrian behaviour is easily observed and recorded in a systematic and non-intrusive way. The use of film or video, together with follow-up inquiries relating to the age and health of the pedestrians observed, would help solve problems concerned with the reliability and validity of observations. In this way it would be possible to identify the special hazards to which older pedestrians are exposed and the unnecessary risks they are inclined to take—for example, slow reactions and the time required to cross a road, and the failure to monitor road conditions after starting to cross.

Accidents can be studied retrospectively, e.g. through accident records or critical incident analysis. In the case of accidents whilst driving a motor vehicle, accident reports and insurance claims can be used to classify the types of accident; their causes; and the age, sex, and driving experience of the drivers involved. Such an analysis reveals that the pattern of accidents for older drivers is different from that for younger drivers—Planek and Fowler (1971). The same sorts of analysis can be carried out for accidents at home or at work.

Other aspects of adult life and old age that can be studied by means of systematic, non-reactive methods of investigation include non-verbal expressive behaviour, spoken language as revealed in ordinary face-to-face or telephone conversations, and written language. Provided the necessary records can be obtained systematically without interfering with the behaviour under investigation, subsequent analysis of the data can be carried out at leisure. One would expect to find effects associated with sensory and motor impairment, interest, arousal and so on in relation to non-verbal expressive behaviour, and effects associated with attention, short-term memory, and practice, for example, in relation to conversational skills and written language.

A logical extension of the systematic non-reactive method of observation is the 'hidden experiment', i.e. the setting up of a contrived situation in which the experimental subjects behave as they would in real life. There is scope for research of this kind in gerontological social psychology provided the ethical restrictions associated with the method can be met. In principle, however, it would be possible to study phenomena such as social interaction, communication, conformity, and cooperation, and a variety of 'demand characteristics', in relation to adult life and ageing.

Simulation and role-playing provide additional techniques for research in behavioural gerontology although they are more often used for training purposes. Sensory and motor disabilities and aspects of behaviour such as dependency and assertiveness might be investigated by these and related methods.

A related method for studying the effects of ageing, not so far used to any great extent, is that of 'unobtrusive observation' (Webb et al., 1966), i.e. the use of traces and records left behind as a result of people's behaviour. Thus letters, diaries, notebooks, and accounts are obvious sources of data, as are registers, membership lists, citations, household possessions, photographs, and medicine bottles (consider what the contents of refuse bins reveal about individual households!). We take note of records and traces in a casual way in daily life, but the professional research worker (as well as the detective or spy) may be able to make more systematic use of them. The alert social worker, for example, observes the state of repair and cleanliness in the house of a patient living alone, and observes the dates on newspapers or envelopes that are lying about. Traces and records are most useful when they accumulate systematically and without reference to the use to which they will be put in gerontological research. So, for example, a series of letters spanning many years may provide the raw data which on analysis might demonstrate changes in attitudes, values, and language ability. The records available to Lehman and other research workers, in the form of citations in journals, history books, source books, and proceedings of learned societies, provided the raw data relevant to his study of achievement in adult life.

The photographs, personal records, artefacts, and other memorabilia we accumulate during our lifetime reflect (in ways that require interpretation and validation) our psychological and social characteristics over long periods of time—see Collier (1967) for an account of photography as a research method in anthropology which has applications in social and behavioural gerontology.

In general, advances in technology, especially in communications and computing, can be expected to greatly increase the range of data available to researchers in gerontology (P. Robinson *et al.*, 1984). Consider, for example, monitoring performance at-a-distance. Advances in technology are likely to have profound effects on many aspects of human ageing—see *Social Behaviour* (1988).

Measurement

Although they are not absolutely essential, measurement and quantification are important aids to scientific inquiry. Measurement and quantification in a sense span the full range of scientific inquiry from simple observational counts and timings to the use of complex standardized psychometric and physiological measures, and from the simplest of descriptive statistics to the most elaborate forms of experimental design and analysis.

Biomedical measurement—height, weight, skinfold thickness, ventilatory capacity, visual activity, blood sugar level, and so on—are fairly direct, although even here measures may not be perfectly reliable and may not indicate what the investigator thinks they indicate—but see Waters *et al.* (1987). By comparison, psychological and social measurements tend to be much less reliable and valid. Consider, for example, measures designed to assess cognitive capacity, emotional well-being, social adjustment, and attitude to retirement. Performance on measures like these depends critically on the sorts of items used, their wording, the way the test instructions are understood, and the way the subjects' responses are scored. It does not follow that a test which is reliable and valid for one group or one type of person will be equally valid for another age group or type of person.

In the case of simple direct observation recorded in note or narrative form, it is usually a question of counting incidents or responses, and timing their duration, from the 'specimen record', as in the study of children in ordinary environments (Barker, 1963). Given that such narrative data are available for certain classes of subject in certain kinds of settings, e.g. residential homes for the elderly, it is possible to make comparisons of behaviour, as for example between males and females, between different times of the day or days of the week, between different institutional arrangements—see Browne and Armstrong-Esther (1984).

In some circumstances it may be advantageous, in terms of economy of resources and standardization of procedure, to use checklists and rating scales rather than narrative accounts. A checklist may provide a more comprehensive list of behaviour items; at the same time it may not discriminate adequately between subjects or patients who display the 'same' behaviour item, e.g. 'complains', 'shows anger'. Rating scales are used in the hope that they enable an observer to make his (or her) judgment more exactly, e.g. friendly (+) vs very friendly (++). Ratings, however, are highly subjective and very much influenced by range effects; one's rating of the behaviour of an elderly person is strongly influenced by prior expectations and by the immediately preceding pattern of ratings, so that one's rating of a particular patient's orientation is influenced by the expectation one has built up about the level and spread of patient behaviour. Thus one's rating of a patient as higher or lower is relative to one's subjective standard; this is particularly damaging if that subjective standard is unreliable. Range effects in ratings can be offset to some extent by forced distributions, by controlling order effects, or by resorting to ranking methods.

In addition to simple checklists and rating scales, there is a wide range of psychometric instruments—questionnaires, tests, and so on—although most are not adequately standardized. Mangen and Peterson (1982a, b, 1984) and Kane and Kane (1981) have reviewed many measures used in social and behavioural gerontology—see also Chapters 3 and 4.

In this chapter the experimental method has been deliberately played down for two reasons. First, it is probably the best-known method of scientific investigation in psychology and needs no special treatment or emphasis in relation to gerontology. Second, it shares, with other methods of systematic observation, some serious deficiencies as a scientific method in psychology. These deficiencies have to do with the reliability and generality of findings from experimental inquiry. It is easy to see that a particular response or performance may be affected by a variety of antecedent conditions, e.g. ability, familiarity, instructions, stress, fatigue, stimulus characteristics, distraction. It follows that a similar response or performance on another occasion is likely to occur only if the antecedent conditions are similar. It is not surprising therefore that the results of a single experiment tend to be unique. Identity (replication) of results can often be achieved only by controlling the outcome very closely, i.e. the experimental effect is not always 'robust' in the sense of being demonstrable across apparently trivial variations in conditions. Often investigators fail to report the extent to which their findings are restricted to the specific circumstances of the experiment.

One way out of this difficulty is to accumulate, or aggregate, experimental results—see Epstein (1983). Thus, for example, although a single measure of choice reaction time would be unreliable as an index of speed of response, yet repeated measures over many trials, especially if they achieve a 'steady state', would be reliable, e.g. as measured by the correlation of odd with even trials over a sample of subjects. There is an obvious analogy with the reliability of psychometric tests of intelligence or personality, where, in general, tests which incorporate a larger number of relevant items tend to be more reliable than shorter tests. The validity and generalizability of psychological measures is a separate issue.

Variations in performance may occur for apparently trivial reasons, for example the choice of words in an experiment on learning, the emphasis laid on speed or accuracy in an experiment on reaction time, the choice of masking stimuli in an experiment on perceptual discrimination, the use of one sort of placebo rather than another. Such variations can lead to inconsistent results in attempts to replicate investigations. As has been pointed out by Epstein, the solution to this problem is not necessarily to tighten up the experimental controls (which may make matters worse) but to aggregate data, thus increasing effect size and robustness in replication studies. Statistical significance is not the only important issue. The need for highly reliable results—from further tests in various conditions on heterogeneous samples—is particularly important in research in ageing because of the unreliability of first-time, single-occasion measures. Remember too that older subjects tend to perform less reliably, so that a larger 'sample' of their behaviour is needed in order to estimate a performance characteristic accurately.

A similar principle applies to the diversity of the experimental (or psychometric) conditions. If an aspect of behaviour—say mental speed, intellectual creativity, or optimism—can be assessed by means of diverse measures, then the aggregate of many such measures tends to be more reliable than any one of them. The problem is to ensure that the aggregated measures are all measuring different aspects of the same thing. We have seen that human behaviour may be affected by a great many antecedent and concurrent variables, some of them not very obvious; so there is no guarantee that the experimental variables are responsible for the outcome even if the level of statistical significance is quite high. The question is: would the experimental outcome be substantially the same, i.e. reliable, if conditions other than those presently under experimental control were changed? In other words would coincidental contextual factors affect the outcome?

Briefly, then, some of the psychological changes associated with adult ageing will be obscure and unreliable if they are based on single occasions of measurement. This might be the case, for example, if practice effects or comprehension of the instructions had a significant influence on performance.

The long periods of time needed to reveal significant ageing effects provide one of the conditions necessary for accumulating the sorts of data needed for robust generalizations. One advantage of this approach is that the problem can be viewed as a set of related sub-problems. For example, we can focus our attention intensively on small groups of subjects homogeneous for a variety of characteristics, including environmental circumstances, over a substantial number of years, say 10. We might examine, age-related changes in the professions, in the use of time and money, in self-appraisal, and moral outlook. The accumulation of repeated observations with a diverse but related set of measures should make it possible to arrive at robust generalizations for subjects of a given sort in circumstances of a given sort over a particular period of life. Similar or related studies of other groups in other circumstances during the same or different periods of life should provide the individual building blocks for a systematic account of the psychology of adult life and old age. The traditional emphasis on between-subject variations would be complemented by an increased emphasis on within-subject variation. This might lead to an increased concern with intervention as a means of testing hypotheses: for example that marital counselling during the menopause improves the health and well-being of couples.

Segmentation

One way of circumventing the methodological difficulties associated with age, cohort, and period effects would be to divide adult life into a series of relatively short overlapping segments, say ten years or less, and study each of these segments in detail. This method would tie in closely with research into stressful life-events, but would be concerned mainly with identifying the *normal* factors governing the organization of behaviour in each age segment. It might be possible in this way to identify critical age periods in adult life, namely those which are associated with substantial normal shifts in the organization of behaviour within or between one segment and another.

This strategy reverses the traditional strategy, which is to try to identify a significant factor in the organization of behaviour by exploring its effects over a wide age range. The justification for this strategy is that chronological age has relatively little effect in the short run and may be outweighed by the effects of education, health, and socioeconomic status.

THE PROBLEM OF AGE, COHORT, AND PERIOD EFFECTS

Basic experimental designs

Most research investigations in behavioural gerontology tend to follow one of two basic designs: longitudinal or cross-sectional. There is a third type of design which combines the longitudinal and cross-sectional methods. It may be referred to as the cross-sequential, time-lag, or more usually the time-sequential method. There have been few investigations of this latter sort, but those that have been carried out have given rise to considerable interest.

The *longitudinal*, or *follow-up*, method measures the performance of a sample of subjects at an initial chronological age, and then on one or more subsequent occasions—over shorter or longer intervals. The results are described in graphs or tables, and the appropriate tests are applied to examine whether the 'effects of age' are statistically significant. Contrasting groups of subjects, for example males versus females, or contrasting experimental treatments, such as nutrition or exercise, can be examined for any differential effects of ageing. If several variables are measured, changes in their relationships over time may be of interest, for example blood pressure and psychiatric symptoms.

The *cross-sectional* method measures the performance of two or more comparable samples of subjects at different age levels. The method of setting up comparable samples varies, depending on whether they are intended to represent actual age groups or a hypothetical set of populations matched for, say, education, health, and intelligence. As with the longitudinal method, contrasting groups or experimental treatments can be examined for any differential effects of ageing. If several variables are measured, their relationships with each other may vary systematically from one age level to another. For example, the relationship between self-confidence and social interaction in middle age may be different from that in later life.

The *mixed* (*cross-sequential* or *time-lag*) method measures the performance of several groups (assumed to be comparable) at different initial ages (in the example below at 45, 50 and 55 years), as in the cross-sectional method, and then follows up each group with similar measures on one or more subsequent occasions. In the example below the subjects are tested initially in 1981–5 and then in 1986–90 and 1991–5. This method combines the advantages and eliminates some of the disadvantages of the longitudinal and cross-sectional methods, and for this reason it is regarded by some as the ideal method.

Note that the cohort by time of measurement data in Table 8.1 (p. 342) could have been set out differently, with chronological ages listed at the head of the rows or columns, with cohort or time of measurement shown in the cells, or heading the column and row totals respectively. The information remains the same in all these arrays. Once the values of *two* of these factors are fixed, the values of the *third* are also fixed. In more elaborate designs the samples compared at different times of measurement need not be the *same* samples as in a 'repeated-measures' study. Instead, they can be *comparable* samples, selected in the same way or matched on an individual or group basis, so that practice and other confounding effects associated with repeated measures can be eliminated.

The *age changes* revealed by the longitudinal method are not always the same as the *age differences* revealed by the cross-sectional method, hence the persisting concern with methodological issues. Combining the two methods is a convenient way of cross-checking results and testing additional hypotheses. By general agreement the term *age change* is used to refer to the results from longitudinal studies—for the obvious reason that changes in score have been observed for the same or equivalent persons. Similarly, the term *age difference* is used to refer to the results from cross-sectional studies—because the scores for different persons are being compared. This familiar and easy usage is misleading, however, because it implies that an observed change or difference is an effect of *age*, when it might be a *cohort* effect, or a *period* effect, or even an *experimental artefact*, such as a fallible measure. Figure 8.1 shows some hypothetical results for two functions observed cross-sectionally and longitudinally. It is assumed that several age groups are tested initially and on a second occasion five years later. The complications arising from sampling errors and measurement errors are ignored. The solid trend line running through the cross-sectional results for fluid ability shows a more rapid decline at younger ages than does the dashed line for the longitudinal results. The dashed lines running through the longitudinal results for crystallized ability show greater improvements at younger ages than does the solid line for the cross-sectional results. The trends, however, are merely illustrative. In practice, different trends may be observed.

Such comparisons have been made, for example, for the effects of age on intelligence, hearing, and weight. The existence of a discrepancy means that one or the other or both methods are failing to show the effects of ageing; and even when no discrepancy occurs it does not follow that an age effect has been conclusively proven. Thus, strictly speaking, the term 'age changes' should refer to changes within persons which are demonstrably due to the effects of increased age; the term 'age differences' should refer to differences between persons which are demonstrably due

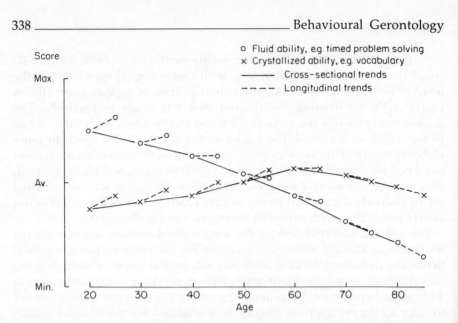

Figure 8.1 A schematic representation of some of the trends expected in cross-sectional and longitudinal studies of ageing. *Note*: In practice, research results are usually less systematic and less clear-cut, depending upon factors such as the population of interest, sampling restrictions, measurement errors, length of time to follow-up, and period effects

to the effects of increased age, similarly with cohort and period effects. Age effects are not necessarily the same as age-related effects. There are a number of reasons why the hypothetical results shown in Figure 8.1 are not as simple as they appear to be.

The cross-sectional method depends upon a number of conditions which are unlikely to be met, such as the following: that there has been no selective loss through death over the age range considered; that samples which are truly comparable and representative of the 'population' under investigation can be selected and tested at each age level; and that the measurements are valid, reliable, and equally applicable to all age groups. Even if all these conditions could be met, there still remains a major source of confusion: each group represents its respective cohort, defined as the people born into the reference population in a specific year, and there may have been systematic secular changes—generation-by-generation changes—in the function(s) under investigation. It is not clear to what extent such secular trends bring about equal changes in all or most members of the population of interest, or systematic differential changes, as between men and women, or between different socioeconomic classes. Secular effects can interact with age, for example in relation to amount of absence from work. Longevity itself shows a secular trend. The average duration of life has been increasing generation by generation, but it has not been increasing equally for all members of a cohort; it has been increasing more for those members with a relatively short life expectation—the upper limit of longevity seems to have remained fixed. It is possible that other psychological capacities are affected by secular trends reflecting the selective effects of social evolution, such as differential fertility rates, migration, and assortative mating.

The longitudinal method also depends upon a number of conditions which are unlikely to be met, such as the following: that the cohort selected for investigation is fairly typical; that the measurements are similarly valid and reliable at each age level on successive occasions of testing, and are sequentially independent; and that there is no systematic loss of subjects from the sample(s) throughout the follow-up period. Even if they could be met, there still remains a major source of confusion: the sample is subject to environmental influences (period or 'treatment' effects), which may affect performance directly or indirectly, and are peculiar to that cohort for those particular times of testing. Effects associated with environmental influence include those arising from socioeconomic conditions, and environmental health hazards—infectious diseases, pollution, radiation, stress. Little is known about such naturally occurring period effects on psychological capacities and behavioural dispositions in adult life. However, in relation to social attitudes and moral values there is evidence to suggest shifts in response to political and economic circumstances, technological and scientific developments, and cultural changes—consider, for example, what 'treatments', i.e. circumstances, have been responsible for effecting changes in social attitudes towards women, towards health, or towards early retirement.

Experimental biology attempts to demonstrate treatment effects as, for example, the effects of an 'enriched' environment on the rat's brain, and the effects of dietary restriction on longevity. The experimental psychology of ageing, similarly, attempts to demonstrate the effects of treatment intervention, for example the effects of cognitive training on mental skills, the effects of increased personal control on life-satisfaction, the effects of relocation and bereavement on further life-expectancy. But these are usually short-term interventions in which cohort and period effects are likely to be negligible.

Epidemiological methods attempt to show a connection between one set of events and another widely separated in time, for example rubella and deafness, drug treatment and birth defects. At present, however, we have little knowledge of such long-range effects affecting psychological functions in adult life and old age. Longitudinal studies have to be prospective if their full value is to be realized; but it is not unusual for a type of longitudinal study to be carried out retrospectively—by making observations in the present on subjects for whom similar or relevant observations were made in the past. The idea of the data-bank, with its standardized records, is already familiar in commerce and in the medical and social sciences, and might be usefully applied in more behaviourally oriented studies of ageing, for example in relation to consumer behaviour, occupational performance, leisure activities.

Longitudinal studies vary in duration. The starting and finishing ages are related to the nature of the problem under investigation: if the suspected ageing process is slow but cumulative, the follow-up period will be long; if critical ages or episodes are hypothesized, for example retirement or the menopause, then the follow-up period will date from shortly before until shortly after these events; and so on. The essential feature of a well-organized longitudinal study of ageing is that the observations should be strategically timed to span the process under investigation, so as to observe the critical phases as they occur.

Sequential patterns

Normally, a dimension of individual differences such as introversion or auditory acuity is investigated by comparing the scores of many individuals observed on one occasion. It has been argued that, in a similar way, a developmental or ageing dimension, i.e. sequence, could be investigated by the analysis of longitudinal changes in one or more subjects observed over many occasions. Presumably, they are analogous to sequential patterns like: the course of an illness, a career path, locomotor development, shifts of interests, or a series of cognitive changes.

The point is that it is not sufficient merely to describe quantitative age effects on a variety of existing dimensions of individual differences; such dimensions were established to describe static differences between persons—they are analogous to the properties of maps in geography. One map does not reveal how the individual parts of a given territory are changing over time; a series of maps, however, might reveal that changes were taking place—just as cross-sequential studies might reveal that biological, social, and psychological changes were taking place. The problem is to devise suitable concepts to describe the changes (in structure or function) thus observed. Using the map analogy, one might speak of silting, erosion, deforestation, subsidence, and so on, which do not correspond to anything on a map, but help to explain changes over a series of maps. In human ageing one speaks of the following dimensions of change: presbycousis, dementia, disengagement, compensatory slowing in perceptual motor performance, the menopause, adjustment to widow(er)hood, dying, and so on. These are concepts referring to observed changes in behaviour, capacity, and experience; they contrast with geographical concepts in that they are less well supported by empirical evidence, and less well embedded in a conceptual system or theory.

The measurement and representation of changes or differences over time are preliminary to the consideration of how these changes or differences are connected. That is, they provide evidence about *empirical* issues relevant to psychological *theories* about ageing. Behavioural gerontology should provide more than a mere narrative or chronology of events in adult life. It should show the causal connections between these events and make a kind of 'path analysis' of the psychobiological sequences of events that we refer to as ageing. Time, or age itself, although it can be easily identified and measured as a distinct variable, needs to be made substantial by showing that it is really a timetable of events. The processes of ageing are sequences of events which at present are known only fractionally and intermittently by reference to changes, usually losses, in function over a given period of time. Path analysis or causal analysis need make little reference to age or the passage of time, except to establish norms. It could be used, for example, to trace the typical sequences of events which lead to social isolation or psychiatric disorders of late onset. One aim is to identify adverse influences leading to increasingly deteriorated states; another aim is to find ways of retarding deterioration, and for renewing or improving functional capacities.

The interrelationships between age, cohort, and period can be seen by considering a hypothetical investigation which compares three age groups on three occasions at five-year intervals. For example, one might wish to investigate the effects of ageing on some aspect of personality, intelligence, or physiological function in women over the menopause years. Suppose we collected data on women in their 40s and 50s over a 10-year period. We might compile a data matrix like that in Table 8.1. The values X_{11} to X_{33} refer to values of the parameters we are interested in, e.g. averages, dispersions, proportions, as calculated from the measurements we take on, say, 100 subjects in each cell of the matrix. We might choose not to collect data for X_{13} and X_{31}, since they would be outside our range of interest and would not contribute to any calculations designed to separate out the effects of age, cohort, and time of measurement. In a repeated-measures design the 100 subjects in the 1931–5 cohort in 1981–5 are the same subjects tested in 1986–90 and 1991–5, and similarly with the 1936–40 and 1941–5 cohorts. There would be a problem of missing data if some subjects were to drop out over these occasions of testing. The 100 subjects in each cell of one matrix could be different from those in

Table 8.1 A data matrix format providing cross-sectional, longitudinal, and cross-sequential comparisons

	Times of measurement		
Cohort	1981–5	1986–90	1991–5
1931–5	X_{11} (50)*	X_{12} (55)	X_{13} (60)
1936–40	X_{21} (45)	X_{22} (50)	X_{23} (55)
1941–5	X_{31} (40)	X_{32} (45)	X_{33} (50)

* Chronological ages in parentheses

any other cell, but they would have to be comparable with each other in the sense of being appropriately 'matched', or 'related'.

The data thus generated enable us to calculate several sorts of differences between cells. We can calculate cross-sectional differences between the three cohorts over the three times of measurement. We can calculate longitudinal differences between the three times of measurement over the three cohorts. We can calculate cross-sequential or time-lag differences between those diagonal entries which have the same chronological age level, namely, 45, or 50 or 55.

Unfortunately, these three sorts of *differences* do not correspond on a one-to-one basis with the three sorts of *effects* we are interested in. Instead, following Palmore (1978), we see that cross-sectional differences combine age effects and cohort effects, longitudinal differences combine age effects and period effects, and time-lag differences combine period effects and cohort effects. This can be grasped intuitively by noting which value (age, cohort, or period) in the matrix remains constant for each of the three types of difference.

We note that once one has fixed any two of the *factors*—age, cohort, time of measurement—the third *factor* is fixed. However, as Palmore points out, this does not mean that the *effects* are similarly fixed. For example, life-satisfaction may vary with age—increasing up to middle age and then declining, it may show long-term secular variations—depending upon prevailing health standards and socioeconomic conditions, it may show short-term period effects—depending upon fluctuations in living standards. 'In other words, each of the three *effects* can vary independently of the other two' (Palmore, 1978, p. 285).

It is important to remember that age, period, and cohort are time factors, not causal mechanisms. Underlying any observed differences between the cells in the above data matrix there may be numerous causal mechanisms acting directly and indirectly to produce the observed effects, and acting in the same or opposite directions.

We already have evidence of secular trends in height, health, age at menarche, and so on. So we should not be surprised to find secular trends related to the menopause or other aspects of adult life. There is growing evidence of secular trends in intelligence for men, so we might expect a similar trend for women. There have been rapid and substantial changes in cultural conditions this century, so we might expect these to have produced cohort effects on measures of personality.

With regard to period (time of measurement), we have to consider whether the particular times of measurement we have chosen might have had an effect on our measurements. Several possibilities come to mind— for example, the availability of the contraceptive pill, new medicinal treatments for menopausal symptoms, cultural changes in diet, exercise, and leisure activities, and social norms affecting the role and status of women. These and other factors might affect the biological, psychological, and social characteristics of our female subjects at those ages over those periods of measurement.

If we consider a wider range of ages and times of measurement we could expect cumulative and complex effects of age, cohort, and period. We can try to overcome these difficulties by holding one of the three factors (age, cohort, period) constant. But this severely restricts the scope of our investigations.

One can argue that confirmation of cohort effects requires an historical perspective (hardly possible to accommodate within the methodology of behavioural gerontology). Even period effects over short intervals of five or 10 years are more appropriately accommodated within a sociological or epidemiological perspective. The study of age effects *in the short run* (minimizing cohort and period effects) is what behavioural gerontology methods are best suited for. Whether it will be possible to assemble the results of consecutive short-run studies to work out the *long-run* cumulative effects remains to be seen.

The argument is that the interrelationships between age, cohort, and period are central not only to the subject-matter of behavioural gerontology, but also to a variety of other disciplines—history, sociology, epidemiology, psychology—working independently of each other or in cooperation. They might or might not be elucidated much by large-scale cross-sequential studies of the sort described above. They are not methodological issues but substantive issues as explained on pp. 352–5. The pattern of effects can be expected to be revealed gradually as empirical findings accumulate, and as theoretical interpretations select and arrange numerous pieces of the multidisciplinary empirical mosaic into meaning-ful patterns.

In view of the attitude we are taking to the so-called 'methodological' problem of separating age, cohort, and period effects, and in view of our preference for short-run studies of ageing, I shall not deal in detail with the related technicalities of experimental design and statistical analysis. These are dealt with at length in other publications and are primarily of interest to the few researchers with access to ample funding for large-scale research.

However, we have an obligation to appreciate how the results of cross-sequential studies might be interpreted. Consider the top left tetrad of cells in Table 8.1. The values one is interested in are as follows, where the Xs are the parameters of interest:

Cross-sectional difference:	$(X_{11} - X_{21})$
Longitudinal difference:	$(X_{22} - X_{21})$
Time-lag difference:	$(X_{22} - X_{11})$

But

$$X_{11} - X_{21} = f \text{ (age + cohort)}$$
$$X_{22} - x_{21} = f \text{ (age + period)}$$
$$X_{22} - X_{11} = f \text{ (cohort + period)}$$

That is to say, each observed *effect* is a function of two *factors*. It is clear that even for a relatively simple data matrix with only three cohorts, three times of measurement, and three initial age levels, the statistical analysis required is complex and subject to a variety of constraints— statistical assumptions, measurement reliability, sampling problems, linearity, and so on. Following Palmore (1978) again, and referring to the above data matrix, we can envisage several possibilities.

The simplest possibility would be to find no significant differences between the parameter of one cell and that of any of its neighbours, i.e. no cross-sectional difference, no longitudinal difference, no cross-sequential (time-lag) difference. Finding small statistical differences of no great effect size might disincline us to pursue a line of inquiry further, since it would seem to offer no great practical or theoretical benefit. However, it is possible that there are substantial effects underlying this result, but that they are cancelling each other out. In this case our experimental design would have failed to reveal them, and if we had good reason to suppose that they existed, then we would have to try again with a modified design.

Next, suppose that some of the observed differences between neigh-bouring cells are significant, but others not. In this case much depends on whether the pattern of differences is consistent across the matrix as a whole. If it is, then we can suppose that the effect is robust and consistent across the ages and periods concerned.

In the simplest case, taking two cohorts and two times of measurement, if two out of the three relevant differences (cross-sectional, longitudinal, time-lag) are significant, then it is possible that one effect (age, cohort, or period) is responsible for these two significant differences, unless, of course, the effects are counteracting each other in some way.

If there are three significant differences, then external evidence is necessary to underpin the assumption that one of the effects is zero or that some combination of effects will account for the observed differences. See Palmore (1978) for further discussion and examples.

The question arises as to why one research design rather than another should be preferred. Apart from administrative considerations, such as cost and time, the choice of design depends upon what we are trying to discover and upon the context of knowledge about the phenomenon we are investigating. For example, if we have reason to believe that the nett effects of age on Function X are small, then we must examine a wide age range in order to increase the likelihood that the cumulative effect will outweigh countervailing influences, sampling variations, errors of measurement, and so on. If we have reason to believe that secular trends in Function X are nil or small, then we may choose to disregard them and feel free to select from a wide range of cohorts. Finally, if we think that time of measurement effects are critical, we may find it possible to restrict ourselves to a given set of retrospective measurement dates, for example those associated with epidemics, social change, or the use of certain drugs, assuming the relevant data are available. We may have reason to believe that the apparent age differences in Function X can be largely accounted for by a secular trend in X. In this situation we obviously wish to look at the effects of age when secular trends are controlled.

The logic of the various designs rests upon the idea that the effect of one of the three factors—age, cohort, or time of measurement—can be made negligibly small in comparison with the effects of the other two. The two main factors can then be examined in relation to each other. As we have seen, however, the observed surface measures and their differences cannot always be accounted for in terms of these factors, for the simple reason that the observed differences are usually compatible with several different interpretations. Exceptions to this general conclusion could occur if there were substantial changes at a critical age level or for a given cohort, or over a particular period. For then the score surface over a matrix like the one above would no longer be smooth but would reveal abrupt shifts or contour effects for say, the ages 45–55 in women (reflecting menopausal changes), or for the cohort 1941–5 (reflecting the stressful effects of wartime on young adults), or for the period 1981–5 (reflecting socioeconomic changes). Unfortunately, contour effects of the sort referred to are unlikely to be observed unless the ages, cohorts, and times of measurement are each measured in narrowly spaced intervals of say one year (rather than in decade or semi-decade intervals). Research designs using very short intervals of time would make sense only if there were strong reasons for supposing that a particular effect was strong and worth investigating.

The measurement of age-related effects

The investigator has to decide whether the *average* differences between age groups are statistically and psychologically significant. This is difficult because age differences are sometimes small, and the score distributions for different age groups overlap considerably. Statistical decision theory is needed to analyse such effects. Further complications arise if the score distributions are not 'normal', if upper and lower score limits artificially restrict the range of observations, if the units of measurement are not at least 'interval' scale units, and if the scores are not reasonably reliable.

A serious disadvantage with psychometric tests is that they may not be applicable, or equally applicable, throughout the whole period of adult life and old age. One reason for this is sheer inconvenience: tests tend to be standardized on readily available samples of subjects, and it is exceptional to find a test which has been standardized on representative samples of subjects at all adult age levels. Even the Wechsler Adult Intelligence Scale—probably the best example—might not qualify if one imposed the kinds of sampling requirements prescribed for social survey work. The consequence is that a test's norms may be in error, particularly at age levels not adequately represented in the standardization sample. Even biometric studies, however, face the more general methodological obstacles described above.

The considerable duration of adult life coupled with the apparently slow rate of change makes it necessary to devise measures which can be sensibly applied to subjects of widely differing ages, or at least makes it necessary to devise a series of measures, each applicable to a narrow age range, overlapping the adjacent ages to which other measures in the series are applicable.

The measurement of *changes* in behaviour, whether through the intrinsic effects of ageing or through some form of treatment or environmental influence, presents some formidable problems in psychometrics and statistics. In the simplest case one can compare a change in score from one occasion to the next, e.g. pre-test versus post-test, in a treatment group against a non-treatment group. Similarly one can compare an age change for one sort of group or treatment with an age change for another sort of group or treatment. Change-scores themselves represent a true change plus an error of measurement; but the error of measurement is compounded by the errors of measurement in the component scores, i.e. the pre- and post-test scores. The psychological measures may not be very reliable or valid, and there is an effect called regression to the mean, whereby high scores tend to decrease on retest and low scores tend to increase; so difference- or change-scores are difficult to interpret, especially over long intervals of time. Tests which are only moderately reliable in the short run will have poor predictive power in the long run.

Any variable which happens to be correlated with the initial (pre-test) score will be correlated with change-scores. Thus, if there is a sex difference on the initial test—for example, if men on average have a higher score than women—then statistical regression effects might make it appear that men and women were differently affected by the period or treatment interval.

Nowadays, statistical techniques such as discriminant analysis, multiple regression, and causal modelling provide ways of dealing with the problem of accounting for ageing effects arising from a multiplicity of interacting sources. They are most effective when used in association with a theory about the processes producing the effects, for the theory makes clear some of the assumptions on which the design of the investigation and the statistical analysis rest. So, for example, we might carry out a study in which chronological age is one of several variables used to predict, say, health status, scientific productivity, or political allegiance. The statistical analysis (applied to appropriate empirical data) would show what weight to attach to chronological age when all the other factors, e.g. sex, education, socioeconomic status, were held constant. Another example would be a study in which we tried to predict further expectation of life by means of indices like age of subject, health status, and rate of cognitive deterioration. The statistical analysis could reveal the nett effect of each variable, but a causal analysis might attribute a greater or lesser effect depending upon the position of each variable in the causal network. Although the statistical complications of measuring age effects are considerable, there appears to be no reason why changes in adult life should not be measured in the same way as changes during the juvenile period—provided the adult measurements can be made sufficiently valid and reliable. On reflection, however, if present-day findings are any guide, adult changes in behaviour and psychological capacities are generally slow and small compared with changes in the juvenile period. In addition, the discriminating power of many psychological scales of measurement may not be sufficient to detect changes. It is sometimes difficult to demonstrate that an observed age change is statistically significant, much less that it is psychologically significant, since the measurement error is usually large, and the 'effect-size' small.

So far we have assumed that errors of measurement on two occasions are uncorrelated. But this assumption may not hold, and ageing may produce systematic bias in measurement error. For example, suppose that, in a test of introversion, measurement errors occur because some items tend to be misconstrued by depressed and anxious subjects—thus leading them to 'appear' more (or less) introverted than they 'really' are. If depression and anxiety increase with age, this particular sort of measurement error will increase, creating a spuriously large increase (or decrease) in introversion. Similarly, the tendency to construe test instructions one way or another may change with age—by preferring one interpretation rather than another or by forgetting them in part. This sort of measurement error then becomes confounded with the validity of the measured age change. It could be argued that the effects are not measurement errors in the technical sense, but sources of invalidity; for all practical purposes, however, they are the same.

The peculiarity of change-scores is that the more closely correlated the initial and final scores are, the less reliable the change-scores are; in the extreme case they reduce to random errors. But if the initial and final scores are not closely correlated, then, in one sense the final test is measuring something different from the initial test. But if that is the case, what is the change-score a measure of? How can one tell whether the subject has changed relative to a stable measure or whether the second test is measuring a different aspect of the subject on the second occasion? The possibility that a follow-up measure is measuring something different from the initial measure seems to be a tenable explanation of the differences sometimes observed between longitudinal and cross-sectional investigations.

This line of reasoning raises a number of problems for the psychometric assessment of age changes and age differences. For example, are the items in personality tests equally valid at different age levels? Does intelligence need to be operationally redefined at different adult age levels, as it is to some extent at different juvenile age levels? There may be changes in test-taking attitudes, a learning effect, response biases, a sensitization produced by the first occasion of testing, or other changes not yet recognized as sources of variation in the measurements obtained by tests. The same principle applies in psychiatric assessment in that symptoms may not have the same diagnostic significance at different ages. If we know that the functional validity of a test is unchanged, we can say the *person* has changed; but if the functional validity of the test changes, how do we become aware of this fact?

The measurement of reliable differences between two or more occasions of measurement is a way of mapping changes in the meaning of standard measuring instruments; that is, it becomes a method of identifying changes in the validity referents over, say, chronological age or intervening environmental influences. Thus differences in the validity of a test for subjects of different ages, which at first sight seem to be a methodological inconvenience, may be seen as a new way of conceptualizing the effects of age. This is another example of translating a 'methodological difficulty' into a 'substantive' issue—see pp. 352–5.

The effects of initial testing are likely to be fairly pronounced in studies of psychological change with age. For example, adaptation to a test situation should be much faster on retest than on the initial test. The natural tendency of older subjects to look back to previous experience to provide a basis for response to a current problem should increase the similarity of behaviour between the two occasions. Hence, repeated measures on the same subjects are likely to create sequential dependencies, especially if the time intervals are short; such time-series call for special methods of statistical analysis. More frequent occasions of measurement, by rendering the test situation more familiar, should have the effect of stabilizing the performance of older subjects, at least after the first few occasions. The problem of devising scales of measurement suitable for frequent repetition is difficult but not insurmountable. Surprisingly, perhaps, time-series analysis appears not to be used often in behavioural gerontology.

A repeated-measures longitudinal analysis is a way of identifying and measuring *dimensions of change* peculiar to development and ageing, i.e. sequential changes associated with groups, treatments, or individuals. If measured age differences in a variable are large, the need for a longitudinal analysis is less, unless there are reasons for supposing that these age differences are spurious. Generally speaking, measured age *changes*—estimated by repeated measures—are sensitive to smaller effects. Cross-sectional studies of ageing usually require a wide age range and fairly large samples, because the spread of individual differences in many behavioural characteristics is large, whereas the changes with age are often relatively small. However, if individual variations are large in respect of the rate or pattern of age changes *within* persons then large samples may be needed, even in longitudinal studies, to stabilize the average pattern of change. A comparison *between* individuals with respect to patterns of change *within* individuals over a period of time can be made only when the *average* pattern of change for individuals of that sort is known. It may also be necessary to shift the focus of attention from chronological age to patterns or rates of change, as was done in studying the growth spurt in adolescence. For example, we might learn more about the early stages of dementia (its rate of onset and the sequential emergence of signs and symptoms) by plotting trends not with reference to chronological age but with reference to some kind of psychological or biological marker.

The commonest type of longitudinal study—using the test–retest method—may fail to take into account the possibility that factors other than ageing might have produced the change: a shift in test validity, incidental experiences unrelated to age, sequential dependency between the tests, sampling bias, and so on. By contrast, a design which establishes a baseline or trend and then introduces a treatment (or establishes a baseline prior to the occurrence of a natural event, like a stress) displays an effect which can be compared with the baseline trend for an untreated or unaffected sample with the same baseline. Naturally, the effect induced by the treatment can only be considered against a background of statistical and theoretical issues like reliability and plausibility.

Thus far, we have discussed change mainly in terms of the difference between two supposedly equivalent measures separated by an interval of time. But change or lack of change can be measured over any number of occasions. Ideally, we would like to describe and explain the *continuous* process of change, over the adult lifespan, of all the variables that are of interest to us. In practice we are usually limited to describing and partly explaining intermittent variations or trends in the behaviour of relatively small samples of subjects, over relatively short intervals of time, on perhaps two or three occasions. The long-range goal, however, is to see whether the surface characteristics shown by psychometric and biometric data can be related to chronological age, and reveal characteristic decay curves, successive transformations in structure, and causal pathways for different characteristics and for different times of life. Hence the need for new theories and concepts and for rigorous quantitative and qualitative methods.

Further comments

Costa and McCrae (1982) take the argument somewhat further. They agree that the effects of age, cohort, and period cannot necessarily be separated out even in complex experimental designs and statistical analyses. However, under certain conditions, where one or more of the effects is constant, the results may provide strong if not conclusive evidence. It is necessary to look at this evidence in the context of the existing state of knowledge in the area. As we have seen, research in behavioural gerontology is liable to a great many faults apart from that of confounding age, cohort, and period effects.

Costa and McCrae (1982) draw attention to some confusion in terminology. In their usage a cross-sequential design is one in which independent but comparable samples of a cohort are tested once only at different points in time. This corresponds to what we have called the longitudinal design in which several independent but comparable cohort samples are each followed up longitudinally on several occasions. In their usage a time-sequential design is one in which independent but comparable subjects of the same age are tested once only at different points in time. This corresponds to what we have called the time-lag or time-sequential design in which comparable samples of subjects of the same age, drawn from the same cohort, are tested on different occasions.

It should be noted that although using separate but comparable samples of subjects tested once only may get over some of the methodological problems, e.g. practice effects, and possibly selective survival, it does not eliminate the confounding of age, cohort, and period effects, as described above.

A point that has been mentioned but not so far discussed is that the selection of particular age levels, cohort dates, and time periods may be important for a given investigation—as for example in studies of the menopause, the effects of certain drugs, or sexual adjustment. Hitherto, research in behavioural gerontology has tended to use arbitrary or administratively convenient values for ages, cohorts, and times of measurement. Careful consideration of the sorts of ways in which ageing, secular trends, and period effects might affect a particular psychological function, e.g. intelligence, stress reactions, spending habits, or use of time, should lead to investigative design features which would reduce ambiguity in interpreting the results.

In elaborate statistical analyses Costa and McCrae (1982) show how a pattern of results based on a variety of 'confounded' measurements can point to firm if not entirely conclusive conclusions, especially if one takes into account knowledge derived from other sources. They point out that statistically significant effects may account for only a tiny fraction of the variance, but argue that such small effects may nevertheless be theoretically interesting. Indeed, in behavioural gerontology we have a situation in which a multiplicity of factors are at work, and it may be the case that we should be looking for explanations which involve many variables each with small effects. Other investigators, however, are likely to argue the opposite—that we should be trying to identify a few major factors which together account for a large part of the variance.

George et al. (1981) compare analysis of variance and multiple regression as methods for analysing age, cohort, and period effects. Using artificial data sets they confirm that analysis of variance will not necessarily separate these effects, and that multiple regression is effective only if certain constraints are imposed.

The problem of separating the effects of age, cohort and period is not a problem that behavioural gerontology on its own can solve. Moreover, it is not one problem but a multiplicity of problems, distributed among all the social and behavioural sciences.

The Baltimore longitudinal studies of ageing (Shock *et al.*, 1984) provide many examples of data collected and analysed in the context of concern with the sorts of methodological considerations we have been discussing.

The point of the present discussion is to show that from the point of view of scientific method there are no final answers, and that it is extremely unlikely that one method or one set of findings, no matter how carefully and convincingly reported, will provide an unequivocal account of the effects of ageing on adult intelligence or on any other human characteristic. What we must look for is not the 'crucial experiment' but *all* the evidence relevant to answering a particular question. Knowledge advances not only by answering questions but also by raising them; what passes for an answer is simply a new interpretation about which new questions can be asked. The advancement of science is a process whereby we use the knowledge structures we have created as the scaffolding and platforms that help us to create new structures of knowledge.

Longitudinal investigations are still relatively rare; yet it is not unusual for their findings to run counter to existing beliefs. Recent longitudinal studies include Aldwin *et al.* (1989), Busse and Maddox (1985), Cooney *et al.* (1988), Hertzog and Schaie (1986, 1988), Palmore *et al.* (1985), Schaie and Hertzog (1983).

ARGUMENTS AGAINST A PREOCCUPATION WITH METHODOLOGY

Levy (1981) argues that so-called 'methodological' problems are really problems about substantive issues which become clearer if we concentrate on what it is we want to know. For example, many assessment procedures are regarded as unfair to older subjects because, say, they impose time limits, or use age-inappropriate materials, or lead to biased sampling through non-completion. Levy seems to argue that problems like these are not impassable methodological barriers but fundamental theoretical issues, susceptible to conceptual clarification in ways that will lead to assertions capable of empirical confirmation or disproof.

With reference to statistical methods, the question is whether the statistical corrections and controls that we impose stand up to close examination from an operational standpoint. That is to say, does the statistical adjustment really correspond to any 'real-world' image of the processes under investigation? The various ways of sampling and matching subjects in cross-sectional studies often leave the underlying theoretical assumptions unexamined, and so fail to reach rationally justifiable conclusions. For example, a study which uses equal numbers of men and women at several age levels in later life is representing male volunteers better than female volunteers at the older levels (because men do not survive as long as women on average, so the 'pool' of volunteers is smaller and diminishing faster). The age/sex comparisons are therefore distorted to the extent that the underlying population distributions are skewed and unequally sampled. Two solutions to this problem are possible: one is to work out the likely biases, given what we know or can reasonably assume about the populations of interest and qualify one's conclusions accordingly; the other is to adjust the recruitment and sampling procedures, according to what we know about the populations, so as to avoid having to qualify our conclusions in that particular way— not forgetting, of course, that all conclusions involving empirical data are necessarily subject to a variety of qualifications, exceptions, and reservations. Broadly speaking, researchers can do what they like *provided* they make their arguments and conclusions clear and show how they collect their data. If the study can be interpreted sensibly, i.e. understood, the data from a survey or experiment can usually be analysed statistically. The key element is not the statistical procedure (provided its assumptions are met and its calculations are correct), but the logic, i.e. the sensible interpretation, of the overall argument. We must also look for effect size and replicability, not just statistical significance, in our experimental and survey investigations.

Consideration of so-called 'procedural' problems in research in ageing— for example, those related to test instructions, practice trials, the effects of fatigue, rate of presentation of stimuli—reveals that they too are not methodological obstacles but substantive problems about which theories can be formulated and empirical evidence collected. To complain that one's research is hampered by methodological obstacles is to complain that the answers to one's questions are unsatisfactory because some more fundamental questions have not been answered. But what is research work if it is not the uncovering of deeper-lying issues?

Consideration of so-called 'measurement' artefacts—for example, those related to the measurement of change, unstandardized *ad hoc* indices, levels of measurement—reveals that the main issue is not whether the 'methodology itself' is sound but whether the study using this method leaves the investigator with only one plausible interpretation of the data.

Errors of measurement may be 'methodological' in the narrow sense of being remediable by modification to the measuring instrument—more items, better choice of content, clearer instructions, and so on, as discussed in Chapter 3. But some limitations and errors of measurement are thought of as methodologically unavoidable, for example those associated with ordinal scales, and sampling distributions. These apparent methodological errors and limitations do not have a separate existence from the actual study in which they occur. They occur because of some substantive inadequacy such as the vagueness or inaccessibility of the process under investigation, e.g. 'subjective well-being', or 'quality of life'. Provided the scales of measurement are the best that can be devised, and provided the logic by means of which the numbers are assigned is explicit and scientifically acceptable, then no methodological measurement problem exists. What does exist is an apparently intractable research problem! Perhaps it should be shelved or reformulated?

Methodological sophistication is no substitute for sensible inference. Perhaps research work in ageing would fare better if we paid more attention to the broader aspects of our findings. Can they be explained in some other way? How plausible are they, all things considered? What are the substantive issues that lie behind the apparent methodological difficulties? Are the findings useful or worth testing out more fully in other contexts?

Most research workers in psychological gerontology nowadays seem to be aware of the methodological obstacles in the path of scientific progress. In particular, there is frequent reference to the limitations of both cross-sectional and longitudinal data, of sampling across a wide spread of ages, of undue reliance on volunteer subjects, of unreliability and invalidity in methods of observation and measurement (especially in single-occasion studies). Indeed, as we have seen, methodology looms so large in the psychology of ageing that sometimes it appears to obscure substantive issues.

It is fairly clear then that observed age differences in, say, social attitudes, activities of daily living, or language usage, may reflect not so much the effects of ageing (as an intrinsic psychobiological process) but rather the effects of time of birth (cohort), or selective mortality, or selective migration. This last-mentioned possibility is rare in psychological gerontology, which tends to rely on relatively small homogeneous samples of subjects, but it is a risk in social gerontology which may have recourse to census data or large-scale survey data collected at intervals over several decades.

Glenn (1976, 1981) maintains, as I have maintained, that the various basic methods—cross-sectional, longitudinal, and cross-sequential—all have their various advantages and disadvantages as logical procedures, apart from differences in cost as regards time, money, and resources.

One's aim should be to choose the method which best suits one's purposes, time, and resources, and to interpret one's results accordingly, stating whatever implications and reservations are appropriate.

Glenn (1981) points out that a longitudinal study of a narrowly defined cohort may produce results which reflect not ageing but 'period' effects, i.e. effects arising from influences exerted in the intervals between periods of observation. Consider, for example, the long-term effects on social attitudes and behaviour of political or religious propaganda, or of health education, or of exposure to television. Panel or cohort studies need to be large and representative if they are to be fully effective; otherwise they may be no better than cross-sectional studies.

An important point to remember is that much of the work of scientific inference and generalization arises from considerations that lie *outside* the procedural framework and findings of the particular investigation. These considerations include the results of previous work and other relevant knowledge. The particular investigation has to be interpreted in a context of existing beliefs and expectations. Put another way, scientific induction and generalization are not narrowly dependent on specific sampling procedures and methods of statistical inference, but broadly dependent on a wide framework of relevant assumptions, methods, and findings. The individual research worker is answerable to a scientific and professional community.

In some instances the effects of age, cohort, and period may be linear and/or offsetting, i.e. counterbalancing, so that it is not possible to separate out these effects. In other instances the effects may be nonlinear and non-offsetting, without necessarily revealing whether the effect is the result of one variable or of two or more variables in combination. The point is that a table of results *by itself* cannot reveal the answer to the problem. The method of analysis adopted (and consequently the result) depends on the investigator's reasons and assumptions, which are to some extent independent of the empirical data, but nevertheless enable the investigator to impose on those data one or more interpretations or patterns of meaning.

SUMMARY

There are two reasons why methodology is so prominent in behavioural gerontology. The first is that psychologists have a long-standing interest in research methods because they aspire to put psychology on a par with the more developed and applicable sciences. The second is that attempts to use scientific (rational and empirical), methods in the study of human ageing have encountered difficult and persistent problems.

For these reasons our treatment of methodological issues is divided into two parts. The first part of this chapter provides a general outline of scientific method in the context of behavioural gerontology. The second part provides a little more technical detail and further discussion of the problem of separating out the effects of age, cohort, and time of measurement. Close examination reveals that it is difficult if not impossible to separate out the effects of age, cohort, and period because cross-sectional differences confound age effects with cohort effects, longitudinal differences confound age effects with period effects, and time-lag differences confound cohort effects with period effects. Even if circumstances permitted one to confidently attribute an observed difference to age, cohort, or time interval, the underlying causal mechanism(s) might still remain obscure.

Further difficulties are revealed when one wishes to compare samples of subjects at different ages, especially if one wishes to draw representative samples from the population at large.

Many psychological measures are not particularly reliable; and some psychological functions are intrinsically variable, e.g. mood, motivation. This reduces the likelihood of identifying stable characteristics, especially over long periods of time. The situation is exacerbated by the tendency for the performance of older subjects to fluctuate more widely (because of the cumulative adverse effects of ageing and disease).

Both psychology and gerontology are multidisciplinary areas of study. Consequently, behavioural gerontology has to find room for a wide range of scientific concepts and methods, and has to face up to questions and criticisms that might arise in the context of other disciplines, including the philosophy of behavioural science, e.g. those concerned with the nature of explanation, theory construction, reductionism, and scientific standards.

Casual observation can provide the starting point for many scientific investigations. Common sense, in its more robust forms, can sometimes raise interesting or awkward questions about claims to scientific knowledge. By contrast, scientific knowledge may contradict common-sense beliefs and come into conflict with prevailing social beliefs and ethical practices.

Scientific method calls for 'controlled observation', i.e. selective, directed observation, in attempts to test explicit theories and hypotheses (expectations). Experiments and surveys are well-known methods of controlled observation, but clinical investigations, case-studies, life-histories, archival studies, and field studies also make use of controlled observation and achieve the status of scientific methods.

Although experimental and survey methods are used extensively in social and behavioural gerontology, there is no guarantee that the findings will be correct. This is because of difficulties associated with unrepresentative sampling, subject variables, inadequate measurement, volunteer effects, and contextual factors affecting the interpretation of results. The analysis of sequential observations calls for considerable statistical expertise, but sophisticated experimental design and statistical analysis cannot make good deficiencies in theory and data collection.

Various factors determine which of the various available methods will be used in a given set of circumstances. These factors include: the nature of the problem, the resources available, the scale of the exercise, the abilities and interests of the investigators, the accessibility of the data, and so on. Many of the effects of ageing can be investigated by different methods: experiments, surveys, field studies, case-studies, life-histories, archival research, unobtrusive observation, critical-incident analysis. The availability of suitable technologies greatly enhances the scope and depth of psychological research.

Any investigation which claims to demonstrate the effects of *ageing* on some aspect of human behaviour has to present arguments which exclude interpretations in terms of cohort effects or period effects. Conclusive evidence may be lacking in spite of the elaborate procedures used to separate out these effects, namely repeated measures over long time intervals on carefully selected samples of subjects of different ages, followed by sophisticated forms of statistical analysis.

From time to time, changes in the way psychological functions are conceptualized, e.g. intelligence and personality, may lead to a reappraisal of the effects of ageing on such functions. Similarly, advances in our knowledge of the physical basis of behaviour may lead to shifts of interest in behavioural gerontology. There are, in a sense, no final answers to scientific questions, but rather a sort of evolutionary selection process that determines which concepts, methods, and findings will survive and continue to be productive and useful.

Conceptual and technological developments in psychometrics should eventually make good some of the deficiencies in the measurement of adult psychological functions and help to overcome the many difficulties encountered in scientific research and professional practice. In particular we need measures which are reliable, valid, useful, repeatable, and acceptable to older persons. We need measures which can be taken 'at-a-distance', and measures which will enable us to aggregate data.

Paradoxically, in view of the amount of space devoted to methodology, we must guard against letting a preoccupation with methodology distract us from the substantive issues in behavioural gerontology and lead us to neglect small-scale research and the diversity of research methods open to us, including the so-called 'qualitative' methods, such as case-studies, life-histories and field studies.

In experiments and surveys, tests of statistical significance are now seen to be less important than measures of effect size and replicability. Studies of human ageing need measures which are robust, i.e. highly reliable and valid, so that they are not unduly in error when used in circumstances or with subjects who differ only in unimportant ways from the comparison group.

Finally, it must be remembered that scientific inference and generalization depend in part on considerations that lie outside the conceptual, methodological, and empirical framework of any particular investigation. In a multidisciplinary area like behavioural gerontology, questions and criticisms can arise from any quarter.

References

Acker, W. and Acker, C. (1982). *Bexley-Maudsley Automated Psychological Screening and Category Sorting Tests*. NFER-Nelson, Windsor.

Adams, C. G. and Turner, B. F. (1985). 'Reported changes in sexuality from young adult to old age'. *Journal of Sex Research*, **21**, 126–41.

Ageing and Society (1984). Special issue on history and ageing (eight articles). *Ageing and Society*, **4**, 379–524.

Aiken, L. R. (1988). *Psychological Testing and Assessment*, 6th edn. Prentice-Hall, Hemel Hempstead.

Åkesson, H. O. (1969). 'A population study of senile and arteriosclerotic psychoses'. *Human Heredity*, **19**, 546–66.

Alderson, M. (1986). 'An aging population—some demographic and health trends'. *Public Health*, **100**, 263–77.

Aldwin, C. M., Spiro III, A., Levenson, M. R. and Bosse, R. (1989). 'Longitudinal findings from the Normative Aging Study: 1. Does mental health change with age?' *Psychology and Aging*, **4**, 295–306.

Alexander, G. J. (1981). 'Age and the law'. In P. W. Johnston (ed.), *Perspectives on Aging*. Ballinger, Cambridge, Mass.

Alexy, W. D. (1982). 'Dimensions of psychological counseling that facilitate the grieving process of bereaved parents'. *Journal of Counseling Psychology*, **29**, 498–507.

American Behavioral Scientist (1988). Special issue: Technology and Aging, **31** (5).

American Psychiatric Association (1987). *Diagnostic and Statistical Manual of Mental Disorders*, 3rd edn, revised. American Psychiatric Association, Washington, D.C.

American Psychological Association (1982). *Ethical Principles in the Conduct of Research with Human Participants*. American Psychological Association, Washington, DC.

Anderson, L. (1984). 'Intervention against loneliness in a group of elderly women: a process evaluation'. *Human Relations*, **37**, 295–310.

Annas, G. J. and Glantz, L. H. (1986). 'The right of elderly patients to refuse life-sustaining treatment'. *Milbank Quarterly*, **64**, 95–162.

Aro, S. and Hanninen, V. (1984). 'Life events or life processes as determinants of mental strain? A 5-year follow-up study'. *Social Science and Medicine*, **18**, 1037–44.

Babcock, H. (1930). 'An experiment in the measurement of mental deterioration'. *Archives of Psychology*, **18**, 117.

Baldwin, R. C. and Jolley, D. J. (1986). 'The prognosis of depression in old age'. *British Journal of Psychiatry*, **149**, 574–83.

Ball, M. J. (1987). 'Pathological similarities between Alzheimer's disease and Down's syndrome: is there a genetic link?' (With commentaries). *Integrative Psychiatry*, **5**, 159–70.

Baltes, M. M. and Baltes, P. B. (eds) (1986). *The Psychology of Control and Aging.* Lawrence Erlbaum Associates, Hillsdale, NJ.

Baltes, P. B. and Schaie, K. W. (eds) (1973). *Lifespan Developmental Psychology: Personality and Socialization.* Academic Press, New York.

Baltes, P. B., Featherman, D. L. and Lerner, R. M. (eds) (1986). *Life-span Development and Behavior*, Volume 7. Lawrence Erlbaum Associates, Hillsdale, NJ.

Baltes, P. B., Featherman, D. L. and Lerner, R. M. (eds) (1987). *Life-span Development and Behavior*, Volume 8. Lawrence Erlbaum Associates, Hove.

Barker, R. G. (ed.) (1963). *The Stream of Behavior.* Appleton-Century-Crofts, Meredith, New York.

Barker, W. A. and Eccleston, D. (1984). 'The treatment of chronic depression, an illustrative case'. *British Journal of Psychiatry*, **144**, 317–19.

Baruch, G. K. and Brooks-Gunn, J. (eds) (1984). *Neither Young Nor Old. Women in Midlife.* Plenum, New York.

Bayles, K. A. and Kaszniak, A. W. (1987). *Communication and Cognition in Normal Aging and Dementia.* Taylor & Francis, London.

Beaumont, J. G. and French, C. C. (1987). 'A clinical field study of eight automated psychometric procedures: the Leicester/DHSS project'. *International Journal of Man–Machine Studies*, **26**, 661–82.

Bebbington, P. E. (1978). 'The epidemiology of depressive disorder'. In A. M. Kleinman (ed.), *Culture, Medicine and Psychiatry*. D. Reidel, Dordrecht, The Netherlands.

Beck, A. T. (1988). *Beck Depression Inventory (BDI).* The Psychological Corporation, Sidcup.

Beck, A. T., Steer, R. A. and Garbin, M. G. (1988). 'Psychometric properties of the Beck Depression Inventory: twenty-five years of evaluation'. *Clinical Psychology Review*, **8**, 77–100.

Beck, A. T., Ward, C. H., Mendelson, M., Mock, J. and Erbaugh, J. (1961). 'An inventory for measuring depression'. *Archives of General Psychiatry*, **4**, 561–71.

Behnke, J. A., Finch, C. E. and Moment, G. B. (1978). *The Biology of Aging.* Plenum, New York.

Bell, J. S. and Gilleard, C. J. (1986). 'Psychometric prediction of psychogeriatric day care outcome'. *British Journal of Clinical Psychology*, **25**, 195–200.

Belmont, J. M. (1983). 'Concerning Hunt's new ways of assessing intelligence'. *Intelligence*, **7**, 1–7.

Belmore, S. M. (1981). 'Age-related changes in processing explicit and implicit language'. *Journal of Gerontology*, **36**, 316–22.

Belsky, J. (1984). *The Psychology of Aging: Theory, Research and Practice.* Brooks/Cole, Monterey, CA.

Bender, M. P. (1986). 'The neglect of the elderly by British psychologists'. *Bulletin of the British Psychological Society*, **39**, 414–17.

Bengston, V. L. and Black, K. D. (1973). 'Intergenerational relations and continuities in socialization'. In P. B. Baltes and K. W. Schaie (eds), Lifespan Developmental Psychology: Personality and Socialization. Academic Press, New York.

Berado, F. M. (ed.) (1982). Middle and late life transitions (14 articles), *Annals of the American Academy of Political and Social Science*, Volume 464. Sage Publications, London.

Beres, C. A. and Baron, A. (1981). 'Improved digit symbol substitution by older women as a result of extended practice'. *Journal of Gerontology*, **36**, 591–7.

Berg, C. A. and Sternberg, R. J. (1985). 'A triarchic theory of intellectual development during adulthood'. *Developmental Review*, **5**, 334–70.

Berger, M. P. F. (1986). 'A comparison of efficiencies of longitudinal, mixed longitudinal and cross-sectional designs'. *Journal of Educational Statistics*, **11**, 171–82.

Bergmann, K. and Cooper, B. (1986). 'Epidemiological and public health aspects of senile dementia'. In A. B. Sorensen, F. E. Weinert and L. R. Sherrod (eds), *Human Development and the Life Course: Multidisciplinary Perspectives*. Lawrence Erlbaum Associates, Publishers, Hillsdale, N.J.

Berrios, G. E. and Brook, P. (1985). 'Delusions and the psychopathology of the elderly with dementia'. *Acta Psychiatrica Scandinavica*, **72**, 296–301.

Bigler, E. D., Hubler, D. W., Cullum, C. M. and Turkheimer, E. (1985). 'Intellectual and memory impairment in dementia. Computerized axial tomography volume correlations'. *Journal of Nervous and Mental Disease*, **173**, 347–52.

Bilash, I. and Zubek, J. P. (1960). 'The effect of age on factorially "pure" mental abilities'. *Journal of Gerontology*, **15**, 175–82.

Binks, M. G. and Davies, A. D. M. (1984). 'The early detection of dementia. A baseline from healthy community dwelling old people'. In D. B. Bromley (ed.), *Gerontology: Social and Behavioural Perspectives*. Croom Helm, London.

Binks, M. G. and Davies, A. D. M. (1985). 'The contribution of the National Adult Reading Test to the detection of dementia amongst community dwelling old people'. In A. Butler (ed.), *Ageing: Recent Advances and Creative Responses*. Croom Helm, London.

Binstock, R. H. and Shanas, E. (eds) (1985). *Handbook of Aging and the Social Sciences*, 2nd edn. Van Nostrand Reinhold, New York.

Birren, J. E. and Bengston, V. L. (eds) (1988). *Emergent Theories of Aging*. Springer, New York.

Birren, J. E. and Renner, V. J. (1977). 'Research in the psychology of aging: principles and experimentation'. In J. E. Birren and K. W. Schaie (eds), *Handbook of the Psychology of Aging*. Van Nostrand Reinhold, New York.

Birren, J. E. and Schaie, K. W. (eds) (1985). *Handbook of the Psychology of Aging*, 2nd edn. Van Nostrand Reinhold, New York.

Blazer, D. G. (1981). 'Social stress and mental disorders in the elderly'. In J. L. McGaugh and S. B. Kiesler (eds), *Aging: Biology and Behavior*. Academic Press, New York.

Blessed, G. and Wilson, I. D. (1982). 'The contemporary natural history of mental disorder in old age'. *British Journal of Psychiatry*, **141**, 59–67.

Block, J. (1971). *Lives Through Time*. Bancroft Books, Berkeley, CA.

Bondareff, W. (1981). 'The neurobiological basis of age-related changes in neuronal connectivity'. In J. L. McGaugh and S. B. Kiesler (eds), *Aging: Biology and Behavior*. Academic Press, New York.

Bondareff, W., Mountjoy, C. Q., Roth, M., Rossor, M. N., Iversen, L. L. and Reynolds, G. P. (1987). 'Age and histopathologic heterogeneity in Alzheimer's disease'. *Archives of General Psychiatry*, **44**, 412–17.

Botwinick, J. (1984). *Aging and Behavior, A Comprehensive Integration of Research Findings*, 3rd edn. Springer, New York.

Bowling, A. (1987). 'Mortality after bereavement: a review of the literature on survival periods and factors affecting survival'. *Social Science and Medicine*, **24**, 117–24.

Brasted, W. S. and Callahan, E. J. (1984). 'Review article. A behavioural analysis of the grief process'. *Behaviour Therapy*, **15**, 529–43.

Bray, J. and Wright, S. (1980). *The Use of Technology in the Care of the Elderly and Disabled*. Greenwood Press, Westport, CT.

Breitner, J. C. S., Folstein, M. F. and Murphy, E. A. (1986a). 'Familial aggregation in Alzheimer dementia—I. A model for the age-dependent expression of an autosomal dominant gene'. *Journal of Psychiatric Research*, **20**, 31–43.

Breitner, J. C. S., Murphy, E. A. and Folstein, M. F. (1986b). 'Familial aggregation in Alzheimer dementia—II. Clinical genetic implications of age-dependent onset'. *Journal of Psychiatric Research*, **20**, 45–55.

British Psychological Society (1985). 'A code of conduct for psychologists'. *Bulletin of the British Psychological Society*, **38**, 41–3.

Broadbent, D., Cooper, P. F., Fitzgerald, P. and Parkes, K. R. (1982). 'Cognitive Failures Questionnaire (CFQ) and its correlates'. *British Journal of Clinical Psychology*, **21**, 1–16.

Brocklehurst, J. C. and Hanley, T. (1976). *Geriatric Medicine for Students*. Churchill Livingstone, Edinburgh.

Brody, E. M., Kleban, M. H., Lawton, M. P. and Silverman, H. A. (1971). 'Excess disabilities of mentally impaired aged: impact of individualized treatment'. *Gerontologist*, **11**, 124–33.

Brody, J. A. (1982). 'An epidemiologist views senile dementia—facts and fragments'. *American Journal of Epidemiology*, **115**, 155–62.

Brody, J. A. (1984). 'An epidemiologist's view of the senile dementias—pieces of the puzzle'. In J. A. Brody (ed.), *Senile Dementia, Outlook for the Future*. Alan R. Liss, New York.

Brody, J. A. and Brock, D. B. (1985). 'Epidemiologic and statistical characteristics of the United States elderly population.' In C. E. Finch and E. L. Schneider (eds), *Handbook of the Biology of Aging*, 2nd edn. Van Nostrand Reinhold, New York.

Brodzinsky, D., Gormly, A. V. and Ambron, S. (1986). *Lifespan Human Development*, 3rd edn. Holt Saunders, London.

Bromley, D. B. (1967). 'Age and sex differences in the serial production of creative conceptual responses'. *Journal of Gerontology*, **22**, 32–4.

Bromley, D. B. (1974a). *The Psychology of Human Ageing*, 2nd edn. Penguin Books, Harmondsworth.

Bromley, D. B. (1974b). 'The history of human ageing'. In D. B. Bromley, *The Psychology of Human Ageing*, 2nd edn. Penguin Books, Harmondsworth.

Bromley, D. B. (1978). 'Approaches to the study of personality changes in adult life and old age'. In A. D. Isaacs and F. Post (eds), *Studies in Geriatric Psychiatry*. John Wiley & Sons, London.

Bromley, D. B. (1986). *The Case-study Method in Psychology and Related Disciplines*. John Wiley & Sons, Chichester.

Bromley, D. B. (1988a). *Human Ageing: an Introduction to Gerontology*. Penguin Books, Harmondsworth.

Bromley, D. B. (1988b). 'The terminal stage: dying and death'. In D. B. Bromley, *Human Ageing: an Introduction to Gerontology*. Penguin Books, Harmondsworth.

Bromley, D. B. (1989). 'The idea of ageing: an historical and psychological analysis'. *Comprehensive Gerontology*, **2**, 30–41.

Brown, B. W. (1974). 'Meaning, measurement and stress of life events'. In B. S. Dohrenwend and B. P. Dohrenwend (eds), *Stressful Life Events: Their Nature and Effects*. John Wiley & Sons, New York.

Brown, N. R., Rips, L. J. and Shevell, S. K. (1985). 'The subjective dates of natural events in very-long-term-memory'. *Cognitive Psychology*, **17**, 139–77.

Browne, K. D. and Armstrong-Esther, C. A. (1984). 'Development of a circadian activity and rehabilitation ward for the elderly'. *Proceedings of the Second National Conference on Gerontological Nursing*, Winnipeg.

Bühler, C. and Massarik, F. (eds) (1968). *The Course of Human Life*. Springer, New York.

Bulbena, A. and Berrios, G. E. (1986). 'Pseudodementia: facts and figures'. *British Journal of Psychiatry*, **148**, 87–94.

Burbank, P. M. (1986). 'Psychosocial theories of aging: a critical evaluation'. *Advances in Nursing Science*, **9**, 73–86.

Busse, E. W. and Maddox, G. L. (1985). *The Duke Longitudinal Studies of Normal Aging, 1955–1980. An Overview of History, Design and Findings*. Springer, New York.

Butler, R. N. (1963). 'The life review: an interpretation of reminiscence in the aged'. *Psychiatry, Journal for the Study of Interpersonal Processes*, **26**, 65–76.

Butler, R. N. and Lewis, M. I. (1982). *Aging and Mental Health*, 3rd edn. Merrill, Oxford.

Canter, D. and Canter, S. (eds) (1979). *Designing for Therapeutic Environments: A Review of Research*. John Wiley & Sons, Chichester.

Cattell, R. B. (1943). 'The measurement of adult intelligence'. *Psychological Bulletin*, **40**, 153–93.

Central Statistical Office (1971). *Social Trends*, 2. HMSO, London.

Central Statistical Office (1986). *Social Trends*, 16. HMSO, London.

Central Statistical Office (1987). *Social Trends*, 17. HMSO, London.

Central Statistical Office (1989). *Social Trends*, 19. HMSO, London.

Cerella, J. (1985). 'Information processing rates in the elderly'. *Psychological Bulletin*, **98**, 67–83.

Chaisson-Stewart, G. M. (1985a). 'Psychotherapy'. In G. M. Chaisson-Stewart (ed.), *Depression in the Elderly: an Interdisciplinary Approach*. John Wiley & Sons, New York.

Chaisson-Stewart, G. M. (ed.) (1985b). *Depression in the Elderly: an Interdisciplinary Approach*. John Wiley & Sons, New York.

Chapman, L. J. and Chapman, J. B. (1978). 'The measurement of differential deficit'. *Journal of Psychiatric Research*, **14**, 303–11.

Charness, N. (1981). 'Visual short-term memory and aging in chess players'. *Journal of Gerontology*, **36**, 615–19.

Charness, N. (ed.) (1985a). *Aging and Human Performance*. John Wiley & Sons, Chichester.

Charness, N. (1985b). 'Aging and problem-solving performance', in N. Charness (ed.), *Aging and Human Performance*. John Wiley & Sons, Chichester.

Church, M. (1983). 'Psychological therapy with elderly people'. *Bulletin of the British Psychological Society*, **36**, 110–12.

Cicerelli, V. G. (1976). 'Categorization behavior in aging subjects'. *Journal of Gerontology*, **31**, 676–80.

Cohen, G. D. (1984). 'Psychotherapy of the elderly'. *Clinical Issues in Geriatric Psychiatry*, **25**, 455–63.

Cole, M. G. (1983). 'Age of onset and course of primary depressive illness in the elderly'. *Canadian Journal of Psychiatry*, **28**, 102–4.

Cole, S. (1979). 'Age and scientific performance'. *American Journal of Sociology*, **84**, 958–77.

Coleman, P. G. (1986). *Ageing and Reminiscence Processes: Social and Clinical Implications*. John Wiley & Sons, Chichester.

Collier, J. (1967). *Visual Anthropology: Photography as a Research Method*. Holt, Rinehart & Winston, New York.

Conley, J. J. (1984a). 'Longitudinal consistency of adult personality: self-reported psychological characteristics across 45 years'. *Journal of Personality and Social Psychology*, **47**, 1325–33.

Conley, J. J. (1984b). 'The hierarchy of consistency: a review and model of longitudinal findings on adult individual differences in intelligence, personality and self-opinion'. *Personality and Individual Differences*, **5**, 1–15.

Conley, J. J. (1985). 'A personality theory of adulthood and aging'. In R. Hogan and W. H. Jones (eds), *Perspectives in Personality*, Volume 1. JAI Press, Greenwich, CT.

Conrad, J. H. (1978). *An Annotated Bibliography of the History of Old Age in America*. Center for Studies of Aging Resources, North Texas State University, Denton, TX.

Conway, M. A. (1987). 'Verifying autobiographical facts'. *Cognition*, **26**, 39–58.

Conway, M. A. and Bekerian, D. A. (1987). 'Organization in autobiographical memory'. *Memory and Cognition*, **15**, 119–32.

Cook, T. D. and Campbell, D. T. (1979). *Quasi-experimentation. Design and Analysis Issues for Field Settings*. Houghton Mifflin, Boston, MA.

Cooney, T. M., Schaie, K. W. and Willis, S. L. (1988). 'The relationship between prior functioning on cognitive and personality dimensions and subject attrition in longitudinal research'. *Journal of Gerontology: Psychological Sciences*, **43**, P12–17.

Copeland, J. R. M., Forshaw, D. M. and Dewey, M. E. (1984). 'The development of a standardised mental state examination and computer assisted psychiatric diagnoses for use in research with the community elderly'. In D. B. Bromley (ed.), *Gerontology: Social and Behavioural Perspectives*. Croom Helm, London.

Copeland, J. R. M., Gurland, B. J., Dewey, M. E., Kelleher, M. J., Smith, A. M. R. and Davidson, I. A. (1987). 'Is there more dementia, depression and neurosis in New York? A comparative study of the elderly in New York and London using the Computer Diagnosis AGECAT'. *British Journal of Psychiatry*, **151**, 466–73.

Cordray, D. S. and Lipsey, M. W. (eds) (1987). *Evaluation Studies Review Annual*, Volume 11, 1986. Sage, Beverly Hills, CA.

Cornelius, S. W. and Caspi, A. (1987). 'Everyday problem solving in adulthood and old age'. *Psychology and Aging*, **2**, 144–53.

Cornell, D. G., Milden, R. S. and Shimp, S. (1985). 'Stressful life events associated with endogenous depression'. *Journal of Nervous and Mental Disease*, **173**, 470–6.

Corso, J. F. (1981). *Aging Sensory Systems and Perception*. Praeger, New York.

Costa, P. T., Jr and McCrae, R. R. (1980). 'Still stable after all these years: personality as a key to some issues in adulthood and old age'. In P. B. Baltes and O. Brim (eds), *Life-span Development and Behavior*, Volume 3. Academic Press, New York.

Costa, P. T., Jr and McCrae, R. R. (1982). 'An approach to the attribution of aging, period and cohort effects'. *Psychological Bulletin*, **92**, 238–50.

Costa, P. T. and McCrae, R. R. (1985). 'Hypochondriasis, neuroticism, and aging. When are somatic complaints unfounded?'. *American Psychologist*, **40**, 19–28.

Costa, P. T., Jr and McCrae, R. R. (1986). 'Personality stability and its implications for clinical psychology'. *Clinical Psychology Review*, **6**, 407–23.

Costa, P. T. and McCrae, R. R. (1988). 'Personality in adulthood—a 6-year longitudinal study of self-reports and spouse ratings on the NEO Personality Inventory'. *Journal of Personality and Social Psychology*, **54**, 853–63.

Counseling Psychologist (1984). Special issue: Counseling Psychology and Aging (nine articles). *Counseling Psychologist*, **12** (2), 13–99.

Craik, F. I. M. (1984). 'Age differences in remembering'. In L. R. Squire and N. Butters (eds), *Neuropsychology of Memory*. Guilford Press, New York.

Craik, F. I. M., Byrd, M. and Swanson, J. M. (1987). 'Patterns of memory loss in three elderly samples'. *Psychology and Aging*, **2**, 79–86.

Craik, F. I. M. and McDowd, J. (1987). 'Age differences in recall and recognition'. *Journal of Experimental Psychology: Learning, Memory and Cognition*, **13**, 474–79.

Craik, F. I. M. and Trehub, S. (eds) (1982). *Aging and Cognitive Processes*. Plenum, New York.

Cresswell, D. L. and Lanyon, R. I. (1981). 'Validation of a screening battery for psychogeriatric assessment'. *Journal of Gerontology*, **36**, 435–40.

Cronbach, L. J. and Associates (1980). *Toward a Reform of Program Evaluation. Aims, Methods and Institutional Arrangements*. Jossey-Bass, San Francisco, CA.

Crook, T. H. (1979). 'Psychometric assessment in the elderly'. In A. Rashkin and L. F. Jarvik (eds), *Psychiatric Symptoms and Cognitive Loss in the Elderly*. John Wiley & Sons, New York.

Cummings, J. L., Houlihan, J. B. and Hill, M. A. (1986). 'The pattern of reading deterioration in dementia of the Alzheimer type: observations and implications'. *Brain and Language*, **29**, 315–23.

Cunningham, W. R. and Brookbank, J. W. (1988). *Gerontology: The Psychology, Biology, and Sociology of Aging*. Harper & Row, New York.

Cutler, R. G. (1981). 'Life-span extension'. In J. L. McGaugh and S. B. Kiesler (eds), *Aging: Biology and Behavior*. Academic Press, New York.

Datan, N., Greene, A. L. and Reese, H. W. (eds) (1986). *Lifespan Developmental Psychology: Intergenerational Relations*. Lawrence Erlbaum Associates, London.

Davies, A. D. M. (1981). 'Neither wife nor widow: an intervention with the wife of a chronically handicapped man during hospital visits'. *Behavioural Research and Therapy*, **19**, 449–51.

Davies, A. D. M., Wilkinson, S. J. and Downes, J. J. (1987). 'Age differences in the rating of life-stress events: does contextual detail make a difference?'. *British Journal of Clinical Psychology*, **26**, 299–303.

Davies, A. D. M., Wilkinson, S. J., James, O. and Newton, J. T. (1989). Life Stress in the Elderly: A Dictionary of Life Events and Difficulties. Unpublished ms.: Department of Psychology and the Institute of Human Ageing, University of Liverpool and Liverpool Institute of Higher Education, Liverpool.

Davies, A. D. M. and Crisp, A. G. (1985). 'The clinical psychology of the elderly'. In M. S. J. Pathy (ed.), *Principles and Practice of Geriatric Medicine*. John Wiley & Sons, Chichester.

Davies, A. D. M., Wilkinson, S. J., James, O. and Newton, J. T. (1989). *Life Stress in the Elderly: A Dictionary of Life Events and Difficulties*. Department of Psychology and the Institute of Human Ageing, Liverpool.

Davies, J. (1987). 'A critical survey of scientific methods in two psychiatry journals'. *Australian and New Zealand Journal of Psychiatry*, **21**, 367–73.

Dennis, W. (1956). 'Age and achievement: a critique'. *Journal of Gerontology*, **11**, 331–3.

Dennis, W. (1958). 'The age decrement in outstanding scientific contributions. Fact or artifact?' *American Psychologist*, **13**, 457–60.

Denzin, N. K. (1984). *On Understanding Emotion*. Jossey-Bass, London.

Dixon, R. A. (1983). 'How to avoid aging effects in free recall'. *Scandinavian Journal of Psychology*, **24**, 335–7.

Dixon, R. A. and Baltes, P. B. (1986). 'Toward lifespan research on the functions and pragmatics of intelligence'. In R. J. Sternberg and R. K. Wagner (eds), *Practical Intelligence*. Cambridge University Press, Cambridge.

Dohrenwend, B. P., Levav, I., Shrout, P. E., Link, B. G., Skodol, A. E. and Martin, J. L. (1987). 'Life stress and psychopathology: progress on research begun with Barbara Snell Dohrenwend'. *American Journal of Community Psychology*, **15**, 677–715.

Dohrenwend, B. P. and Shrout, P. E. (1985). '"Hassles" in the conceptualization and measurement of life stress variables'. *American Psychologist*, **40**, 780–5.

Dohrenwend, B. S. and Dohrenwend, B. P. (eds) (1974). *Stressful Life Events: their Nature and Effects*. John Wiley & Sons, New York.

Doll, E. A. (1919). 'The average mental age of adults'. *Journal of Applied Psychology*, **3**, 317–28.

Dorfman, L. T. (1985). 'Retired academics and professional activity: a British-American comparison'. *Research in Higher Education*, **22**, 273–89.

Dorland, W. A. N. (1908). *The Age of Mental Virility. An Inquiry into the Records of Achievement of the World's Chief Workers and Thinkers*. Century Co., New York.

Dowd, J. J. (1980). 'Exchange rates and old people'. *Journal of Gerontology*, **35**, 596–602.

Downing, A. and Smoker, B. (eds) (1986). *Voluntary Euthanasia: Experts Debate the Right to Die*. Peter Owen, London.

Dunkle, R. E., Haug, M. R. and Rosenberg, M. (eds) (1984). *Communication Technology and the Elderly*. Springer, New York.

Eagles, J. M. and Whalley, L. J. (1985). 'Ageing and affective disorders: the age at first onset of affective disorders in Scotland, 1969–1978'. *British Journal of Psychiatry*, **147**, 180–7.

Eisdorfer, C., Lawton, M. P. and Maddox, G. L. (eds) (1985). *Annual Review of Gerontology and Geriatrics*, Volume 5. Springer, New York.

Eisner, D. A. (1983). 'Down's syndrome and aging—is senile dementia inevitable?'. *Psychological Reports*, **52**, 119–24.

Ekman, P. (ed.) (1982). *Emotion in the Human Face*, 2nd edn. Cambridge University Press, Cambridge.

Eppinger, M. G., Craig, P. L., Adams, R. L. and Parsons, O. A. (1987). 'The WAIS-R Index for estimating premorbid intelligence: cross-validation and clinical utility'. *Journal of Consulting and Clinical Psychology*, **55**, 86–90.

Epstein, S. (1983). 'Aggregation and beyond: some basic issues on the prediction of behavior'. *Journal of Personality*, **51**, 360–92.

Erikson, E. H. (1963). *Childhood and Society*. Norton, New York.

Erikson, E. H. (1978). 'Reflections on Dr Borg's life cycle'. In E. H. Erikson (ed.), *Adulthood*. Norton, New York.

Estes, C. L. (1986). 'The aging enterprise: in whose interests?'. *International Journal of Health Services*, **16**, 243–51.

Eysenck, H. J. (1987). 'Personality and ageing: an exploratory analysis'. *Journal of Social Behaviour and Personality*, **3**, 11–21.

Eysenck, H. J. and Eysenck, S. B. G. (1969). *Personality Structure and Measurement.* Routledge and Kegan Paul, London.

Fairburn, C. G. and Hope, R. A. (1988). 'Changes in behaviour in dementia—a neglected research area'. *British Journal of Psychiatry,* **152**, 406–7.

Fillenbaum, G. G. (1984). *The Well-being of the Elderly. Approaches to Multidimensional Assessment.* World Health Organization, Geneva.

Fillenbaum, G. G. and Smyer, M. A. (1981). 'The development, validity, and reliability of the OARS multidimensional functional assessment questionnaire'. *Journal of Gerontology,* **36**, 428–34.

Finch, C. E. and Schneider, E. L. (eds) (1985). *Handbook of the Biology of Aging.* Van Nostrand Reinhold, New York.

Fiske, D. W. (1961). 'The inherent variability of behavior'. In D. W. Fiske and S. R. Maddi (eds), *Functions of Varied Experience.* Dorsey Press, Homewood, IL.

Fiske, M. (1979). *Middle Age: The Prime of Life?* Harper and Row, New York.

Fitzpatrick, J. J. and Friedman, L. J. (1983). 'Adult developmental theories and Erik Erikson's life-cycle model. A critical assessment'. *Bulletin of the Menninger Clinic,* **47**, 401–16.

Flanagan, J. C. (1979). *Identifying Opportunities for Improving the Quality of Life of Older Age Groups.* American Institutes for Research, Palo Alto, CA.

Flanagan, J. C. (1982). *New Insights to Improve the Quality of Life at Age 70.* American Institutes for Research, Palo Alto, CA.

Flicker, C., Ferris, S. H., Crook, T. and Bartus, R. T. (1987). 'Implications of memory and language dysfunction in the naming deficit of senile dementia'. *Brain and Language,* **31**, 187–200.

Flynn, J. R. (1987a). 'Massive IQ gains in 14 nations: what IQ tests really measure'. *Psychological Bulletin,* **101**, 171–91.

Flynn, J. R. (1987b). 'The rise and fall of Japanese IQ'. *Bulletin of the British Psychological Society,* **40**, 459–63.

Flynn, J. R. (1987c). 'The ontology of intelligence'. In J. Forge (ed.), *Measurement, Realism and Objectivity.* Reidel, Dordrecht, The Netherlands.

Fozard, J. L. and Popkin, S. J. (1978). 'Optimizing adult development: ends and means of applied psychology of aging'. *American Psychologist,* **33**, 975–89.

Frank, G. (1983). *The Wechsler Enterprise. An Assessment of the Development, Structure and Use of the Wechsler Tests of Intelligence.* Pergamon Press, London.

Freedman, N., Bucci, W. and Elkowitz, E. (1982). 'Depression in a family practice elderly population'. *Journal of the American Geriatrics Society,* **30**, 372–7.

Freeman, J. (1979). *Aging. Its History and Literature.* Human Sciences Press, New York.

Frijda, N. H. (1986). *The Emotions.* Cambridge University Press, Cambridge.

Frolkis, V. V. (1977). 'Aging of the autonomic nervous system'. In J. E. Birren and K. W. Schaie (eds), *Handbook of the Psychology of Aging.* van Nostrand Reinhold, New York.

Gaber, L. B. (1983). 'Activity/disengagement revisited: personality types in the aged'. *British Journal of Psychiatry,* **143**, 490–7.

Gardner, H. (1985). *Frames of Mind. The Theory of Multiple Intelligences.* Paladin Books, London.

George, L. K. and Okun, M. A. (1976). 'Misuse of analysis of covariance in aging research revisited'. *Experimental Aging Research,* **2**, 449–59.

George, L. K., Siegler, I. C. and Okun, M. A. (1981). 'Separating age, cohort and time of measurement: analysis of variance and multiple regression'. *Experimental Aging Research*, **7**, 297–314.

Gergen, K. J., Fisher, D. C. and Hepburn, A. (1986). 'Hermeneutics of personality description'. *Journal of Personality and Social Psychology*, **50**, 1261–70.

Ghiselli, E. E., Campbell, J. P. and Zedeck, S. (1981). *Measurement Theory for the Behavioral Sciences*. W. H. Freeman, San Francisco, CA.

Gibson, A. J. and Kendrick, D. C. (1979). *The Kendrick Battery for the Detection of Dementia in the Elderly*. NFER, Windsor.

Gilbert, J. G. (1952). *Understanding Old Age*. Ronald Press, New York.

Gilleard, C. J. (1980). 'Wechsler memory scale performance of elderly psychiatric patients'. *Journal of Clinical Psychology*, **36**, 958–60.

Gilleard, C. J. and Pattie, A. M. (1979). *Clifton Assessment Procedures for the Elderly*. NFER-Nelson, Windsor.

Glamser, F. D. (1981). 'The impact of preretirement programs on the retirement experience'. *Journal of Gerontology*, **36**, 244–50.

Glenn, N. D. (1976). 'Cohort analysts' futile quest: statistical attempts to separate age, period, and cohort effects'. *American Sociological Review*, **41**, 900–4.

Glenn, N. D. (1981). 'Age, birth cohorts, and drinking: an illustration of the hazards of inferring effects from cohort data'. *Journal of Gerontology*, **36**, 362–9.

Golden, C. J., Hammeke, T. A. and Purisch, A. D. (1980). *The Luria–Nebraska Neuropsychological Battery—Form 1*. NFER-Nelson, Windsor.

Golden, R. R., Teresi, J. A. and Gurland, B. J. (1984). 'Development of indicator scales for the Comprehensive Assessment and Referral Evaluation (CARE) interview schedule'. *Journal of Gerontology*, **39**, 138–46.

Goldstein, H. (1979). *The Design and Analysis of Longitudinal Studies: their Role in the Measurement of Change*. Academic Press, London.

Grana, J. M. and McCallum, D. B. (eds) (1985). *The Impact of Technology on Long-Term Care. Project HOPE*. Millwood, VA.

Gregory, R. J. (1987). *Adult Intellectual Assessment*. Prentice-Hall, Hemel Hempstead.

Grellner, B. M. (1986). 'Age salience in older adults' spontaneous self-concept'. *Perceptual and Motor Skills*, **63**, 1196–8.

Guilford, J. P. and Hoepfner, R. (1971). *The Analysis of Intelligence*. McGraw-Hill, New York.

Gurland, B., Copeland, J. R. M., Kuriansky, J., Kelleher, M. J., Sharpe, L. and Dean, L. L. (1983). *The Mind and Mood of Aging—Mental Health Problems of the Community Elderly in New York and London*. Haworth Press, New York.

Gurland, B., Copeland, J. R. M., Sharpe, L. and Kelleher, M. J. (1976). 'The Geriatric Mental Status Interview (GMS)'. *International Journal of Aging and Human Development*, **7**, 303–11.

Gurland, B. and Wilder, D. E. (1984). 'The CARE interview revisited: development of an efficient systematic clinical assessment'. *Journal of Gerontology*, **39**, 129–37.

Gurland, B., Golden, R. R., Teresi, J. A. and Challop, J. (1984). 'The SHORT-CARE: an efficient instrument for the assessment of depression, dementia and disability'. *Journal of Gerontology*, **39**, 166–9.

Guttentag, R. E. (1985). 'Memory and aging: implications for theories of memory development during childhood'. *Developmental Review*, **5**, 56–82.

Haemmerlie, F. M. and Montgomery, R. L. (1987). 'Self-perception theory, salience of behavior, and a control-enhancing program for the elderly'. *Journal of Social and Clinical Psychology*, **5**, 313–29.

Haier, R. J., Robinson, D. L., Braden, W. and Williams, D. (1983). 'Electrical potentials of the cerebral cortex and psychometric intelligence'. *Personality and Individual Differences*, **4**, 591–9.

Haley, W. D. (1983). 'A family-behavioral approach to the treatment of the cognitively impaired elderly'. *Gerontologist*, **23**, 18–20.

Hall, G. S. (1923). *Senescence: The Last Half of Life*. Appleton-Century-Crofts, New York.

Hamilton, M. (1967). 'Development of a rating scale for primary depressive illness'. *British Journal of Social and Clinical Psychology*, **6**, 278–96.

Hamsher, K. D. and Benton, A. L. (1978). 'Interactive effects of age and cerebral disease on cognitive performances'. *Journal of Neurology*, **217**, 195–200.

Harris, C. W. (ed.) (1967). *Problems in Measuring Change*. University of Wisconsin Press, Madison, WI.

Harris, D. K. (1985). *The Sociology of Aging. An Annotated Bibliography and Sourcebook*. Garland, New York.

Harris, D. K. and Cole, W. E. (1980). *Sociology of Aging*. Houghton Mifflin, Boston, MA.

Hart, S. (1988). 'Language and dementia: a review'. *Psychological Medicine*, **18**, 99–112.

Hart, S., Smith, C.M. and Swash, M. (1986). 'Assessing intellectual deterioration'. *British Journal of Clinical Psychology*, **25**, 119–24.

Hartley, J. and Burnhill, P. (1977). 'Understanding instructional text: typography, layout and design'. In M. J. A. Howe (ed.), *Adult learning: Psychological Research and Applications*. John Wiley & Sons, Chichester.

Hasher, L. and Zacks, R. T. (1979). 'Automatic and effortful processes in memory'. *Journal of Experimental Psychology: General*, **108**, 356–88.

Haynes, S. G. and Feinleib, M. (eds) (1980). *Second Conference on the Epidemiology of Aging*. National Institute of Aging, National Institutes of Health, Bethesda, MD.

Hayslip, B. and Panek, P. E. (1989). *Adult Development and Aging*. Harper and Row, London.

Hazan, H. (1983). 'Discontinuity and identity: a case study of social reintegration among the aged'. *Research on Aging*, **5**, 473–88.

Hazan, H. (1984). 'Continuity and transformation among the aged: a study in the anthropology of time'. *Current Anthropology*, **25**, 567–78.

Hearnshaw, L. S. (1979). *Cyril Burt: Psychologist*. Hodder & Stoughton, London.

Hebb, D. O. (1980). 'An inside look at aging'. *American Psychological Association Monitor*, **11**, 4–5.

Hellman, L. H. (1985). 'Geriatrics and the law'. *Journal of Legal Medicine*, **6**, 421.

Helmes, E., Csapo, K. G. and Short, J. A. (1987). 'Standardization and validation of the Multidimensional Observation Scales for Elderly Subjects (MOSES)'. *Journal of Gerontology*, **42**, 395–405.

Hendricks, J. and Hendricks, C. D. (1977). *Aging in Mass Society. Myths and Realities*. Winthrop, Cambridge, MA.

Herbst, P. G. (1970). *Behavioural Worlds. The Study of Single Cases*. Tavistock, London.

Hersch, E. L. (1979). 'Development and application of the extended scale for dementia'. *Journal of the American Geriatrics Society*, **27**, 348–54.

Hersen, M. and Barlow, D. H. (1976). *Single Case Experimental Designs. Strategies for Studying Behavior Change*. Pergamon Press, New York.

Hertzog, C. and Schaie, K. W. (1986). 'Stability and change in adult intelligence: 1. Analysis of longitudinal covariance structures'. *Psychology and Aging*, **1**, 159–71.

Hertzog, C. and Schaie, K. W. (1988). 'Stability and change in adult intelligence: 2. Simultaneous analysis of longitudinal means and covariance structures'. *Psychology and Aging*, **3**, 122–30.

Hertzog, C., Schaie, K. W. and Gribben, K. (1978). 'Cardiovascular disease and changes in intellectual functioning from middle to old age'. *Journal of Gerontology*, **33**, 872–83.

Herzog, A. R. and Rodgers, W. L. (1981). 'Age and satisfaction: data from several large surveys'. *Research on Aging*, **3**, 142–65.

Hewitt, K. E., Carter, G. and Jancar, J. (1985). 'Ageing in Down's syndrome'. *British Journal of Psychiatry*, **147**, 58–62.

Hier, D. B., Hagenlocker, K. and Shindler, A. G. (1985). 'Language disintegration in dementia: effects of etiology and severity'. *Brain and Language*, **25**, 117–33.

Hinchcliffe, R. (ed.) (1983). *Hearing and Balance in the Elderly*. Churchill Livingstone, London.

Hoinville, G. (1983). 'Carrying out surveys among the elderly: some problems of sampling and interviewing'. *Journal of the Market Research Society*, **25**, 223–37.

Holden, U. P. and Wood, R. T. (1982). *Reality Orientation*. Churchill Livingstone, London.

Holmes, T. E. and David, E. (1984). *Life Change Events Research, 1966–1978. An Annotated Bibliography of the Periodical Literature*. Praeger, London.

Holmes, T. E. and Rahe, R. (1967). 'The social readjustment rating scale'. *Journal of Psychosomatic Research*, **11**, 213–18.

Horn, J. L. and Cattell, R. B. (1966). 'Age differences in primary mental ability factors'. *Journal of Gerontology*, **21**, 210–20.

Horn, J. L. and Cattell, R. B. (1967). 'Age differences in fluid and crystallized intelligence'. *Acta Psychologica*, **26**, 107–29.

Horn, J. L. and Donaldson, G. (1980). 'Cognitive development in adulthood'. In O. G. Brim and J. Kagan (eds), *Constancy and Change in Human Development*. Harvard University Press, Cambridge, MA.

Howe, M. J. A. (ed.) (1977). *Adult Learning. Psychological Research and Applications*. John Wiley & Sons, Chichester.

Howe, M. L. and Hunter, M. A. (1985). 'Adult age differences in storage-retrieval processes: a stages-of-learning analysis of developmental interactions in concreteness effects'. *Canadian Journal of Psychology*, **39**, 130–50.

Howe, M. L. and Hunter, M. A. (1986). 'Long-term memory in adulthood: an examination of the development of storage and retrieval processes at acquisition and retention'. *Developmental Review*, **6**, 334–64.

Hoyer, W. J., Raskind, C. L. and Abrahams, J. P. (1984). 'Research practices in the psychology of aging: a survey of research published in the *Journal of Gerontology*, 1975–1982'. *Journal of Gerontology*, **39**, 44–8.

Hughes, J. R., O'Hara, M. W. and Rehm, L. P. (1982). 'Measurement of depression in clinical trials: an overview'. *Journal of Clinical Psychiatry*, **43**, 85–8.

Hussian, R. A. (1981). *Geriatric Psychology: A Behavioral Perspective*. Van Nostrand Reinhold, New York.

Hyland, D. T. and Ackerman, A. M. (1988). 'Reminiscence and autobiographical memory in the study of the personal past'. *Journal of Gerontology: Psychological Sciences*, **43**, P35–9.

Incagnoli, T., Goldstein, G. and Golden, C. J. (eds) (1985). *Clinical Applications of Neuropsychological Test Batteries*. Plenum, New York.

International Journal of Behavioral Development (1985). Special Issue: Development of the self in lifespan perspective, **8** (4), 375–482.

International Journal of Psychology (1984). Special issue: Changing conceptions of intelligence, **19** (4–5).

Jacobs, S., Kal, S., Ostfeld, A., Berkman, L. and Charpentier, P. (1986). 'The measurement of grief—age and sex variation'. *British Journal of Medical Psychology*, **59**, 305–10.

James, O., Davies, A. D. M. and Ananthakopan, S. (1986). 'The Life-Satisfaction Index: Well-being: its internal reliability and factorial composition'. *British Journal of Psychiatry*, **149**, 647–50.

Jarvik, L. F. and Blum, J. E. (1971). 'Cognitive declines as predictors of mortality in twin pairs. A twenty year longitudinal study of aging'. In E. Palmore and F. C. Jeffers (eds), *Prediction of Life Span*. D. C. Heath, Lexington, MA.

Jarvik, L. F. and Russell, D. (1979). 'Anxiety, aging and the third emergency reaction'. *Journal of Gerontology*, **34**, 197–200.

Jorm, A. F. (1985). 'Subtypes of Alzheimer's dementia: a conceptual analysis and critical review'. *Psychological Medicine*, **15**, 543–53.

Jorm, A. F., Korten, A. E. and Henderson, A. S. (1987). 'The prevalence of dementia—a quantitative integration of the literature'. *Acta Psychiatrica Scandinavica*, **76**, 465–79.

Journal of Personality (1988). Special issue: Psychobiography and life narratives, **56** (1), 1–326.

Kahnemen, D., Slovic, P. and Tversky, A. (eds) (1982). *Judgment Under Uncertainty: Heuristics and Biases*. Cambridge University Press, Cambridge.

Kalish, R. A. (1985). *Death, Grief and Caring Relationships*, 2nd edn. Brooks/Cole, Monterey, CA.

Kaminsky, M. (ed.) (1984). *The Uses of Reminiscence: New Ways of Working with Older Adults*. Haworth Press, New York.

Kane, R. A. and Kane, R. L. (1981). *Assessing the Elderly. A Practical Guide to Measurement*. D. C. Heath, Lexington, MA.

Kastrup, M. (1985). 'Characteristics of a nationwide cohort of psychiatric patients—with special reference to the elderly and the chronically admitted'. *Acta Psychiatrica Scandinavica*, **71**, 107–15.

Kaszniak, A. W. and Allender, J. (1985). 'Psychological assessment of depression in older adults'. In G. M. Chaisson-Stewart (ed.), *Depression in the Elderly. An Interdisciplinary Approach*. John Wiley & Sons, New York.

Kaszniak, A. W., Sadek, M. and Stern, L. Z. (1985). 'Differentiating depression from organic brain syndromes in older age'. In G. M. Chaisson-Stewart (ed.), *Depression in the Elderly. An Interdisciplinary Approach*. John Wiley & Sons, New York.

Kausler, D. H. (1982). *Experimental Psychology and Human Aging*. John Wiley & Sons, New York.

Kay, D. W. K. (1989). 'Genetics, Alzheimer's disease and senile dementia'. *British Journal of Psychiatry*, **154**, 311–20.

Kay, D. W. K. and Bergmann, K. (1980). 'Epidemiology of mental disorders among the aged in the community'. In J. E. Birren and R. B. Sloane (eds), *Handbook*

372 Behavioural Gerontology

Kemper, S. (1986). 'Imitation of complex syntactic constructions by the elderly'. Applied Psycholinguistics, 7, 277–88.

Kemper, S. (1987). 'Life-span changes in syntactic complexity'. Journal of Gerontology, 42, 323–8.

Kemper, S. and Rash, S. J. (1988). 'Speech and writing across the lifespan'. In M. M. Gruneberg, P. E. Morris and R. N. Sykes (eds), Practical Aspects of Memory: Current Research and Issues. John Wiley & Sons, Chichester.

Kemper, S., Kynette, D., Rash, S. J., O'Brien, K. and Sprott, R. (1989). 'Lifespan changes to adults' language: effects of memory and genre'. Applied Psycholinguistics, 10, 49–66.

Kemper, T. D. (1987). 'How many emotions are there? Wedding the social and autonomic components'. American Journal of Sociology, 39, 263–89.

Kendrick, D. C. (1982). 'Psychometrics and neurological models: a reply to Dr Rabbitt'. British Journal of Clinical Psychology, 21, 61–2.

Kendrick, D. C. (1985). Kendrick Cognitive Tests for the Elderly. NFER-Nelson, Windsor.

Kenney, R. A. (1982). Physiology of Aging: A Synopsis. Year Book Medical Publishers, Chicago, IL.

Kerlinger, F. N. (1986). Foundations of Behavioral Research, 3rd edn. Holt, Rinehart & Winston, New York.

Kermis, M. D. (1984). The Psychology of Human Aging. Allyn & Bacon, Boston, MA.

Kettel, E. and Chaisson-Stewart, G. M. (1985). 'Planning a therapeutic environment'. In G. M. Chaisson-Stewart (ed.), Depression in the Elderly. An Interdisciplinary Approach. John Wiley & Sons, New York.

Kimmel, D. C. (1980). Adulthood and Aging. An Interdisciplinary Developmental View, 2nd edn. John Wiley & Sons, New York.

Kinsbourne, M. (1974). 'Cognitive deficit and the aging brain: a behavioral analysis'. International Journal of Aging and Human Development, 5, 41–9.

Klein, H. A. and Shaffer, K. (1985). 'Aging and memory in skilled language performance'. Journal of Genetic Psychology, 146, 389–97.

Klesges, R. C. and Troster, A. I. (1987). 'A review of premorbid indices of intellectual and neuropsychological functioning: what have we learned in the past five years?'. International Journal of Clinical Neuropsychology, IX, 1–11.

Kline, P. (1986). A Handbook of Test Construction. Introduction to Psychometric Design. Methuen, London.

Knight, B. (1986). Psychotherapy with Older Adults. Sage, London.

Koeppl, P. M., Bolla-Wilson, K. and Bleecker, M. L. (1989). 'The MMPI: regional difference or normal aging?'. Journal of Gerontology: Psychological Sciences, 44, 95–9.

Kozma, A. and Stones, M. J. (1987). 'Social desirability in measures of subjective well-being: a systematic evaluation'. Journal of Gerontology, 42, 56–9.

Labouvie-Vief, G. (1980). 'Adaptive dimensions of adult cognition'. In N. Datan and N. Lohmann (eds), Transitions of Aging. Academic Press, New York.

Labouvie-Vief, G. (1985). 'Intelligence and cognition'. In J. E. Birren and K. W. Schaie (eds), Handbook of the Psychology of Aging. Van Nostrand Reinhold, New York.

Lachman, M. E., Baltes, P. B., Nesselroade, J. R. and Willis, S. L. (1982). 'Examination of personality-ability relationships in the elderly: the role of contextual (interface) assessment mode'. Journal of Research in Personality, 16, 485–501.

Lamb, M. J. (1977). *Biology of Ageing*. Blackie & Sons, Glasgow.

Language and Communication (1986). Special issue: Language and communication and the elderly, **6** (1–2).

Larrabee, G. J., Largen, J. W. and Levin, H. S. (1985). 'Sensitivity of age-decline resistant ('hold') WAIS subtests to Alzheimer's disease'. *Journal of Clinical and Experimental Neuropsychology*, **7**, 497–504.

Larson, R. (1978). 'Thirty years of research on the subjective well-being of older Americans'. *Journal of Gerontology*, **33**, 109–25.

Lashley, K. S. (1929). *Brain Mechanisms and Intelligence*. University of Chicago Press, Chicago.

Lawton, M. P. (1980). *Environment and Aging*. Brooks/Cole, Monterey, CA.

Lawton, M. P. (1984). 'The varieties of well-being'. In C. Z. Malatesta and C. E. Izard (eds), *Emotion in Adult Development*. Sage, Beverly Hills, CA.

Lawton, M. P. and Maddox, G. L. (eds) (1985). *Annual Review of Gerontology and Geriatrics*, Volume 5. Springer, New York.

Lawton, M. P., Moss, M., Fulcomer, M. and Kleban, M. H. (1982). 'A research and service-oriented multilevel assessment instrument'. *Journal of Gerontology*, **37**, 91–9.

Lawton, M. P., Windley, P. G. and Byerts, T. O. (eds) (1982). *Aging and the Environment: Theoretical Approaches*. Springer, New York.

Lehman, H. C. (1953). *Age and Achievement*. Oxford University Press, London.

Lehman, H. C. (1956). 'Reply to Dennis' critique of age and achievement'. *Journal of Gerontology*, **11**, 333–7.

Lehman, H. C. (1962). 'More about age and achievement'. *Gerontologist*, **2**, 141–8.

Leng, N. (1985). 'A brief review of cognitive–behavioural treatments in old age'. *Age and Ageing*, **14**, 257–63.

Leon, G. R., Kamp, J., Gillum, R. and Gillum, B. (1981). 'Life stress and dimensions of functioning in old age'. *Journal of Gerontology*, **36**, 66–9.

Lesnoff-Caravaglia, G. (ed.) (1984). *World of the Older Woman: Conflicts and Resolutions*. Human Sciences Press, New York.

Leszcz, M., Feigenbaum, E., Sadavoy, J. and Robinson, A. (1985). 'A men's group: psychotherapy of elderly men'. *International Journal of Group Psychotherapy*, **35**, 177–98.

Levenson, A. J. (ed.) (1979). *Neuropsychiatric Side-Effects of Drugs in the Elderly* (*Aging*, Volume 9). Raven Press, New York.

Levinson, D. J. (1978). *The Seasons of a Man's Life*. Knopf, New York.

Levinson, D. J. (1981). 'Explorations in biography: evolution of the individual life structure in adulthood'. In A. I. Rabin, J. Arnoff, A. M. Barclay and R. A. Zuckers (eds), *Further Explorations in Personality*. John Wiley & Sons, New York.

Levinson, D. J. (1986). 'A conception of adult development'. *American Psychologist*, **41**, 3–13.

Levy, P. (1981). 'On the relation between method and substance in psychology'. *Bulletin of the British Psychological Society*, **34**, 265–70.

Lewinsohn, P. M. and Teri, L. (eds) (1983). *Clinical Geropsychology. New Directions in Assessment and Treatment*. Pergamon Press, London.

Liang, J., Levin, J. S. and Krause, N. M. (1989). 'Dimensions of the OARS mental health measures'. *Journal of Gerontology, Psychological Sciences*, **44**, P127–38.

Light, L. L. and Burke, D. M. (eds) (1988). *Language, Memory and Aging*. Cambridge University Press, New York.

Litwin, H. (1987). 'Applying theories of aging to evaluation of social programs for the elderly'. *Evaluation Review*, **11**, 267–80.

Loewenstein, D. A., Amigo, E., Duara, R., Guterman, A., Hurwitz, D., Berkowitz, N., Wilkie, F., Weinberg, G., Black, B., Gittelman, B. and Eisdorfer, C. (1989). 'A new scale for the assessment of functional status in Alzheimer's disease and related disorders'. *Journal of Gerontology: Psychologial Sciences*, **44**, 114–21.

Lofland, L. H. (1985). 'The social shaping of emotion: the case of grief'. *Symbolic Interaction*, **8**, 171–90.

Lord, F. M. (1953). 'On the statistical treatment of football numbers'. *American Psychologist*, **8**, 750–51.

Lovell, B. (1980). *Adult Learning*. Croom Helm, London.

Lowenthal, M. F., Thurner, M. and Chiriboga, D. (1975). *Four Stages of Life*. Jossey-Bass, San Francisco, CA.

Ludeman, K. (1981). 'The sexuality of the older person: review of the literature'. *Gerontologist*, **21**, 203–8.

Lumsden, D. B. (ed.) (1985). *The Older Adult as Learner: Aspects of Educational Gerontology*. Hemisphere, Washington, DC.

Lynn, R. (1987). 'Japan: land of the rising IQ. A reply to Flynn'. *Bulletin of the British Psychological Society*, **40**, 464–8.

McAllister, T. W. (1983). 'Overview: pseudodementia'. *American Journal of Psychiatry*, **140**, 528–33.

McCluskey-Fawcett, K. A. and Reese, H. W. (eds) (1984). *Life-span Developmental Psychology. Historical and Generational Effects*. Academic Press, Orlando, FL.

McCrae, R. R., Arenberg, D. and Costa, P. T. Jr (1987). 'Declines in divergent thinking with age: cross-sectional, longitudinal, and cross-sequential analyses'. *Psychology and Aging*, **2**, 130–7.

McCrae, R. R. and Costa, P. T. Jr (1984). *Emerging Lives, Enduring Dispositions: Personality in Adulthood*. Little, Brown and Company, Boston, MA.

McCrae, R. R. and Costa, P. T. Jr (1988). 'Age, personality, and the spontaneous self-concept'. *Journal of Gerontology: Social Sciences*, **43**, S177–85.

MacDonald, E. T. and MacDonald, J. B. (1982). *Drug Treatment in the Elderly*. John Wiley & Sons, New York.

McGaugh, J. L. and Kiesler, S. B. (eds) (1981). *Aging: Biology and Behavior*. Academic Press, New York.

McKee, P. L. (ed.) (1982). *Philosophical Foundations of Gerontology*. Human Sciences Press, New York.

McLanahan, S. and Sorensen, A. (1984). 'Life events and psychological well-being: a re-examination of theoretical and methodological issues'. *Social Science Research*, **13**, 111–28.

McLean, S. (1987a). 'Review: assessing dementia. Part I: Difficulties, definitions and differential diagnosis'. *Australian and New Zealand Journal of Psychiatry*, **21**, 142–74.

McLean, S. (1987b). 'Review: assessing dementia. Part II: Clinical, functional, neuropsychological and social issues'. *Australian and New Zealand Journal of Psychiatry*, **21**, 284–304.

McLeish, J. A. B. (1981). 'The continuum of creativity'. In P. W. Johnson (ed.), *Perspectives on Aging*. Ballinger, Cambridge, MA.

McNair, D. M., Lorr, M. and Droppelman, L. E. (1982). *Profile of Mood States: Bipolar*. NFER-Nelson, Windsor.

Maddi, S. R. (1980). *Personality Theories: A Comparative Analysis*, 4th edn. Dorsey Press, Homewood, IL.

Maddox, G. L. (1985). 'Intervention strategies to enhance well-being in later life: the status and prospect of guided change'. *Health Services Research*, **19**, 1007–32.

Maddox, G. L. (editor-in-chief) (1986). *The Encyclopedia of Aging*. Springer, New York.

Magni, G., de Leo, D. and Schifano, F. (1985). 'Depression in geriatric and adult medical inpatients'. *Journal of Clinical Psychology*, **41**, 337–44.

Malatesta, C. Z. and Culver, L. C. (1984). 'Thematic and affective content in the lives of adult women'. In C. Z. Malatesta and C. E. Izard (eds), *Emotion in Adult Development*. Sage, Beverly Hills, CA.

Malatesta, C. Z. and Izard, C. E. (eds) (1984). *Emotion in Adult Development*, Sage, Beverly Hills, CA.

Malatesta, C. Z., Fiore, M. J. and Messina, J. J. (1987a). 'Affect, personality, and facial expressive characteristics of older people'. *Psychology and Aging*, **2**, 64–9.

Malatesta, C. Z., Izard, C. E., Culver, L. C. and Nicolich, M. (1987b). 'Emotion communication skills in young, middle-aged, and older women'. *Psychology and Aging*, **2**, 193–203.

Malde, S. (1988). 'Guided autobiography: a counseling tool for older adults'. *Journal of Counseling and Development*, **66**, 290–3.

Mangen, D. J. and Peterson, W. A. (eds) (1982a). *Research Instruments in Social Gerontology*, Volume 1: *Clinical and Social Psychology*. University of Minnesota Press, Minneapolis, MN.

Mangen, D. J. and Peterson, W. A. (eds) (1982b). *Research Instruments in Social Gerontology*, Volume 2: *Social Roles and Participation*. University of Minnesota Press, Minneapolis, MN.

Mangen, D. J. and Peterson, W. A. (eds) (1984). *Research Instruments in Social Gerontology*, Volume 3: *Health, Program Evaluation and Demography*. University of Minnesota Press, Minneapolis, MN.

Manton, K. G. (1982). 'Changing concepts of morbidity and mortality in the elderly population'. *Milbank Memorial Fund Quarterly/Health and Society*, **60**, 183–244.

Marshall, V. W. (ed.) (1986). *Later Life. The Social Psychology of Aging*. Sage, Beverly Hills, CA.

Martin, A., Brouwers, P., Lalonde, F., Cox, C., Teleska, P. and Fedio, P. (1986). 'Towards a behavioral typology of Alzheimer's patients'. *Journal of Clinical and Experimental Neuropsychology*, **8**, 594–610.

Martin, M. (1986). 'Ageing and patterns of change in everyday memory and cognition'. *Human Learning*, **5**, 63–74.

Marvel, G. A., Golden, C. J., Hammeke, T. A., Purisch, A. D. and Osmon, D. (1979). 'Relationship of age and education to performance on a standardized version of Luria's neuropsychological tests in different patient populations'. *International Journal of Neuroscience*, **9**, 63–70.

Matarazzo, J. D. (1986). *Wechsler's Measurement and Appraisal of Adult Intelligence*. Williams & Wilkins, Baltimore, MD.

Mattis, S. (1976). 'Mental status examination for organic mental syndrome in the elderly patient'. In L. Bellack and T. Katusa (eds), *Geriatric Psychiatry: A Handbook for Psychiatrists and Primary Care Physicians*. Grune & Stratton, New York.

Maxwell, J. (1969). 'Intelligence, education and fertility: a comparison between the 1923 and 1947 Scottish surveys'. *Journal of Biosocial Science*, **1**, 247–71.

Meer, B. and Baker, J. (1966). 'The Stockton Geriatric Rating Scale', *Journal of Gerontology*, **21**, 392–403.

Meier, D. E. and Cassel, C. K. (1983). 'Euthanasia on old age: a case study and ethical analysis'. *Journal of the American Geriatrics Society*, **31**, 294–8.

Mintz, J., Mintz, L. I. and Jarvik, L. F. (1985). 'Cognitive–behavioral therapy in geriatric depression: reply to Riskind, Beck and Steer'. *Journal of Consulting and Clinical Psychology*, **53**, 946–7.

Mintz, J., Steuer, J. and Jarvik, L. F. (1981). 'Psychotherapy with depressed elderly patients: research considerations'. *Journal of Consulting and Clinical Psychology*, **49**, 542–8.

Morris, R. G. (1987). 'Identity matching and oddity learning in patients with moderate to severe Alzheimer-type dementia'. *Quarterly Journal of Experimental Psychology (Sec. B: Comparative and Physiological Psychology)*, **39**, 215–28.

Mortimer, J. A., Pirozzolo, F. J. and Maletta, G. J. (eds) (1982). *The Aging Motor System*. Praeger, New York.

Moses, J. A. (1985). 'The relative contributions of Luria–Nebraska neuropsychological battery and WAIS subtest variables to cognitive performance level'. *International Journal of Clinical Neuropsychology*, **VII**, 125–30.

Mosher-Ashley, P. M. (1986–7). 'Procedural and methodological parameters in behavioral–gerontological research: a review'. *International Journal of Aging and Human Development*, **24**, 189–229.

Mossey, J. and Shapiro, E. (1982). 'Self-rated health: a predictor of mortality among the elderly'. *American Journal of Public Health*, **72**, 800–8.

Mottaz, C. J. (1987). 'Age and work satisfaction'. *Work and Occupations*, **14**, 387–409.

Mowbray, R. M. (1972). 'The Hamilton rating scale for depression: a factor analysis'. *Psychological Medicine*, **2**, 272–80.

Mueller, J. H. and Ross, M. J. (1984). 'Uniqueness of the self-concept across the lifespan'. *Bulletin of the Psychonomic Society*, **22**, 83–86.

Munnichs, J., Mussen, P., Olbrich, E. and Coleman, P. G. (eds) (1985). *Life-span and Change in a Gerontological Perspective*. Academic Press, New York.

Murphy, E. (1983). 'The prognosis of depression in old age'. *British Journal of Psychiatry*, **142**, 111–19.

Murphy, M. D., Sanders, R. E., Gabriesheski, A. S. and Schmitt, F. A. (1981). 'Metamemory in the aged'. *Journal of Gerontology*, **36**, 185–93.

Nahemow, L. and Pousada, L. (1983). *Geriatric Diagnostics. A Case Study Approach*. Springer, New York.

Nelson, A., Fogel, B. S. and Faust, D. (1986). 'Bedside cognitive screening instruments: a critical assessment'. *Journal of Nervous and Mental Disease*, **174**, 73–83.

Nelson, H. E. (1982). *National Adult Reading Test (NART) for the Assessment of Premorbid Intelligence in Patients with Dementia*. NFER-Nelson, Windsor.

Nelson, H. E. and O'Connell, A. (1978). 'Dementia: the estimation of premorbid intelligence levels using the new adult reading test'. *Cortex*, **14**, 234–44.

Nesselroade, J. R. and Harkins, S. W. (eds) (1980). 'Methodological issues' (eight chapters), in L. W. Poon (ed.), *Aging in the 1980s. Psychological Issues*. American Psychological Association, Washington, DC.

Neugarten, B. L. (ed.) (1968). *Middle Age and Aging*. University of Chicago Press, Chicago, IL.

Neugarten, B. L. and Associates (1980). *Personality in Middle and Late Life*. Arno Press, New York.

Nilsson, L. V. (1983). 'Personality changes in the aged. A transectional and longitudinal study with the Eysenck Personality Inventory'. *Acta Psychiatrica Scandinavica*, **68**, 202–11.

Nilsson, L. V. (1984). 'Incidence of severe dementia in an urban sample followed from 70 to 79 years of age'. *Acta Psychiatrica Scandinavica*, **70**, 478–86.

Nilsson, L. V. and Persson, G. (1984). 'Personality changes in the aged. A longitudinal study of psychogenic needs with the CMPS'. *Acta Psychiatrica Scandinavica*, **69**, 182–9.

Nisbett, R. E. and Ross, L. (1980). *Human Inference: Strategies and Shortcomings of Social Judgment*. Prentice-Hall, Englewood Cliffs, NJ.

Norman, A. (1980). *Rights and Risks: A Discussion Document on Civil Liberty in Old Age*. Centre for Policy on Ageing, London.

Norman, K. D. (1984). *On Understanding Emotion*. Jossey-Bass, San Francisco, CA.

Notman, M. (1979). 'Midlife concerns of women: implications of the menopause'. *American Journal of Psychiatry*, **136**, 1270–4.

Nydegger, C. N. (ed.) (1977). *Measuring Morale: A Guide to Effective Assessment*. Gerontological Society, Washington, DC.

Ober, B. A., Koss, E. and Friedland, R. P. (1985). 'Processes of verbal memory failure in Alzheimer-type dementia'. *Brain and Cognition*, **4**, 90–103.

Obler, L. K. and Albert, M. L. (eds) (1980). *Language and Communication in the Elderly. Clinical, Therapeutic and Experimental Issues*. Lexington Books, Lexington, MA.

O'Brien, G. E. (1981). 'Leisure attitudes and retirement satisfaction'. *Journal of Applied Psychology*, **66**, 371–84.

O'Carroll, R. E. (1987). 'The inter-rater reliability of the National Adult Reading Test (NART): a pilot study'. *British Journal of Clinical Psychology*, **26**, 229–30.

O'Carroll, R. E., Baikie, E. M. and Whittick, J. E. (1987). 'Does the National Adult Reading Test hold in dementia?'. *British Journal of Clinical Psychology*, **26**, 315–16.

O'Carroll, R. E. and Gilleard, C. J. (1986). 'Estimation of premorbid intelligence in dementia'. *British Journal of Clinical Psychology*, **25**, 157–8.

Office of Population Censuses and Surveys (1989). *Mortality Statistics, 1987. England and Wales*. HMSO, London.

Oliver, C. and Holland, A. J. (1986). 'Down's syndrome and Alzheimer's disease: a review'. *Psychological Medicine*, **16**, 307–22.

Ordy, J. M. and Brizzee, K. R. (eds) (1979). *Sensory Systems in Communication in the Elderly*. Raven Press, New York.

Orford, J., O'Reilly, P. and Goonatilleke, A. (1987). 'Expressed emotion and perceived family interaction in the key relatives of elderly patients with dementia'. *Psychological Medicine*, **17**, 963–70.

Osgood, N. J. and McIntosh, J. L. (1986). *Suicide and the Elderly. An Annotated Bibliography and Review*. Greenwood Press, London.

Overall, J. E. (1987). 'Estimating sample size for longitudinal studies of age-related cognitive decline'. *Journal of Gerontology*, **42**, 137–41.

Owens, R. D. (1987). 'Effects of age, education and attitudes on learning by older adults from a documentary programme'. *Journal of Educational Television*, **13**, 95–113.

Oyer, H. J. and Oyer, E. J. (eds) (1976). *Aging and Communication*. University Park Press, Baltimore, MD.

Palmore, E. (1978). 'When can age, period and cohort be separated?'. *Social Forces*, **57**, 282–95.

Palmore, E., Busse, E. W., Maddox, G. L., Nowlin, J. B. and Siegler, I. C. (eds) (1985). *Normal Aging. III. Reports from the Duke Longitudinal Studies, 1975–1984.* Duke University Press, Durham, NC.

Palmore, E. and Kivett, V. (1977). 'Change in life satisfaction: a longitudinal study of persons aged 46–70'. *Journal of Gerontology*, **32**, 311–16.

Parker, K. C. H. (1986). 'Changes with age, year-of-birth cohort, age by year-of-birth cohort interaction, and standardization of the Wechsler adult intelligence tests'. *Human Development*, **29**, 209–22.

Parkes, C. M. (1986). *Bereavement. Studies of Grief in Adult Life,* 2nd edn. Penguin Books, Harmondsworth.

Patterson, R. L., Dupree, L. W., Eberly, D. A., Jackson, G. M., O'Sulliven, M. J., Penner, L. A. and Kelly, C. D. (1982). *Overcoming Deficits of Aging. A Behavioral Approach.* Plenum, New York.

Patterson, R. L., Eberly, D. A. and Harrell, T. L. (1983). 'Behavioral assessment of intellectual competence, communication skills, and personal hygiene skills of elderly persons'. *Behavioral Assessment*, **5**, 207–18.

Pattie, A. M. and Gilleard, C. J. (1979). *Clifton Assessment Procedures for the Elderly (CAPE).* Hodder & Stoughton, Sevenoaks.

Paykel, E. (1983). 'Methodological aspects of life events research'. *Journal of Psychosomatic Research*, **27**, 341–52.

Perlmutter, M. and Hall, E. (1985). *Adult Development and Aging.* John Wiley & Sons, New York.

Pfeiffer, E. (ed.) (1978). *Multidimensional Functional Assessment: The OARS Methodology. A Manual,* 2nd edn. Center for the Study of Aging and Human Development, Durham, NC.

Pinkston, E. M. and Linsk, N. L. (1984). 'Behavioral family intervention with the impaired elderly'. *Gerontologist*, **24**, 576–83.

Planek, T. W. and Fowler, R. C. (1971). 'Traffic accident problems and exposure characteristics of the aging driver'. *Journal of Gerontology*, **26**, 224–30.

Plemons, J. K., Willis, S. L. and Baltes, P. B. (1978). 'Modifiability of fluid intelligence in aging: a short-term longitudinal approach'. *Journal of Gerontology*, **33**, 224–31. (See also correspondence and references in *Journal of Gerontology*, **36**, 634–8, 1981).

Plewis, I. (1985). *Analyzing for Change: Methods for the Measurement and Explanation of Change in the Social Sciences.* John Wiley & Sons, Chichester.

Plough, A. L. (1986). *Borrowed Time: Artificial Organs and the Politics of Extending Lives.* Temple University Press, Philadelphia, PA.

Plutchik, R. (1980). *Emotion: a Psychoevolutionary Synthesis.* Harper & Row, New York.

Pollinger-Haas, A. and Hendin, H. (1983). 'Suicide among old people: projections for the future'. *Suicide and Life-threatening Behavior*, **13**, 147–54.

Poon, L. W. (ed.) (1980). *Aging in the 1980s. Psychological Issues.* American Psychological Association, Washington, DC.

Poon, L. W. (1985). 'Differences in human memory with aging: nature, causes, and clinical implications'. In J. E. Birren and K. W. Schaie (eds), *Handbook of the Psychology of Aging.* Van Nostrand Reinhold, New York.

Poon, L. W. (ed.) (1987). *The Handbook for Clinical Memory Assessment of Older Adults.* American Psychological Association, Washington, DC.

Poon, L. W., Fozard, J. L., Cermak, L. S., Arenberg, D. L. and Thompson, L. W. (eds) (1980). *New Directions in Memory and Aging, Proceedings of the George Talland Memorial Conference.* Lawrence Erlbaum Associates, Hillsdale, NJ.

Poon, L. W., Rubin, D. C. and Wilson, B. C. (eds) (1989). *Everyday Cognition in Adulthood and Late Life*. Cambridge University Press, New York.

Powell, R. A. and Porndorf, R. H. (1971). 'Comparison of adult exercisers and nonexercisers on fluid intelligence and selected physiological variables'. *Research Quarterly*, **42**, 70–7.

Prigitano, G. P. and Parsons, O. A. (1976). 'Relationship of age and education to Halstead Test performance in different patient populations'. *Journal of Consulting and Clinical Psychology*, **44**, 527–33.

Pruchno, R. A., Kleban, M. H. and Resch, N. L. (1988). 'Psychometric assessment of the Multidimensional Observation Scale for Elderly Subjects (MOSES)'. *Journal of Gerontology: Psychological Sciences*, **43**, P164–69.

Psychological Corporation (1986). *WAIS-R Microcomputer-assisted Interpretive Report (WAIS-R Micro)*. Psychological Corporation, Sidcup.

Quattrochitubin, S. and Jason, L. A. (1983). 'The influence of intro-version—extroversion on activity choice and satisfaction among the elderly'. *Personality and Individual Differences*, **4**, 17–22.

Rabbitt, P. M. A. (1980). 'A fresh look at changes in reaction times in old age'. In D. G. Stein (ed.), *The Psychobiology of Aging*. Elsevier, North Holland, New York.

Rabbitt, P. M. A. (1981). 'Cognitive psychology needs models for changes in performance with old age'. In J. Long and A. D. Baddeley (eds), *Attention and Performance*, IX. Lawrence Erlbaum Associates, Hillsdale, NJ.

Rabbitt, P. M. A. (1982a). 'How to assess the aged? An experimental psychologist's view. Some comments on Dr Kendrick's paper'. *British Journal of Clinical Psychology*, **21**, 55–9.

Rabbitt, P. M. A. (1982b). 'Development of methods to measure functional activities of daily living in the elderly'. In S. Corkin, K. L. Davis, J. H. Growdon, E. Usdin and R. J. Wurtman (eds), *Alzheimer's Disease—A Report of Progress in Research*. Raven Press, New York.

Rabbitt, P. M. A. (1986). 'Cognitive effects of mild deafness'. *Journal of the Royal National Institute for the Deaf*, June.

Rachels, J. (1986). *The End of Life: Euthanasia and Morality*. Oxford University Press, London.

Radebaugh, T. S., Hooper, F. J. and Gruenberg, E. M. (1987). 'The social breakdown syndrome in the elderly population living in the community: the helping study. *British Journal of Psychiatry*, **151**, 341–46.

Rando, T. A. (ed.) (1986). *Loss and Anticipatory Grief*. Lexington Books, Lexington, MA.

Ratna, L. and Davis, J. (1984). 'Family therapy with the elderly mentally ill. Some strategies and techniques'. *British Journal of Psychiatry*, **145**, 311–15.

Raven, J. (1977). *Education, Values and Society: The Objectives of Education and the Nature and Development of Competence*. H. K. Lewis, London.

Raven, J. C. (1982). *Revised Manual for Raven's Progressive Matrices and Vocabulary Scales*. NFER–Nelson, Windsor.

Ray, J. J. (1988). 'Lie scales and the elderly'. *Personality and Individual Differences*, **9**, 417–18.

Reason, J. T. (1977). 'Skill and error in everyday life'. In M. J. A. Howe (ed.), *Adult Learning. Psychological Research and Applications*. John Wiley & Sons, Chichester.

Reichard, S., Livson, F. and Peterson, P. G. (1962). *Aging and Personality: A Study of Eighty-seven Older Men*. John Wiley & Sons, New York.

Reinert, G. (1970). 'Comparative factor analytic studies of intelligence throughout the human life-span'. In L. R. Goulet and P. B. Baltes (eds), *Life-Span Developmental Psychology*. Academic Press, New York.

Reiser, B. J., Black, J. B. and Abelson, R. P. (1985). 'Knowledge structures in the organization of autobiographical memories'. *Cognitive Psychology*, **17**, 89–137.

Renvoize, E. B., Mindham, R. H. S., Stewart, M., McDonald, R. and Wallace, D. R. D. (1986). 'Identical twins discordant for presenile dementia of the Alzheimer type'. *British Journal of Psychiatry*, **149**, 509–12.

Riley, M. W., Hess, B. B. and Bond, K. (eds) (1983). *Aging in Society: Selected Reviews of Recent Research*. Lawrence Erlbaum Associates, Hillsdale, NJ.

Riley, M. W., Matarazzo, J. D. and Baum, A. S. (1987). *Perspectives on Behavioral Medicine: The Aging Dimension*. Lawrence Erlbaum Associates, Hove.

Riskind, J. H., Beck, A. T. and Steer, R. A. (1985). 'Cognitive behavioral therapy in geriatric depression: comment on Steuer *et al.*'. *Journal of Consulting and Clinical Psychology*, **53**, 944–5.

Robinson, D. L. (1985). 'How personality relates to intelligence test performance: implications for a theory of intelligence, ageing research and personality assessment'. *Personality and Individual Differences*, **6**, 203–16.

Robinson, D. L. (1986). 'The Wechsler Adult Intelligence Scale and personality assessment: towards a biologically based theory of intelligence and cognition'. *Personality and Individual Differences*, **7**, 153–9.

Robinson, D. L., Haier, R. J., Braden, W. and Krengel, M. (1984a). 'Psychometric intelligence and visual evoked potentials: a replication'. *Personality and Individual Differences*, **5**, 487–9.

Robinson, D. L., Haier, R. J., Braden, W. and Krengel, M. (1984b). 'Evoked potential augmenting and reducing: the methodological and theoretical significance of new electrophysiological observations'. *International Journal of Psychophysiology*, **2**, 11–22.

Robinson, K. (1986). 'Older women—a literature review'. *Journal of Advanced Nursing*, **11**, 153–60.

Robinson, P. K., Livingston, J. and Birren, J. E. (eds) (1984). *Aging and Technological Advances*. Plenum, New York.

Rodin, J. (1983). 'Behavioral medicine: beneficial effects of self control training in aging'. *International Review of Applied Psychology*, **32**, 153–81.

Rodin, J. and Langer, E. J. (1977). 'Long-term effects of a control-relevant intervention among the institutionalized aged'. *Journal of Personality and Social Psychology*, **35**, 897–902.

Rodin, J., Timko, C. and Harris, S. (1985). 'The construct of social control: biological and psychosocial correlates'. In M. P. Lawton and G. L. Maddox (eds), *Annual Review of Gerontology and Geriatrics*, Volume 5. Springer, New York.

Rogers, D. (1986). *The Adult Years. An Introduction to Aging*, 3rd edn. Prentice-Hall, Englewood Cliffs, NJ.

Romaniuk, M., McAuley, W. J. and Arling, G. (1983). 'An examination of the prevalence of mental disorders among the elderly in the community'. *Journal of Abnormal Psychology*, **92**, 458–67.

Rosoff, A. J. and Gottlieb, G. L. (1987). 'Preserving personal autonomy for the elderly'. *Journal of Legal Medicine*, **8**, 1–48.

Rosow, I. (1974). *Socialization to Old Age*. University of California Press, Berkeley, CA.

Rosow, I. (1985). 'Status and role change through the life cycle'. In R. H. Binstock and E. Shanas (eds), *Handbook of Aging and the Social Sciences*, 2nd edn. Van Nostrand Reinhold, New York.

Roth, D. L. and Crosson, B. (1985). 'Memory span and long-term memory deficits in brain-impaired patients'. *Journal of Clinical Psychology*, 41, 521–7.

Rothstein, M. (ed.) (1983). *Review of Biological Research in Aging*, Volume 1. Alan R. Liss, New York.

Rowe, A. (1989). 'Continued engagement by professional scientists'. *Psychological Reports*, 65, 250.

Rozenbilds, U., Goldney, R. D., Gilchrist, P. N., Martin, E. and Connelly, H. (1986). 'Assessment by relatives of elderly patients with psychiatric illness'. *Psychological Reports*, 58, 795–801.

Rubin, D. C. (ed.) (1986). *Autobiographical Memory*. Cambridge University Press, Cambridge.

Rubin, E. H., Morris, J. C. and Berg, L. (1987). 'The progression of personality changes in senile dementia of the Alzheimer's type'. *Journal of the American Geriatrics Society*, 35, 721–5.

Ruddle, H. V. and Bradshaw, C. M. (1982). 'On the estimation of premorbid intellectual functioning: validation of Nelson and McKenna's formula and some new normative data'. *British Journal of Clinical Psychology*, 21, 159–65.

Runyan, W. McK. (1982). *Life Histories and Psychobiography. Explorations in Theory and Method*. Oxford University Press, New York.

Runyan, W. McK. (1984). 'Diverging life paths: their probabilistic and causal structure'. In K. J. Gergen and M. M. Gergen (eds), *Historical Social Psychology*. Lawrence Erlbaum Associates, Hillsdale, NJ.

Sadavoy, J. and Leszcz, M. (eds) (1987). *Treating the Elderly with Psychotherapy*. International Universities Press, New York.

Salthouse, T. A. (1982). *Adult Cognition: An Experimental Psychology of Human Aging*. Springer, New York.

Salthouse, T. A. (1985a). *A Theory of Cognitive Aging*. Elsevier, Amsterdam.

Salthouse, T. A. (1985b). 'Speed of behavior and its implications for cognition'. In J. E. Birren and K. W. Schaie (eds), *Handbook of the Psychology of Aging*. Van Nostrand Reinhold, New York.

Salthouse, T. A. (1987). 'Sources of age-related individual differences in block design tests'. *Intelligence*, 11, 245–62.

Salthouse, T. A., Kausler, D. H. and Saults, J. S. (1988). 'Utilization of path-analytic procedures to investigate the role of processing resources in cognitive aging'. *Psychology and Aging*, 3, 158–66.

Salthouse, T. A. and Prill, K. A. (1987). 'Inferences about age impairments in inferential reasoning'. *Psychology and Aging*, 2, 43–51.

Salthouse, T. A. and Somberg, B. L. (1982). 'Isolating the age deficit in speeded performance'. *Journal of Gerontology*, 37, 59–63.

Santrock, J. W. (1985). *Adult Development and Aging*. Merrill, Oxford.

Sarason, I. G., Levine, H. M., Basham, R. B. and Sarason, B. R. (1983). 'Assessing social support: the Social Support Questionnaire'. *Journal of Personality and Social Psychology*, 44, 127–39.

Sarteschi, P., Cassano, G. B., Castrogiovanni, P. and Conti, L. (1973). 'The use of rating scales for computer analysis of the affective symptoms in old age'. *Comprehensive Psychiatry*, 14, 371–9.

Sartorius, H. and Ban, T. A. (eds) (1986). *Assessment of Depression*. Springer, Berlin.

Savage, R. D. and Britton, P. G. (1969). 'The factorial structure of the WAIS in an aged sample'. *Journal of Gerontology*, **23**, 183–6.

Schaie, K. W. (ed.) (1983). *Longitudinal Studies of Adult Psychological Development. Adult Development and Aging*. Guilford Press, New York.

Schaie, K. W. and Hertzog, C. (1983). 'Fourteen-year short-sequential analyses of adult intellectual development'. *Developmental Psychology*, **19**, 531–43.

Schaie, K. W. and Willis, S. L. (1986). *Adult Development and Aging* (2nd edn). Little, Brown, Boston, MA.

Schaie, K. W., Willis, S. L., Jay, G. and Chiuer, H. (1989). 'Structural invariance of cognitive abilities across the adult life span: a cross-sectional study. *Developmental Psychology*, **25**, 652–62.

Schank, L. R. and Abelson, R. P. (1977). *Scripts, Plans, Goals and Understanding: An Enquiry into Human Knowledge Structures*. Lawrence Erlbaum Associates, Hillsdale, NJ.

Schatzberg, A. F., Liptzin, B., Satlin, A. and Cole, J. O. (1984). 'Diagnosis of affective disorders in the elderly'. *Psychosomatics*, **25**, 126–31.

Schmitt, J. F. and McCroskey, R. L. (1981). 'Sentence comprehension in elderly listeners: the factor of rate'. *Journal of Gerontology*, **36**, 441–5.

Schneider, E. L. (1982). *Biological Markers of Aging*. National Institute on Aging, National Institutes of Health, Bethesda, MD.

Schuessler, K. F. (1982). *Measuring Social Life Feelings: Improved Methods for Assessing How People Feel About Society and their Place in Society*. Jossey-Bass, San Francisco, CA.

Schulz, R. (1976). 'The effects of control and predictability on the psychological and physical well-being of the institutionalized aged'. *Journal of Personality and Social Psychology*, **33**, 563–73.

Schulz, R. (1982). 'Emotionality and aging: a theoretical and empirical analysis'. *Journal of Gerontology*, **37**, 42–51.

Schulz, R. (1985). 'Emotion and affect'. In J. E. Birren and K. W. Schaie (eds), *Handbook of the Psychology of Aging*. Van Nostrand Reinhold, New York.

Schulz, R. and Hanusa, B. H. (1980). Experimental social gerontology. *Journal of Social Issues*, **36**, 30–46.

Schwarz, N. and Clore, G. L. (1983). 'Mood, misattribution, and judgments of well-being: informative and directive functions of affective states'. *Journal of Personality and Social Psychology*, **45**, 513–23.

Scialfa, C. T. and Games, P. A. (1987). 'Problems with step-wise regression in research on aging and recommended alternatives', *Journal of Gerontology: Psychological Sciences*, **42**, P579–83.

Seligman, M. E. P. and Elder, G. Jr (1986). 'Learned helplessness and life-span development'. In A. B. Sorensen, F. E. Weinert and L. R. Sherrod (eds), *Human Development and the Life Course: Multidisciplinary Perspectives*. Lawrence Erlbaum Associates, Hillsdale, NJ.

Shallice, T. (1979). 'The case study approach in neuropsychological research'. *Journal of Clinical Neuropsychology*, **1**, 183–211.

Shanan, J. (1985). *Personality Types and Culture in Later Adulthood*. Karger, Basel.

Sheehy, G. (1976). *Passages: the Predictable Crises of Adult Life*. Dutton, New York.

Shock, N. W., Greulich, R. E., Andres, R., Arenberg, D. L., Costa, P. T., Jr., Lakatta, E. G. and Tobin, J. D. (1984). *Normal Human Aging: The Baltimore Longitudinal Study of Aging*. US Government Printing Office, Washington, DC.

Shuchter, S. R. (1986). *Dimensions of Grief. Adjusting to the Death of a Spouse*. Jossey-Bass, San Francisco, CA.

Shulman, K. I. and Silver, I. L. (1985). 'Hysterical seizures as a manifestation of "depression" in old age'. *Canadian Journal of Psychiatry*, **30**, 278–80.

Siegler, I. C. (1975). 'The terminal drop hypothesis: fact or artefact?'. *Experimental Aging Research*, **1**, 169–85.

Silverstone, B., Whittington, F. J. and Roberts, J. (1986). 'Introduction and case history of Mr S'. *Gerontologist*, **26**, 595–8.

Simonton, D. K. (1977). 'Creative productivity, age and stress: a biographical time-series analysis of 10 classical composers'. *Journal of Personality and Social Psychology*, **35**, 791–804.

Skinner, B. F. (1983). 'Intellectual self-management in old age'. *American Psychologist*, **38**, 239–44.

Smyer, M. A. and Gatz, M. (eds) (1983). *Mental Health and Aging. Programs and Evaluations*. Sage, Beverly Hills, CA.

Social Behaviour (1988). Special issue: Ageing, technology and society. *Social Behaviour*, **3** (2), 59–196.

Sorensen, A. B., Weinert, F. E. and Sherrod, L. R. (eds) (1986). *Human Development and the Life Course: Multidisciplinary Perspectives*. Lawrence Erlbaum Associates, Hillsdale, NJ.

Spiers, P. (1981). 'Have they come to praise Luria or to bury him? The Luria Nebraska Battery controversy'. *Journal of Consulting and Clinical Psychology*, **49**, 331–41.

Spiers, P. (1982). 'The Luria–Nebraska Neuropsychological Battery revisited: a theory in practice or just practising?'. *Journal of Consulting and Clinical Psychology*, **50**, 301–6.

Spilich, G. J. (1985). 'Discourse comprehension across the span of life'. In N. Charness (ed.), *Aging and Human Performance*. John Wiley & Sons, Chichester.

Spinnler, H., Della Sala, S., Bandera, R. and Baddeley, A. (1988). 'Dementia, ageing, and the structure of human memory'. *Cognitive Neuropsychology*, **5**, 193–212.

Starr, B. D. (1985). 'Sexuality and aging'. In M. P. Lawton and G. L. Maddox (eds), *Annual Review of Gerontology and Geriatrics*, Volume 5. Springer, New York.

Stearns, P. N. (ed.) (1982). *Old Age in Preindustrial Society*. Holmes & Meier, New York.

Sternberg, R. J. (1985). *Beyond IQ. A Triarchic Theory of Human Intelligence*. Cambridge University Press, New York.

Sternberg, R. J. and Wagner, R. K. (eds) (1986). *Practical Intelligence, Nature and Origins of Competence in the Everyday World*. Cambridge University Press, Cambridge.

Steuer, J., LaRue, A., Blum, J. E. and Jarvik, L. F. (1981). '"Critical loss" in the eighth and ninth decades'. *Journal of Gerontology*, **36**, 211–13.

Stevens, S. (1985). 'The language of dementia in the elderly'. *British Journal of Disorders of Communication*, **20**, 181–90.

Stevens-Long, J. (1984). *Adult Life: Developmental Processes*, 2nd edn. Eurospan, London.

Stoller, E. (1984). 'Self-assessments of health by the elderly: the impact of informal assistance'. *Journal of Health and Social Behavior*, **25**, 261–70.

Strongman, K. T. (1987). *The Psychology of Emotion*, 3rd edn. John Wiley & Sons, Chichester.

Swenson, W. M. (1985). 'An aging psychologist assesses the impact of age on MMPI profiles'. *Psychiatric Annals*, **15**, 554–7.

Tennant, C. (1983). 'Life events and psychological morbidity: the evidence from prospective studies'. *Psychological Medicine*, **13**, 483–6.

Teresi, J. A., Golden, R. R. and Gurland, B. J. (1984a). 'Concurrent and predictive validity of indicator scales developed for the Comprehensive Assessment and Referral Evaluation Interview Schedule'. *Journal of Gerontology*, **39**, 158–65.

Teresi, J. A., Golden, R. R., Gurland, B. J., Wilder, D. E. and Bennett, R. G. (1984b). 'Construct validity of indicator-scales developed from the Comprehensive Assessment and Referral Evaluation Interview Schedule'. *Journal of Gerontology*, **39**, 147–57.

Terry, R. D. (ed.) (1987). *Aging and the Brain*. Raven Press, New York.

Terry, R. D. and Davies, B. (1980). 'Dementia of the Alzheimer type'. *Annual Review of Neurosciences*, **3**, 77–96.

Thienhaus, O. J., Hartford, J. T., Skelly, M. F. and Bosmann, H. B. (1985). 'Biological markers in Alzheimer's disease'. *Journal of the American Geriatrics Society*, **33**, 715–26.

Thomae, H. and Lehr, U. (1986). 'Stages, crises, conflicts, and life-span development'. In A. B. Sorensen, F. E. Weinert and I. R. Sherrod (eds), *Human Development and the Life Course: Multidisciplinary Perspectives*. Lawrence Erlbaum Associates, Hillsdale, NJ.

Thoms, W. J. (1873). *The Longevity of Man: Its Facts and Fictions*. John Murray, London.

Thornton, E. W. (1984). *Exercise and Aging. An Unproven Relationship*. Institute of Human Ageing, Liverpool.

Thornton, S. and Brotchie, J. (1987). 'Reminiscence: a critical review of the empirical literature'. *British Journal of Clinical Psychology*, **26**, 93–111.

Tinker, A. (1985). *The Elderly in Modern Society*, 2nd edn. Longman, London.

Todd, M., Davis, K. E. and Cafferty, T. P. (1984). 'Who volunteers for adult developmental research? Research findings and practical steps to reach low volunteering groups'. *International Journal of Aging and Human Development*, **18**, 177–84.

Tomlinson, B. E. (1982). 'Plaques, tangles and Alzheimer's disease'. *Psychological Medicine*, **12**, 449–60.

Troll, L. E. (1985). *Early and Middle Adulthood*, 2nd edn. Brooks/Cole, Monterey, CA.

Turner, J. S. and Helms, D. B. (1986). *Contemporary Adulthood*, 3rd edn. Holt Saunders, London.

Turner, R. R. and Reese, H. W. (eds) (1980). *Life-span Developmental Psychology: Intervention*. Academic Press, New York.

Ulatowska, H. K. (ed.) (1985). *The Aging Brain*. Taylor & Francis, London.

Ulatowska, H. K., Hayashi, M. M., Cannito, M. P. and Fleming, S. G. (1986). 'Disruption of reference in aging'. *Brain and Language*, **28**, 24–41.

Umlauf, R. L. and Frank, R. G. (1987). 'Cluster analysis, depression and ADL status'. *Rehabilitation Psychology*, **32**, 39–44.

United States Department of Health and Human Services (1982). *Final Report of the 1981 White House Conference on Aging*, Volumes 1, 2 and 3. US Department of Health and Human Services, Washington, DC.

Vaccaro, F. J. (1988). 'Successful operant conditioning procedures with an institutionalized aggressive geriatric patient'. *International Journal of Aging and Human Development*, **26**, 71–9.

van Heeringen, A. and Dijkwel, P. A. (1987a). 'The relationship between age, mobility and scientific productivity. Part I. Effect of mobility on productivity'. *Scientometrics*, **11**, 267–80.

van Heeringen, A. and Dijkwel, P. A. (1987b). 'The relationship between age, mobility and scientific productivity. Part II. Effect of age on productivity'. *Scientometrics*, **11**, 281–93.

Vannieuwkirk, R. R. and Galbraith, G. G. (1985). 'The relationship of age to performance on the Luria–Nebraska neuropsychological battery'. *Journal of Clinical Psychology*, **41**, 527–32.

van Toller, C. (1979). *The Nervous Body: An Introduction to the Autonomic Nervous System and Behaviour*. John Wiley & Sons, Chichester.

Verbrugge, L. M. (1984). 'Longer life but worsening health? Trends in health and mortality of middle-aged and older persons'. *Milbank Memorial Fund Quarterly/ Health and Society*, **62**, 475–519.

Vernon, P. E. (1983a). 'Speed of information processing and general intelligence'. *Intelligence*, **7**, 53–70.

Vernon, P. E. (1983b). 'Recent findings on the nature of *g*'. *Journal of Special Education*, **17**, 389–400.

Volans, P. J. and Levy, R. (1982). 'A re-evaluation of an automated tailored test of concept learning with elderly psychiatric patients'. *British Journal of Clinical Psychology*, **21**, 93–101.

Volans, P. J. and Woods, R. T. (1983). 'Why do we assess the aged? Comment'. *British Journal of Clinical Psychology*, **22**, 213–14.

Wagenaar, W. A. (1986). 'My memory: a study of autobiographical memory over six years'. *Cognitive Psychology*, **18**, 225–52.

Warner, H. R., Butler, R. N., Sprott, R. L. and Schneider, E. L. (1987). *Modern Biological Theories of Aging*. Raven Press, New York.

Wasserman, I. M. (1987). 'Cohort, age and period effects in the analysis of U.S. suicide patterns: 1933–1978'. *Suicide and Life-threatening Behavior*, **17**, 179–93.

Waters, W. F., Williamson, D. A., Bernard, B. A., Blouin, D. C. and Faulstick, M. E. (1987). 'Test–retest reliability of psychophysiological assessment'. *Behavioural Research and Therapy*, **25**, 213–22.

Webb, E. J., Campbell, D. T., Schwartz, R. D. and Sechrest, L. (1966). *Unobtrusive Measures. Nonreactive Research in the Social Sciences*. Rand, McNally, Chicago, IL.

Wechsler, D. (1986). *Wechsler Adult Intelligence Scale-Revised (WAIS-R)*. Psychological Corporation, Sidcup.

Wechsler, D. (1987). *Wechsler Memory Scale-Revised (WMS-R)*. Psychological Corporation, Sidcup.

Weg, R. B. (ed.) (1983). *Sexuality in the Later Years. Roles and Behavior*. Academic Press, New York.

Welford, A. T. (1958, reprinted 1977). *Ageing and Human Skill*. Oxford University Press, London.

Welford, A. T. (1985a). 'Changes of performance with age: an overview'. In N. Charness (ed.), *Aging and Human Performance*. John Wiley & Sons, Chichester.

Welford, A. T. (1985b). 'Practice effects in relation to age: a review and a theory'. *Developmental Neuropsychology*, **1**, 173–90.

Wharton, G. F. III (1981). *Sexuality and Aging: An Annotated Bibliography*, 2nd edn. Scarecrow Press, Metuchen, NJ.

Wheatley, D. (ed.) (1983). *Psychopharmacology of Old Age*. Oxford University Press, New York.

Whitbourne, S. K. (1985). *The Aging Body. Physiological Changes and Psychological Consequences*. Springer, New York.

Whitbourne, S. K. (1986). *Adult Development*, 2nd edn. Praeger, New York.

Willis, S. L. and Schaie, K. W. (1986). 'Practical intelligence in later adulthood'. In R. J. Sternberg and R. K. Wagner (eds), *Practical Intelligence*. Cambridge University Press, Cambridge.

Wisner, E. and Green, M. (1986). 'Treatment of a demented patient's anger with cognitive–behavioral strategies'. *Psychological Reports*, **59**, 447–50.

Wisocki, P. A. (1984). 'Behavioral approaches to gerontology'. In M. Hersen, R. M. Eisler and P. M. Miller (eds), *Progress in Behavior Modification*, Volume 16. Academic Press, Orlando, FL.

Woodruff-Pak, D. (1988). *Psychology and Aging*. Prentice-Hall, Hemel Hempstead.

Woods, R. T. and Britton, P. G. (1985). *Clinical Psychology with the Elderly*. Croom Helm, London.

Wright, A. F. and Whalley, L. J. (1984). 'Genetics, ageing and dementia'. *British Journal of Psychiatry*, **145**, 20–38.

Yerkes, R. M. (1921). Psychological Examining in the U.S. Army, Part III, Chapter 14. Memoirs of the National Academy of Science, Volume 15, Washington, DC.

Yesavage, J. A., Brink, T. L., Rose, T. L., Lum, O., Huang, V., Adey, M. B. and Leirer, V. O. (1982–3). 'Development and validation of a geriatric depression rating scale: a preliminary report'. *Journal of Psychiatric Research*, **17**, 37.

Yost, E. B. and Corbishley, M. A. (1985). 'Group therapy'. In M. G. Chaisson-Stewart (ed.), *Depression in the Elderly. An Interdisciplinary Approach*. John Wiley & Sons, New York.

Zabrucky, K., Moore, De W. and Schultz, N. R. Jr (1987). 'Evaluation of comprehension in young and old adults'. *Developmental Psychology*, **23**, 39–43.

Zeman, F. D. (1942–50). 'Life's later years. Studies in the medical history of old age', articles in the *Journal of the Mount Sinai Hospital* (from Volume 8), 1942, 1944, 1945, 1947, 1950, parts 1 to 12 (part 2 not traced). See Bromley (1974a) for further details.

Zemore, R. and Eames, N. (1979). 'Psychic and somatic symptoms of depression among young adults, institutionalized aged and non-institutionalized aged'. *Journal of Gerontology*, **34**, 716–22.

Zepelin, H., Wolfe, C. S. and Kleinplatz, F. (1981). 'Evaluation of a yearlong reality orientation program'. *Journal of Gerontology*, **36**, 70–7.

Zimmerman, M. (1983). 'Methodological issues in the assessment of life events: a review of issues and research'. *Clinical Psychology Review*, **3**, 339–70.

Zisook, S., Devans, R. A. and Click, M. A. (1982). 'Measuring symptoms of grief and bereavement'. *American Journal of Psychiatry*, **139**, 1590–2.

Zung, W. W. K. (1965). 'A self-rating depression scale'. *Archives of General Psychiatry*, **12**, 63–70.

Zung, W. W. K. and King, R. E. (1983). 'Identification and treatment of masked depression in a general medical practice'. *Journal of Clinical Psychiatry*, **44**, 365–8.

Zusné, L. (1976). 'Age and achievement in psychology'. *American Psychologist*, **31**, 805–7.

Author Index

Morris, R.G. 202, *376*
Mortimer, J.A. 21, *376*
Moses, J.A. 79, 179, *376*
Mosher-Ashley, P.M. *376*
Moss, M. *373*
Mossey, J. 82, *376*
Mottaz, C.J. 303, *376*
Mountjoy, C.Q. *361*
Mowbray, R.M. 122, *376*
Mueller, J.H. 56, *376*
Munnichs, J. 26, *376*
Murphy, E. 119, 121, *376*
Murphy, E.A. *362*
Murphy, M.D. 227, *376*
Mussen, P. *376*

Nahemow, L. 93, *376*
Nelson, A. 131, *376*
Nelson, H.E. 125, 132, *376*
Nesselroade, J.R. 317, 372, *376*
Neugarten, B.L. 33, 286, *376*
Newton, J.T. *365*
Nicolich, M. *375*
Nilsson, L.V. 88, 108, 109, *377*
Nisbett, R.E. 198, 238, 284, *377*
Norman, A. 25, *377*
Norman, K.D. 264, *377*
Notman, M. 33, *377*
Nowlin, J.B. *378*
Nydegger, C.N. 89, *377*

Ober, B.A. 256, *377*
Obler, L.K. 202, *377*
O'Brien, G.E. 303, *377*
O'Brien, K. *372*
O'Carroll, R.E. 62, 132, *377*
O'Connell, A. 125, *376*
Office of Population Censuses and Surveys, 3, 6, *377*
O'Hara, M.W. *370, 372*
Okun, M.A. 326, *367*
Olbrich, E. *376*
Oliver, C. 111, *377*
Ordy, J.M. 21, *377*
O'Reilly, P. *377*
Orford, J. 293, 308, *377*
Osgood, N.J. 114, *377*
Osmon, D. *375*
Ostfeld, A. *371*
O'Sulliven, M.J. *378*
Otis, 165
Overall, J.E. 328, *377*

Owens, R.D. 216, *377*
Oyer, E.J. 202, *377*
Oyer, H.J. 202, *377*

Palmore, E. 300, 317, 342, 344, 345, 352, *377, 378*
Panek, P.E. 26, *369*
Parker, K.C.H. 181, 182, 183, *378*
Parkes, C.M. 297, *378*
Parkes, K.R. *362*
Parsons, O.A. 179, *366, 379*
Patterson, R.L. 129, *378*
Pattie, A.M. 94, 123, *368, 378*
Paykel, E. 317, *378*
Penner, L.A. *378*
Perlmutter, M. 26, *378*
Persson, G. 88, *377*
Peterson, P.G. *379*
Peterson, W.A. 62, 291, 310, 333, *375*
Pfeiffer, E. 94, 106, *378*
Piaget, J. 204
Pinkston, E.M. 135, *378*
Pirandello, 39
Pirozzolo, F.J. *376*
Planek, T.W. 330, *378*
Plemons, J.K. 164, *378*
Plewis, I. 317, 326, *378*
Plough, A.L. 71, 140, *378*
Plutchik, R. 291, 293, *378*
Pollinger-Haas, A. 114, *378*
Poon, L.W. 26, 197, 215, 255, *378, 379*
Popkin, S.J. 146, *367*
Porndorf, R.H. 164, 168, *379*
Pousada, L. 93, *376*
Powell, R.A. 164, 168, *379*
Prigitano, G.P. 179, *379*
Prill, K.A. 179, *381*
Pruchno, R.A. 94, *379*
Psychological Corporation, 72, 173, *379*
Purisch, A.D. *368, 375*

Quattrochitubin, S. 285, *379*

Rabbitt, P.M.A. 20, 62, 80, 132, 161, 167, 186, 188, 190, *379*
Rachels, J. 25, 114, *379*
Radebaugh, T.S. 105, 106, *379*
Rahe, R. 47, 51, 54, 60, *370*
Rando, T.A. 297, *379*
Rash, S.J. 201, *372*
Raskind, C.L. *370*

Subject Index